THE
WARSAW
DIARY OF
CHAIM A.
KAPLAN

REVISED EDITION

TRANSLATED AND EDITED BY

Abraham I. Katsh

COLLIER BOOKS • NEW YORK, NEW YORK

In memory of six million Jews, martyrs for humanity,

and in honor of the righteous men who never forgot

that man is made in the image of God

"Therefore, but a single man was created in the world, to teach that if any man has caused a single soul to perish from the world, Scripture imputes it to him as though he has caused a whole world to perish; and if man saves alive a single soul from the world, Scripture imputes it to him as though he had saved alive a whole world."—*Maimonides*

"I believe with perfect faith in the coming of the Messiah; and though he tarry, none the less do I believe."—*Song of the ghetto martyrs*

Street. The actual name of the school was the "Sixth Grade Grammar Elementary School of Ch. A. Kaplan."

Kaplan was an exponent of the direct method of language teaching, in which Hebrew was taught as a spoken language. He used the Sephardic dialect, the one now used in Israel. In spite of strong opposition from exponents of traditional methods, he stubbornly followed this system and published several Hebrew textbooks advocating it. As an ardent Hebraist he participated actively in the Society of Writers and Hebrew Journalists in Warsaw and contributed to many Hebrew periodicals.

Kaplan visited the United States in 1921 and Palestine in 1936. He intended to settle in Palestine in order to be with his two children who had emigrated there earlier, but for personal reasons he returned to Warsaw the same year, hoping eventually to revisit Palestine. (The same personal reasons, along with his compulsion to record the holocaust for posterity, were decisive influences in Kaplan's decision to stay in Warsaw in 1941, when according to him, he could have secured an exit visa.) In 1937, Kaplan published a book called *Pizzurai*, a collection of the essays and articles on the Hebrew language and Jewish education that he had published during his forty years of teaching. While in New York he published a Passover Haggadah for children. This illustrated Passover story was republished recently in New York. He was also the author of a Hebrew grammar book and textbooks for children dealing with Jewish history and customs. His full name was Chaim Aron Kaplan, but his name in his own writings appears as Ch. A. Kaplan.

Kaplan's Judaism seems to have been based more on national and historic allegiance than on traditional observances. He felt that his personal philosophy was a legacy from his father and he was very grateful. He once remarked that had he received merely a financial inheritance, it would finally have been lost, but this spiritual legacy would remain with him forever. From his early youth Kaplan was what we would call an introvert: books were his friends and the walls of the academies his companions. At times he felt that his ambition to be independent was a primary obstacle to him in attaining leadership in the Warsaw community, and for that reason he was unable to develop his full talents and intellectual abilities. On the other hand, the fact that he was a respected member of the community gave him satisfaction and comfort.

The author began a personal diary as early as 1933. This trained him for the mission he undertook at the beginning of World War II, to devote all his efforts to preserving a record for posterity. No diarist, of course, can be fully objective, even in a less tormented time than Kaplan's. Yet his intention of objectivity is carried out with remarkable tenacity, and with increasing personal nobility, as the dreadful events increased his own physical and emotional suffering and his anguish at the mounting tragedy of those around him. It is significant that although he had suffered from diabetes since 1928, there is no mention of his illness in the war years, though the difficulties of obtaining medicines may be imagined.

The chronicler kept his diary in small notebooks, similar to the ones that grade-school children in the United States use today. The entries in this edition are from the time of the invasion of Poland on September 1, 1939, to August 4, 1942.

Because it was smuggled out of the ghetto before the total liquidation, the diary comes to us without lacunae. By a miracle or perhaps by decree of historic faith, which commands us to know all and remember everything, these entries are finally seeing the light of today. Kaplan himself was largely responsible for the miracle of preservation. In late 1942, when he knew that the Nazi noose was around his neck, he gave the diary to a Jewish friend named Rubinsztejn, who was working daily at forced labor outside the ghetto, returning each evening. Rubinsztejn smuggled the notebooks out singly and passed each one on to Wladyslaw Wojcek, a Pole, who was a resident of Liw, a small village near Warsaw. Wojcek, who subsequently emigrated to the United States, claimed to have been active in ghetto underground activities.

Kaplan was a habitual diarist. He wrote a record of his times through much of his life, but he wrote in virtual secrecy. Nobody seems to have known about his chronicles, not even his family. Only at the very end of his life did Emmanuel Ringelblum and a few others learn about his diary.

In his *Notes from the Warsaw Ghetto*, Volume II (pages 339–340), published in Warsaw, Ringelblum refers to Kaplan's diary: "Several times I implored Kaplan to let me preserve his diary, assuring him that after the war he would get it back. The most he agreed was to have me copy the manuscript, but that was a physical impossibility because of the hardships. The whole manuscript was lost when the author was taken to the *Umschlagplatz* [the assembly point for transport to the concentration camps]." Kaplan and his wife are believed to have perished in the Treblinka extermination camp in December 1942 or January 1943.

Interestingly, Kaplan never mentioned his own name in the entries, perhaps because he feared discovery—especially during the war years. Because of this lack of self-identity on Kaplan's part, it took me a year and half to establish the author's identity beyond a doubt before I began to translate and edit the diary.

Significant clues to Kaplan's identity were given in the notebooks of 1935–1936, in which he mentions his problems with the teachers in his school as well as personal family matters. Throughout these entries he emerges as an understandably bitter man, but one with an obviously wide circle of contacts, who had access to data when information was a scarce commodity. Yet he remained a loner. He also comes through as a confirmed egotist.

In 1962, when Wojcek emigrated to New York, he called on the late Surrogate Judge Maximilian Moss and me with a letter of introduction from the late Professor Berl Mark, then the Director of the Jewish Historical Institute in Warsaw, who had suggested that we might help him get a job. During our conversation Wojcek showed me an old envelope which contained several notebooks of the Kaplan diary. I purchased the material from Mr. Wojcek for the New York University Jewish Cultural Foundation Library of Judaica and Hebraica where the original material is now located. Wojcek told me that in 1952 he had given other Kaplan notebooks to Professor Mark, and that the ones he brought with him had been discovered by him before he left for the United States, and for this reason he had had no chance to give them to Professor Mark.

The diaries Wojcek brought to the United States covered the years 1935–1936, 1939, several entries for 1940, and a few entries for 1942, and I had thought the notebooks in the Jewish Historical Institute in Warsaw covered only the prewar period. In 1963, the late Moshe Sharett obtained for me for the Hebrew edition, which was published in Israel by Am Oved, microfilm of several Kaplan notebooks in Warsaw, and I discovered that these entries included the missing part of 1940, and some for 1941. I had already decided not to include the prewar material and to give as much space as possible to the crucial war years. Thanks to Moreshet I am now able to present the missing entries from April 4, 1941, to May 2,

15

1942, which were not included in the original edition and thus give a more comprehensive picture of Kaplan's detailed history of these years.

The entries are presented here in a form which seeks to remove the repetition inevitable in a diary, without sacrificing the factual record; but to translate is really to "traduce" when one is forced to abridge. Kaplan uses a fine Hebrew; at the same time his style is interwoven with classical allusions, Biblical and Talmudic passages, and folkloristic expressions and images. At times he coins his own terms or uses a German or Polish expression. Therefore, to translate for a reader in another time and place is a perilous undertaking, and some errors of omission and commission must occur in such a difficult and exacting task. But I have tried to the best of my ability to be faithful to the author's words and spirit.[1]

Kaplan himself never expected to have his diary published in toto. In his entries of November 15, 1941, he writes: "This journal is my life, my friend, and ally. I would be lost without it. I pour my innermost thoughts and feelings into it and this brings relief. When my nerves are taut and my blood is boiling, then I am full of bitterness. In my helplessness I drag myself to my diary and at once I am enveloped by a wave of creative inspiration, although I doubt whether the recording that occupies me deserves to be called 'creative.' Let it be edited at some future time as it may be. The important thing is that in keeping this diary I find spiritual rest. That is enough for me."

My own royalties for this book have been designated by me for a Chaim A. Kaplan scholarship at The Dropsie University. I have devoted all my energies to this diary without ever receiving any compensation whatsoever. The reasons are many. One cannot fail to be deeply moved by Kaplan's words and his record of the awesome days through which the Jewish people lived. Although I never knew or heard of Kaplan before involving myself with the diary, I did feel a personal tie as the Director of Hebrew Studies at New York University during the Holocaust. I organized many meetings trying to stir up the community about the indescribable Nazi atrocities. Later on when I had a chance to visit places where ghettos existed in Poland, Hungary, and Russia, I found no traces

[1] The footnotes are mine, as are the occasional bracketed explanatory words in the text.

16

of cemeteries or even monuments that showed that Jews ever lived or existed. They had all evaporated into thin air. The thought was constantly in my mind, "It could have been the reverse. We there and they here!"

I am grateful to the late Mrs. Cecily Gesundheit-Gerrard and to her husband Benjamin, daughter and son-in-law of Mr. Kaplan, and to Mr. Kaplan's son, Mr. Lionel Kenneth.

My deep appreciation goes to my former students and colleagues, Dr. Israel M. Biderman, for his help during my negotiations with Mr. Wojcek; Dr. Aaron Citron, for his painstaking reading of the entire manuscript in its early stages; and Dr. Shimon Redlich, for his help with the maps.

I owe a debt of gratitude to Dr. Felix Zandman for his genuine interest and encouragement in making this edition possible.

I am indebted to my dear wife, Estelle, and my children, Ethan, Salem, and Rochelle, who encouraged me in this task and for their infinite patience.

Last, but not least, my profound thanks to my editor, Mr. Benton M. Arnovitz at Macmillan, for his advice and literary guidance in the final stages of the publication.

July, 1972   ABRAHAM I. KATSH

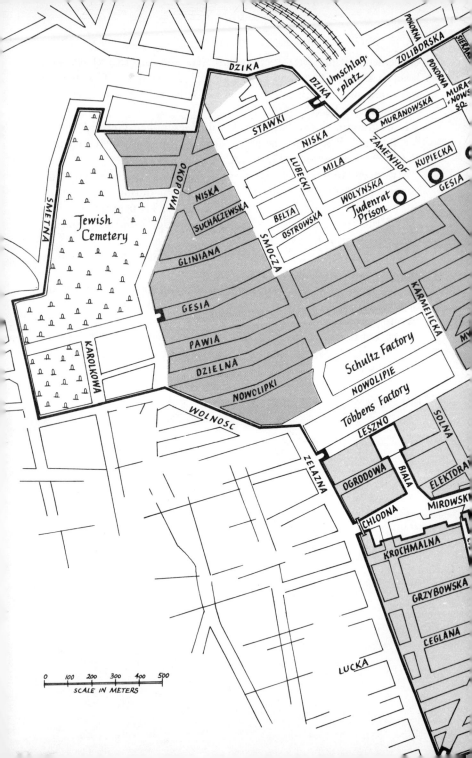

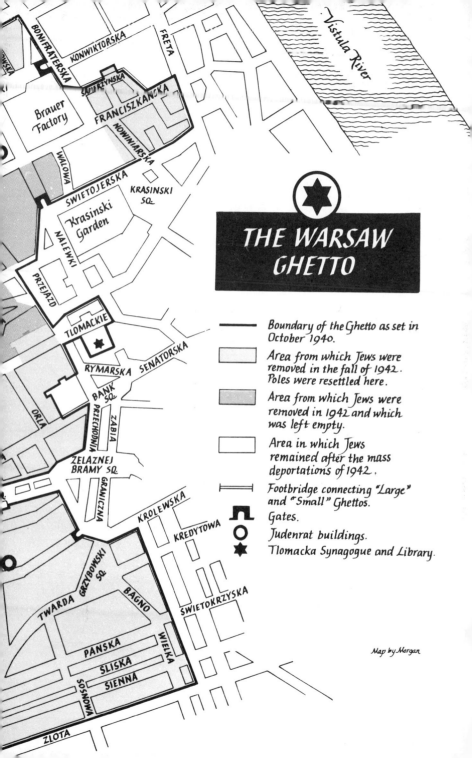

THE WARSAW GHETTO

Boundary of the Ghetto as set in October 1940.

Area from which Jews were removed in the fall of 1942. Poles were resettled here.

Area from which Jews were removed in 1942 and which was left empty.

Area in which Jews remained after the mass deportations of 1942.

Footbridge connecting "Large" and "Small" Ghettos.

Gates.

Judenrat buildings.

Tlomacka Synagogue and Library.

Map by Morgan

Vilna

Novogrudok

Baranowicze

Slonim

Vno

dno

k

sk

awa

elm

Hrubieszow

Rowne

Ostrog

REICHSKOMISSARIAT

Kremenets

UKRAINE

T

GALICIA

Lwow

l

bycz

aw

Stryj

Buczacz

Stanislawow

Kolomyja

Map legend (top)

■	Third Reich in 1937
▨	Territories annexed & "incorporated" into the Third Reich
▥	"Protectorate of Bohemia & Moravia" and "General Government"
░	Territories under German civil & military administration
≈	Countries cooperating with & controlled by the Third Reich

OSLO · STOCKHOLM · HELSINKI · LENINGRAD

DUBLIN · RIGA · RZHEV · MOSCOW

THE HAGUE · COPENHAGEN · SMOLENSK · OREL · VORONEZH

LONDON · BERLIN · WARSAW · STALINGRAD

BRUSSELS · PRAGUE · CRACOW · DNEPROPETROVSK

PARIS · VIENNA · BUDAPEST · MOSDON

VICHY · BERN · ZAGREB · BUCHAREST

LISBON · MADRID · BELGRAD · SOFIA · ANKARA

ROME · TIRANA

ATHENS

NAZI EXPANSION IN EUROPE

Map by Morgan

Legend (bottom)

▨▨	Frontier of the Greater German Reich
- - -	Province boundaries
▓	Territories "incorporated" into the Reich
░	"General Government"

CHAPTER
ONE

DURING THE MORNING hours of the first of September, 1939, war broke out between Germany and Poland and, indirectly, between Germany and Poland's allies, England and France. This time the allies will stick to their word and not betray Poland as they betrayed Czechoslovakia. For the time being, Poland alone will suffer all the hardships of the war, because there are no common frontiers between Poland and her allies. We are witnessing the dawn of a new era in the history of the world.

This war will indeed bring destruction upon human civilization. But this is a civilization which merits annihilation and destruction. There is no doubt that Hitlerian Nazism will ultimately be defeated, for in the end the civilized nations will rise up to defend the liberty which the German barbarians seek to steal from mankind. However, I doubt that we will live through this carnage. The bombs filled with lethal gas will poison every living being, or we will starve because there will be no means of livelihood.

How will I support myself? The schools won't be opened for a long, long time, and even if they should open, there would be no students in them. Parents will not let their children go outdoors for fear of air raids. I invested all I could in repairing my school (2,000 zloty[1]), and now it is bright, clean, repaired, and redecorated. But it will stand empty.

Poland is the chosen one, and the first arrows of the war between civilization and barbarism are falling upon her. But she will be joined by other nations, and united they will destroy the modern Huns. Since our enemy is the enemy of the whole human race, someone or other will come and avenge our spilled blood. And even the Poles who rejoiced at our misfortune, and not only expressed no word of consolation to us, but threatened to do to us what Hitler has done unless we emigrate from Poland—well, now the Poles themselves will receive our revenge through the hands of our cruel enemy.

The country is full of patriotic fervor. All classes and all nationalities, even those that suffered persecution at the hands of the Poles in time of peace, are ready to sacrifice their strength and wealth for the sake of the Fatherland. They make donations, they send declarations of submission and obedience to the chief of staff, Marshal Smigly-Rydz, etc., etc., as is customary at the beginning of every war.

As for the Jews, their danger is seven times greater. Wherever Hitler's foot treads there is no hope for the Jewish people. Hitler, may his name be blotted out, threatened in one of his speeches that if war comes the Jews of Europe will be exterminated. The Jews comprehend and sense all that is in store for them wherever Hitler's armies make a temporary conquest. It should therefore not be surprising that the Jews show their devotion to their fatherland in a demonstrative fashion. When the order was issued that all the inhabitants of the city must dig shelter trenches for protection from air raids, the Jews came in numbers. I, too, was among them. I took with me A.W.,[2] whose friend and supporter I have become in this time of tribulation. We signed up with the group of diggers who volunteered on behalf of the Jewish Journalists and Authors Association, and we went to dig at 29 Dluga Street. This was almost the first time in my life that I had done such physical labor, but I did not lag in my work. I returned home tired, but I couldn't eat.

[1] The zloty was worth approximately 20 cents at that time.
[2] Anka Welcer. A writer who translated Zalman Shneour's novel, *Noah Pandre,* into Polish.

The second day of the Polish-German war, which ultimately will turn into a world war and a slaughter of nations. England is in no hurry to declare war on Germany, and France too is delaying. But there is no doubt that the two allies will declare war at the same time. This time they will not betray us. Their representatives have already left Berlin, and their ultimatum to Hitler is that he withdraw his armies from the borders of Poland. In his usual fashion, Hitler has ignored the request. Tomorrow or the next day the cannons will begin to speak. From the moment when England and France join with Poland, the war will cease to be local. Then all of England's allies, such as Turkey and Rumania, will awaken, and the world catastrophe will grow.

Today there were four air raids in Warsaw. The inhabitants have already grown accustomed to them and know what they have to do. We have indeed entered upon a new era. We feared its coming and greeted it with anxious hearts, but since it has come and assumed a definite shape, this era will become second nature. Even abnormal living becomes normal when it becomes constant. But our nerves are working hard. Almost the entire day is filled with air raids whose results are unknown because the communiqués are delivered in a terse, clipped style, and conceal more than they reveal. As is customary, each side proclaims its victories and conceals its defeats, but it is not hard to understand why Poland's defeats are great, for the full force of war with a cruel and barbaric enemy, armed from head to foot, is directed against her. The aid which will eventually come from her allies will be indirect rather than direct.

My brain is full of the chatterings of the radio from both sides. The German broadcast in the Polish language prates propaganda. Each side accuses the other of every abominable act in the world. Each side considers itself to be righteous and the other murderous, destructive, and bent on plunder. This time, as an exception to the general rule, both speak the truth. Verily it is so—both sides are murderers, destroyers, and plunderers, ready to commit any abomination in the world. If you want to know the character of any nation, ask the Jews. They know the character of every nation.

The hour is fateful. If a new world arises, the sacrifices and troubles and hardships will be worthwhile. Let us hope that Nazism will be destroyed completely, that it will fall and never rise again. But our hearts tremble at the future . . . what will be our destiny?

21

And in these strange times of ours, wondrous things are taking place. Mussolini, Hitler's vassal, has remained neutral in the Polish-German war. No one imagined that. Some people think Mussolini will remain outside the war camp, but truly this is nothing but naïveté. The neutrality of this killer is merely a strategy instigated by Hitler. The moment England and France declare war on Germany, Mussolini will make his grand appearance. Hitler and Mussolini intend to localize the war, as if it were a minor territorial dispute between two neighbors which they could not resolve by peaceful means, not a world-wide matter. Actually Hitler has no need of any military aid from Mussolini as long as he is facing only Poland. But the dictators have erred. They are both as afraid of an international war as of the Russian bear, for they are fully aware that they will be defeated; and therefore their tactic is for each one to fall upon his prey at a time when the world is immersed in some other matter, and thus avoid a showdown. In keeping with this tactic it was decided that Mussolini would proclaim neutrality, and remain alone in his corner waiting to pounce when the right time came. Will such a time come? Everything depends on England.

September 3, 1939

Historic events! One cannot guess at the results of them. If a German bomb doesn't cut our lives short, and we are privileged to reach the end, it will yet be worthwhile living. England and France stood by their word, their promise to their ally, and the world conflagration has been ignited. There is no counting the number of victims which this slaughter will bring as sacrifices on the altar of Hitlerian barbarism. But there was no alternative. It was impossible to sit in silence and abandon Europe, carved up into small states, to the savage domination of the German terror. The end of this war is not in doubt. The tyrant will receive his punishment, his payment in kind. At that time Providence will also avenge the spilled blood of the German Jews.

It is now six years since the day Hitler rose to power and made the nullification of the Versailles Treaty his objective. He started from the Rhineland and ended with Czechoslovakia. For six years he stole, looted, and subjugated nations and lands to whom the treaty had promised protection and freedom. No one stopped him. The scoundrel began to see himself as the pampered child of Providence, born to be a Messiah for his people. Nearly all of the clauses of the treaty were made null and void by his ruthlessness. Only super-fluous paragraphs were left in it—Danzig continued to be a free city, and Poland retained Pomerania. Thus my question is: Why did the allies keep silent all this time, whereas now they have moved against Hitler with their armaments? I know in advance that they have no answer.

One must admit it: With all his successes, Hitler erred. And this error will bring ruin and destruction upon him. He erred by starting from Czechoslovakia and not from Poland. Had he started from Poland, no one would have lifted a finger for her sake. She is not very popular. The dispute would have remained local, and perhaps it would not have come to the point of war. But this terrorist put the cart before the horse. He preceded Poland with Czechoslovakia, rather than Czechoslovakia with Poland.

A moment ago Radio Moscow announced that the German army has captured Czestochowa. We were not informed of this here. Still more: flight hangars were demolished by bombs dropped from airplanes in the cities of Poznan, Lublin, Cracow, and others. But all these victories will be as naught when the day of retribution comes.

Today (from 2:30 to 7:00 P.M.) we again went to dig at 29 Dluga Street and worked for four hours. By immersing myself completely in the physical labor, I freed myself from the sad thoughts which darken my world. There is no happier moment now than the one which is free of thoughts!

From the communiqués it appears that there are no victories. If there were any they would be proclaimed in the loudest of voices. But one cannot describe how great the rejoicing in the capital city is upon hearing that England and France have declared war on Hitler. In an instant the entire city was bedecked with flags.

The joy of the Poles is unbounded. They are fighting for freedom, for the progress of humanity, for international ethics, and for all the lofty ideals for which the chosen few of the human race have sacrificed their lives. A true metamorphosis! The time is not long past when Hitler was their prophet. When they mentioned his name they were greatly pleased, and he served as an example to them, particularly in regard to the Jews. Now everything has changed completely.

How would my mother-in-law have said it? We have a father in heaven!

That Czestochowa was taken by the Germans was just verified

a moment ago by the Polish radio as well. "The enemy concentrated immense forces and forced us to leave the city of Czestochowa."

> Woe unto the Jews of Czestochowa.
> There is no calamity like unto theirs!

September 4, 1939

Bit by bit we are beginning to feel wartime living conditions. Normal life has ceased and our world has turned into chaos. There is no mail; there is no train travel unless one has a permit; the banks are paying their depositors just a part of their deposits; and there is no way to earn a living. All trade has stopped except in food stores and medical supply houses, which are being besieged by customers. Every day I receive telephone demands that I pay my bills, and I, of course, contrary to my usual practice, am not paying them because my small cash reserve is decreasing from day to day.

Half of today passed peacefully, but during the other half of it we had the taste of an air raid the like of which had never taken place till now. The enemy dropped bombs, each of which deafened us, and sometimes it seemed to us that they were exploding over our heads. Women fainted, cowards hid, and little children cried. The official communiqués do not usually inform us of the actual results of these raids, but simply underscore small incidents of real or fancied valor and conceal important conquests of the enemy. However, by reading between the lines we can learn that our armies are retreating little by little—abandoning great and important cities. In the course of four days, the enemy attacked on the northern front, where he reached Przasnysz, and on the southwestern front, where he reached Ostrow, and he is approaching Cracow. I am a novice in matters of military tactics and therefore it is difficult for me to determine whether this retreat is a stratagem or weakness. In any case, it is not a good sign. Where is Poland's strength, its might? If this is not a stratagem but rather a weakness, the enemy will reach Warsaw in another couple of days. And what will become of us? In the meantime Poland is being devastated. This is not the Germany of 1914—bad as it was, it had some conception of moral principles and international law.

Poland does have important and wealthy partners, but this partnership will not protect her from being turned into a place of desolation. As much as our allies harass the enemy on the Western front, he does as he pleases on the Eastern front. And until victory comes, women and innocent children who have never tasted sin will be killed.

I have made a rule for myself in these historic times not to let a single day go by without making an entry in my diary. Great Warsaw, from its center to its suburbs, is cloaked in a terrible darkness, comparable to the plague which was visited upon Egypt— darkness so thick it can be felt. They are very strict about the blackout, and night traffic in the streets has practically ceased. In the hope of keeping the people calm, the theaters are open, trolleys are operating, and the same is true of many other outward manifestations of life in the city. But no one is using them. Everyone prefers to remain in the house, because this is an awesome darkness which casts fear into everyone within it. Our noisy, gay city seems to have stopped breathing.

In truth, no one would have imagined that within five days the enemy would attain such great victories. Just now the Breslau radio announced the German communiqué in the Polish language. It is misfortune upon misfortune and defeat upon defeat. The Polish army is retreating in disorder and the Germans are pursuing and destroying them. The defeat of one division was so complete that all its officers were captured.

We are left abandoned and the shadow of death encircles us. When you see all that is taking place, evil thoughts awaken within you and disturb your rest. The Germans destroyed the Catholic church in Czestochowa, the most important Catholic shrine in Poland. The Poles call the Germans all sorts of derisive names and threaten them with revenge. Good! They are bitter. And when a nation is bitter, it cries out to avenge its blood and the desecration of its holy things.

But why did not the Poles join in our sorrow when Hitler ordered the burning of our synagogues, which were consumed in smoke together with scrolls of the Torah? We didn't hear a word of consolation. On the contrary, they enjoyed it; they were happy at our misfortune. We, however, share their sorrow and pray to the God of Israel to avenge their blood and ours.

The Poles complain against Germany, and justifiably, for she wishes to steal their native land from them and make them into slaves. But one question concerns me: Why didn't the Poles protest when the Germans decided to force the Jews, citizens of this country from earliest times, to leave Poland and to rob them of the land of their birth? The Poles renounce what befell them, but not what they did. And again I return to the essence of Jewish ethics: "Because thou drowndest, they drowned thee; and in the end they who drowned thee shall be drowned."[3]

September 6, 1939

Cracow, burial place of the kings of Poland, an ancient royal city with tradition and prestige, has been conquered by the European Huns. Is this not a dream? You get the impression from the Breslau radio that the Polish army is not an equipped army led by officers trained for warfare, but a flock of sheep. Whoever saw or heard of such a thing in the history of the wars of nations—that a rich country with thirty-five million citizens, with an organized army, would become something to be stepped on by the German villain within five days?

In Warsaw an evacuation has begun of government departments and of the government itself in all its glory, this pompous government which pursues praises and accolades. According to the Breslau radio, this government fled for its life to Lublin while there was still time. The government is fleeing and at the same time tries to soothe and placate the panicked masses.

All day long thousands of wagons come into the city laden with personal possessions—the "property" of the refugees, inhabitants of the cities where the enemy is wreaking destruction. The unfortunate Jews are running for dear life from the wrath of the oppressor. O God! Who can reveal to me what is yet to come?

September 7, 1939

The enemy is at the gates of Warsaw, and we are a beleaguered city. The masses have an eye that sees and an ear that hears. I too perceived it in the darkness of the night. The window of my bedroom faces toward Karmelicka Street, and even though I was sunk in slumber, voices and the noise of passersby reached my ears. I got up and looked out the window, and I knew at once that the government was fleeing.

[3] *Ethics of the Fathers* 2:9. A moral epigram by the sage Hillel: As you have done, so it will be done to you.

Today the government fled to Lublin and left not even a shadow of an administration in a city of a million three hundred thousand people.

There is no bread! Long lines of several hundred people formed in order to get a loaf of bread. The cries arose to the heart of the heavens. The beast in man came to the surface, for hungry mobs are capable of all manner of violence. One man struck his neighbor on his side and on his shoulder and there was no policeman to keep order. Whoever managed, after much effort and labor, to grab a loaf of bread, which is nothing but a bit of dough, was fortunate and his joy knew no bounds. This scene awakened revulsion in me, and pity for the unfortunates.

When the air-raid alarm is heard, the streets empty at once and a terrible silence reigns. The echoes of the bombs dropped from the planes of the enemy are answered by the beating of our pained and aching hearts. These are horrible moments. You prepare yourself to meet death. You are carried away on the wings of your sick imagination, as though the ceiling were already falling on your head and you would not even be privileged to see those dearest to you before your death. Women cry and faint. Frightened Jews recite the Psalms, and heretics accept their judgment. No, this is not life!

Life has gone off its straight course and becomes increasingly awry. A long, long time will pass before our lives become livable again.

September 9, 1939

In my psychological state it is hard to hold a pen in my hand, and my pen is not the one to describe what befell us last night. We have seen death face to face, and even the strong-hearted and the brave-spirited were gripped by trembling when they perceived that there was but a step between life and destruction. The thing is wondrous! In time of danger they all hold on to life and don't want to be separated from it. None of them, not even the old, the sick, and people who know poverty and endure sufferings, want to pass from the world by a bomb from Hitler's soldiers. In my eyes as well this is a senseless death. And here, perhaps, lies all the tragedy of it.

The enemy is at the gates, and he sends his angels of death to proclaim his coming. One must admit that the bombs are not being dropped deliberately to harm the peaceful inhabitants. Hitler kept his word. And gas bombs are not being used, so all the preparations for them were superfluous. But our torments from the bombs he is aiming at military objectives within the city are affecting residential neighborhoods. In my beautiful apartment on the first floor a few panicky, frightened neighbors gathered from among the residents of the courtyard whose apartments are on a higher floor, and who are hence in greater danger. And then—suddenly—the clap of thunder! We ran downstairs to the cellar, even though we might be buried alive there if the walls collapse. This was a shattering scene.

The defense of Warsaw has been turned over to the Polish General Czuma and he is fortifying himself within the city. Well, and where will we be? In the cellars! When I think of this war I shudder. Our sacrifices will reach into the tens of thousands.

Warsaw will be turned into a second Madrid.

September 10, 1939

The streets are sown with trenches and barricades. Machine guns have been placed on the roofs of houses, and there is a barricade in the doorway of my apartment house, just under my balcony. If fighting breaks out in the street no stone will remain upon another in the wall within which I live. We have therefore fled to my wife's sister's at 27 Nowolipki Street, which is nearby. Her apartment is supposed to be safer, since it faces a courtyard.

The enemy of the Jews attested long ago that if war broke out, Jews would be eliminated from Europe. Now half the Jewish people are under his domination. Why has God embittered our lives so cruelly? Have we indeed sinned more than any nation? We are more disgraced than any people!

September 11, 1939

Because there is no commerce or any sort of trade, there are many idlers who stand near the gates and gossip. They tell all sorts of fabricated tales, and since the newspapers have stopped, rumors are flourishing. Everyone expresses some stupid conjecture, which he transmits as fact, and at once it makes wings for itself.

Today a rumor spread that things have become a bit easier for us; that the enemy has been pushed back, and that our situation is growing better. How fortunate we would be had these rumors any basis! To my great sorrow, even if there is a bit of truth in them, they have no decisive value. We are careless in our thinking habits.

We are happy that England will come to our aid, but we do not ask ourselves: How? In what way?

The length and breadth of Warsaw is covered with trenches and barricades. The Supreme Commander has issued a proclamation that the capital is to defend itself to the last drop of blood. Should fighting break out in the streets, the German pirates would be greeted with a hail of bullets from the machine guns stationed on every rooftop and balcony. In his great anger the enemy would destroy every stone of every wall, and our homes would become our graves.

Why? For what purpose are such precious sacrifices offered up from among the civilian population?

In two more days it will be Rosh Hashanah, our New Year. Our humanitarian and pacifist prayers will be in sharp dissonance to all that is going on around us.

Jacob goes his way and Esau goes his.

Warsaw is full of refugees from all corners of the country. In the midst of the turmoil an unplanned and undirected exodus started, with some fleeing from Warsaw and others fleeing to Warsaw. Among the refugees there is a preponderance of people from the left bank of the Vistula. They were so frightened by the approach of the barbarian enemy that they left a lifetime's labor behind in order to save their skins. Camps, camps of tens of thousands, filled with movable property and children, line all the roads that lead to the capital, when the capital itself is not safe from disaster.

September 12, 1939

It is beyond my pen to describe the destruction and ruin that the enemy's planes have wrought on our lovely capital. Entire blocks have been turned into ashes and magnificent palaces into rubble. Every incendiary bomb dropped in the stillness of the night brings havoc and death to hundreds of people. Dante's description of the Inferno is mild compared to the inferno raging in the streets of Warsaw. Today the Jewish Polish-language newspaper, *Nasz Przeglad*, published a description of last night's raid and I couldn't read it through. A kilo of potatoes costs one zloty. It is impossible to get coal; the gas has been shut off; meat can no longer be found and it is now three days since we last tasted it. The lovely Anka Welcer, her sick mother, and her artist sister have not tasted bread for three days. Yesterday she came to me and I gave her a half-kilo of bread, one pickled herring, and a quarter-kilo of sugar. It was heartbreaking to see her distress.

I myself still have something to eat as well as some money. But how long will it last? I am now out of work. Despite all this, however, I still live with hope. This too shall pass. We will yet come out of this alive!

September 14, 1939

Eight in the morning, the first day of Rosh Hashanah, 5700

I have returned to my own apartment. The danger is great everywhere. There is no hiding from fate.

It is difficult to write, but I consider it an obligation and am determined to fulfill it with my last ounce of energy. I will write a scroll of agony in order to remember the past in the future. For despite all the dangers I still have hopes of coming out of this alive.

Yesterday was a day of horror and destruction. Between five o'clock and seven o'clock on the eve of Rosh Hashanah[4] there was an air raid on the North Quarter, which is predominantly Jewish. From where I was, I could see with my own eyes all the horror that such a murderous attack can bring upon quiet residents, who in their innocence were busy preparing themselves for the approaching holiday. A rumor had spread that Hitler had ordered the cessation of air attacks. He was forced to do this by Stalin "the merciful," who threatened to "void" their pact unless attacks against the peaceful civilian populace ceased. Despite my bitterness, I could not help smiling at this bit of "consolation." And immediately we were all shown the veracity of this rumor.

The enemy mercilessly poured his wrath on the Jewish quarter with incendiary bombs. We too experienced such a bomb at 22 Nowolipki Street, opposite where we are. The effect is like an earthquake. But worst of all is the chaos which follows among the victims. No one knows where he is running. Each one runs to a place that has already been abandoned by another as unsafe. Carrying babies and bundles, distracted and terrified people desperately look for a haven. Tens of thousands of broken refugees find themselves lost in a strange city. These people fill every courtyard and

[4] Most air attacks and evil decrees later on in the ghetto were launched on Jewish holidays and Sabbaths.

every stairway, and during the turmoil of the fires there are none more miserable. Afterward you hear details that curdle the blood. Hundreds of families are left with nothing—their wealth has been burned, their apartments destroyed, their possessions lost.

How has Warsaw, the royal, beautiful, and beloved city become desolate!

September 15, 1939

Second day of Rosh Hashanah, 5700

Everything and everyone bears the stamp of war. Instead of Jews wearing prayer shawls and carrying prayer books rushing to the synagogue, one sees stretcher bearers carrying the dead and wounded dug out from the ruins of bombed buildings. Yesterday passed uneventfully, and already the populace of the besieged city seems hungry for amusements, promenades, work. That is—outwardly. Inwardly, everyone is busy preparing himself for death. Everyone senses that what we have already experienced is nothing compared to what we will yet experience.

According to a decision made by the Supreme Commander, the city of Warsaw has turned into a special "position," a military zone of the front. The big shots have deserted us; they fled like cowards while there was still time. They also saved their families by sending them to a neutral country, Rumania. This is what the Foreign Minister, Beck,[5] did, the man who with his great diplomatic skill brought this tragedy upon the country. The exalted and cowardly government sits in Kremenets, near the Rumanian border—just in case of trouble. It is bad enough that the government ran out on us, the citizens, and offered us no guidance whatsoever during this crisis. Now it wants to sacrifice our lives and the lives of our families by ambushing the enemy as he enters the besieged and broken city; in other words, to mark our houses as our graves. What compels it to such criminal decisions? Especially since the German radio repeats at least four times a day that the Supreme German Command threatens the entire population of each city with dire consequences if any civilian groups try to stop the German army. Such cities will be wiped off the face of the earth. And there is no reason to doubt that Hitler's army will keep its word.

[5] Colonel Jozef Beck.

Actually, our strategic situation is horrible. The three richest parts of the country, from the point of view of military supplies, are in the hands of the enemy. The incompetent and haughty Polish government has practically nothing left to govern. It has dug itself into a distant corner on the southeast border and waits to be forced out. Never before in history has any people suffered a defeat as shameful as this. And even if a hundred thousand unarmed civilians should give their lives for the capital—would they save it? Only a murderous government could make such a criminal decision.

Will we be destroyed by this war? My heart tells me no. But we will pay a very dear price for our lives.

September 16, 1939

Yesterday was quiet. Today, however, in the afternoon, Hitler's emissaries returned again to imbue us with the fear of death. Until now we hoped that even if war broke out, Hitler's downfall would inevitably come, as would the destruction of Nazism. We were prepared to accept the labor pains of peace as long as the world would be assured of a bright future. Now, as military events have developed, there is a danger that Hitler may yet prevail. There was a mistaken calculation here. One ally—Poland—let down all the other allies. Who ever dreamed of this kind of military catastrophe for a people who took as a motto: "By thy sword shalt thou live"? They spoke so highly of their military prowess that they misled all the other nations with their vain boasts and overblown conceit. At their first contact with the Germans they melted like wax and proved that their valor was an empty disguise. There is good reason to believe that within a month Hitler will have finished off the entire Polish front, and the remnants of the Polish army will either be taken prisoners or escape disarmed to a neutral country.

Then no one will envy France or England even though they stand together.

I received a sad piece of news from one refugee who had left and then returned; that is to say, he fled to Kaluszyn, wandered about, and finally decided to return to Warsaw. My friend and companion, the Yiddish writer Szymon Horonczyk, has committed suicide in Kaluszyn, where he had fled with the other refugees. The reason for his death is also known: his son disappeared during the flight from Warsaw.

Warsaw, a city of two million, is being laid waste by fire and sword.

In the pitch dark, close to three o'clock, we turned on the radio in the hope of hearing a voice from the outside, from the wide world, even though I knew very well not to expect any comfort in the news. There was a voice—from the German sector of Breslau. The voice said, "The murderous Polish government is inciting the populace of Warsaw to fight against the German army. Therefore Warsaw is now considered a military front. The German Military Command sent an emissary to the commander in charge of the defense of Warsaw with a demand for surrender, in order to spare the innocent populace. The emissary was not received. Therefore, know full well, residents of Warsaw, your own military commander is bringing all this strife upon you."

In the early morning the telephone rang. It was my friend Dr. A. W. Perhaps I could recommend a baker who would sell him a daily loaf of bread so he would not have to wait in line. I offered to give him one of my loaves, and within the hour he was at my apartment to pick it up. When I saw him I was startled. Never had I seen him in so despairing a state, so broken and crushed. He had turned gray, his voice was hoarse and low, he was sloppily dressed—the inner beauty that had always illumined the face of this scholar was gone. He was a broken man.

The city's newspapers, whose number has been diminished by two-thirds and whose texts are ever more closely censored, are full of "victories." According to them, our military position is secure. The fact that the enemy is at the city gates is only incidental. If I want to know the truth, I must tune in Radio Breslau, which has a tendency to exaggerate—or better yet, Radio Moscow.

Yesterday Radio Moscow announced a piece of terrifying information. The Soviet army has crossed the Polish-Russian border and penetrated into the western Ukraine and western White Russia with the intention of annexing these lands to Soviet Russia. Now the cat is out of the bag. In the Hitler-Stalin pact, which took the whole world by surprise, there was a secret paragraph that has not been revealed. The other side (England and France) could not present Stalin with as meaningful a historical achievement as the annexation of the Ukraine and White Russia; that could come about only through the destruction of Poland. Now that Poland's military might has been broken, and the government has escaped—now is the right time to act. This is the level of international morality. Just as Poland acted toward Czechoslovakia when she had the upper hand, so the Soviets act toward Poland now that they have the upper hand. When the ox is fallen, sharpen the knife. Because you drowned others, they drown you.

The Soviet army is "conquering" (bloodlessly, of course) all of the western Ukraine and western White Russia, with Hitler's approval and aid. This is what is called a united front. The city where I was born, Horodyszcze,[6] became a Bolshevik city one bright morning. And the same for the city of Korelicze, and all the trembling cities of that poor and wretched region. A socialist revolution in the guise of a military revolution. Worlds are destroyed and worlds are created.

We had a day of rest and our taut nerves relaxed a bit. At moments such as these we tend to forget that human beings are killing one another and men are attacking their brothers, bent upon murder. Why do they do it? It is difficult to find an answer. Perhaps the correct answer is that men are basically corrupt, swayed by primitive passions—laws that consider darkness to be light, and wrath righteousness.

The Soviets have come from the east, bearing "peace, order, and bread" to their Ukrainian and White Russian blood brothers. Stalin's government seems to be supported by strong public sympathy in this move. A really historic surprise! Hitler is helping Stalin spread his Communist regime to White Russia and the western Ukraine, and Stalin is helping Hitler to strengthen his hold on us. These two extremes find a common meeting ground in their hatred of democracy. It is this ideological affinity that brought about the nonaggression pact and the terrible war that has followed it.

September 20, 1939

One day without an entry. Besieged Warsaw is now a world of primeval chaos. It is difficult to recognize the city. At times it seems to me that I am in an alien land, entirely unknown to me.

[6] In White Russia, near Minsk.

The enemy has surrounded the city from four sides, no one is permitted to leave or enter, and there is no way of getting bread The stored provisions are all but exhausted. Of the mills near the city, one was burned and the rest captured by the enemy. Once some hungry people went searching for potatoes in the nearby fields and found death instead. They were shot at and killed.

It is interesting that in the midst of all the turmoil and haste, the Polish government did not forget to take the national treasury to Rumania, and from there to England. The masses say that the ministers will divide the treasury amongst themselves, and that this is a good thing since in this way the money will remain in Polish hands. In any event, we, the citizens of the country, are left to die and starve and suffer all the other horrors of war with freshly printed, valueless bills. As long as the government was still in existence, prices remained fairly stable, but now there is no fixed price for anything, and very little food is available at any price.

Things have come to such a pass that the mayor, Stefan Starzynski, who has shouldered the responsibility of the government and who several times daily comforts and encourages the unfortunate residents of the city, announced over the radio today that the merchants must open their stores to enable the people to buy clothes and shoes for the winter. The merchants always know what's in it for them. Why should they open their stores? Let the merchandise lie unsold. Every day its price goes up. Long lines of customers wait in front of the Bata shoe store to convert the fallen government's notes into merchandise. As usual, the professional man is in a difficult position since he cannot find work and does not have ready cash to fall back upon; and even when he does find work, the salary offered falls short of the prices asked. How will the teachers live? I only wish I knew.

Human beings spend all their energies and talents in the pursuit of bread. Man has become an animal, concerned only with brute existence and fear of starvation. Holidays and festivals no longer exist. During Rosh Hashanah, haphazard public prayers were held in some synagogues, but will we be able to recite the Kol Nidre?[7] I doubt it! Israel's prayers in a city surrounded by German soldiers—what dissonance!

[7] A prayer that is part of the service on the eve of Yom Kippur, the Day of Atonement.

Our holy day is over. Mourning is on every face. As our prophet said, "The whole head is sick and the whole heart faint." There is not one family who has not endured a sacrifice of some sort, human or material. Many of my friends have turned gray. It is hard to recognize them.

On the Day of Atonement the enemy displayed even greater might than usual. He did not give us an hour's respite. The heavy artillery rained fire and iron upon our heads, destroying one apartment house after another and killing dozens of people with every burst. Perhaps it is good to die. Anticipating death is worse than death itself, since death brings release from consciousness, and an end to one's suffering. Everyone feels that his staying alive is merely a matter of chance. Last Thursday the Free Burial Society buried eighty people who had been killed by bombs and grenades. This is an everyday occurrence.

September 25, 1939

Our minutes are numbered. For forty-eight hours the enemy has unleashed the furies of death upon us. It is impossible to describe them.

September 26, 1939

Blessed is the eye that does not see Warsaw desolate and destroyed, still at the enemy's mercy.

I have seen people consumed by the desire for a livelihood, or money, or amusements—which was foolish enough; but to see people consumed by the desire for life when an awful danger hovers over their heads—this is the most foolish of all foolish things. Man's nothingness is then exposed in high and ugly relief.

When the air demons go out for a "stroll" in the skies of the unfortunate city, everyone runs for cover to the dark holes commonly called shelters. Everyone is hushed in the face of death. The Christians immediately go down on their knees and start chanting our psalms. Orthodox Jews recite the prayers for death. Hysterical women gasp and wail and beat their breasts.

We lack all the necessities of life: bread, water, gas, electricity;

and it goes without saying that such "luxuries" as meat, butter, and milk are unobtainable at any price.

Our days are taken up with one pursuit—to hide from death.

And Starczynski sends releases all over the world: Warsaw is fighting with marvelous valor! Warsaw is full of hope for victory! Life is continuing in normal fashion!

There is an end to everything, except to the lies of the mayor.

September 28, 1939

Thursday, first day of Sukkot,[8] *5700*

Blessed be God for bringing me out of this alive!

Last night will go down in history as another St. Bartholomew's Massacre—the terror of the former surpassing the terror of the latter, the victims of the former far outnumbering the victims of the latter. During the St. Bartholomew Massacre, the killing was done by hand-wielded weapons; during Warsaw's Night, the killing was done by heavy artillery trained on a metropolis full of quiet citizens.

Hitler has kept his promise. In order to destroy without mercy and yet remain "legally blameless," should the conscience of the world (if there is such a thing!) bring him to trial, he has wrapped himself in legalities.

General Czuma, who is in charge of Warsaw's defense, and who doesn't know his right hand from his left, sent out a proclamation to the citizens of Warsaw ordering them to defend the city. Of course he did not bother asking their advice, nor did they consent. During a war the civilian citizens are in the category of dumb sheep. They are filled to overflowing with false patriotism, compelled to obey every word that comes out of the commanders' mouths, and the commanders regard thousands of lives as nothing when compared to a little military prestige. And here lies the root of our catastrophe. The murderous supervision of the military staff turned Warsaw into a defensive position. Though the citizens hadn't been asked, Hitler considered it to be an actual military position on the front lines. It cannot be denied that the German military staff, through Radio Breslau, warned us at the beginning that the population of the city would be considered frontline soldiers and would have to bear all the consequences of war.

[8] The feast of thanksgiving, commemorating the ingathering of the harvest.

And oh, how we are bearing them! The murder of masses of people through a legal technicality—why not?

And so Hitler's army has encircled a metropolis of two million people with heavy artillery, shut off the water supply, damaged the electricity, and deprived them of all food and provisions. And for ten hours let loose a barrage of fire and brimstone and red-hot iron upon them.

Suddenly, however, a new wind blew among the people of the city. We instinctively felt that a change had taken place for our good. That the next hours would bring some sort of salvation was whispered from mouth to mouth, brightening every dark and gloomy face. Various rumors were spread in whispers. From the nearby front many soldiers started to pour into the city and were immediately besieged by civilians waiting for some sort of word.

Suddenly a proclamation swept through the city: Armistice!

September 29, 1939

I have seen Warsaw in its utter devastation. Woe is me!

This is a topic fit for a classical elegist, capable of creating a new expression to describe the magnitude of destruction. Beautiful Warsaw—city of royal glory, queen of cities—has been destroyed like Sodom and Gomorrah. There are streets which have been all but wiped off the face of the earth. Hundreds of houses have been destroyed by fire or changed into islands of rubble. Dozens of streets have turned into desolate heaps of gravel. All this happened on that bitter and unforgettable day, August 25.[9] It is difficult to walk among the still smoldering and smoking ruins. Only long walls are left, walls that stand unsupported, endangering the passersby, for they are liable to fall at any minute. In the midst of the ruins thousands of human beings lie buried. This is the third day that the bodies of people who did not manage to escape are being pulled out from among the ruins. The members of the Burial Society collect the bodies and arrange them in piles to be taken to the cemetery.

There is no end to corpses of horses. They lie fallen in the middle of the street and there is no one to remove them and clear the road. They have been rotting for three days and nauseating all the passersby. However, because of the starvation rampant in the city, there are many who eat the horses' meat. They cut off chunks and eat them

[9] Apparently one of the diarist's rare errors in date. September 25 is undoubtedly meant.

to quiet their hunger. There isn't a store that hasn't been burned or damaged and whose goods were not ruined or stolen. In this transitional period when there is no government authority, pillaging and robbery are committed in broad daylight everywhere, and have increased in those stores which were not emptied by their owners. Warm winter clothes are most often stolen. Storekeepers have been known to invite passersby in off the street to take what they want, since the merchandise would be ruined anyway.

And we are waiting for Hitler's army. Once again, woe to us!

After all the horrors that we have endured, we wait for Hitler's army as for the spring rains. We are without bread and without water. Our nerves are shattered from everything that has happened during the last awful days. In such a condition, our only desire is to rest awhile, even if it is under Hitler's rule. And so, today at 8:00 P.M., Hitler's soldiers will enter the gates of Warsaw like victorious heroes.

Poland has fallen. Will she yet arise?

September 30, 1939

And so, theoretically speaking, we are already under Nazi rule. The city is wide-open. Rommel[10] has shown his "heroism" by killing thousands of people and burning down the palaces in the capital; he has turned a bustling city into a desolate heap of ruins; he has made tens of thousands of people penniless and homeless; he has created widows and orphans without number—all this has happened so that his Polish colleague, who is as "smart" as he, might be able to announce to the world: Warsaw fights! Warsaw displays bravery! Warsaw fights to her last drop of blood! Warsaw will not surrender! Warsaw is our pride: every house—a fortress; every courtyard—a stronghold! Not one handful has been relinquished to the arrogant foe; here he will meet his downfall, etc., etc. These empty phrases were spoken by military experts who were aware of the enemy's strength and who knew that aside from victims and havoc nothing was to be gained from such empty rhetoric!

We laymen who were not military experts were capable of accurately evaluating the comparative strength of the two warring countries. We knew and felt the great danger hovering over our heads —mortal danger and financial ruin. As civilians, commanded and prepared to be patriotic, we were afraid to open our mouths and voice

[10] This is apparently not a reference to Erwin Rommel, the "Desert Fox," but to Polish Major General Juliusz Rommel.

any sort of criticism against the leaders controlling our fate. But in secret, among ourselves, wherever a small group of Jews gathered—even in the dark, cold cellar—we whispered our doubts to one another: These fools! These pompous idiots! For what purpose do they lead a city of two million people to slaughter? There isn't even any military prestige involved here! Everything they say is a lie! Is civilian Warsaw really fighting? We were commanded by a military order that does not recognize surrender to dig ditches, pits, and holes in the streets—and so we dug. As we were digging we knew that it was a useless labor—but we were impelled to comply. We spent most of our time hiding in cellars. I never knew that I was "fighting ferociously" in a knightly manner; I never knew that the eyes of the whole world were upon me and that people marveled at my courage and wished me success. I was like a broken vessel—motivated by fear and genuine cowardice. I sat, shrunken and shriveled, in a dank cellar, overcome with fear and trembling at the terror of the bombs. Rommel and Starzynski suddenly made a "military hero" out of me!

The blood of the masses is boiling. Everyone is full of rebellion and bitterness, prepared to tear the nation's leaders to pieces, although a short while ago they were unanimously shouting: "Lead us to Berlin!" After the Warsaw front was dismantled yesterday, large disarmed regiments returned home. I talked to a few of the soldiers and they too are happy and sad—happy to be out of danger and sad at the futility of their effort, at Poland's defeat, at the loss of their political freedom, at the shortsighted diplomacy of their beautiful and beloved country:

"Here, in the capital, thousands of tons of provisions and food went to waste and at the front we starved."

"Now the French and British will come and smoke their pipes on Poland's ruins."

"For the sake of justice, they must not be pardoned for this heinous deed! Doesn't the blood of infants demand vengeance? Has all sense of responsibility departed with the coming of war? Has anything like this ever been heard of before—to turn over the lives of an entire city into the hands of people demented by a sick desire for military prestige?"

Great political changes will yet take place in Poland. When peace comes, this sin will also be recalled, demanding punishment.

But the enemy is not here; he delays his entry. Why? People in the know say that he is waiting for the streets to be fixed up, for the ditches to be filled in, and for the barricades to be torn down. I foresaw this from the beginning; jokingly, I used to say that the hands that dug would also fill in—now it has come to pass.

October 1, 1939

Now I will try to put the whole thing down in an orderly fashion. I was surrounded by disorder, and therein lay the difficulty—how was it possible to describe a disorderly thing in an orderly fashion?

I find it hard even to hold a pen. My hands tremble; I have lived through a catastrophe that has left me crushed and physically broken. And what is worse, even as I sit writing these lines, I am still not certain that the catastrophe is over; I only comfort myself with the hope that I will come out of this alive.

The Germans entered the capital in a disciplined way. They immediately announced that they are distributing free bread to the needy. Before the entry—bombs; after the entry—loaves of bread to the starving. They appear to be a charitable army, but in the midst of their charitableness, their planes did not forget to circle over Warsaw and take pictures of the long lines waiting for free bread from the "charitable" enemy. Thus two birds were killed with one stone: material for propaganda and for films to prove it.

I also stood in line, but not to receive bread—only impressions. I wanted to see the Nazis when they are engaged in charitable work. Also, at that time the entry into the city was being completed, and this too was a good opportunity for impressions. I studied Hitler's army into which he had sunk, according to his own words, ninety million marks within six years—and I was amazed to see how well fed, sleek, and fat it was. The Germans who entered the city amazed you with their healthy appearance and marvelous uniforms. You almost began to believe that this was indeed a people fit to rule the world by virtue of power and strength. But perhaps this too was merely a propaganda display, since everything the Nazis do is motivated by a plan to impress the masses. But even if it was only propaganda, it must still be reckoned with. A doubt stole into my heart: perhaps it was I who had been deceived? Until now I had been certain that they were starving and we were well fed; now I see the exact opposite. We are hungry and they give us free bread. They are well fed and wealthy, and we are starving and impoverished.

41

Yesterday I wrote my scroll of agony by the dim light of a candle, and so I was unable to detail and complete the record of my experiences. Therefore I am returning to it today.

I was suddenly informed that the newly arrived Germans had already managed to requisition five houses on Nowolipki Street—numbers 12, 14, 16, 18, 20—and to expel all their Jewish inhabitants. They did not permit them to take even a shoelace out of their apartments; they did not permit them to don even an overcoat. In a matter of minutes, all the Jews were expelled and all the houses cleared. The Jews went out afraid and shocked, in a state of confusion and wearing house clothes. Two or three soldiers arrogantly and noisily stormed into every apartment and shouted: "Jews, *heraus!*"

They were not permitted to utter a syllable. Within minutes, hundreds of families were left without a roof, without clothes, without food, without an apartment, without money—and I among them. And to add to my misery, I had left all my savings in my apartment. My last straw to cling to in an hour of need had been taken from me. Up to now, during the dangerous days, I had left my money in safekeeping with my wife; after things quieted down a bit, we put it in a box which we locked in a chest in the closet. Now I am stripped of all my possessions. I don't even have a roof over my head.

They comfort us with the promise that the apartments were taken for only a few days; that the Germans will not ransack them; that everything will be returned to us in perfect condition. This does not appease me. I am caught between the jaws of the lion; will I emerge unscathed?

According to rumor, the German Supreme Commander has let it be known that he wants no difficulties set in the way of the Jews; but this is merely a political move. In the reality of everyday, the Jews are discriminated against. Perhaps the soldiers do this on their own accord, since they are rabidly anti-Semitic, but it matters little to us from whence the evil stems. We are always candidates for double troubles.

We run around like madmen trying to obtain help in entering our apartments and taking out some clothes and other necessities from them, but all our efforts are in vain. It is impossible to return to the apartment without permission, and permission can only be granted by the Commandant, and his office is surrounded with long lines of thousands of waiting people. My sick wife got up at four o'clock this morning and (at 3:00 P.M.) has not yet returned. And I am certain that after waiting ten hours she will return empty-handed. Broken, depressed, and weak, running a fever, hungry and thirsty, she will return home in despair and disappointment.

I am like the man who watches his ox being slaughtered: sad to lose a companion and hungry for meat. From time to time I walk along the left side of Karmelicka Street and gaze at the windows of my lovely apartment, now in the hands of strangers; the sons of Ham took over my property as though it belonged to them. My heart is broken: I sank a whole lifetime's work into that apartment: I lived in it for twenty-four years; I decorated it and beautified it and adorned it; and in one confused hour I lost it.

October 4, 1939

We are at the mercy of shameless murderers. The "charitable" army distributes bread and pottage to the hungry, and the poor unfortunates must wait in line long hours to get their meager portions; but when it comes to a Jew's turn, he is roughly pushed aside and compelled to return home shamed and mauled as well as hungry and thirsty. Incidents of daylight robbery are on the rise. My friend Szlofsztejn told me today that his son was robbed in broad daylight yesterday of 1,000 zloty. A Nazi invited him to the gate, pointed his pistol at him, searched him, and took 1,000 zloty out of his pocket. And this is typical. They rob in secret; the Commandant claims to know nothing about what is going on. But the troops know which way the wind is blowing. People are so overcome with fear that they are afraid to shout. The pillage and plunder are committed only against Jews. The Christians are spared these troubles. They are treated "charitably"; they are given food and drink and offered sympathy, because their government deceived them and brought this great misfortune upon them.

We are in a state of double darkness. Physical darkness, because the electricity has been shut off; and mental darkness because the news from the outside world has been shut off. The same day that the electricity stopped, the radio and newspapers also stopped. Undoubtedly, great events have taken place outside our dark world.

Since we have no reliable means of receiving news, rumors abound about the political situation in the world and the military situation on the Western front. Some say that the Soviets are eying Warsaw and a war is bound to break out between them and the Germans. A peculiar rumor, but one that does not cease. The interminable voice of the people. Others say the Germans are being beaten and battered on the Western front; in fact, the French have already captured twelve cities! In view of the deteriorating and dangerous situation on the Western front, the German Command has decided to transfer several divisions from here to there. In spite of all these peculiar rumors whispered from mouth to ear, no one really knows what is going on.

But politics is far removed from our world. We simply do not have the time to engage in it. We are too busy fighting for a piece of stale bread, a sip of water, the primary necessities of life which even money can no longer buy.

We have turned into animals: some of us into domestic animals; and some of us into carnivorous animals.

The requisitioned apartments have not been returned. They lied to us. About five hundred displaced people stand at the corner of Nowolipki and Karmelicka streets every day, gazing at their former apartments, now occupied by strangers. From time to time the sentries threaten the poor unfortunates with their guns in an effort to disperse them. Actually, the people have but one request: that they be permitted to take out their most necessary belongings. But obstacles are deliberately placed in their path. In an effort to get rid of these "rebels," the sentries send them to the Commandant to obtain a *Passier-schein*. At the Commandant's office, thousands of people wait in long lines. Cold and damp, hungry and thirsty, they wait for long hours and then return home empty-handed. The "efficient" Germans do not display their efficiency in this case. On the contrary, they treat the Jews as though they were positively averse to efficiency. Dozens of people appear before them and do not receive any satisfaction, but as soon as some well-dressed, beautiful woman appears, she gets what she wants. As far as they are concerned, beautiful women are in a top priority category.

The Nazis promised that at 8:00 A.M. the senior officer of the division would appear and permit all the displaced people to enter their apartments, and take out their possessions. But as usual, they lied. A few were permitted to enter their apartments; most of us stood by passively and lost hope of ever entering at all. One of our women

44

friends succeeded in getting into her apartment and nearly fainted. Chaos and disorder reigned everywhere. Everything had been thrown together and the apartment looked as though a pogrom had taken place in it. I took a daring step and decided to get our things out through the window facing Karmelicka Street. Since our apartment is on the first floor, it was easy for our things to be lowered outside. Our maid Irka and our friend Aniuta went into the apartment and handed out everything they could lift. We stood outside—in sight of hundreds of passersby with nothing better to do than watch us for diversion—and caught the things as they came out. It was a scene worthy of being filmed. We worked under these circumstances for about two hours, until we had managed to retrieve all our possessions. With the aid of the women we made packages and bundles which we placed at the gate near 24 Karmelicka Street. Afterward, we brought them to our relative's house.

October 5, 1939

Eve of Simhat Torah,[11] *5700*

Our holiday is no longer celebrated. Fear has displaced gladness, and the windows of the synagogues are dark. Never before have we missed expressing our joy in the eternal Torah—even during the Middle Ages. After 7:00 P.M. there is a curfew in the city, and even in the hours before the curfew we live in dread of the Nazi conquerors' cruelty. The Nazi policy toward Jews is now in full swing.

Every day brings its share of grievous incidents. Here are some typical occurrences: Bearded Jews are stopped on the streets and abused. During the morning prayers on Shemini Atzeret,[12] a hundred and fifty men were pulled out of the Mlawa Street synagogue, herded into a truck, and taken to enforced labor. A Jew was stripped of his coat in the street and the coat was given to a Christian, so that he could benefit from the theft. A broken Jew, standing in a food line for long hours, was picked up for a twenty-four-hour work detail, hungry and thirsty as he was.

Midian and Moab have joined forces in order to oppress Israel.

[11] The holiday of "Rejoicing in the Torah," at the end of Sukkot, when the weekly Sabbath reading of the Pentateuch is completed and begun anew for the coming year.
[12] The Eighth Day of Assembly, celebrated after the seventh day of Sukkot, as the concluding festival of the harvest season.

The last lesson has not yet been learned by our wise Polish neigh-bors, for even though they have suffered a national catastrophe as horrible as hell, they have not forgotten their animosity toward the Jews. Even though they are dull-witted and uncultured and do not know German, they have nevertheless learned to say: *"Ein Jude!"* in order to get him thrown out of line.

Dark and heavy clouds darken our sky. There is no gleam of hope, no ray of light.

The masses comfort themselves with groundless rumors, offsprings of their own imaginings. Man believes what he wants to believe. In the thick darkness surrounding us, we have ample opportunity for imaginings. This time, they are not Messianic dreams but political fantasies: in a little while the Nazis will leave and the Soviets will take over; war will break out between Germany and America; war will break out between Turkey and Germany; there are Nazi defeats on the Western front; Berlin has been destroyed like Warsaw, etc.

Where are we to look for salvation? It seems as though even our Father in Heaven—the mainstay of our fathers—has deserted us. Are we indeed to sing with the poet[13]: "Heavenly spheres, beg mercy for me. Behold, the path to God no longer exists! God of Israel, where art thou?"

October 6, 1939

The unfortunate Jews of Nowolipki Street have not yet been permitted to enter their requisitioned apartments and take out their belongings. The few who have succeeded in entering the apartments find everything in a state of disorder and disarray. But even the pillage is not carried out systematically. Everything de-pends upon the individual soldier, and the human material of the army is composed of varied elements. Churls and boors rob and plunder; decent and honest people do not touch anything.

When the Nazis confiscated our apartment, they permitted our Christian maid to remain. Since she is exempt from the Nuremberg Laws, they raped her. After that they beat her so that she would reveal where I had hidden my money.

For various reasons most of my possessions were saved. Thanks to the window, instead of a quarter of an hour—the time allotted to those permitted to enter their apartments—we worked three full hours, and everything that had not been stolen was removed. Even

[13] Ch. N. Bialik, 1873–1934, then considered the national Hebrew poet.

so, when I took stock of my possessions afterward, I saw that many valuable things were gone.

At this point I must record the double miracle that happened to me.

I had placed all my money, along with some importmant documents, in an expensive copper box decorated with Bezalel art work. I had 600 zloty in the form of twelve notes, each worth 50 zloty. The notes were in a sealed envelope. The envelope and some other papers were in a small linen bag inside the box. The soldiers of the "ruling race" broke the lock of the box, took out the bag, and cast it aside as valueless. When the open and broken box was handed out the window to me I thought I would faint, so certain was I that my money had been stolen. But when we returned to our new apartment and began arranging our things—what joy when among our other possessions—which are practically valueless—we found the bag containing the money and documents.

From all the excitement my wife came close to fainting. The money found in the bag was our last bit of security in these turbulent times.

I, to whom this miracle happened, do most certainly appreciate my good fortune. Sinful and murderous men searched for my money in order to rob me of it, and they were smitten with blindness. A double miracle!

October 7, 1939

The conquerors and the conquered find common cause in their hatred of Israel. Jewish morality demands: If a man suffers misfortune, let him examine his deeds. Not so Christian morality. Misfortune does not trouble the hearts of these practitioners of the "religion of love." When they suffer misfortune, they merely cause others to suffer in turn—especially if they are strangers and not friends. During these confused times, when everyone grieves and worries about the most basic problems, when a common enemy has overrun the country and threatens to swallow both peoples, when their misfortune is even greater than ours since theirs involves a nation and ours involves individuals—and since we are used to suffering and punishment from time immemorial and for them it is a new experience—despite all this, animosity toward Jews continues to grow even during these times of poverty and distress.

The conquered people flatter the conquerors, open their houses to them, socialize with them, and with a submissiveness that is down-right ugly they eagerly accept any little kindness that the cruel conqueror metes out. They permit themselves to be stepped on and are prepared to eat gall, as long as they can inform on the Jews. We are lucky that they do not know German. In the long run, sign language is not enough. But animosity finds its way; it is strong enough to enable the dumb to speak.

October 10, 1939

Only Jews are taken for forced labor. Young, energetic, muscular Poles stand and mock from afar the Jews who kneel under the burden of their toil. The enemy picks Jews particularly for the most distasteful work—cleaning toilets, scrubbing floors, and other jobs of this sort. And there was an occurrence that I heard of from a youth—"It happened to me, myself!" he said. They caught him for work and ordered him to clean out filthy places and gave him no tools. When he asked for tools, they advised him to do it with his hands and to use his coat in place of a vessel. When he objected to this they beat him. Some soldiers were present at the time who couldn't stand to see an innocent man tortured, and explained to the strongarm that one should not behave in that manner toward a human being. The officer replied to this that the Jews wanted the war so it was just that such great misfortune befall them; that more than ten thousand German soldiers have already fallen victim, and that the Jews are making a business out of this war. Afterward they beat him some more, and after seven hours of degrading and despicable work, without tasting bread or water, he returned home.

October 12, 1939

Today a new order was published: All deposits, whether of gold, silver, notes, or other currency left in banks, are closed. The financial institution is authorized to give a Jew only 250 zloty a week against his deposits, and if he needs larger sums for business, such as buying goods or paying salaries to workers and staff, he is required to submit documentary proof. It is forbidden for a Jew and all his relatives living with him in the same house to keep more than 2,000 zloty in his pocket at a time; any amount over 2,000 must be deposited in the bank. All manner of jewelry and trinkets whether of silver, gold, platinum, or other precious metals must be turned over to him—the conqueror.

The conquered Poles also suffer and are tormented, but theirs are tortures that flow from the general situation. On the contrary, the enemy smiles upon them and assists them in rebuilding their ruins. They promise them the establishment of a Polish state, and the masses who don't understand much of such matters are nevertheless glad that "Poland will be" (*Polska bedzie*). Not so the Jews. They are paying the costs of the war. The Nazis justify themselves: You want the war, so you must bear its sufferings and expenses. Something along the lines of the Biblical law, "He that kindled the fire shall surely make restitution." We've fallen into the trap and there's no way out.

October 13, 1939

The electricity has been only partially restored. I am still immersed in darkness. And because of the curfew in the city, it seems as though we are under house arrest. But worse than that is the mental darkness. We are cut off from the democratic world and all that is taking place there. All the newspapers, even the Polish ones, are suspended. This week, in their place, a Polish-language paper— a rag, the conquerors' brainchild—has begun appearing. The news from the world at large filters out through this paper, given, to be sure, a particular slant and coloration. Germany is praised above all; conversely, England has no equal for ugliness. In spite of that, they praise and laud Soviet Russia, a Communist state, the nest of world filth with whom, only a few months ago, the Führer refused even to negotiate. The local wits want to find a contradiction in the Führer's approach. Bolsheviks and Jews are one and the same thing, and therefore whoever likes the Bolsheviks likes Jews.

But you can't ask a Führer hard questions, and the mystique of his world is unknown to us. Furthermore, the first victims of Russian Bolshevism were the Jews, and the Jewry of Russia, too, has been driven from the earth. There are no signs of Jewishness at all in Russia. Yet nevertheless, when the news reached us that the Bolsheviks were coming closer to Warsaw, our joy was limitless. We dreamed about it; we thought ourselves lucky. Thousands of young people went to Bolshevik Russia on foot, that is to say, to the areas conquered by Russia. They looked upon the Bolsheviks as redeeming Messiahs. Even the wealthy, who would become poor under Bolshevism, preferred the Russians to the Germans. There is plunder on the one hand and plunder on the other, but the Russians plunder one as a citizen and as a man, while the Nazis plunder one as a Jew. The former Polish government never spoiled us, but at the same time never overtly singled us out for torture. The Nazi is a sadist, however. His hatred of the Jews is a psychosis. He flogs and derives pleasure from it. The torment of the victim is a balm to his soul, especially if the victim is a Jew.

Thus there is little wonder that the Bolsheviks became, in our eyes, the saviors of mankind. Everyone rejoiced as they neared Warsaw. Ceaseless rumors passed from person to person: the Messiah is coming! It was said, as if it were an actual fact, that war had broken out between the Russians and the Nazis. But to the sorrow and misfortune of tens of thousands of young people, it was only a pleasant dream. The Bolsheviks, it is true, marched forward, paying no attention to the line of demarcation established at the outset between them and Germany; but later a change took place. The Russians turned on their heels; they began to retreat to the east, and the Germans marched after them—and our fate was sealed.

October 14, 1939

The food supply has improved. All kinds of food and produce are being brought in from the nearby villages in great quantities, because the villager is even more anxious to sell than the city dweller to buy. In the days of battle the roads were so dangerous that no one traveled to buy or sell for fear of death. The enemy was able to seize whatever he found to satisfy his own hunger. But when the country quieted down, the villagers came out of their holes and brought the fruits of their soil to the city.

Warsaw has become full of all good things, but they are not being sold in the normal way. The stores are still closed and the markets have been burned and destroyed, therefore all the trade has been brought out to the street. Whatever used to be done indoors is now being carried on outside, and the streets have begun to resemble a fair. They are full to capacity. There is no room to pass; everywhere selling and bargaining, trade and barter are going on under the sky.

This is the order of trade: the street vendors buy secretly from the owners of the closed stores at high prices, then sell the produce out of doors to the passersby at still higher prices. Never have there been so many vendors among the Jews as in our own days.

Tens of thousands of people are left without a source of livelihood. There is no possibility under current conditions for them to return to their previous occupations, so they turn to new ones. And there is no better source of livelihood than trade in produce—in necessities. Now—everything is saleable. Rotten, stinking goods that used to be considered unfit to eat or use are now brought outside, and at once long lines are formed to grab up the bargain.

All trade, except the trade in produce, has stopped. And just as everyone is selling, everyone is buying. Men who until now were totally ignorant in matters of food, who always found their table laid with all kinds of delicacies without their having lifted a finger to prepare it, now get up at the crack of dawn to fetch water, to look for bread, to search for potatoes, or to find a butcher shop open to sell them a kilo of kosher meat for the price of ten zloty. Every important man now carries a bag full of potatoes on his back, and a live chicken or a duck in his hand, and he wears a look of triumph for having managed to supply himself with food. No one is interested in anything but matters of eating.

The conquerors have left this whole business alone. They haven't even attempted to make any sort of order in regard to profiteering, so each man can charge as much as he wants. It is quite possible that free trade is the better arrangement. The prices go up sometimes and down sometimes. Everything finds a level without pressure from any direction. There is one constant: Warsaw is Warsaw. You can find all manner of delicacies and luxuries, provided you have the money.

October 15, 1939

The offices of the Joint[14] are like a madhouse. There are tens of thousands of needy. All the rooms are full of people. The noise and tumult never cease throughout the working day. At the door there is a guard who sticks to his orders but not to his place—the people who wish to enter ignore him, and push their way in by force. All manner of entrepreneurs have attached themselves to the Joint and everyone wants to enjoy pleasure and profit. The whole thing is marvelous—this whole "country fair" going on without the conqueror's knowledge or interest. In general, the Nazis have no dealings with the wielders of power among the Jews simply because there really is no such power. Our leaders abandoned us in time of

[14] The Joint Distribution Committee, popularly known as Joint or JDC, an American overseas relief and rehabilitation organization.

danger. They scattered in all directions like mice, and so we are left neither a nation nor a community, but rather a herd.

Life moves along by itself. There is no transportation, no water, no electricity. Everything creeps, and this has given foundation to flourishing rumors that the conquerors won't remain here. But there is one thing the conquerors do not ignore, that they return to incessantly, as though from the very outset they had come here for that purpose alone. A certain psychosis of hatred and loathing toward "the *Jude*" has infected them, and if they do anything with care and forethought, it is in the Jewish area.

Here are a few pearls in the course of one day: First, Mayor Starzynski, in the name of the local commissar appointed by the German military command, announced with special pleasure that the German-appointed courtyard commandants are required to furnish a list of the residents of each courtyard who require public assistance, and on the basis of this, everyone will receive a legal document entitling him to receive, free of charge, bread, meals, clothing, and linen which the city will furnish at its own expense— except for the Jews.

Second, in a conversation which lasted two minutes, and which assumed the character of an order through the addition of a threat that "otherwise, they alone are responsible for their lives," the Jewish Council[15] was ordered to furnish a list of the Jewish residents of Warsaw from sixteen to sixty years of age. For what purpose? Nobody knows. But it is certain that it's not for the benefit of the Jews. Our hearts tell us that a catastrophe for the Jewry of Poland is hidden in this demand.

Third, Rosensztat, a Jewish pharmacist from Grzybowska street, came to the conquerors with a request for "spirits," without which no drugstore can function. They asked him if he was a Jew. When he said yes, they informed him that he wouldn't receive any until he fired his Jewish employees, and that the manager, who until now

[15] The Jewish Community Council (Hebrew: *Kehillah*) had been replaced, at German orders, by the Jewish Council (German: *Judenrat*) on October 4, 1939. The last head of the *Kehillah*, Mauryc Majzel, was not elected but was appointed by the Polish Government. He fled Warsaw immediately after the outbreak of the war, and Adam Czerniakow was the appointed head of the *Judenrat*.

had been Rosensztat himself, must also be an Aryan. Henceforward it is forbidden for the Jewish owner to cross the threshold of his own pharmacy. The Aryan manager will send the monthly accounts to him at home.

Fourth, the price of merchandise has gone down unnaturally—because everyone is afraid of confiscation. Jews plead with their Christian acquaintances to accept certain sums for safekeeping, so that they won't have to deposit anything in excess of 2,000 zloty in the bank under the supervision of the conqueror. But the Christian "friends" refuse, because their merchants' association has forbidden its members to give assistance to Jews in any form whatsoever.

Fifth, today Moshe Indelman,[16] an editor of the newspaper *Hajnt*, was arrested. They told his wife that if her husband didn't return, she could find out about his fate at Third of May Street. M.I. is my friend and comrade.

Sixth, there is a widespread rumor that Vladimir Jabotinsky has founded a Jewish Legion of 200,000 men; that England has proclaimed a Jewish State in Palestine and an Arab State in Syria; that Chaim Weizmann has been made President, and so on. I don't believe any of these rumors. I record them only for remembrance.

October 18, 1939

Our lives grow gloomier from day to day. Racial laws have not yet been formally decreed, but actually our defeat is inevitable. The conqueror says bluntly that there is no hope for Jewish survival. There is room for the assumption that a beginning is being made now.

So far there has been free trade in the streets. This is a trade of pennies, whose practitioners are boys and girls, young men and women driven to this sort of business by poverty. It is destined to be forbidden. It too will be taken out of the hands of the Jews. Every public place shows hatred and loathing toward the Jews. Isolated incidents of blows and violence against Jews have grown too numerous to count. Eyewitnesses tell horrifying stories, and they are not exaggerations.

The future of the schools for Jewish children is not yet known. In general the conquerors have no dealings with Jewish representatives. We are like grains of sand. There is no prior consultation

[16] Moshe Yinnon, now in the United States and the editor of *Hadoar*, a Hebrew weekly.

53

regarding our own lives. They make decrees by themselves and there is no changing them. Reasons are not required. There is only one reason—to destroy, to kill, to eradicate.

Let anyone who wishes to consider the depths of the tragedy of Polish Jewry come to the Joint building (13 Leszno Street) and see the vale of tears. But even the Joint has no legal authority, and the conqueror knows nothing of its existence. It is our good fortune that the Joint's funds are in the hands of the American consulate and the enemy has no access to them. Otherwise he would confiscate them to the last cent. But the Joint's relief money is like a drop in the ocean. Great God! Are you making an end to Polish Jewry? "The populace" cannot understand: Why is the world silent?

October 19, 1939

There are no schools, elementary or high, Jewish or Polish. Many school buildings were burned, and a school that has been burned will never rise again, with so many people homeless. Even the schools that remain are in ruins. There isn't a building in Warsaw whose windows haven't been broken, particularly on the side facing the street—and when any glass is available, they raise the prices so exorbitantly that glass for a double window costs 200 zloty. There are school buildings in which the cost of glass would run to several thousand zloty.

October 20, 1939

Besides the economic disaster, we suffer from particular misfortunes—Jewish misfortunes. Eyewitnesses tell that even officers and high military officials are not ashamed to chase after an old Jew with scissors in their hands to cut off his beard. When they start chasing a bearded Jew, an uproar starts in the street and all the passersby and tradesmen flee. It strikes fear into all the Jews, and they are afraid to go outside. Their fear is far from groundless. First of all, they are seized for forced labor; second, they are seized for beard cutting; and third, they are afraid in general of Esau and Amalek. In the light of all this, our lives are no life at all; we are not secure either outside or at home. In the house they are afraid, "Lest they come . . . ," outside, lest they be seized for forced labor. Everyone goes outside wearing old, torn clothes, and I know one clever Jew who doesn't permit his house to be cleaned, so that it

54

will have the look of a poor man's dwelling—thus he will fool the conquerors.

The *Judenrat*, which was orphaned when its money was stolen and its appointed president (commissar) fled, attempted to organize the matter of seizing people for labor. Czerniakow offered to supply a certain number of workers if only they would stop seizing for forced labor whoever comes to hand in the streets. They scarcely listened to this proposal, merely explained in passing that it was not detailed enough. Finally they agreed that the *Judenrat* will supply five hundred laborers a day, and that the street captures will stop. Tomorrow will be the first day for this new arrangement. The *Judenrat* will pay each worker four zloty a day out of its treasury. Let us see if they find people willing to work, if the *Judenrat* can meet its obligation, and if the conqueror will be satisfied with the new arrangement. If, heaven forbid, the contract with the enemy doesn't succeed, the evil will be worse than it has been up to now. We have all become orphans. Out of the depths I called thee.

October 21, 1939

Some time ago I stated that our future is beclouded. I was wrong. Our future is becoming increasingly clear. Today the legal destruction began, with an order barring Jews from the two branches of the economy in which 50 per cent of the Jewish community supported itself. It makes one's blood freeze, and a man is ready to commit suicide out of desperation. This isn't just a small economic deprivation that makes things difficult but will not endanger our survival. It is a savage slash that has no equal in the history of the oppression of the Jewish people. The cruel decree is short and decisive, comprising only seven paragraphs, but it suffices to topple our entire economic structure. The decree says: It is strictly forbidden for Jews to trade in textile goods (manufactures) and processed hides (leather) and any sort of manufacturing that involves these materials. With terrible savagery the ax has struck at the most active artery of the Jewish economy. All violators of this order will be severely punished, even by capital punishment.

After this it will be proper to say "blessed be the righteous judge"[17] for Jewish business in Poland. Besides the traders in hides and fabrics, thousands of Jews who were indirectly supported from this will be deprived of all livelihood.

[17] The prayer said at funerals and upon hearing of a death.

But in the decree there is one detail that arouses various thoughts: it affects only the left bank of the Vistula, and excepts the right bank. This is hard to understand. For what reason was the left bank set apart from the right bank? Those who understand politics seek to prove by this that the right bank will belong to the Russians. Thus Warsaw for the Germans, Praga for the Russians. This is the comedy of life.

October 22, 1939

Our only source of news is the two-page rag called *Nowy Kurier Warszawski*, the conqueror's organ of expression, which is beneath criticism as a newspaper. The important thing here is not its point of view but its news content, which is evidence of his mental poverty. In the conqueror's circles there isn't a single man capable of heading a daily newspaper worthy of the name. He has no professionals capable of giving color to the newspaper, even in the Nazi spirit. It is therefore no wonder that there is no demand for it, and that it has shrunk from four pages to two, which are filled mainly with decrees against the Jews.

Radios are being confiscated. Through the long chilly evenings we sit desolate and mournful, and there is no end to our tears. In every family there is misfortune and in every house, destruction. The "legal" destruction has darkened our world, but even this has become a subject for Jewish jokes. But this is gallows humor. I am afraid of a despair psychosis which is permeating our whole lives. We have stopped reacting. Even if they forbid us to breathe, we will make peace with that too. This too will furnish a subject for a new joke.

October 25, 1939

There aren't enough words to describe the confusion in our minds. Blatant signs prove that some terrible catastrophe, unequaled in Jewish history, is in store for Polish Jewry.

There is no end to the rumors, and one must admit that there is some basis to them, for the Führer in his speech before the Reichstag on June 10 listed, among the aims of the war, the uprooting of various national groups in the areas under his domination. In all this strange business there is one central objective: to Germanize the conquered areas and to settle German populations in them which will become rooted there and turn the occupied areas into German regions joined to the Reich as one German-national unit.

The migration of communities, meaning the uprooting of communities from their native soil and the resettling of them in a strange land, is an economic catastrophe for the communities themselves. But wherever there is politics, no attention is paid to economics. And here the Jews will be the victims. The Tyrolians, the Letts, and the Estonians are under the administration of a government which seems to take care of them with friendship. For them the government is a solution; it is concerned with them and fulfills all their wants. But for us Jews the government is an enemy out to annihilate us.

Yesterday we heard over the London radio that the Jews of Vienna have received an order to be ready to leave their native city and migrate to the Lublin district of Poland. This means: Prepare yourselves for total destruction.

Another sign that bodes ill: Today, notices informed the Jewish population of Warsaw that next Saturady (October 29) there will be a census of the Jewish inhabitants. The *Judenrat* under the leadership of Engineer Czerniakow is required to carry it out. Our hearts tell us of evil—some catastrophe for the Jews of Warsaw lies in this census.[18] Otherwise there would be no need for it.

The day before yesterday, like true Vandals, the conquerors entered the Tlomackie Library, where rare spiritual treasures were stored. They removed all the valuable books and manuscripts, put them on trucks, and took them to some unknown place. This is a burning of the soul of Polish Jewry, for this library was our spiritual sanctuary where we found respite when troubles came to us. Now the fountain which slaked our thirst for Torah and knowledge is dried up. The hands of Nahum Sokolow and other men of stature established it. They invested great spiritual powers in it and lately had even built a beautiful building.

October 26, 1939

The Exile of Poltawsk

In our scroll of agony, not one small detail can be omitted. Even though we are now undergoing terrible tribulations and the sun has grown dark for us at noon, we have not lost our hope that the

[18] This census showed about 360,000 Jews in Warsaw.

era of light will surely come. Our existence as a people will not be destroyed. Individuals will be destroyed, but the Jewish community will live on. Therefore, every entry is more precious than gold, so long as it is written down as it happens, without exaggerations and distortions.

The community of Pultusk has been exiled. I was told by one of the exiles all the details that I am writing down here. He is a communal functionary, a bookkeeper in the free loan fund of the Joint named Majer Szejnberg. My heart is confident that these are the facts and that a future historian will find material here that may be relied upon, not just stories out of the imagination.

"The conqueror entered Pultusk on September 18, 1939, and right after that the rabbi received an order from the commander of the division to make two lists, one dealing with personal items, the other a list of the assets of the entire Jewish community. He was given until September 25.

"On September 26 I went to the rabbi to get the lists and pass them on to the conqueror. The rabbi had a pupil, a protégé in Hasidic clothes and wearing a beard, who accompanied me. On our arrival the conqueror made my companion get up on the table and dance for two whole hours. I, the 'European,' tried to convince the officer that he ought to let him go and give him a rest, but the officer answered, 'It's nothing! Let him dance another hour.'

"The rabbi's list included nine hundred and sixty families, and at ten in the morning the lists were turned over to the officer. After two hours, at noon, the expulsion order was issued. Soldiers went from house to house and also seized the passersby in the market. They made no distinctions between old men and boys, healthy and sick, men and women. They seized every living soul, just as they found them at that time in whatever they happened to be wearing. They collected them all in a park near the *Starosta*[18] and ordered the whole community to leave the town at once and cross the Narew River. Those who had managed to pack a valise or a bundle were allowed to take it with them. Whoever didn't manage to do so was not allowed to go back for his things.

"As I said, there were no exceptions. Even old men with canes and sick people on the point of death were exiled. They did except one mother who had given birth that day. They left her alone for

18 Administrator; by extension, administrative building.

one day, and on the next day they laid her down in a wagon and exiled her too.

"All of this was done at noon, September 26, 1939. The exiles crossed the Narew River, and their first stop was the village of Poplawy, which is on the opposite bank. But their rest didn't last long. On Saturday, September 30, they exiled them from the village of Poplawy as well. Some died on the way. The tumult and confusion cannot be described. The rabbi went with the exiles to Poplawy. That night the Polish inhabitants of the village attacked the rabbi, beat him up, and stole his last few pennies. They stole the money from the rest of the exiles as they were leaving the village. The crowd searched them all and emptied their pockets."

This much was related by Majer Szejnberg, one of the exiles on the Narew River.

October 27, 1939

We continue to live in chaos. There is disorder and confusion everywhere. No order is visible among the conquerors either, for whatever they do bears the seal of haste and temporariness. There is a program in only one area—robbery and looting of the Jews.

The edicts of the conquerors are not clear. The decree forbidding Jews to trade in textiles and leather specifically said that it did not apply to the right bank of the Vistula, and the Jews hastened to transfer their goods to Praga. Later it became clear that the order did not apply to the city of Warsaw either, which is on the left bank of the Vistula—and there was a respite. True, this is only temporary, but there is some relief in it. But what is clear beyond any doubt is the aim of uprooting everything. The conqueror adds that in the new Poland there will be no room for political agitators, profiteers, and Jewish black-marketeers. Under the cloak of accusations of black-marketeering they will utterly destroy us.

October 28, 1939

We move along the earth like men condemned to death. It is clear to us that we will die by expulsion, but we don't know when the sentence will be carried out. Such a beginning was made in Berlin before the expulsion there. The order for a census stated that it is being held to gather data for administrative purposes. That's a neat phrase, but it contains catastrophe.

In the eyes of the conquerors we are outside the category of human beings. This is the Nazi ideology, and its followers, both common soldiers and officers, are turning it into a living reality. Their wickedness reaches the heights of human cruelty. These people must be considered psychopaths and sadists, because normal people are incapable of such abominable acts. There are army officers whose greatest pleasure is to lie in wait for bearded Jews on Nalewki Street, to attack them, and to cut off half their beards. The unfortunate Jew is afraid to oppose this, lest his opposition be considered a crime for which he will be punished. Jews are pulled out of lines and beaten for no reason. Nevertheless, one must admit that there are also some soldiers who possess human feelings. P.K. told me that a certain German officer ran into his wife at the corner of Chlodna and Zelazna streets. He asked her if she was a *Judin* and gave her half a loaf of bread.

Our tragedy is not in the humane or cruel actions of individuals, but in the plan in general, which shows no pity toward the Jews. We are certain that this census is being taken for the purpose of expelling "nonproductive elements." And there are a great many of us now. No one knows whose lot will be drawn and therefore sorrow is on every face. We are caught in a net, doomed to destruction.

Now the sad news has reached us that the border has been closed; some people say temporarily, others say it is for good.

October 30, 1939

Sometimes it seems that the conqueror hasn't the slightest interest in getting the ruined city to function again. Therefore there are widespread rumors that the enemy is, as it were, standing on one foot, and that in the end he will leave the city and turn it over to the "Reds." The rumor as it stands is a strange one, and it is hard for an intelligent person to believe it. Yet no one knows how things will turn out in a few days. In our day anything is possible, even something contrary to logic and common sense.

These rumors were strengthened by the arrival of the Soviet delegation which has come to discuss the boundary settlement. Intelligent Jews never stop saying that Hitler is deathly afraid of Stalin because his fate is in Stalin's hands, and that Stalin has found the times propitious for demanding the borders of 1914, in order to annex Communist Poland to the Soviet Union. This is plausible. Our people are awaiting this fortunate moment as a pious Jew awaits the coming of the Messiah. Even fat, rich Jews are satisfied with a moldy crust and physical labor, as long as they are treated as human beings.

The enemy, who is not expert in Polish trade, wished to take the trade in leather and textiles out of the hands of the Jews, but he was immediately forced to nullify the prohibition because the German (*Volksgenossen*)[19] merchants opposed it for fear it would cause losses to their own businesses. The repeal was not made in writing, but was merely an oral nullification. Such is the power of Jewish business in Poland. The enemy erred in thinking he was in Berlin, dealing with his own "*Juden.*" After the prohibition forbidding a Jew to keep more than 2,000 zloty in his home, the naïve Jews of Germany would probably have stood in line at the banks the next day by the tens of thousands to fulfill the Führer's commandments. But the Polish Jews said emphatically, "No!" They didn't deposit a single penny, but you won't find a single Jew whose strongbox contains more than 2,000 zloty! All these ridiculous decrees, which attest to low culture and sadistic wickedness, arouse laughter among the Jews of Poland. "My troubles I'll give him, the crook!" and they stick to their word; they don't deposit one cent.

Soon the Jewish schools will be opened. They will be opened because it is hard to wait any longer and let the children remain idle. But in this area too the conquerors have done nothing to make their position on the problem clear. We searched for some sort of office of educational affairs to give us specifics to guide our actions, but the Polish educational administration has been thrown out. Only a puppet in the form of a Polish-speaking clerk remains, and he knows nothing. The Poles are urging us to reopen our schools without permits, on the authority of the charters we have had up to now. It has been decreed that everyone must go back to work. So we have gone back to work! With trembling hearts, and full of doubts, we have decided to do so. The existence of the schools is in danger, and therefore we have decided to make the effort.

Will students come? Their parents have been beaten, robbed, and looted. Will impoverished, homeless parents still find the heart to send their children to study Torah? Will the Eternal break His promise?

[19] Polish citizens of German descent.

CHAPTER TWO

November 1, 1939

TODAY WAS A day of terror in unhappy Warsaw—that is, in Jewish Warsaw. The conqueror is pouring out all his wrath upon the people he wishes to exterminate, and their distress is unbearable. People are ready to take their own lives. Without a doubt, there are many suicides among the Jews, but because of the city's size and the lack of newspapers they are not generally known.

Recently they began to beat young women. A girl who works as a clerk for the *Judenrat* told me that when the officers entered the *Judenrat* office to arrest her, they held whips (*Spitzruten*) in their hands and chased the clerks as one chases a flock of sheep or cattle. She herself turned to one of the conquerors with a question, and instead of an answer received a lash of his whip.

The conqueror wanted to open the law courts. The dean of lawyers, Jan Nowodworski, in peaceful days a well-known anti-Semite, was called up and two requests were made of him: to insert an Aryan clause in the judicial code, and second, to take a loyalty oath to the Führer. Nowodworski did not agree to either, on the grounds that they were both against the Polish Constitution. He said, in so many words, If the Jews are to be deported, let us be the ones empowered to do so, not you! There were also political motivations for opposing the demand for an Aryan clause: they were ashamed to let their allies see it. This reply caused the negotiations for the opening of the courts to collapse. Later, negotiations were renewed with the court clerks, with the judges, public prosecutors, etc. Here a new obstacle arose: In whose name were legal decisions to be issued? The conquered demanded that verdicts be pronounced in the name of the Polish Republic which is no longer in existence. The conqueror would not agree to this, and the negotiations again collapsed.

November 4, 1939

The conqueror has surrounded himself with spies, traitors, and talebearers, some of whom are found even among our Jewish brethren. The Jews fill a triple role here. First, they are "informers" pointing out the way for the thieves. Visits are made to one place and then another, and each visit ends in a loss of money and life. Valuables are brazenly stolen, accompanied by threats and most often by blows and injuries. A merchant from Gesia Street, Mr. Czerwonykamien, told me all his goods were stolen and he himself was cruelly beaten in the presence of his young son, a child of twelve, who watched, crying and screaming.

The second role filled by the Jews is to serve as sacrificial victims. As a result of our sacrifices, they take nothing from the Christians except in unusual cases. A third role is, to our shame, filled by those Jews who buy the stolen goods from the robbers. But we should not be ashamed of this. In all ages and in every generation we have had destroyers from our own midst.

Because of the lack of newspapers, from time to time I buy that Lodz rag of a paper *Deutsche Lodzer Zeitung.* When I read it, my skin crawls. The greatest punishments are meted out to the Jews of Lodz, an "ancient German city," according to the conquerors, which was cut out from the Polish territories and annexed to the Reich. The newspaper prints inflammatory statements against the Jews every day, and the smallest of sins committed by a Jew is emphasized with added explanations and interpretations about "sinful and criminal Jewry," which does not obey the regime, and sucks the blood of the Christian population. The chief of police himself abets this loathing for the Jews in his proclamations. There is no official order, proclamation, opinion, or announcement of any kind in which the Jews are not mentioned deprecatingly, and in which they are not depicted as a lowly race.

They find all kinds of excuses. The Jews caused the devaluation of the currency, and if there is no currency devaluation they blame "sinful Jewry" for cruelty toward animals. These barbarians have pity on animals, which they claim the Jews treat with cruelty. Thus, in view of this terrible situation, one cannot wonder that the Jews, even wealthy ones, await the arrival of the Soviets as their rescuers and redeemers. Rumors spread endlessly that "the murderers are leaving the city." It is difficult to ascertain what these rumors are based upon, but one cannot deny that something new is brewing—something that will bring changes—for "the voice of the people is like the voice of God." Verily, if we jump out of the frying pan we will land in the fire, but a drowning man clutches at straws. All we ask is a crust of bread and a cup of water, and to be treated as human beings. The Soviets have law and order; the Nazis, insolence and violence.

November 5, 1939

"The will is the father of the idea," and thus in time of distress rumors of redemption and liberation spread. Until now our pride was "the indestructibility of Israel." I doubt if anyone still believes in this. The horrible persecutions of the Middle Ages are as nothing in face of the terrible troubles in which the Nazis enmesh us. In primitive times, methods of torture were also primitive. The oppressors of the Middle Ages knew only two alternatives: life or death. As long as a man lived, even if he were a Jew, they let him live. He also had an opportunity to live out his days by choosing conversion or exile. The Nazi inquisition, however, is different. They take a Jew's life by throttling his livelihood, by "legal" limitations and cruel edicts, by such sadistic tortures that even a tyrant of the Middle Ages would have been ashamed to publicize them. It was part of the concept of that generation to burn a sinning soul, but it was not their habit to torture a man because he was born "in sin," according to the hangman's ideas.

What has today brought us? Nothing less than a Jewish ghetto! A ghetto in Jewish Warsaw! Who could have believed it? Proclamations have not yet been posted, but our fate is already known to us. The conqueror has decided to establish a Jewish ghetto, consisting of some ten streets which the 360,000 Jews of Warsaw will be permitted to occupy.

Besides the insult inherent in this decree, it will create a social catastrophe for the entire population of Warsaw, even for the non-Jews; and the livelihood and occupations of the Jews who will be evicted from their homes will be lost. Those who are dispossessed will lose their property and become unemployed. Where will this great mass of people go? This order strikes especially at the wealthy Jews, the rich professional intelligentsia whose Judaism has been only surplus baggage, and whose suffering as Jews makes no sense.

Tomorrow we shall know the details. Rumor says that a delegation of Germans and Poles appeared before the conqueror to ask that the verdict be eased—but to no avail.

November 7, 1939

The ghetto decree, in its first draft, affected 160,000 Jews. But then it was eased, and in its latest appearance it affects only (!) 25,000 Jews.

This time the conqueror entered into negotiations with a Jewish delegation which succeeded in having the law eased. Dr. Szoszkes,[1] a member of the delegation, spoke in the courtyard of the *Judenrat* yesterday about the details of the negotiations, and talked about the painful difficulties the delegation went through in order to convince the conqueror to take various arguments into consideration and reduce the sentence. The result was that the Jewish ghetto has been expanded from fifty-four streets to over ninety. The decision particularly affects Marszalkowska Street and the streets branching off it, from Graniczna to the main railroad station. But in other districts throughout the city there are also streets in which Jews are forbidden to live. Furthermore, in the restricted streets the Jews may live on one side of some streets, but not on the other, such as Twarda Street, in which they can live in the even-numbered houses, but not in the odd-numbered ones. Pinska Street is also divided, but in length, not in width. Jews are allowed only up to a certain point. A "compromise" was reached by which some streets in which Jews had originally been forbidden to live are now open to them, but only *post factum*—that is, Jews who had been living there and whose

[1] Dr. Chaim (Henryk) Szoszkes, who escaped soon afterward and was, until his death in 1964, a columnist on the Yiddish newspaper *The Day-Jewish Journal*, in New York.

removal it would be difficult to accomplish may remain, but other Jews are forbidden to move there from now on. In short, the medieval institution—a ghetto!

But, thank God, they did not carry the decree to its logical conclusion. It does not affect businesses and shops, which for the time being remain in possession of their Jewish owners. In the same fashion, professionals such as doctors, dentists, lawyers, engineers, etc., may continue their practices as heretofore. Will they be allowed to live there? It has not yet been decided.

November 8, 1939

The ghetto decree gnaws away at our depressed world. No one had foreseen this catastrophe, even though the conqueror's treatment of the Jews in Germany was known to us. The Gestapo is devoting its complete attention to this problem, with its boundless evil and cruelty. Those in the know say secretly that the military authority was opposed to this, that there was a disagreement between the two authorities.

In the meantime a Jewish delegation has gone to Cracow, to see Dr. Frank[2] and plead with him to set aside the severe decree. Dr. Szoszkes heads the delegation. I doubt whether they will accomplish anything. This is the Führer's method, and one cannot swerve from it. At the moment we are awaiting Monday, when the delegation will return. But the delegation's trip and the faint hope attached to its mission have not calmed the confusion. Thirty thousand Jews girded, packed, and with money in their hands, are filling the streets open to them, searching for apartments. Finding one is as difficult as parting the waters of the Red Sea. It is painful to witness the distress of these poor evicted people. Despair overwhelms them.

Terrible rumors reach us from the country. Dozens of Jewish towns have been burned, wiped off the face of the earth. In Wyszkow, for example, only three houses remain. As for the towns that were not burned—the Jews were exiled anyway. First their property was confiscated, then they were beaten and seized for forced labor, and finally, after they were searched and their money

[2] Dr. Hans Frank (1900–1946) had just been appointed governor of the "General Government," the part of occupied Poland that was not incorporated into the Reich. After the war, he was tried at Nuremberg and executed as a war criminal. Frank kept a diary of some forty-three volumes, a summary of which has been published in Poland.

stolen, they were forced to flee. The unfortunate exiles have been burned, robbed, assaulted, left naked and penniless and exiled from their birthplaces. This has happened to the Jews of Pultusk, Mlawa, Wloclawek, and other Jewish towns too numerous to list.

Almighty God! Are you making an end to the remnant of Polish Jewry?

November 11, 1939

I am one of the people of Nowolipki Street evicted by the conqueror on the first day he entered the city (October 1). One battalion seized our homes and remained in them for three weeks. After that the battalion left the homes they had occupied, but another, even more cruel group of soldiers arrived. Almost all were middle-aged; their faces were coarse and heavy; most of them were evidently peasants with primitive ideas, who knew nothing beyond the Führer and his orders. The first group had permitted some Jewish families to live in the occupied courtyard. Some humane reasons had weighted the decision in their favor. But when the second group arrived, these families also were evicted. A Jew and an Aryan cannot live side by side.

I was almost certain that this occupancy would last the entire winter. We sighed bitterly and gave up hope. But a miracle occurred and the second group remained in our homes only about ten days. Suddenly we were saved, for an apartment these days, after the fires, the destruction and demolition, and on the eve of the ghetto, is more precious than gold and pearls. If one has an apartment, he has everything; without an apartment, he has nothing.

We returned, unfortunately, not to homes but to stables. Everything is broken and destroyed, stolen and plundered. Not one unbroken lock remains. Every possession with a selling price was taken. Even the electric fixtures were removed, and brooms were stolen. In short, we have been cleaned out.

This is not the eve of destruction, but destruction itself. Our personal degradation is calamitous, and material impoverishment is bound up in our degradation. The entire administrative machinery is geared toward this end. Everywhere—"no Jews allowed." Czarism used to do this, but without sadism. With all its savagery, it had laws which it was careful to obey; there were certain limitations to its persecutions. Beyond such a point it is no longer "law" but barbarity, and Czarism refrained from barbarity. Not so the unclean

Nazi! Everything is permitted him; he has no restrictions. That shame which keeps one from sinning has abandoned him. On the contrary, cruelty to Jews is a national *mitzvah*.[3] He who causes them the most suffering is the most praiseworthy. And so we are trodden upon like mud in the streets.

And the upright, ordinary Jew asks himself and his fellows-in-distress: Is there no justice in the world?

Just as darkness rules the streets of Warsaw, so does it dominate our minds. The conqueror depletes the spirit along with more material things. Every spark of light is a potential breach in the kingdom of darkness of bestial Nazism; therefore everything that ties us to the democratic world is denied us, except for those speeches made by "friend" Molotov, in which he reviles the democracies.

First, the newspapers were shut down. Only one special newspaper exists, fruit of their hands and their spirit. Through this rag all outside news is filtered, and its single topic is invective and vituperation against England: she is unequaled in lying, stealing, murdering, and all the sins in the world; she is being defeated on all fronts and within the country there is starvation and illness. The French are not touched. Altogether the newspaper has two pages, one of them for announcements. This is the well from which we draw our political and military information.

Second, the radio station was shut down and all receivers were taken away. To be exact, they didn't come and take them; the owners took the sets to the commissariat of their police districts. They stood in line and were "overjoyed" when it was their turn to give them up. This time there was no difference between Jews and Aryans. The only exceptions were soldiers and the Aryans of German birth. I had to hand over two expensive sets, costing more than 1,000 zloty. My heart was broken, but there was no alternative.

Third, there is no community life. All the political parties have been disbanded, every philanthropic organization closed. Wild rumors spread in whispers. There is a rumor that Mussolini is fighting against Hitler. Can it be possible? A comment crept into the conqueror's press that the Duce wishes to activate his army. Against whom? Will salvation come from an unexpected source? We try to comfort ourselves that our liberation is close at hand, and our distress makes room for all kinds of fantasies and visions.

[3] Literally, commandment; colloquially, a good or charitable deed.

Besides the conqueror's "legal" pillage, illegal robbery has broken out among the Polish masses. Today I was an eyewitness to such a theft in Gesia Street. A dreadful outcry arose. Jews were screaming violently, calling *"Polizei!"* with all their strength—and the plundering continued. Dozens of gentiles with stolen merchandise under their arms scattered in all directions, and our Jews continued to shout. No one dared to go up to the thieves and take back the stolen goods they held. It would have been easy to do, but they were afraid. Such scenes are played out each day. The thief steals and the Jews shout.

November 14, 1939

Complete destruction has befallen Polish Jewry—especially in the Warta River district, which the conqueror annexed to "Greater Germany." In the legal and administrative sense, this district does not belong to the Polish zone, where the laws of Dr. Frank of Cracow are operative. The Warta district is reserved only for Germans, and every foreign element is being uprooted from it. To a certain extent even Poles are being driven out—and the Jews, of course. It is holy ground! The conqueror claims that the superior German culture cannot exist side by side with low cultures such as that of the Poles and the Jews. From the first days of its existence the Warta district was German land, and through the compassion of Providence it has now returned to its original owners.

Wherever the land has become German and has been annexed to the Reich, woe betides its people, especially its Jewish inhabitants. Prosperous Lodz, the mercantile center of the country, has become a hell for its Jews. Those who flee from there to Warsaw draw a new breath and say that this is a paradise. God have pity on them, and on us too.

News—a bombshell! A plot against the Führer. Even before the news was announced officially, rumors had spread that his assistant, Hess,[4] was killed in the plot. Never has there been so ripe a time for those who exaggerate, for sowers of frightening rumors, and for spreaders of panic as in our days. And now the fantasies have happily become a reality.

[4] Rudolph Hess, the Führer's deputy, was not killed. In 1941 he flew to Great Britain on a "private peace mission." He is now serving a life sentence as a war criminal.

It was as if we were all in the plot together. We were happy that the "affair" had already begun; that the organized revolt was secretly under way and had dared to bring its plot into the open. It is a sign that the time is ripe for revolt, that its strength is growing; that not only among the intelligentsia but even in the ranks of the workers, the spirit of rebellion is growing. But at the same time we are aghast that the revolt was not successful. If it had succeeded, we would have seen therein the finger of God—instead, He has disappointed us.

Nonetheless, we were hopeful. We waited for additional news, for details, for reactions to the uprising in and outside of Germany. But the news is meager, now that our radio sets have been taken away and everybody who listens to broadcasts in secret is liable to punishment. There is therefore a broad field for the imagination, which in time of distress is very active.

November 15, 1939

There is no end to the "flight" of the Jews to the Führer's "friends." One must admit that our sages' words were justified: "The Almighty prepares the remedy before the sickness." Were it not for Soviet Russia we would be strangled to death.

Tens of thousands of young Jews are without means of sustenance. Jewish youth has no present and no future, and it is fleeing for its very life. The escape is accomplished in various ways: on foot, by automobile, by train, in carts, and in all sorts of other vehicles. There is no obstacle from the Soviet side, and the Nazi conqueror has no established policy. One never knows what is prohibited and what is permitted. For the same offense they sometimes tend to be lenient and sometimes strict. This is understandable, for wherever there is stubbornness and arrogance there can be no specific policy.

Moreover, what one authority permits the other prohibits. Right after the conquest, the border was open. You could cross it without a permit, and whoever wanted to queue up for three days could even receive a permit explicitly stating that the bearer was entitled to cross the border into Russia, with his baggage and possessions, using any means of transportation. But in reality the route is full of dangers. According to the law, those crossing the border are permitted to take only 20 zloty with them. Since this is a regulation which cannot possibly be obeyed, people connive to smuggle out larger sums, and here many fail. On the way they are assaulted and robbed. The border guards know that Jewish lives and money are public property and they deal with those who cross in whatever fashion strikes their fancy.

People therefore prefer to cross without permission: they do not trust the legalities of the conqueror. When they cross secretly they feel more secure, for there is no refugee that does not take with him a larger sum of money than the law permits. And so the "green border" has been publicized among the refugees, and experts in border crossings earn tremendous sums at their "profession."

Those in the know estimate that over a million refugees have fled to Russia. And no matter how the numbers swell, they are welcomed. But where will this large mass of people settle? Some particularly skilled workers have already been transferred to the interior of Russia, but the majority either have some cash and are managing, or have nothing and are hungry and thirsty. As always, there are those who are successful and those who have no luck and suffer. But all in all, one must not deprecate Soviet Russia, which opened its gates to the Polish exiles and saved them from bitter suffering. The Soviets charge America and England, the wealthy democracies, with closing their gates and turning a deaf ear to the heartrending cries of the refugees from the Germans at the very hour of their most terrible persecution. The Soviets, on the other hand, say, "Come, we will give you work; just join us."

But *Realpolitik* does not allow these "friends" to goad the Nazis into abandoning their abominable acts toward the Jews.

Here is what happened to us in a single day:

After much work and trouble, the schools were opened. They exist only by a miracle, since the teachers, because of a dearth of students, don't earn enough for a crumb of bread. One school of 300 students dwindled to 100 and one school of 100 to 20. Teaching is not being done well, because of frustration and insufficient pay. Now even this is coming to an end. Because of the contagious diseases spreading throughout the city, especially typhoid fever, all schools have been ordered closed. From now on we may look forward to lives of hunger and poverty, of ugliness and degradation.

November 17, 1939

Material impoverishment is not enough. Over and above this, the Nazis act ruthlessly toward the unfortunate exiles and attach to their sleeves the "yellow badge." Yes, with my own eyes I saw the "badge of shame" which the conqueror awarded the exiled Jews of Sierpc.

It is a yellow patch on which is written *Jude*, sewn to one of the coat lapels. All the officials of the Joint saw it too, and their faces were filled with shame. I advised that Jew to add, next to the word *Jude*, the words *Mein Stolz* (my pride). But the Jew answered as one who knows, that the conqueror calls such things "sabotage" and condemns the guilty one to death.

Besides the yellow badge, each Jew wears an identification tag on which is stamped his name, his parents' names, his age, occupation, and address. From 5:00 P.M. to 8:00 P.M. Jews may not leave their homes. This is to prevent them from hiding during the hours when the conqueror's minions enter their homes to take them out for forced labor.

In Cracow there is a Jewish ghetto; the center of the city is closed to the Jews. In Warsaw a ghetto has been postponed for the time being. And here there is room for various fantasies which can be created only in the sick imaginations of the unfortunates who are in the midst of these troubles. Sometimes the storytellers throw themselves on the mercy of Stalin, "the compassionate"; sometimes on Roosevelt, who "has pity on the poor" and who threatened the Führer that if he did not stop persecuting Jews, the Germans would be thrown out of America.

The soil is ready even for religious Messianism.

November 18, 1939

The conqueror feeds us news of the wide world. The news is limited and colored with a brown tint. Sometimes we learn more from what is not reported than from what is. According to the conqueror, everything is fine; everything is being accomplished with the greatest success, and there is no one who can be compared to the Nazi in energy, culture, and expertness in each and every area. There is no end to his boasting and pride. As for the enemy, everything is bad and unsuccessful. The English and French do not come up to the Nazis' boots. Their soldiers are starving. Every front has been abandoned. Hore-Belisha,[5] the Jew, does not pay a salary to the officers of his army. In wintertime these defenders of their homeland have no woolen undershirts to protect their bodies from the cold.

"Miserable" England especially is getting her just deserts, for from the day the war broke out, poverty and privation have roosted there,

[5] Leslie Hore-Belisha, British Secretary for War from 1937 to 1940.

and all life has become a hell. The Nazis laugh at the "blockade," which is aimed at Germany but which hits England itself. If anyone has reason to fear starvation, it is England. The conqueror has everything in abundance. Not only is the army dressed and equipped with all that is necessary, from food to ammunition, but all of Greater Germany wallows in abundance, wealth, all kinds of luxuries, etc. The conqueror's pride is nauseating. With our own eyes we see the opposite of all this, but it is best to be silent.

Altogether, two daily papers appear. One is from "German" Lodz. In its seventeen years it has always been under Polish influence, taking Poland's side against the Führer in the conflict over Danzig. Now it has changed its opinion and its line, and become a hundred per cent Nazi. Instigations against the Jews bloom from it like flowers from Aaron's staff. The exhortations are ugly, coarse, pogrom-like, and stupid. A "Kraut" work! Sometimes the paper contradicts itself within two successive lines. But what it must do, it does, and it finds favor and grace in the eyes of the men in power. This is the organ of the holy Warta district, which becomes more and more Germanized, with such efficiency that in Lodz, Jews are now prohibited from walking on Piotrkowska Street.

The second paper is the *Warschauer Zeitung*, which is not printed in "provincial" Warsaw, but in the capital, Cracow, the seat of Frank's administration. Frank's region is still a Polish area and as an administrative unit it consists of four districts—Cracow, Warsaw, Radom, and Lublin. Special "laws" apply to this region. It is self-understood that these are the administrative laws of a cruel satrap, who condemns to death all those who sabotage the conqueror, and this term includes even the tearing up of a poster.

The new Cracow-Warsaw paper is superior to the other one as a newspaper, and its instigations against "the excommunicated people" are more "cultured." Nevertheless, it constantly attacks the Jews. No place is free of them, it complains, and it considers us an "inferior race" whose habit is to harm others and to contaminate the surroundings. Its stinging words do not directly incite to action—everything is done by innuendo—but the poison which it foments seeps into the depths of the reader's soul.

Nazi pride is unlimited. The Poles and the Jews are classed together as if they were both "natives" in African jungles. Both were supposedly created only to serve the conqueror. The Nazis have come to teach order and culture, to raise this unfortunate nation from the low level to which the previous criminal and barbaric government reduced it by its dependence upon vile England.

Truly we are cattle in the eyes of the Nazis. When they supervise Jewish workers they hold a whip in their hands. All are beaten unmercifully. If I were to start recounting all the things I have heard from injured people, I would never be able to finish. The details of Nazi cruelty are enough to drive you crazy. Sometimes we are ashamed to look at one another. And worse than this, we have begun to look upon ourselves as "inferior beings," lacking God's image. Our only hope is that the defeat of the Nazis will surely come. We have only one doubt—whether we shall live to see that day.

And I say: Yes, we will live; we will reach that day! No power endures forever.

News of the Mussolini affair penetrates our world. That the Duce supports treachery and is ready to betray, of this there is no doubt. By nature, politics is like prostitution. You sell yourself to the highest bidder. But here is the question: In whose favor will Mussolini decide? If, God forbid, in favor of the Führer, his close ally—we are lost.

November 23, 1939

I have taken a short leave from my diary, because the nature of its contents, which are nothing more than lamentations and mourning and tales of woe, wearied me. How long can I lament?

It is hard to watch the death of an entire community, which with all its limitations did have its positive features; and the features were completely and entirely Jewish. There is also a Jewish cultural tragedy here, but our hearts are not free now for spiritual-cultural affairs. We do not have the spiritual strength of our forefathers, whose souls were tempered, and who in the midst of terrible privation did not forget their spiritual needs and sacrificed themselves for these things. In the face of the persecution which endangers our physical existence, we are ready to give up everything that has heretofore been dear and holy to us. Polish Jewry—Hasidic, ultrareligious, God-fearing, loyal to the Torah of Israel—is extending its hands to Stalin. In our plight we welcome help from any quarter, as long as we do not fall into the hands of the slaughterer.

Amidst the general horror, the tragedy of the individual is neutralized and ignored. There is no one whose existence has not been devastated. There is no one who has not had a member of his family killed. And those who remain alive are without work. The busiest and most necessary economic arteries have been paralyzed. In the face of the general disruption and destruction of the foundations of life, the tragedy of the individual is not distinct. Before a companion opens his mouth to tell of his troubles, I can anticipate all the details in advance. His words almost remain suspended in air, and his frightful story makes no impression upon me.

But sometimes even the individual's tragedy assumes a half-recognizable importance. Sometimes, from among tens of thousands of the ravaged, your eyes are drawn to a face which haunts you no matter where you turn, does not leave you alone, follows you like a shadow and disturbs your rest. It is hard to understand why this is so. But so it is. The tragedy of a particular individual disturbs me to such an extent that I find myself obliged to make special mention of it. This is the tragedy that occurred to my cherished friend Reb Jakub Zajac.

The word "cherished" doesn't describe the man's essence. He is a merchant, learned in the Torah, secularly educated, and a person with a warm heart. He is modest, compassionate, and fond of religious traditions. And he is a philanthropist, the first to contribute to every charity. He loves his fellow man and he is far above envy, hate, and all these human weaknesses whose roots lie in life's struggle. And even though he is both pure in heart and honorable in deeds, pleasant to people and generous with his wealth, he has also been successful in business and become wealthy. His shop on Kosciuszko Street brought in a sizable income. One must admit that Providence did not err: its trust was left in worthy hands. Jakub contributed from his wealth to every good cause, both openly and secretly. No one left him empty-handed or embarrassed. He belonged to no party, but to the people of Israel as a whole; he respected its Torah and culture and gave his strength and his wealth for their support. This loyal Polish Jew was undoubtedly unique among the tens of thousands of his coreligionists.

Sometimes it bothered me that he was a superior person among the millions of lesser people, for as a type he contradicted my opinion about Polish Jewry. That is, the existence of Jakub Zajac clashed with my opinions about the Jews of Poland, which are not too positive. Forty years ago I settled among the Jews of Poland and I am known among them. I deal with them and I am well acquainted with their way of life and their cultural level as human beings and as Jews. To my great sorrow, I have not always spoken well of them. My opinions are based upon concrete examples, and from year to year the instances proving the validity of my opinions multiplied. Then here came Jakub and demolished all I had built up. If Polish Jewry can bring forth such a person, it is a sign that within it there exists something of the very finest.

Each week a few of us who were steeped in Torah and secular education would meet. For the most part we studied the Talmud and reminisced about the days that were gone; we tried to create a learned atmosphere saturated with knowledge and wisdom. On the Sabbath, Jakub would treat us to fruits and candy. Not only did he spend his own money, but he used to wait upon us and serve each one with his own hands. So it was every Sabbath. He himself would carry in the food in order to give pleasure to his companions in study and contemplation. No one asked him to undertake this expense. On the contrary, more than once we objected to it as unnecessary, but Jakub stood firm.

And thus was this precious soul rewarded: his wife and two daughters were killed by a bomb; his home was razed; his shop was burned; he was left without a loved one and without belongings. Everything was destroyed, everything was burned. He was left alone and childless. Only the skin covering his flesh remained. Is this the way the Almighty looks after His dear ones?

November 25, 1939

Nine families left for Palestine last week, with the permission of the Gestapo, which was supposedly not aware of their departure. Their sight failed, they were stricken with blindness, and one may imagine that the families had in their money bags more than the allotted 20 zloty apiece.

Rumor has it that the Gestapo was given a gift of 30,000 zloty, but the problem of Jewish emigration will not be solved by such means. This is no solution for the masses, nor even for the middle class. And yet there is no way to be saved except by emigration. Where is world Jewry? Where are the peaceful, quiet, affluent, and influential

Jewish communities? Is it possible that they will permit an entire tribe of Israel to be cut off?

Polish Jewry has become public property; but first come is not first served, for no one wants it; no one will step into the breach and defend it. The so-called leaders of Jewry fled for their lives earlier, and three million Jews have been left orphaned, abandoned to the claws of a cruel beast who knows no pity.

Unorganized emigration to Soviet Russia has therefore increased. Overnight Lwow, Rowno, Brisk, Bialystok, and Grodno became "Russian" territory. In tens of thousands our youths flee to this "Russia" from the inferno awaiting them under the rule of Nazism. At first they were well received. As a persecuted group they were considered excellent material for Bolshevism. But the stream was endless, and in the swelling stream, elements not at all desirable for Bolshevism entered.

Finally the Soviet government noticed them. True Bolshevism cannot live side by side with financiers, middlemen, black marketeers, exploiters, and extortionists. Didn't Communism come to uproot all such things from the world? And the effects are already noticeable. The border has been closed. Along the border, barbed-wire fences are being erected, and border smugglers are being shot. Speculators are under special surveillance and can look forward to severe punishment. I do not feel for them in their "troubles," God forbid, but my heart aches to see that thousands of other Jewish refugees must be punished, not for their own crimes but for the sins of their evil brethren.

With all this—the forbidden emigration continues. The "green border" is secretly crossed. In our oppression, the wishes of the Bolsheviks are not taken into account. Secret "firms" of border guides have been formed in which Jews and Aryans divide up the work. The Jews produce the "livestock" and the Aryan, usually a person who lives in the area and for whom the border routes are clear, smuggles the merchandise across.

November 28, 1939

One Jew told me of an incident in which he was involved, one typical of many other happenings which number in the hundreds each day. This Jew traveled to Praga in an ordinary cart. Due to lack of street cars, plain carts carrying travelers from Warsaw to Praga and back have increased in number. This Jew looks like any European non-Jew. A soldier approached the cart and beckoned: "Come!" The unfortunate man had no choice but to go. He was taken to a certain place and the soldier ordered him to shine his shoes. The poor fellow obeyed. While he worked, the German rebuked him for being careless with the polish and using more than was necessary. And he immediately added: "You will pay for this." After he finished his work, the Jew took out his wallet to pay for the damage. "How much must I pay?" The soldier replied: "How much do you have?" He stood and counted the Jew's money and found that he had 32 zloty. He took thirty for himself, i.e., "for the extra polish which the Jew used unnecessarily," and out of the goodness of his heart left the owner two zloty, and went off. The Jew was satisfied with the outcome, for the German had not beaten him. Dozens of such incidents occur every day.

November 30, 1939

Today two harsh decrees reached us. First, the "Star of David" decree—just like the one in Cracow, except that in Cracow the authorities announced the decree in advance, about two weeks before it became effective, and the leaders of the community had time to prepare the Zionist symbols, whereas in Warsaw, or rather in the Warsaw district, the decree was published on November 30, to become effective on December 1. Most likely this was done on purpose, in order to catch many Jews in the act of sabotage; but perhaps for technical reasons the matter will be postponed for a few days.

In any event, the conqueror is turning us into Jews whether we like it or not. Nobody is being discriminated against. The Nazis have marked us with the Jewish national colors, which are our pride. In this sense we have been set apart from the Jews of Lodz, the city which has been annexed to the Reich. The "yellow badge" of medieval days has been stuck to them, but as for me, I shall wear my badge with personal satisfaction.

I shall, however, have revenge on our "converts." I will laugh aloud at the sight of their tragedy. These poor creatures, whose number has increased radically in recent times, should have known that the "racial" laws do not differentiate between Jews who become

Christians and those who retain their faith. Conversion brought them but small deliverance. The conqueror was accustomed to ask the Jews seized for forced labor, "*Jude!*" The convert could of course "tell the truth" and say no. But now the conqueror will not ask, and the convert will not "tell the truth."

This is the first time in my life that a feeling of vengeance has given me pleasure.

On the same day another decree was announced. Beginning December 1, 1939, every Jewish shop and business must indicate its Jewish ownership. The owners must conspicuously display a sign with a Star of David, but without any special wording. Here, too, we have been set apart from the Jews of Lodz, who had to put up signs with the words: "Jewish business."

In the future, everywhere we turn we shall feel as if we were in a Jewish kingdom. The national colors will flutter everywhere. From now on Jerusalem will not only crown our every joy, but also our ordinary weekdays, as we get up and as we lie down, as we trade and conduct business. "Poland-Judea" will no longer be a false accusation.

Our forefathers, who were experienced in adversity, immortalized their sufferings in lamentations. The dirge "O inquire, You who are burned" was written by Rabbi Meir of Rothenburg to commemorate the burning of the Talmud by the Dominicans in France in the thirteenth century. This dirge has become part of our national religious poetry, immortalized forever.

Who will immortalize our troubles? The national splendor inherent in religious poetry is not expressed in newspaper reports. It is a pity. A catastrophe that becomes part of poetry, even non-religious poetry such as Bialik's "The City of Slaughter," which commemorated the Kishinev pogrom, spreads among the people and is transmitted to future generations. A poet who clothes adversity in poetic form immortalizes it in an everlasting monument. And this monument provides historic material from which future generations are nourished.

Who will write of our troubles and who will immortalize them? Where is the folk poet of Polish Jewry, who will gather all the tragedy in our lives and perpetuate and guard it in the reliquary of his tears?

Poet of the people, where art thou?

Today we learned officially that on November 22, 1939, fifty-three Jews were shot for the "offense of rebellion." All these victims lived at Number 9 Nalewki Street. The majority were frightened merchants and landlords; some were learned in Torah and others just plain Jews whose eyes and hearts were turned only toward their dwindling businesses, and to whom the thought of rebellion was as distant as east from west—and suddenly they were imprisoned and killed.

The terrible event began when some Jewish thief shot and killed a Polish policeman and wounded another. The investigation and inquiry indicated that the murderer was one Jakub Pinchas Zylbring, whom the Jewish merchants had perhaps never seen before and certainly did not know; and if they knew him they had had no dealings with him. In every courtyard in Warsaw there live various elements, and two neighbors who are separated by only a thin wall may not know each other even after many years of living side by side. What does a merchant who is mainly occupied with his business have to do with a ne'er-do-well who lives in the same courtyard and whose occupation is theft and robbery? But there is no place for legal logic when there is an excuse to bring catastrophe upon fifty-three Jewish families. All those who lived in the courtyard were imprisoned and taken to an unknown place. After two weeks they were all shot.

There is a rumor that the *Judenrat* is partly to blame for this terrible incident. If so, it is a crime that cannot be forgiven. I shall make inquiries and investigate this. Since I have not yet verified this rumor, I find it difficult to believe. I shall refrain, for the time being, from disclosing its details. I will postpone it for a few days.

December 1, 1939

The liquidation of Polish Jewry is in full force, but it is not proceeding everywhere at a uniform rate. It is a mistake to think that the conqueror excels in logic and orderliness. We see quite the opposite of this. Everything that is done by those who carry out his exalted will bears the imprint of confusion and illogic. The Nazis are consistent and systematic only with regard to the central concepts behind their actions—that is, the concept of authoritarianism and harshness; and in relation to the Jews—the concept of complete extermination and destruction.

Our national colors are to fly throughout the capital city. There
was not enough time to prepare the arm bands, but in fear of death
not a moment was lost, and all of us, wives, sons and daughters over
twelve, are equipped; clothed in shame, in the conqueror's opinion,
but in our opinion clothed in honor. Say what you will, there are
no colors more splendid than our national colors. The matter was
arranged according to certain rules. In the Warta district, which
was annexed to the Reich and whose land is now reserved only for
elite Germans, even Polish citizens are compelled to wear a distinctive badge on their arms. Furthermore, the Poles too are being
deported. However, in the ethnic Polish land under Dr. Frank's
authority, where the German population is but a drop in the bucket,
the Poles are exempt from wearing their badge. The conqueror
tramples upon both "inferior" races, but the Jews are on the lowest
rung and the Poles on the next to lowest.

The teaching profession—whether Polish or Jewish—is treated as
a stepchild by the conqueror. All communal aspects of life have
been taken over by his cruel and mighty hand, to be reorganized and
disposed of; but education, whether at the elementary, intermediate,
or higher level, has been entirely neglected. Internal administration
of the elementary schools was left in Polish hands under the supervision of some *Schulrat*. The school directorate, banished from its
quarters and moved to 13 Hoza Street, is open, and the employees
sit like mourners, answering every question with "We don't know.
This is what we were ordered to do."

The elementary schools, some of which had been set aside for
Jewish children and were closed on Saturdays and Jewish holidays,
were opened briefly, then closed again because of the epidemics. In
the meantime everyone has been inoculated against typhus, and the
danger has passed to some extent. Permission has been granted to
reopen the elementary schools for Polish children, but not for
Jewish children. Thousands of them are out in the streets because
there are no schools for them. They remain untutored, uneducated,
and above all unfed. The aim of the conqueror is to exclude them
from the network of schools being supported by state and municipal
funds. Nazi justice does not permit Jews to benefit from public
funds. In general, it does not recognize that Jews have any rights,
and all the rights which the Jews enjoyed under Polish law have been
abrogated and annulled. This exclusion enters even the area of

general taxation. Frank's decree states that taxes are collected on the basis of the Polish laws in effect heretofore, but at the same time all Jewish exemptions and dispensations have been canceled. From now on all Jewish institutions of any kind, whether philanthropic, religious, cultural, or artistic, will have to pay taxes. Even the *Judenrat* schools and hospitals are included in this. This decree alone will cause them to perish.

December 4, 1939

Masses of exiles stream daily to the unfortunate capital city, downtrodden refugees who were uprooted one fine morning from the town of their birth. One's heart bleeds at the sight of these despairing people. Because of the extent of the catastrophe, one cannot even think about giving constructive aid. The only institution which is extending temporary relief, beggarly handouts that are only enough for a day at a time, is the Joint office at 13 Leszno Street.

December 5, 1939

The conqueror is condemning us to ignorance. Jewish education of all kinds has ended in Poland. After a transitional period, the elementary schools for Polish children have been opened and are being supported by the municipality. Only these, no others. The private schools of all kinds—even the Polish ones—remain closed. The Jewish teachers in the city-supported schools for Jewish children have been dismissed, although up to now they had been considered state employees. Their families await hunger, want, and a miserable existence.

At last even the Poles have begun to understand that the hatred of the Jew which the conqueror spreads among them is an opiate, an intoxicating drink to blind them and turn their attention away from the real enemy. We thought that the "Jewish badge" would provide the local population with a source of mockery and ridicule —but we were wrong. There is no attitude of disrespect nor of making much of another's dishonor. Just the opposite. They show that they commiserate with us in our humiliation. They sit silent in the street cars, and in private conversation they even express words of condolence and encouragement. "Better times will come!"

The matter of the fifty-three Jewish martyrs has been sufficiently clarified. On no account should the *Judenrat* be blamed. On the contrary, the *Judenrat* outdid itself. After the event (the shooting of the policeman), the conqueror demanded payment of 300,000 zloty to the murdered man's family. The *Judenrat* immediately set about collecting the money from among the wealthy Jews. The first payment of 150,000 was made immediately. It was difficult to collect the remainder of the sum in ready cash, so the *Judenrat* turned in checks drawn against "closed" accounts. These were also accepted. Therefore the required sum was paid in full; but in spite of this, innocent blood was spilled. More than seventy people were jailed, and fifty-three of them were killed.

Rumors continue that the Nazis are going to leave us within the next few days. This gossip deserves consideration. There are indications of demoralization within the army. Many units are changing their military uniforms for civilian clothes and running away. Where? To the Russian border. Someone came and told us that some officers entered a clothing store and ordered the proprietor and the salesmen to leave the place for two hours. When they returned they found everything in order, except that the officers had changed clothing: they had left their military uniforms on the table and taken civilian suits from the store's stock.

Someone else came and told us: The Führer is dead. But they are keeping his death a secret from the army so that it will not be demoralized. A third party adds another detail: Someone saw the Führer's picture draped in black.

Such is the imagination of a despised people which has nothing left but imagination. The downtrodden masses are waiting for a miracle; the ground is ripe for Messianism. Every stupidity finds a listening ear. Healthy common sense is gone: He Who dwells on High is all-powerful.

December 7, 1939

Besides confiscating and stealing, and emptying the leather and textile shops in "legal" fashion, the soldiers come to the stores and buy ready-made merchandise, especially Jewish merchandise. In this the rule of "desecration of the race" does not hold. Soldiers come to "buy" like decent people, and pay the "full" price. But God protect the shopkeeper from such customers. They pay whatever they want, and you can't protest. If you don't accept the price he suggests, the soldier will take it for nothing, and that's your hard luck. It is sufficient that you have not been beaten; it is sufficient that you are safe, and the financial loss is your expiation.

It is not necessarily the real soldiers who behave in this manner; even the *Volksgenossen,* who have risen high, try their hands at robbery. Through theft and various threats, they grab everything they fancy from the Jews. With my own eyes I saw a German civilian enter a bookstore to buy a dictionary priced at five zloty. He offered to pay two, giving as his "reason" that if he wished he could take it for nothing, since he is a German and could easily call in a soldier.

December 8, 1939

The Nazi authority in the occupied zones of Poland is full of joy. Today is its holiday. Representatives of their former archenemy, the Bolshevik-Jewish government, are now guests in this zone and have been received with royal honors. The head of the Soviet delegation is a Jew, the Nazis' "friend" Litvinov. When it is time to engage in politics, nobody cares about race. This is Jewish revenge—but it will not redound to our benefit.

The conqueror's newspapers do their job. On the front page they glorify "the wise and farsighted Stalin" and his emissary Litvinov, who although born of an "inferior race" is toasted by Dr. Frank himself, while on the third page they incite terribly against the Jews of Czestochowa, "who are not desirable residents, who busy themselves with theft, robbery, and other forms of white-collar work." Litvinov is not insulted by this. At this point he is the Nazis' "pet Jew." The Nazi newspapers—there are no others—are filled with words of praise for the Soviet Union and with flattery *ad nauseam.* This is our fate. Good deeds by prominent men of Israel do not help us in our hour of distress, and the bad deeds are credited to our account, so that the Jew suffers no matter what. More than once has the conqueror severely punished the Jews of Krochmalna Street because Hore-Belisha, the Jewish minister in England, fights against the Nazis. But when "the Bolshevik *Zyd*" from Moscow comes to the conqueror's aid, this is not to our credit.

Our political and personal deterioration at the hands of the conqueror proceeds at a rapid pace. From day to day the noose around our necks grows tighter. Just as in the Reich, the conqueror has excluded us from human society. Each day new pressures. Every morning a new insult. Almost every hour a new economic deprivation. Here is the harvest he reaped in a single week:

1. Pinning a "Jewish badge" on every Jewish man and woman without exception, not excluding converts and children of converts.
2. Forbidding Jews to enter the central post office on Warecki Street.
3. Placing Aryan commissars in loan and mortgage establishments owned by Jews.
4. Prohibiting the opening of Jewish schools, whether elementary or intermediate, municipal or private, for Jewish children. Jewish children do not have to study.
5. Prohibiting the support of retired Jews, even from assets of the Community Retirement Fund, although this is money they paid in monthly over many years.
6. Compelling every Jewish business and store to have a Star of David hung in a conspicuous place.

I think this is enough for one week.

December 9, 1939

Sunday morning, 4th day of Hanukkah,[6] *5700.*

Our festival has lost its meaning. All joyousness has been canceled. Sadness is on every face and dumb fear in every heart. There is no sign or memory of the glorious national holiday which used to bring such gaiety and happiness into our hearts during the long years of exile.

A freezing cold penetrates one's broken and aching heart. Moments occur when you are really ready to take your own life.

A simple old woman asks me each day: "Why is the world silent? Does Israel have no God?" I wished to comfort her in her agony, and so I lit four Hanukkah candles. And as I kindled the lights I felt that they were as humiliated as I. This is not a festival, this is not a light. The real flame is missing.

December 13, 1939

Three days without an entry. Not because our life has been quiet, but because we are so tired. There is no strength left to cry; steady and continual weeping leads finally to silence. At first there is

[6] An eight-day holiday, "the festival of lights," celebrating the victory of the Maccabees against the Syrians and the rededication of the Temple.

screaming; then wailing; and at last a bottomless sigh that does not leave even an echo. We live broken and shattered lives; lives of shame and dishonor; lives of suffering and grief. But the power of adaptability within us is miraculous. Conditions change—the mode of work changes too. We have drawn together within ourselves; we have shriveled and shrunk; we follow the advice of the prophet: "Come, my people, enter thou into thy chambers, and shut thy doors about thee: hide thyself for a little moment, until the indignation be overpast." From historical experience we have learned that there is no permanence in life; that everything changes; that all is transitory.

Every one of us hides from the cruel conqueror's eye, so as not to be noticed. The splendid starched and decorated hats have vanished from the heads of the women of Warsaw; they wear plain kerchiefs so that no evil eye will fall upon them. The Karakul furs are no more. Everyone wears old clothes, without ornament or attractiveness. Whoever has a holiday suits keeps it packed away and hidden and does not take it out even for the Sabbath or holidays. Splendor arouses suspicion of wealth. And the wealthy are the special object of the plundering Nazis' lust. He doesn't need paupers.

December 14, 1939

The unemployed Jewish teachers have found a way to partially save themselves from starvation. They got together and organized small groups of children who come to the teacher's home to be taught for two or three hours. Hundreds of teachers support themselves in this fashion. It is possible that the ban against study also applies to such small groups, and if questions were asked they would have to be stopped. But no one asks questions. The matter is done quietly, underhandedly. There is no other solution. I too want to make a living, and I have organized three small groups from among my pupils and meet with them in my apartment. Two women teachers from my school teach them general subjects twenty hours a week, and I teach them Hebrew subjects. For this purpose I have set aside a special room and have placed in it five desks for ten pupils. From this I support myself. I have thus relieved myself of the administration of the school, which has a staff of ten waiting for a salary. This is a temporary, transitory livelihood born of necessity, the child of adaptability.

Contrary to my custom since the outbreak of the war, I have written this personal entry in my diary today.

December 16, 1939

The beast within the Nazi is whole, completely healthy—it attacks and preys upon others; but the man within him is pathologically ill. Nature has struck him with the illness of sadism, and this disease has penetrated into the very fiber of his being. There is no Nazi whose soul is not diseased, who is not tyrannical, sadistic, homosexual.

People who may be trusted told me today of incidents of sadism toward Jews which only a sick mind would be capable of originating.

In Lodz some Jewish girls were seized for forced labor. Women are not given hard work, but instead perform various services, generally in homes. These girls were compelled to clean a latrine—to remove the excrement and clean it. But they received no utensils. To their question: "With what?" the Nazis replied: "With your blouses." The girls removed their blouses and cleaned the excrement with them. When the job was done they received their reward: the Nazis wrapped their faces in the blouses, filthy with the remains of excrement, and laughed uproariously. And all this because "Jewish England" is fighting against the Führer with the help of the *Juden*.

There was another incident, of a rabbi in Lodz who was forced to spit on a Torah scroll that was in the Holy Ark. In fear of his life, he complied and desecrated that which is holy to him and to his people. After a short while he had no more saliva, his mouth was dry. To the Nazi's question, why did he stop spitting, the rabbi replied that his mouth was dry. Then the son of the "superior race" began to spit into the rabbi's open mouth, and the rabbi continued to spit on the Torah.

And here is a third incident. This time I know the person to whom it happened. It is my friend Grynberg, a man close to fifty, a clerk by occupation, unsuited for any physical work. When he was seized for labor he was ordered to carry up whiskey barrels from a cellar. Because the weight of the load was beyond his strength, he asked for a helper, but his request was turned down. "You are just lazy," the Nazi scolded. But because, after all, a man is not capable of doing anything beyond his physical strength, they transferred him to still heavier labor—as a punishment. This was

87

digging. Again he stopped working. Then, ordering him to stretch out upon the ground, they measured the length of his body and asked his friends to dig a grave for the lazy fellow. The candidate for burial was taken to a room, turned with his face to the wall, and some object that he could not identify was hung on his back. The poor fellow was ready and waiting for death. He went through terrible moments of fear. Clear in thought and in possession of all his faculties, he waited for the fearful moment. But the Nazi was merely playing a joke. He didn't shoot his victim, he was content to have implanted the fear of death. Broken and shattered, half-dead and half-alive, my friend was transferred to new work. They tortured him in such fashion all day—until he was freed and abandoned.

December 17, 1939

This period, so full of darkness and catastrophe, through which Polish Jewry is now passing, is unparalleled since we became a people. Looting and plundering continue. Every day there are new victims. Each morning, new family tragedies. We have ceased to be a people or even a community. Like dumb lambs we are led to the slaughter, whether it is a killing of the body or a killing of the soul.

Nor are we an ordinary flock of lambs, but one which is scattered. In bits and pieces we are beaten and tortured; each group in a different sadistic fashion. The Jews of Lodz were marked with a double "yellow patch" on their right arms and on their backs; the Jews in the Polish zone (Cracow, Warsaw, Radom, Lublin) were decorated with our national colors. All those who have any means are fleeing Lodz for their lives, but even flight is forbidden.

December 19, 1939

The savage, preying Nazi has sunk his claws into the Jews of Lodz, and without pity, like an animal, he sucks their blood and breaks their bones. I am far from the place where this is happening, for I live in Warsaw and have no way of gathering exact information to set down in orderly fashion. But the exiles of Lodz are fleeing to Warsaw, and there is no house which does not shelter a Lodz refugee and his family. You can recognize them on every street and on every corner. Their fearful stories harrow your soul, and you feel like a worm instead of a man. Never, since the day that violence and devastation came into the world, have men been robbed and pillaged in such a cynical and cruel manner.

The enemy's hand has fallen upon the remainder of our precious treasure. Some weeks ago, only part of the books of the Tlomackie Library were removed, for the most part bound sets of daily news-papers, weekly and monthly journals. The shelves were still laden with volumes that the enemy had not touched. When he left, he placed a seal upon the locked doors, and this week he returned to complete his work of looting. Trucks stood before the library and Jews who were innocently passing by were seized and made to load the trucks with the remaining books.

In general, the conqueror displays a weakness for libraries which other hands have accumulated and preserved. The Sejm[7] Library has also been looted and its contents taken to an unknown place. It was unequaled in its wealth of books and manuscripts. Jews in the street were seized for labor in the Sejm Library also. One of the "porters," a friend of mine, told me that he was compelled to work in the Sejm Library for two days. When I asked why he had not said he was an attorney-at-law, he replied with astonishment, "On the contrary, when they asked me my occupation, I hid the fact that I am a lawyer and said that I am a laborer. They don't like educated people."

This week the Jewish lawyers were on the agenda. Their end— to die of starvation! All Jewish lawyers (including converts) with-out exception are required to answer a questionnaire which aims at their exclusion from the legal profession. Among the questions are these: religious affiliation—past and present; religious affiliation of parents—past and present. The intentions are obvious.

The Soviet commission to arrange for Slavic migration has begun to function. Long, snake-like lines stand before its door and wait to enter. But most of those waiting in line are Jews. Slavs do not come in large numbers.

Whether there is a formal prohibition excluding Jews from this organized migration I don't know, but there is a grudge in the Soviet heart against Jewish emigrants who are Polish-born, of that

[7] The Polish parliament.

89

there is no doubt. To my great sorrow, I must admit that "we have truly sinned." The bad behavior of some of our people in the border towns which were annexed to Russia has made us all hated and unwanted even in the eyes of the Russian government, which does not discriminate among peoples and whose basic attitudes are generally humane toward every person who accepts its authority. Many Jews did not migrate to become Soviet citizens and find work, but only to find temporary refuge, a night's shelter, hoping that conditions would improve and they could return to their former homes. In the meantime, until the storm should subside, they occupied themselves with all kinds of ugly speculation, which has since become their livelihood and life's work. The émigrés created an atmosphere of profiteering, which the Soviets hate, and therefore they have a feeling of contempt for all Jews.

The Soviet government took steps to lessen the crowding and congestion in the border towns, where thousands of immigrants are sleeping under the stars. It decreed that 2,000 people would be sent to work in inner Russia. Immediately 2,000 people appeared who were pining for work and manual labor. They received 50 rubles apiece and two changes of linen. To our shame, only 800 returned to accept the work and take the journey—the rest disappeared without a trace. They simply expressed their gratitude to the Soviet government, which has extended its protection and opened its borders to them, with trickery. There were also incidents of stealing from private people. Polish-born Jews are rather high-handed in matters of "yours" and "mine," and if they don't actually steal, they "take." We have thus garnered a bad reputation with the Soviet government, which has been liberal with us. For years and years she had weeded out middlemen and profiteering. Will she be silent now in the face of the ugliness which has again entered her cities?

There can be no atonement for such shameful behavior. It reflects on the character of an entire people. The Soviet-German treaty for legal immigration would have brought us salvation. Without it we are public property, open to all kinds of looting and evils. Now we have brought ruin upon ourselves and lost our only hope.

We are dealing with a nation of high culture, with "a people of the Book." An article in the *Deutsche Allgemeine Zeitung*, "Books,

Books, Books," reports on the mania for reading that has seized all of Germany. The Germans have simply gone crazy for one thing—books. At every bookstore there are long lines of people waiting for the moment when they will be able to buy a book. They are hungry, not for bread, not for water, nor for any tangible worldly pleasure, but for the German writer. Editions of tens of thousands are sold in a few days, and the publishers cannot keep up with the tremendous demand, a demand that has never been equaled, even in the inflationary days of World War I. Because of the crowding and congestion at the bookstores, the police intervene at times to avoid incidents, and order a store closed in midday. In such cases the shopkeeper hangs a sign on the door of his shop: "Due to crowding, this store has been closed by order of the police," and those waiting in line return home, full of disappointment, empty-handed, only to come back and try their luck again on the morrow. The customers' orders are only partially filled; if one orders four copies, he gets two. Obviously the printers and binders are not in a position to meet the gigantic demand that shouts: "Give me! Give me!" Germany has become a madhouse—mad for books.

Say what you will, I fear such people! Where plunder is based on an ideology, on a world outlook which in essence is spiritual, it cannot be equaled in strength and durability. Such a nation will not perish. The Nazi has robbed us not only of material possessions, but also of our good name as "the people of the Book." The Nazi has both book and sword, and this is his strength and might.

December 25, 1939

We have a "holiday" today, for all the nations of the world are celebrating the birthday of their Savior; their Savior—and not our Savior. Here is the cause of the entire Jewish tragedy. Were we to say "our Savior, too," the hatred against us would not be so great, and even the principle of racism would not find such a broad field for deepening the hatred of the world against us.

The principles of Nazism are not, after all, terribly original. The nullification of all hitherto accepted ideals was adopted from Bolshevism. The starling did not visit the crow for nothing, but because they are two of a kind. They share an ideological affinity, which becomes one at the first opportunity.

Nor did Nazism carry on original work in the field of hatred toward the Jewish people. They merely plowed more deeply, fertilized the field and its seeds, so that it would yield new, flourishing crops. Nazism found the primeval matter of religious hatred all prepared as a heritage of the Middle Ages. It merely reinforced it with economic hatred, in which it mixed various drugs—bits of ideology from Nietzsche, from Houston Stewart Chamberlain, and from other bigots and racists.

Today is also a holiday for Nazism, although it injects its own meanings and nuances. The "newborn babe" is not to be mentioned; he is born of an inferior race and is not to be glorified. The teachings of love for all who are born in the image of God—this is not for them. But in spite of this, through peculiar ideological arguments they too find an association with the festival of love. Men of mediocre intelligence among the leading columnists of the Nazi press minutely detail the basic and lofty principles of the Nietzsche-Chamberlain teachings:

The Feast of the Nativity ushers in the first tidings of the victory of light over darkness. Just as in that distant time a never-ceasing war began between light and darkness, which ended in the victory of light, so is a new war beginning now, a war for the creation of a new world order. The old world, which English plutocracy supports, has been shaken to its foundations and is rotting from within; one push will topple it. For a new force has arisen in the world, called Nazism, and it will establish a new world order upon the wreckage of the old. Its principles and foundations are made of completely different stuff. The right to live is given only to the strong. The tender and weak have no place in the world. Strength is the source of law. All the laws of nature are laws of strength. Only the strong can take possession. Humanism is a stumbling block to the world, humanism weakens and rots it, and this is against the laws of nature, established since the world was created. One should aspire to create an elite and aristocratic world, a world full of strength and splendor; and such a world can only be the creation of chosen ones, bearers of the legacy of authority, trained from birth to rule and dominate.

"Domination" is another outstanding psychosis of Nazism. All other nations are as nothing compared to Germany. It has been chosen by nature to rule, to command, to dominate, and to force the lesser and inferior nations to serve and obey it. The German people need "room to live" (*Lebensraum*), and are ready to achieve it at any cost. Is it justice for 42,000,000 Britons to rule 400,000,000 souls, in an empire spread over 40,000,000 square kilometers, while 82,000,000 Germans are crowded into an area of 500,000 square kilometers? This is the lesson of Christmas for Nazism.

There has been a short interruption in my entries, due to the one-sidedness of our lives. Again and again complaints; again looting and violence; again deportees; again insults and indignities; again deterioration and spiritual impoverishment. Silence reigns everywhere. The screams of those suffocated and killed do not reach us; only the voice of the Nazi is heard in his newspapers. He publishes lies upon lies, spreads falsehoods upon falsehoods every day, casts filthy epithets upon Jew and Pole alike—and there is no way to deny them, for one cannot utter a sound. The Feast of the Nativity (oh, how great is the shame; the birth of a Jew) passed with special celebration in Nazi circles. They used all kinds of publicity, discovered by modern technology, to bolster up the spirits and inject hope into their hearts. The lords and masters of the nation made speeches in honor of the defense forces: army, navy, air force, and submarine. They glorify every overblown metaphor; they publicize it in gigantic headlines with capital letters—and all to still the pain of not having shoes and winter clothing and other physical needs.

The *Volksgenossen* are the first everywhere, for they are the tree on which the Führer hangs his Polish policy. They are the killed and slaughtered ones whose cries touched the Führer's heart; they are those who "suffered the tortures of hell" because of their loyalty to their Germanness. The fury of the Poles against the conqueror is great, but it is seven times greater against the *Volksgenossen*, who previously were Polish citizens and who had truly dwelled in peace with no one harming them. The conqueror arranged holiday parties, concerts, and plays in their honor, loaded them, their wives, and children with a wealth of gifts, and fed them of the best.

In his press the conqueror admits that up to 50,000 refugees have entered the capital. But as usual he lies. More than 100,000 Jews have actually come to Warsaw. Piled high with belongings and babies, their carts form long lines along the city streets. No organized help has been given them. Each one helps himself in his own way and on his own initiative. Some move in with a relative, a friend, or a distant acquaintance. The poor ones fill the synagogues, which have become refugee centers. One cannot describe the crowded conditions, the congestion and filth in these shelters.

You can recognize the deportees and refugees by their faces and mode of walking through the bustling city streets. They stop the passerby and ask for this or that street. Sometimes you see a provincial Polish Jew, who truly presents an exotic appearance in a European city. Even his brethren, fellow Jews of Warsaw, are not accustomed to him, and in gentile eyes he is the object of ridicule and mockery. Some go out with their yellow patches in the shape of a Star of David. In such cases they are rebuked and forced to change them for the blue and white patch—symbol of the Jewishness of the Jews of Warsaw.

December 31, 1939

The usual persecution is not enough for us. An extraordinary persecution has been added, which leaves us in danger of death, and we have become daily candidates for stoning, burning, murder, strangulation, and all manner of unnatural deaths.

Apparently a secret military group is quietly functioning in Polish circles. Pilsudski once said about his fellow Poles that they are expert conspirators. When Poland was revived and political activity no longer required conspiracy, Pilsudski scolded them for retaining their early patterns. With their recent defeat, the Poles are returning to their old habits. Again conspiracy, again undermining what exists, again the striving for political freedom, which is only a hymn to the future. Poles and Jews always hover between destruction and construction. In their destruction they long for construction, and after they build, destruction comes again. Living side by side for thousands of years, they are joined in one historic fate. But this is not the point here.

Some military organization has begun to plot against the Nazis' lives. Obviously its work will be clandestine. This is merely an activity born of despair and spiritual depression. The terrible conqueror who knows no pity will not stand idly by. His revenge will know no bounds. In place of one, he will kill a hundred. The officers in the reserve, who were at first relieved of duty at the front to return home and enjoy their freedom, have been exiled to prisoner-of-war camps within the Reich. But this is only an introduction to what will be worse.

When evil is afoot, the conqueror turns into an attacking lion. He preys upon and devours guiltless people, free of crime, and dips himself in the blood of innocents, even in the blood of children who have never known sin. When a plot comes to light there is no room for legal investigation, for the clarification of an individual's degree of guilt or the verification of details and results. A terrible revenge is wrought by the vengeful sword.

Such an incident occurred a few days ago in Wawer, near Warsaw. Two German officers were shot to death in some tavern, evidently while drunk, and a horrible misfortune has befallen the surrounding area. Every home was entered, every man was seized, and thus 102 victims were led to the scaffold, giving up their souls for a sin that they had not committed. Of them a hundred were Poles and two were Jews. The tavern owner was hanged, and his corpse was not taken down from the gallows for several days so that it would serve as a warning.

CHAPTER
THREE

January 5, 1940

I HAVE RESTED for a few days. It is not pleasant for a musician to tune his instrument for an elegy. This is also true for the chronicler of events—it is not pleasant for a man to lament constantly. But to my great sorrow there are only lamentations and dirges in our lives. When a day passes and there is no new decree, we can hardly believe it. Through his representatives in authority the conqueror openly says: "There is no solution for the Jews other than to disappear from the world." We are sure that this will not happen. Nonetheless, it is possible that he will succeed in making us persons utterly despised and contemptible.

To compound our tragedy, the Joint's official representatives have all left us. The leaders of Polish Jewry pushed themselves to the fore in peaceful days when a monthly salary of 1200 zloty, equivalent to that of a senator or a deputy, attracted them; but in time of danger to us—and to them as well, if the truth be told—they fled for their lives. Will their sin be remembered on the Day of Reckoning? I doubt it.

In any event, there is nobody trained in proper organizational work and the Joint's administration is in the hands of unemployed teachers, idle actors, and loafers, who lack the ability to grasp the situation, do their work expertly, and set up an organizational framework suitable for the needs of the hour. I sympathize with these paid public servants. They are good-hearted and willing, but they are sinking under the weight of their burden. Truthfully, even public officials more educated and experienced than they would not do better. Such a gigantic undertaking needs governmental initiative and the help of an administrative machine.

The Russian commission of immigration is carrying out the letter of the law. Even the Jews who were born in the Ukrainian and White-Russian zones which were annexed by the Bolsheviks are now to be excluded. But the entire matter has assumed a ludicrous aspect. The migration of Slavs is to be permitted, but they do not wish to emigrate at all; and in their place at "the *Rathaus*" are long lines of the Jews whom the Russians refuse to accept. This is perhaps the first time in Bolshevik history that they are following an "except for Jews" rule—and it is probably not their fault. When asked. "Why do you too exclude Jews?" the Russian officer replies, "The conqueror did not consent to any privileges for his hated Jews."

Those in the know add some details about the negotiations between the conqueror and Molotov. The Russian side asked that every migrant, whether Slav or Jew, be permitted to take with him up to 2,000 zloty in cash and up to 100 kilos of baggage; the German side agreed in principle to Jewish migration, but limited each Jewish migrant to only 50 zloty in cash and only 20 kilos of baggage. This is why there was no agreement about the Jews. It is difficult to know how much truth there is in this rumor. The voice of the people in days as mad as ours is not exactly the voice of God.

January 6, 1940

Inflation has reached a point where the entire population without exception faces starvation. Place yourself in this position: A kilo of meat has gone up to seven zloty, and a kilo of fish to eight zloty. The costs of other foodstuffs are in proportion to this. Household expenses for even meager nutrition have increased four- or fivefold, while a broad section of the public remains without work and without income. The Jews joke that they no longer have to travel to Carlsbad, for the spa has come to them. Their weight has dropped, and their drawn, thin faces show poverty and privation.

Aside from hunger, we also suffer from cold. For the hard, bitter winter has come, and there is not a piece of coal in any house to warm our miserable bodies. The coal mines are in the hands of the conqueror, and he is killing us with cold. The fuel that was prepared and stored away before the war has been confiscated and looted, and no new supplies are being brought into the city. The warehouses stand empty. Obtaining a cartload of coal is as difficult as parting the waters of the Red Sea, and it is fraught with mortal danger, especially for Jewish merchants. Instead of coal being sold from warehouses, it is sold in the streets from handcarts brought by Poles, and each piece is worth its weight in gold. For 120 pounds of coal we pay 25 zloty; one firing of the stove comes to five or six zloty. Who can withstand such inflation?

And clothing? It is the most expensive of all. All the textile stores, like stores for other types of merchandise, are closed. The merchandise was looted, and only a few individuals succeeded in hiding a small amount of goods. There is no one from whom to buy; everything is closed and locked. To buy yard goods you need a personal recommendation; you will find the merchant hidden in a back room, and if he doesn't know you, he will not sell you anything for any amount. If you are fortunate enough to be led there by some go-between who indicates to the merchant that "everything is kosher," only then will the seller let you enter the inner sanctum and do you the favor of showing you what goods he has. You have no right, God forbid, to question the quality, for there is no choice. Hence one is obliged to buy the poorest merchandise, which is absolutely worthless, for fantastic prices. There are goods whose price is more than 100 zloty a yard. This is the first stop. And when you reach the second stop, a tailor, you'll be stunned again. The price of tailoring is three times higher than it was; an average suit will cost up to 600 zloty. I would be surprised if, under such circumstances, one could find a Jew to utter the blessing, "He who clothes the naked," over new clothing—and not fear that his blessing is in vain.

January 8, 1940

The terrible cold freezes our bodies, shrunken and cramped for lack of a warm stove. At the coal warehouses the Warsaw paupers stand in long lines. All the different queues which were seen in great numbers in the city streets during the early months of the war have disappeared, except for the coal line. From far off the angry voices of people being pushed and shoved reach your ears.

Everyone wants to get ahead of his friend and push into the treasure house of the "black pearls." You witness ugly scenes that shake you to your depths, even if you are not squeamish. The cries of those who are fighting and struggling fill the entire street, and when you come a little nearer and scrutinize them more closely, the inferno within your heart begins to burn, and you feel pain for the humiliation of these creatures which God has created in His world. These same unfortunate people danced for joy because they escaped alive from the air bombardment.

To compound the tragedy, there is in all this ugliness a most painful "Jewish angle." While hundreds of people are standing in line struggling to be first to get coal—the warehouse owner does not even contemplate selling it. When the merchant succeeds in getting a cartload of coal, he transports it furtively to some hidden cellar and tells the buyers on the street, to whom he is obliged to sell at a fixed price, that he has none. Then he distributes his smuggled coal among his steady customers, mainly wealthy people who can pay him an exorbitant price. The rest go home empty-handed, after long hours of waiting in the cold and snow, after their thin bodies have absorbed blows and kicks from all sides, be it from their fellow paupers or a police representative who keeps "order."

There is yet another Jewish angle enveloping us in shame and justifying some of the severe decrees which the conqueror loads upon us with a generous hand. With the outbreak of the war, people stopped paying rent. People born in Warsaw do not like to pay a debt even if morality demands it; how much more do they dislike paying a debt in which their morality is not involved. When there are no courts and there is no fear of dispossession of tenants, they will not give the landlord a penny. In the midst of the suffering brought by the war and later by the conqueror, there was no physical possibility of paying rent, but such a situation cannot and must not continue for long. The landlord is burdened with expenses and debts and taxes, and therefore he begins to demand his rent emphatically—and no one pays. There is, indeed, legal recourse, but it is lengthy. The conqueror and the *Volksgenossen* showed the landlords a short cut, although it is not entirely legal. You simply come and forcibly remove the stubborn tenant from the apartment. But only a *Volksgenosse* is permitted to use force; he has entry into Nazi circles, and the rulers will listen and obey his wishes.

The masses grit their teeth. Can such a despicable thing occur among Jews? Can Jews surrender their coreligionists to the hands of their archenemies, especially in time of such terrible material oppression? But the landlords did what they did. Their end will be that the *Volksgenossen* will be the main candidates for these houses, and the landlords will be driven from their own homes, but it is not the way of the world for people to pay attention to what will happen later. The Jew lacks community feeling and a sense of collective responsibility. I am sure that not one Polish landlord would allow himself to be safeguarded by means of such a disgusting action. And if he dared do such a thing, he would be ostracized like a leper. But in our camp? Mr. K., a Jewish landlord who is also president of the Society for the Aid of the Poor, transferred the management of his house on Karmelicka Street to a German *Volksgenosse* so that he could oppress his tenants and terrorize them.

January 12, 1940

Within the Reich, patriotism is reaching its zenith. The conqueror senses that after the passing of the first cycle, studded with victories, a turning point will be reached and the front will change from passive to active. The allied powers—England and France—are preparing themselves for some new military initiatives, and the conqueror is quaking with fear of the coming day. He has a premonition of defeat, and therefore he has mobilized the entire population. Everything is being reorganized, repaired, and mechanized. Everything is pulsing and vibrating; everything is changing form and taking on a new shape and adjusting itself to the needs of the war.

Hermann Goering[1] has been appointed dictator of the war economy, which heretofore had been under the control of Minister Frank. Everything is being concentrated under one man, in order to adapt it more readily to the needs of the hour and to improve its fitness for any need that may arise. This is first. And secondly, in the schools of higher learning the semesters were eliminated and trimesters were initiated in their stead. The time required to complete a higher education was thus reduced by one year. During war and threat of war there is no time to acquire knowledge with reflection; there isn't time for academic work which is by nature

[1] Field Marshal Goering (1893–1946) was Hitler's Minister of Interior and head of the *Luftwaffe*. He committed suicide just before he was scheduled to hang as a war criminal.

more research than study. When the time comes to serve one's homeland, research which is only theoretical must be laid aside In its place one must substitute studies leading to practical results. The Fatherland needs doctors, engineers, technicians, mechanical workers, and artisans. Therefore it is proper that their preparation be speeded up.

Third, academic work cadres were organized. The academician is not exempt from the physical labor which the Fatherland requires. When the homeland must be served, all laws may be changed. This is an ancient rule of every nation and every state in time of danger. More than the Fatherland needs men with diplomas, it needs working hands. Millions of people are at the front; there is thus a shortage of workers. Let the hands which had heretofore been occupied with delicate tasks now come and grasp a hoe. So it is wherever you turn. We see the results. Life is invigorating. The people stand alert, ready, and prepared. Say what you will, it is hard to defeat such an enemy.

January 13, 1940

There are groups who enjoy spreading the frightening rumor that from January 15 to January 18 there will be "three days of killing" of Jews, that the Poles, aided and abetted by the conqueror, will slaughter them. I am sure that this will not happen. The Polish people as a whole will not permit itself, in a moment of depression or spiritual passivity, to become an instrument for pogroms in the hands of the conqueror, its eternal enemy. But it is not impossible that isolated attacks will occur by those Polish groups which maintain their existence through theft and depredation. Terrorists and troublemakers are not lacking among any people, and at all times and places they can be found in sufficient numbers.

It is not my custom to write in my diary about rumors. I always think that only actual facts are worthy of note. This time I only wished to show our mood, our state of mind, the atmosphere which causes such frightening rumors to spread. An evil rumor, when it is being spread, is worse than the event itself when it comes to pass.

January 14, 1940

A new catastrophe for Polish Jewry.

When I wrote in my diary yesterday, I did not know what was happening at the time, for I had not read the conqueror's newspaper

101

of January 13, 1940, in which the terrible new decree was published. This decree will uproot all of Polish Jewry and bring utter destruction upon it. If we are not saved by some outside help, our end is complete annihilation, for nothing like this has been inscribed before in our historical scroll of agony. If this decree is even partially carried out, we shall not be able to survive.

The cruel Nazi, full of murder and tyranny, is creating forced-labor camps for *Juden* for a two-year period. This is not to be work for its own sake, but work that will educate and accustom us to hard physical labor, labor under the supervision of tyrannical Nazis, who will oppress us as one might enslave a camp of criminals and felons in order to cleanse them of their sins.

When we read the details of the decree—which is not signed by the established administrative authority but by the head of the S.S., Otto Krüger[2]—our knees sagged and our hearts turned to water. All of Polish Jewry is to be deported for hard labor, for forced labor, in order to be strangled by our archenemies, by tyrants and oppressors who are commanded and ready to turn us into doormats for their sadistic appetites and to annihilate us to the very last one. Neither more nor less: Every Jewish man from the ages of twelve to sixty and every Jewish woman from fourteen to sixty, all of them, without exception, whether merchants or artisans, workmen or clerks, and even young children with their mother's milk still on their lips, are required to register in the office to be established for this purpose by the *Judenrat*. After the registration is completed the work camps are to be established—naturally in various gradations and of various types—and the workers will be deported for two years!

January 15, 1940

We feel with some sixth sense, with that unnamed sense which prisoners and all those condemned to lengthy solitude possess, that we are living in a time of transition. The first period of the war was a war without battles. Tremendous, heavy camps on both sides, armored and equipped with all the destructive tools of modern technology, camps which cost tens of millions a day to supply, stood idle. The front was silent. In contrast, the "rear" battled in the

2 Obergruppenführer W. F. Krüger was police chief and State Secretary for Security in the General Government until February 18, 1943. Kaplan was apparently mistaken about his first name.

editorial columns. Each side was proud of itself and mocked the other side. Each side glorified its victories which had not yet taken place. It appears that the two sides came to the realization that this situation could not continue. The final preparations therefore came to an end.

It is true that we have no clear news of all that is happening among the Allied Powers, for news about them is strained through the conqueror's sieve, through newspapers in which one finds only scraps of news about the opposing side. But from between the lines some feeble echoes reach one's ears. The discussions and polemics in the press hide a great deal, but also disclose a little. Anyway, even if the "news" is slow, the heart has a presentiment of it.

If defeat comes, it will be decisive and eternal. Tender, sensitive democracy will harden its heart this time. There will be no place for Kerenskys or Wilsons. One does not take pity on a serpent. The "new" world of Nazism will be destroyed before it is established.

January 16, 1940

The forced labor decree gnaws away at our people. Because of the extent of the catastrophe, the Jews do not believe that it will come to pass. Even though they know the nature of the conqueror very, very well, and his tyrannical attitude toward them has already been felt on their backs; even though they know he has no pity or human feeling in relation to the Jews—in spite of all this, their attitude toward the terrible decree he has published is one of frivolity. I do not join them in this. Thousands and perhaps tens of thousands will become slave laborers—that is, if the tyrant's defeat does not intervene.

In the past few days a frightful new rumor has brought grief to thousands of families whose children had fled from the tyrant to Russia, that is, to Bialystok and along the zone occupied by the Soviets. To our great grief, there is a basis to this rumor, and it is not impossible that it will come to pass, even though its political and strategic motivations are a complete mystery to us.

They say that the Germans are going to enter, or have already entered, Bialystok, which is filled with myriads of Jewish refugees from Poland, some of whom have settled down there and have found a meager livelihood. Is it possible that the Soviets are giving up

103

Bialystok and its environs? For what purpose? What will they get in exchange? Only the diplomats know. Whatever it is, we will be the first victims. Again a flight of tens of thousands of refugees! Again economic disaster for thousands of families. Again the physical and mental tortures of a psychopathic tyrant who knows no shame. Where will the people flee now?

Among the paragraphs of the new decree there is one that forcibly confiscates all the specialized tools owned by Jewish craftsmen. From now on no Jewish craftsman may sell his working tools, give them away as gifts, hide them, or destroy them, and he may not even buy new tools without a permit.

But another paragraph provides relief for craftsmen who can present documentary proof that they are candidates for migration to Russia. In spite of the fact that the Russian commission for migration was originally formed for the benefit of Slavs, it does not exclude Jews who have skills that the country needs. Candidates for migration are therefore exempt from forced labor. Immediately after this became known, there was a change in those waiting on line before the doors of the Russian commission. Now most of them are vigorous men and craftsmen who wish to escape the jurisdiction of the conqueror. There is no doubt that some lucky individuals will be successful. And the rest? They are condemned to slow and gradual death.

This cruel winter is increasingly severe, and its heavy hand rests upon us with a temperature of thirteen below zero. There is no coal to alleviate it.

I don't know whether anyone else is recording daily events. The conditions of life which surround us are not conducive to such literary labors. I am one of the fortunate ones whose pen does not run dry, even in this hour of madness. Anyone who keeps such a record endangers his life, but this does not frighten me. I sense within me the magnitude of this hour, and my responsibility toward it, and I have an inner awareness that I am fulfilling a national obligation, a historic obligation that I am not free to relinquish. My words are not rewritten; momentary reflexes shape them. Perhaps their value lies in this. Be that as it may, I am sure that Providence sent me to fulfill this mission. My record will serve as source material for the future historian.

Are we lacking in tumults? Now another one has been added.

At the time the new edict was born an old one expired. This was the decree for registering Jewish property (in cash, goods, debts, and real estate). We had been given until January 19, that is to say, a month's time, but as usual in paying off notes, people delayed until the last minute. But they forgot one small detail, which the conquerors established with premeditation: the forms were sold at low prices only until January 1. Most people didn't pay attention to this: "A matter of a few cents." "There won't be any shortage even after the deadline." The profiteers and those who trade on the troubles of their neighbors made use of this. They went and bought up all the remaining forms and are selling them to the latecomers at a price of ten zloty a copy. (Imagine! Ten zloty for half a sheet of printed paper!) To every form various extra sheets must be affixed, according to the various categories of possessions and businesses. Thus a Jew who is late in filing his declaration is forced to pay a sum of 30 or 40 zloty, just for some paper forms.

And so—panic upon panic! Crowding, pushing, toil and unnecessary expenses!

Until now there was no shortage of bread. It was expensive (150 zloty a kilo), but it was available in abundance all over. Besides its usual place in the food stores, it was also sold in the street. Hundreds of people in all parts of the city would go out with loaves of bread under their arms (hygiene, who even remembers its name?) and find buyers for their wares. And not just ordinary bread was to be found in plenty, but even white bread, and baked goods from ordinary cake to honey cake, and all sorts of luxurious rolls and pastries.

As long as the conquerors took no notice of this, everything went smoothly. We got used to the cost. You raise the price of your goods and I raise the price of mine, and neither is deprived by the other. This is not a healthy phenomenon, but it is a necessary one. Such is the way of war. But every time a regime, especially a despotic, foreign regime, desires our "good" we find ourselves in the midst of all evil. And so it is in this case. One fine morning notices were posted that profiteers and all those who sell their goods, including

105

essential foods, above the fixed prices will be sentenced to death. Immediately afterward bread and baked goods disappeared, and we are doomed to deprivation and famine as though in a city besieged. The fixed prices, as usual, were set in a bureaucratic fashion. It is life which sets them at naught, not the bakers; therefore they have stopped baking. When it comes to beheading, the conqueror sticks to his word. And who wants to endanger his life?

January 22, 1940

Yesterday notices were posted in the streets: A certain Jew named Kot[3] is accused of murder and has disappeared. Following are his identifying characteristics. Anyone having some knowledge of him should inform the police and will receive a reward of 2,000 zloty.

The word *Zyd* was written with the letters spaced so as to accentuate his Jewishness, for there is no sin that the Nazis don't lay at the Jews' doorstep. But steeped in lies as they are, this time too they concealed the truth.

This Kot was born into Christianity; his father was a Christian, born and bred. Not only that: even the third generation on his father's side, his grandfather, was a Christian. On his father's side, his whole family tree is Christian. His Judaism comes to him from his grandmother, with whom his grandfather, a descendant of untold generations of Christians, fell in love and raised another generation of pure Christians. But the addled conquerors go along their merry way. This time they paid no attention to the rule they themselves laid down—that everything goes according to the father; that the third generation may enter into the congregation of the Nazis and is considered a pure Aryan in all matters.

This Kot was caught in some political crime; he was the leader of a diversionist group. He did whatever he did, and fled, and here the conquerors found an open field for revenge against their forfeit people. Kot's grandmother was a Jew three generations back, and the whole Jewish people must bear the sin of her Jewishness. Logic would indicate that this Kot was also an anti-Semite, as is customary in Poland, but all this has nothing to do with the basic matter of the punishment. In connection with this event, the conquerors have arrested several hundred Jews from among the intelligentsia and the

[3] Andrzej Kot was accused by the Nazis of being the leader of an underground resistance group. He was arrested and then managed to escape.

wealthy merchants, as well as from among the elite and the influential. A rumor is going around that Rabbi Icchak Nisenbaum,
the head of the Mizrachi party, was also among those "responsible"
for Kot's sin and is required to atone for it.

Every house is filled with sadness and a spirit of depression. The
Kot affair brought misfortune to a number of families among the
intelligentsia whose husbands or sons were arrested for no legal
reason. And those who have not yet been arrested live in mortal
fear. Every echo of footsteps on the stairs in the dark of night drives
mute panic into their hearts. Especially in danger of arrest are young
people, who are suspected of being especially capable of diversion-
ary tactics.

There is no chance of hiding out from the conquerors. When
someone is listed by them as a candidate for imprisonment and cannot be found in his home, his closest relatives are given strict orders
to produce him within a few hours; if not, they will be shot. And
they are shot. Under such circumstances there is no alternative, and
the missing ones are forced to come "voluntarily," and bare their
necks for slaughter. This insecurity debilitates the nerves and
weakens one's powers in the war of survival.

Today you are here, tomorrow in prison.

This week all places of worship—whether in rented quarters or in
their own splendid buildings—were closed. It is hard to delve into
the secret of a barbaric decree such as this: whether it is because of
the epidemics that are spreading through the city, or because of the
conquerors' desire to embitter our lives. The conquerors, according
to their statements, greatly esteem the spirit. Their barbarism in
relation to the Jews is ideological; and here lies the source of the
evil. Ideological filth is hard to vanquish, and there is no ugliness, no
baseness which the enemy ideologists are incapable of justifying with
nauseating slogans. May I live to see the restoration of my people!

I read a lead article this very week in the *Deutsche Allgemeine
Zeitung* in which the author rambles around the notion of the twofold aspect which every war assumes. There is war which is nothing
but power and worldliness, and there is war whose source is in the
spirit—and it is self-evident that this Nazi war is no less than a war
whose roots are inspired with spirit.

A small ray of light has shone forth from between the clouds that are spread across our skies. The information has reached us that the American Quakers will send a rescue mission to Poland. This time the aid will be offered in American fashion, without regard to race or religion, and even the Jews will be able to benefit from the proffered aid. May they be blessed! For us this is the first time that, instead of "except the Jews," the expression "including the Jews" has reached us, and it rings in our ears with a strange sound. Is it really true?

What is more, the conqueror's Polish newspaper[4] found it necessary (voluntarily or under duress?) to make this known publicly. Thanks to America, we are in good standing for once. They are deathly afraid of America and afraid of antagonizing the American public. That is why there is no restriction on the Joint's offering aid to the Jewish population, and why the conquerors didn't demand that the American Quakers exclude the Jews from their charitable undertaking. When a rumor spread abroad that the Quaker delegation was encountering obstacles in its path to the conquered territory the conquerors hastened to deny it, and to raise on a banner their good intentions of giving this American philanthropic organization the opportunity to furnish material assistance to the conquered population who had come to this downfall through the guilt of their government.

Their hearts are full of compassion for all creation. It is self-evident that in all this there is no contradiction to the information purveyed in the same newspaper, that the Jews do not enjoy the right to receive 200 zloty in small denominations when they "deposit," by force of the latest decree, their 100 and 500 notes. This concession was made for the sake of the poor depositors whose entire fortune doesn't exceed 200 zloty in two 100-zloty notes. What would they support themselves from? One cannot take away the last crust of the poor man with which he sustains his soul as his last support. Yes, but none of this applies to Jews. From them one must extract the last penny. Let them waste away in hunger and cold. They have no atonement but utter destruction.

With a heavy heart the conquerors allowed the charitable Quakers to offer assistance "even to the Jews."

The fear of America is upon them.

4 *Nowy Kurier Warszarwski.*

Historical events capture the imagination completely only after their time. Like paintings, they require perspective. Through the passage of time and the flow of generations they assume their true form, while in proximity of place and time they are passing occurrences that make no impression. Men who have been privileged to witness great events busy themselves nonetheless with day-to-day needs, with little things and little events that order individual life and suit it for the needs of the moment and the hour. Here they are spilling human blood like water; and here they are profiteering and amassing fortunes. In one place there is a sea of troubles and injuries, in another, someone else grows opulent from those very troubles. Men grow rich by robbing the poor and exploiting the destitute. In one place there is sighing and weeping, in another wedding feasts and dancing. Perhaps in this lies the secret of the perpetuation of life. It is in the nature of life that it cannot be stilled.

The paltry bread cards are inadequate. In Germany you'd never get anything beyond the card, but we are adept in conspiracy. Never before has profiteering flourished as in the past few days. It is thus clear that the conquerors have accomplished nothing "for the sake of order." But maybe I'm wrong: they have accomplished much. Prices have risen tenfold.

The rationale is that the Lord provides the remedy before the sickness. He created permitted things and forbidden things. And in time of crisis the forbidden things become permitted and enable us to survive. For some it is a degrading, narrow survival; for some it is survival with a moderate income; and for others it is survival in wealth and abundance. All of them live and support themselves, and not one is entirely "kosher." There isn't one who doesn't break the law; not one who doesn't deserve death under penalty of the conqueror's decrees. The words of the prophet have almost come true: "No weapon that is formed against thee shall prosper."

Arrests never cease. No one knows when his day will come, so every heart is fearful. The intellectuals in particular are being arrested, and not necessarily famous people, but rather "everybody is welcome." The prison cells are full of young lawyers and doctors who were arrested for no crime; they are not accused of any sin, nor are there any complaints against them. They must atone for the sin of Kot, whom they never so much as laid eyes on.

Unexpectedly I ran into Moshe Indelman, who was sent to a concentration camp some months ago. Where to? Indelman is not allowed to say. One rumor is that he went to Dirschau. He himself says neither yes nor no. He is afraid to say, because he signed a declaration to keep everything strictly secret, and he wants to keep his word. But he revealed a little of what was permitted. He says that he didn't hesitate to argue with the Nazis who conducted the investigation in his case, when he was arrested in Warsaw. He wholeheartedly affirmed to them: It is no sin to rage at those who seek my very life, who persecute me, who undermine my existence and wish to eliminate me from the earth. Nazism is anathema to the Jewish people, and anyone who says otherwise is lying. The Jewish world outlook is Zionistic. In this there is no contradiction to the Nazi's world outlook as regards the Jewish question, because both of them want emigration and both say that the Jews have no place within foreign cultures. Zionism endorses the "desimilation" which Nazism has begun to put into living practice. These words seemed new to the Nazis. They couldn't believe their ears. In the future, when the danger is past, he will write about everything.

I was as happy to meet him as though I found a great treasure. This is the first time in my life that I have met a human being who returned alive from the torments of hell.

January 30, 1940

The conditions of life affect the appearance of the streets. In general, they look different at every period of the day. Any perceptive person who looks out his window can identify the period of day from the appearance of the street, even if he doesn't know the time.

The latest happenings have also totally changed the face of the streets of Warsaw. This is not the Warsaw that used to be.

There is crowding and congestion on the sidewalks. One person shoves another on side and shoulder without any malice and without any apology. Both sides concede that no other way is possible. At a time of general trouble a person has no right to say "I'm crowded!" They all share the same fate. In everyone's face the terrible happenings of which he is himself the subject are reflected. A certain silent sorrow is cast on all their faces. Everyone shares his neighbor's troubles even if they are unknown to him in detail. The vicious conqueror has made them all equal. A single drawn sword hovers over the heads of all of them. Trembling before the immediate future fills the hearts of all of them. And thus their hearts have grown warmer and drawn closer to one another. A single wordless glance from one of my brothers in misfortune is enough to show me what is going on deep within his heart.

Many reasons have combined to bring about a situation in which the clothing, too, is the same, as though everyone had been in the same prison and had to wear the same uniform, and had been set free at one and the same time. Formerly there was a special "Jewish hat" in Poland which Hasidic groups used to wear. This Jewish hat was famous, even among the gentiles. It was a small black hat with a short visor. It is hard to see what symbols of Judaism the religious found in this shape, but that doesn't change the fact. Whole generations of enlightenment, of Zionism and rationalism, had no influence on removing the Jewish hat from the heads of the Hasidim. From the esthetic side, there is nothing but ugliness in it; whoever wears a hat of this sort is really an exotic type. But nothing availed, for once the Hasidim latch on to a custom they stick to it forever. But when the conquerors started seizing only Jews for forced labor, everyone at once began to erase the symbols of his Judaism. People exchanged their hats for "gentile hats" of a different shape. "Perhaps this will help." This gentile hat has a cloth visor; but some people are careful to wear gentile hats with blocked brims—a clearer proof of one's being a Gentile.

January 31, 1940

And again days of twilight have come, a time of transition. When the shadows of misfortune cover every ray of light, our ancient hope, which has sustained us thus far, comes to our aid. In actual reality there is disappointment upon disappointment, yet hope flourishes. A nation which for thousands of years has said daily, "And even if he tarries, I will await the coming of the Messiah every day," will not weaken in its hope, which has been a balm of life and has strengthened it in its miserable survival.

Today the first step was taken to put the terrible forced-labor decree into effect. The Jews didn't want to believe it and invented a political dialectic: This is only a threat which won't be put into practice; the conquerors are greedier for our money than for our labor. And experts were found who told wild stories of negotiations

111

between the conquerors and the *Judenrat* about a contribution of tens of millions. Now the enactments for putting it into practice have been made public, and our eyes have darkened with pain. Everyone from a child of twelve to a father of sons who is sixty years old is obliged to register at the *Judenrat* as a candidate for forced labor. There are families in which both father and sons will be forced into exile in a work camp, to become despised and degraded slaves of the Führer. The registration must be effected within the ten days from February 1 to February 10.

And even at the very moment when this sharp sword rests on their necks, the Jews do not cease to console themselves—with politics. I am astounded. Where does this nation get such nerve, such inner confidence that they will come out unscathed?

I have heard one current bit of consolation, that in spite of all, the days of the conqueror's occupation of Warsaw are numbered; that during February (and some people even specify the date, February 15) the conqueror will abandon us to joy; that because of a shortage of oil they will make a trade with their "friend and admirer" Stalin. The Russians will give up the oil wells in Boryslaw and Drohobycz and the Germans will give up the "General Government" to the Russians. A sign of this: the Russians passed several German divisions through Bialystok toward the Rumanian border by permission. Rumanian oil is of the utmost importance to the conquerors. Without it their downfall is assured and they will go to destruction. But even the Rumanian wells aren't enough and they'll give anything for additional oil. And such oil is right at hand, in Russian Galicia, Rumania, Boryslaw, and Drohobycz are the springs of salvation for the conqueror.

And therefore the registration means nothing; they're getting out of here!

And the popular imagination, which in dark times has an open field for its delusions, supports these "political deceptions" with evidence drawn from real life: A certain Jew who was riding in a trolley car with his companions in misfortune guessed the amount of money each one had with him with absolute accuracy. Afterward they asked him, "If you tell fortunes, make a guess as to when Haman will leave us." And this amazing Jew answered with absolute certainty: "The departure will not be later than the fifteenth of February, 1940." Isn't this evidence drawn from life?

Then there was the case of a boy, a candy vendor on Swietokrzyska Street. A Nazi soldier passed by him, kicked him, turned his box over, and trampled on his wares. The boy started to cry, and at the sound of his crying a group of passersby gathered around him. Within a few moments a military car drove up to the scene and a German officer got out, and asked the man who told me of this incident what had happened. When he learned of the incident he at once took 20 zloty out of his pocket, and gave it to my informant with a request that he give them to the injured boy at once. And at the same time he added: "Go and tell your brethren that their suffering will not last much longer!"

And so saying, he disappeared! Here you have a second bit of evidence.

February 1, 1940

The first Germans reduced the pride of the might of Rome. They brought its world hegemony to earth, but they accepted its teachings and adhere to them scrupulously to this very day.

In all their tributary provinces the Romans conducted themselves on the principle of divide and conquer. In a subjugated state one must not inculcate peace and amity among the various races dwelling there. There is danger for the conqueror in every such union. There is no more tried and tested means of strengthening one's rule over foreign tribes than civil strife. Our new lords put this into practice.

Even before the war broke out, hatred of the Jews spread through Poland with the help of the Nazis. At that time their objective was different. Racial hatred would undermine Poland's survival; it would weaken her military strength, create internal enemies, and render her incapable of looking out for her survival.

Since the conquest of Poland the conqueror has become the "father and patron" of the Polish people, and he is saving the country from the Jews. Propaganda for hatred of Jews suited the tastes and wishes of many Polish circles, and perhaps the entire Polish public. It is as if the Nazis were saying: "We have taken your political independence away from you; but in its place we will give you economic independence. Up to now all economic life was controlled by Jews. From now on it will pass into your hands. All your lives you have fought against the Jewish plague and you have accomplished nothing. We will show you the way. Under our rule the

Jews will be eliminated from all their occupations and you will take their place."

But the oppressed and degraded Polish public, immersed in deepest depression under the influence of the national catastrophe, has not been particularly sensitive to this propaganda. It senses that the conquerors are its eternal enemy, and that they are not fighting the Jews for Poland's sake. Common suffering has drawn all hearts closer, and the barbaric persecutions of the Jews have even aroused feelings of sympathy toward them. Tacitly, wordlessly, the two former rivals sense that they are brothers in misfortune; that they have a common enemy who wishes to bring destruction upon both at the same time.

Such a stand on the part of the Poles in relation to the Jews has endangered the entire strategy of the conquerors, and for this reason they approach the matter with greater efficiency. No nation lacks hooligan elements, and the conquerors have paved the way for them. They have hinted that the Jews are expendable, that the government will not adhere to the letter of the law when the victims are Jews. And a hint is enough for hooligans. In the past few days there has been no end to attacks upon Jews in public places in broad daylight. The conquerors' eyes look on, but they are struck with blindness.

February 2, 1940

Social visits have ceased. Everyone remains locked in his own unheated room, imprisoned in his own sorrowful thoughts. You sit like a mourner, and the monotony of the long winter evenings consumes your heart like a flame. The fear of death stares at you from every hidden corner. Every knock at the door after six o'clock is an evil omen which frightens you to the core.

The stories of the day's happenings are still fresh in memory: In one street they detained a Jew who was riding in a carriage, stripped him of his fur coat, emptied his wallet, beat him up, ordered him to pay the driver for the ride—and set him free. In another street, a Jewish youth "dared" to go outside without the Jewish "badge"; an insignificant soldier noticed him and ordered him from a distance to halt; the Jew panicked and began to flee—and he paid with his life, because a bullet was sent after him. Such occurrences are innumerable.

This week we are under the influence of the Führer's speech, which was overflowing with murder and revenge. With the coming of spring a cataclysm on a scale that has never before existed will take place, and we are caught in the middle. If they suffer defeat, we caused it; if, heaven forbid, they score a victory—they will be our masters. In either case, we are helpless.

February 3, 1940

If anyone in the democratic lands is attempting to write a book on the nature of Nazism, I know without seeing it that the author will not be able to express the truth of Nazism's cruelty and barbarism. Nazism has two faces. On the one hand, it is full of hypocrisy and submissiveness when it is necessary to obtain some benefit from someone; and on the other hand, it is full of brutal strength, trampling all humanism under foot, hardening its heart against the most elementary human emotions.

Descriptive literary accounts cannot suffice to clarify and emphasize its real quality. And moreover, no writer among the gentiles is qualified for this task. Even a Jewish writer who lives the life of his people, who feels their disgrace and suffers their agony, cannot find a true path here. Only one who feels the taste of Nazi rule in all his "248 organs and 365 sinews"; only one who has bared his back to the lashes of its whips; only one who has examined the various nuances of its administrative and legal tactics in relation to the Jews, unequaled in hard-heartedness, sadistic cruelty, warped sensibility, petrification of human feeling, and stupidity—only such a writer, if he is a man of sensitivity, and if his pen flows, might be able to give a true description of this pathological phenomenon called Nazism. Only those afflicted with a disease of the soul are capable of being joined to a party such as this. Only one who has a defect of the soul and of the senses is able to be numbered in its ranks. It is not impossible for an entire class of human beings to suffer a mental illness, and attempt to put into practice a diseased, unclean ideology by such barbaric means as the human race has never recognized and never known, and which it would have been incapable of inventing even in the remotest Dark Ages.

Do the foreign visitors who come to Germany for some academic or athletic event, who marvel at the sight of the "exemplary order and advanced technology," and who enjoy the exaggerated friendship which surrounds them on all sides, know that their "cultured" hosts torture pregnant women and children? I would swear they don't.

February 4, 1940

From the outset, the People of Hope did not believe that the decree of forced labor for Jews would be put into effect. As is the way with Jews, they didn't understand the decree in its simple sense. Because of the magnitude of the destruction contained therein, they didn't believe that even so fierce an enemy as the Führer would put it into actual practice. They tried to find in it some hint for an enormous financial contribution instead. This, however, was the theory of an undiscerning people. They didn't properly assess the character of the conquerors, who have more active and effective hints. They steal outright, and whatever decrees they make are the literal law. Now it has been proved to the hopeful ones that they erred in evaluating the situation.

February 5, 1940

This week an incident occurred involving a certain Jew which emphasizes the ethical face of the Nazis. This unfortunate was caught for forced labor. The work consisted of transferring cakes of ice from one place to another. The terrible cold pierces the flesh. Who could endure the icy chill? But there was no choice. It was the Nazis' order and, as such, could not be avoided. The Jew did his job with gloves, but the Nazi overseer forced him to do the work barehanded. The Jew was forced to fulfill the wishes of the oppressor, and with terrible suffering he moved the ice cakes barehanded, in below-zero cold. The Jew fell under the agony of this torture. His palms were so frozen that they are beyond help and his hands will have to be amputated.

February 8, 1940

Two days without an entry. My pen is tired.

Each one's thoughts are according to the brooding of his heart and the color of his bile. We are confident of the downfall, but no one knows how quickly it will come. Comforting rumors, which are the fruit of the imagination of some politician of the back-fence, kitchen-store variety, never cease. But their origin is no hindrance to their spread. More than once or twice they have killed off the Führer with their misty breath, and people are pleased to note that in Berlin "not one stone remains on top of another." And promptly some stranger appears who claims that he himself hid out for three days and three nights in a dark cellar without bread or water.

In short, they enjoy this idle chatter, the unfounded stories, the exaggerations, the unlimited flights of fancy. Old women, wise in experience, add: "And so what? Even if consolation comes, death will come first."

February 9, 1940

There is a well-known saying that the appetite comes with the eating, and this is true in political projects or social improvements. When one starts them he has only a minimal ultimate aim. When the beginning is successful, the ultimate aim progresses and increases until it reaches a maximal level. The appetite grows stronger. A limited measure no longer suffices; it is forced to make way for a wider measure.

Political figures too are not different from the rest of mankind and its weaknesses. I am referring to the Führer, whose might encompasses the world.

In the beginning the hatred of Jews was not so deep or so radical. At first he wanted only to diminish the Jewish influence. The creator of Nazism had a special interest in hatred of the Jews as a party strategy, and the reward was to be Jewish wealth—not just wealth, but the Jews' economic positions and their businesses. All this was in theory. In practice, even the leaders of Nazism didn't dare to think of the realization of a hundred per cent maximal program. The writings of the greatest among the enemies of the Jews— Alfred Rosenberg, editor of the *Voelkischer Beobachter*—can testify to this. In his day he wrote a book on the war with the Jews according to the doctrine of Nazism. Even in theory, which naturally demands the maximum, he didn't dare think of a process of destruction which would uproot everything. There isn't even half of what has come to pass in reality in Rosenberg's program. The Jews of Germany would have signed their names to Rosenberg's program with both hands, for in comparison to what actually happened later, it was paradise. In its day it was upsetting, because seven years ago the hand of liberalism was still strong, but with the demise of liberalism and the victory of a National Socialist state, it was still nothing more than a compromise program, a program for national

117

protection, a halfway measure, a palliative which in no way endangered the survival of the German Jewish community.

But as the program developed, the appetite grew. The stratagem was successful. Tens of thousands of hands grabbed at the wealth of the Jews. Thousands of positions became available. Jewish ownership was eliminated from thousands of businesses bringing in huge profits. Nazism filled itself on the destruction of German Jewry. But their appetite for destruction grew strong before they had their fill. In the mind of the Führer, for whom the hour was propitious, there grew the psychological possibility of directing his "I am, and there is none else beside me" even at the Jews, his victim nation. "You say that whatever is done against them does not succeed? Against me there is no remedy. I am omnipotent. Pharaoh, Haman, and Nebuchadnezzar did not succeed, but I will succeed!" Here the party tactic receded, and in its place came personal prestige. "Many projects have been undertaken by me which no statesmen would have dared to think possible, and they were successful. In the destruction of the Jews as well, I will show wonders that my predecessors never imagined."

There is no remedy for the Jews but *"Krepieren"* [to die like animals]. But the Jews refuse *"Krepieren."* It appears to me that the Führer is mistaken, as were Pharaoh, Nebuchadnezzar, and Haman.

February 12, 1940

No day goes by in which dozens of Jewish families are not impoverished. The stores are already empty, as they were looted immediately. Eleven freight buses full of goods were removed from the manufacturing firm of Rubin Rotenburg, and the same is true of all the other stores on Gesia, Nalewki, and Franciszkanska streets and vicinity. This was the first stage. As soon as it ended the second stage began: the looting of apartments. They came in carrying a pistol in one hand and a *Spitzrute* in the other. At first they used to come on the pretext of "searching for arms." When the chests and cabinets were opened, they stole whatever came to hand. As time passed, there was no longer a need for formal pretext: they simply come and take not only gold, silver, jewelry, and precious stones, but also pillows and blankets, and often linens, clothing, furs, and even furniture. You are never sure but that in an hour you will be left naked, and be beaten besides.

I have already mentioned that the Jews have been extremely careful in observing the curfew and have undertaken to observe it from six, instead of from eight, because of the dangers facing a Jew who is on the street during the evening hours. From six o'clock on, all flesh is silent. They shut themselves up in rooms within rooms, with drawn shades and extinguished candles, listening for the echo of footsteps reaching them from beyond the door.

I swear that I neither distort nor exaggerate.

February 14, 1940

We are used to seeing the victims of the sword in war. We are used to counting the dead, the wounded, the physically maimed, and the mentally disturbed. Whoever goes to war expects to kill or be killed. In the previous wars the front had almost no organic connection with the nation in the rear, its creator. The daily lives of the masses were almost unchanged even in time of war, which was concentrated, in the main, on the borders of the country. In the interior of the country, the people met their obligations by paying taxes in money and men and by shouting hurrah, patriotism! Not so today: modern war is a people's war. Its front extends to the dwellings of paupers and the halls of princes. All of life is geared toward the war. It penetrates into every corner of life, whether industrial, commercial, or artistic. Every citizen is a soldier on the battlefield.

Lately a new tribulation has been added. This is the tribulation of the "small change." One fine morning the small change disappeared from the commercial market, and it is almost impossible to get change for a paper bill. It has become so difficult that the unfortunate consumer is forced to stop buying, and must return empty-handed.

Where has this small change disappeared to? Everyone asks this question, but the answer is obvious to a first-grader. First of all, the "honest and upright" villagers, upon whose produce our lives depend, have no faith in paper money. They don't spend the small change (specie) they take in in exchange for their wares. In their eyes, specie has value, while paper money, signed by ministers of a now defunct government, does not.

What a tragic situation this is! Your pocket is full of bills and your stomach is empty. The storekeeper greets you with the question: "Do you have small change?" They won't give you so much as ten groszy in change. And this applies not only to private individuals. At the post office, on the street car, and in court as well, you must have the exact change or you lose the difference.

In order to lessen the problem, instead of giving you coins, the merchants give you change tickets for various sums. You are entitled to present a ticket of this sort in place of cash toward any new purchases you make in the same store. Some storekeepers have gotten smart. They've put their prices in round numbers so as to eliminate the problem. Rounded prices are advantageous to the seller, because he can thus raise the price of his goods, and they are advantageous to the buyer, as they enable him to make purchases.

Who is responsible for all this? It is not the villagers alone. Everyone has had a hand in creating this situation. Each one blames the other and sheds tears about the speculating in "small change," while he himself is not innocent of this crime.

I know of one storekeeper who has a dairy on Nowolipki Street and who during a search was found to have seven kilos in small change. He was arrested, and will be punished severely.

February 16, 1940

There is no more terrible government program than one put into effect by psychopaths. And psychopathy accompanied by sadism is seven times as bad. The Jews of Poland sense this, and thus react with scorn to all the terrible edicts which are pregnant with doom and destruction for our survival as individuals and as a people. There is no room in our inner feelings for despair and depression. We greet every edict with a deprecating smile, although we are conscious that the creators and enactors of these cruel decrees are psychopaths. In every one of them one can find signs of madness, of a psychopathy affecting an entire community in the form of a monomania. A poison of diseased hatred permeates the blood of the Nazis, and therefore all their stupid decrees, the fruit of this hatred, are doomed to failure. Such an awareness saves us from despair. Anything founded upon insanity must not last long.

A short time ago the conquerors started capturing Jewish women for forced labor. During a search a Gestapo member will thrust his hand into a young woman's breast the same as he would with a man. They search the private parts of a woman's body in full sight of her husband and children with no regard for her honor or her modesty. Animals! Moreover, they are proud of this "fine" quality of theirs.

I know an intelligent, highly educated woman who, before going outside, always puts a scrub rag into her purse as a precaution in case of trouble, but she has no certainty that the Nazis won't order her to do the work with her blouse or her dress in any case. This is the face of Nazism unmasked.

The time may come when these words will be published. At all events, they will furnish historiographic material for the chronicle of our agony. This obligates those who are writing impressions to record every event, every small detail which might shed light upon the darkness of foul, depraved souls. It is beyond my capabilities to record every event in organized form. Perhaps other people will do this when the appropriate time comes. But even events recorded in reportorial style are of historical value. In them the truth is reflected —not a dry, embalmed truth, but a living, active truth proclaiming before the world: "Behold, there is no pain like unto mine." Listen, and you will hear.

My colleague K., once a school principal and now twice burned out—both his own home and his school were destroyed by fire—got up early in the morning and prepared to go out. When he opened the door, he at once saw a pistol pointing at him, held by a Nazi soldier who threateningly ordered the "*Jude*" to go back inside. There was no alternative. K. went back into his apartment with the soldier behind him. Holding the pistol, the Nazi began an interrogation: Who lives here? All the doors were opened for him and he examined the furniture and household goods in every room. Do you have any German marks? None. Have you got a radio? No. He looked over every item, examined the quality of everything and nothing suited his taste. It was not worth taking. The apartment is rented out, room by room, to the burned-out people of Warsaw and the exiles of Lodz. Everything is neglected and disordered. The robber was unlucky. Bitterly he turned to the residents of the building and demanded that they show him where a rich Jew lived. Otherwise he'd confiscate everything in the apartment. The residents were caught between two evils. How can you turn an innocent Jew over to a thief? How can you knife some innocent Jew in the back, endangering both his property and his life? Some said they didn't know. But nonetheless one was found among them, a refugee from Lodz, who was afraid for his life and gave the robber the ad-

121

dress of the rich Jew Sz. in Elektoralna Street. The Nazi left the apartment with the address of a rich Jew in his hand.

When they asked the man from Lodz what prompted him to do something so abominable he rationalized by saying, "I'm a refugee and have 200 zloty in my pockets—my whole fortune, all that's left of my property. I was afraid he'd search me and leave me without a penny. Warsaw is strange to me, and I have no means of support here. I had no other choice. Besides, this Sz. whose address I gave to the thief won't lose by it, because he's not in Warsaw. Whatever he had has already been confiscated by the Gestapo. Woe unto this villain when he comes to steal from an apartment which has already been confiscated by those more powerful than he. Thus I have saved my own life, and the thief is the loser."

February 21, 1940

The Joint keeps its tireless vigil and brings some minor help to Polish Jewry, along with major help to the barbarian conquerors. These paupers have begun spreading a new doctrine—that gold and wealth are not the main thing, but rather labor, manufacture, human energy utilized at the right time and place. The hateful, depraved plutocracy of England has no strength but gold, which is no longer worth much. But this is all theoretical, for the purpose of encouraging a despairing public. In practice they try every deceitful trick—including common thievery—in order to get a carat of gold or a certain sum in dollars or pounds.

More than we, the conquerors benefit from the gold which flows to us from noble, philanthropic America, and therefore they overlook principles and permit the rescue work of the Joint. Eighty per cent of every dollar goes into the conqueror's pockets; only twenty per cent of its actual value reaches us. Every dollar must be converted into Polish zloty at the rate established by the conquerors, that is, 5.20, at the same time that its real value may approach 200. Thus the barbarians grow rich from the Jews' misfortunes, which they themselves caused and fashioned. But even a little is better than nothing. But for the Joint's support we would die of hunger and cold. This is especially true of the unemployed intelligentsia, all of whose sources of livelihood have been cut off. In the days of the First World War, the Joint's support was necessary. Now it is *imperative*. Its main functions are to set up shelters for the refugees and soup kitchens to still their hunger; to sew linens and make clothes to cover their nakedness; to give financial support to those burned out of their homes, and medical care to the sick and the weak.

The story of the Joint isn't finished yet. One Jew pointed to the truth when he said that the Joint is the Jewish government. Its budget approaches that of a small state, and is certainly greater than that of Luxembourg. I am therefore justified in pointing out the social side of its activities and describing its most conspicuous features. Those close to it and those on the inside, who have all the numerical and statistical data, will no doubt do this when the appropriate time comes. I am only an outsider who gets certain impressions from the official work carried on in its various departments. Impressions generally are not objective truth, but rather subjective. They are dependent on the personality of the observer. But even subjective truth testifies to the state of affairs, and in observer from a distance as a rule has an open, uncorrupted eye which sees a composite truth, partly subjective and partly objective.

Tens of thousands of refugees and fugitives benefit from the Joint's soup kitchens and are supported at its expense. Tens of thousands of people have been clothed and shod. Hundreds of refugee rabbis and religious functionaries eat its bread and drink its water. Hundreds of professional intellectuals, among them journalists, actors, and teachers, have found work in its offices. Its waiting rooms are full of functionaries from the provincial cities who unburden themselves of all their perils and troubles. No one leaves empty-handed. Journalists, actors, and teachers are not bureaucrats with petrified hearts who relate to petitioners like automatons. On the contrary you see a paternal attitude, a humane attitude of compassion toward all the sore and driven masses, who cause them unwarranted trouble and work because of lack of understanding and because of the bitterness of their souls. I marvel at where these people of flesh and blood get such angelic patience. All that is fine, and may our dear brethren in America be blessed for it. But in reality all this good has a drawback. The real truth is that the genuinely needy people do not benefit to a degree that accords with the size of the subsidies the Joint has set aside for them. The reason is the middlemen who stand between the Joint and the needy ones. By middlemen I mean the public servants to whom the huge sums are given for the benefit of the members of their organization or congregation. There is a basic rule in life: Whoever sits closest to the bowl shoves his fork in first.

In Poland there is no such thing as selfless work for society. Those engaged in social service say that they too belong to society. Every fat portion, to begin with, remains in the hands that hold it. The miserable and the oppressed get crumbs; their portion is the leftovers, the scraps—and there is no remedy for this situation. The central offices have no technical facilities to deal directly with the individual needy. They are forced to maintain a system of leaders, to deal with representatives, and these latter don't carry out their missions halfheartedly. On the contrary, they do everything in their power to increase the size of the subsidies. They are eloquent on the subject of the condition of those who sent them. Their hearts melt at the sight of the abysmal poverty and depression. But whatever they do, they do for themselves. Every soup kitchen director is sure of his livelihood. Thus there are now a multitude of nonexistent "chairmen" and committees who come forth with requests to establish soup kitchens for their members, who were never before organized or existent as organizational units. They spread out like locusts on the Joint, which finds it difficult to separate the wheat from the chaff.

February 24, 1940

The public thefts which are committed in broad daylight in full view of the entire Jewish and Polish public never stop, so that dozens of Jewish families are reduced to beggary. Apparently the Nazis have a special regiment set up for this purpose, because it does its murderous work in such an organized fashion. The past few days have been the season for stealing furniture. They come in and take all the furnishings down to the last item, leaving behind empty rooms. It goes without saying that during the inspection and the search, they take anything of any value while emptying the closets. Young Dr. Rakower was arrested. Not many days passed before the Nazis came to take all the expensive furnishings from his apartment at 19 Nowolipki Street. His young, desolate wife pleaded with the thieves to leave her at least the furniture in her husband's office. She got a cynical reply to this, that her husband would not be returning to her very soon, so what use would his furniture be to him?

Today as well, expensive furniture has been taken from many

Jewish apartments in Nowolipki Street, and innocent Jewish passersby have been forced to remove it and load it onto the truck.

A terrifying occurrence of foul murder took place in Bagno Street, where there is a store for plumbing supplies whose owner is a Jew. One day they came to him and ordered him to be present in his store, which had been closed earlier, at nine in the morning the next day. What occurred at the time of his meeting with the murderers no one knows. All that is known is that after an hour he was found dead in his store. Some say he was killed because he was five minutes late; others say he was killed because he had emptied his store and the thieves could find nothing to take. It is difficult to determine the truth, and in any event it is unnecessary. The whole thing serves only to prove that a Jew's life is worthless. There is no one before whom you can cry out over the innocent spilled blood.

The kidnapers have begun stopping trolleys and taking off Jews whose clothing indicates that they are more or less wealthy. Their lot will be backbreaking toil and lashes of the whip; moreover, the enemy searches their pockets and steals their last cent, and frequently strips them of their clothing and furs.

February 27, 1940

In the matter of certificates,[5] which are the aspiration of every Jew in Poland, even the anti-Zionists, oppressed and tortured Poland has received only twenty-five. It is a heartrending joke. Obviously those who had made a living out of Zionism all their lives were the first to get them, and perhaps it must be like this. In all nations and in every state such customs are widespread. When a political party achieves any semblance of victory, its founders and leaders are the first to benefit. Our Jews, however, object to such a practice.

A whole group of functionaries like Kirszenbaum Ajnzauner, and the engineer Reis, historians like Dr. I. Schiper, journalists like A. Einhorn, M. Indelman, and officials like D. Radunski, Bloch, and several of their friends will leave us and go to Palestine.

Rabbi Icchak Nisenbaum got one of the certificates—a man who has devoted his entire life to propagating Zionism. In his preaching he combines religion with nationalism and makes propaganda for both at once. No one is as deserving as he to go to Palestine. Nevertheless, he gave up his right to a certificate, and for the time being does not intend to leave the bitter exile. The formal pretext is that

[5] For immigration to Palestine.

he needs 4,000 zloty for travel expenses and he doesn't have it. Of him may be said: "You may view the land from afar, but you shall not enter it."

Just as troubles impoverish, so too do they enrich. Whenever chaos comes to the world, those on the bottom rise, and those on top fall. Practical people who are clever adjust to any situation, and every new situation creates new opportunities. Old businesses have fallen and new businesses have cropped up, businesses which had no place before the recent upheaval. When the conquerors came and terrible calamity fell upon Polish Jewry, everyone began to think of escape, but the Nazis don't allow escape. And thus middlemen and procurers have cropped up who claim to perform miracles and promise that the Nazis will give up their intentions in favor of the middlemen and allow escape.

First of all, the passport. Getting one is harder than parting the Red Sea. But there are some former Polish officials who are familiar with the ways of the *Starosta* and all its secrets. During the time of confusion they were left with a certain number of blank passport books, as well as the departmental seal. Blank paper has one great virtue, which is that a man can write whatever he wishes on it, and so they invented a scheme of the following sort: The official writes the passport information in the booklet and stamps it with his pre-war seal. A passport of this kind is valid for a year, and afterward you can get an extension. The files of that department were either burned or lost, and thus there is no possible way of determining whether the passport was legally issued before the war or made to order afterward. The Nazis believe what they see.

This is the first station, the more expensive one. The number of blank books, a legacy from the former Polish government, is small, and there are many ready customers for them—particularly among the Jews, and therefore the Jew pays.

The second stop is the consulate of the country to which the Jew wants to emigrate. There too they recognize the form of a coin, and its officials are by no means oblivious to profit. A visa of this sort is very expensive. The consuls are pampered and show a special preference for real currency which can be readily exchanged, such as dollars and pounds. And after having successfully gotten through the first two stages with money, you reach the third stop: the

Gestapo, in order to get a permit to leave the country. A permit of this sort is not granted until after the emigrant brings a "proper, valid" passport containing a visa to a country from which the Nazi government is assured that it need not fear the possibility of your return. Then, "by law," you are required to empty your money box, and your pockets, and your purse, and any other hidden places which you use to keep your money in, leaving yourself 20 zloty per person for travel expenses.

And after you have met all these obligations you may leave the Nazi paradise. There is no restriction on taking your luggage with you after it has been inspected, but it is forbidden to employ a porter to put your luggage on the train. The Jewish emigrant must do it himself. Even if he is sick, he is forbidden to engage an Aryan porter. What logic is there to a decree like this? But there is no analyzing the Nazi soul. Pathology, nothing more!

In short, the way of the Jewish emigrant is paved with Polish zloty amounting to as much as 20,000 apiece. For beside the three steps mentioned above, there is another mobile one. This is the middleman, who also has a soul, also a desire for profit. And with it all, there are still customers for a "bargain" who will gladly give away the "rags" (a term for the Polish zloty) if only they are allowed to escape.

And so you see that the counterfeiting officials are growing rich; the consuls are making an excellent living; the Gestapo gets a goodly portion; and the Jewish procurers, as well, are doing a nice business. And all of this from the Jewish tragedy.

March 1, 1940

The Nazi press speaks most loftily of the human ideals which only Nazism can bring into reality. England and France are the representatives of the plutocracy whose days are numbered. A new world is going to be created, and its makers are the representatives of Nazism. They allow Mussolini and Stalin to be its helpers. The new world will be built on justice and righteousness, on healthy social foundations without jealousy and hatred between one class and another.

The conquerors boast that there are no unemployed in the Reich. When they entered Poland they began currying favor with the masses, trying to convince them that they will be better off under the scepter of the Reich than they were under the scepter of their previous government. The Nazis' first step is thus to give work to the unemployed, and not only to give it to them, but to force them to accept it. Obviously work for pay is meant. Here too it is "except the Jews"—"except" only when it comes to getting paid, not in regard to getting work.

Some time ago hundreds of young Jewish professionals were arrested and transported to some unknown place, and it is now six weeks since all contact ceased between the prisoners and the outside world. Even their relatives have not been informed of their where-abouts. A rumor has begun to circulate that they are being held in the Mokotow prison, but the relatives who went there were threat-ened with death and driven away shamefully. Thus their families spent six weeks in frightened anticipation. A certain hope lingered that maybe in the end they would be liberated from their imprison-ment.

Now it has become known to me through a certain *Volksgenosse* who told me in a whisper, that all the prisoners were deported the day before yesterday to the concentration camp in Oswiecim [Auschwitz]; the Kot sacrifices have already been placed on the altar.

March 4, 1940

During the last third of February it seemed to us that spring was drawing near. Clear days came. The sky was bluish-gray, and in it was the sun of the eve of spring. Not much warmth, but enough to melt the snow which was piled into bank upon bank at the edges of the sidewalks—sure signs of spring taking its first steps. We thought we were already saved. The freezing cold of a coal-less winter had eaten into our flesh, but now our limbs began to stretch out toward the sunlight. Our bent and huddled bodies began to straighten up. The worry about coal disappeared as doors to the rooms which weren't heated during the cold months were opened. The sunlight began to spread some joy into our sore and aching hearts. But this joy was premature. Apparently there is a fierce battle going on be-tween the retreating winter and the advancing spring. Sometimes one falls and the other rises. On the next day, it is the reverse. Again the skies have clouded over and turned gray. Cold winds begin to blow again. Again we are covered by the snow which has begun falling in abundance. And again worry enters our hearts. When will we be rid of the drawn-out winter that casts its ice into our homes and our hearts?

When snow begins to fall, we have additional trouble. According to the agreement between the *Judenrat* and the government, the Jews are liable for the forced labor of snow removal throughout the whole city. Every morning several hundred Jews, at the order of the *Judenrat*, go out to forced labor. You can recognize them not only by the "Jewish insignia" on their sleeves, but by their gestures, by the sorrow implanted on their faces. They receive no pay for this, not even food. The Gentiles too are required to work, but they are paid.

March 7, 1940

Our desolate and miserable lives go on without the spark of hope to which our people have always been accustomed. The days when the oppressed Jewish masses would console themselves with nonsensical political rumors are past. Reality shows us that our redemption is still far from us. Those who understand the military and political situation well are going about like mourners. There is no ground for hope that the decisive action will come this spring, and lack of a decision means that our terrible distress will last a long time.

March 9, 1940

The administration of the Joint spreads its wings over all of Polish Jewry, which is cut off from the Jewish communities scattered throughout the world. There is no one to ask for advice, no one to stand in the breach. Our community is abandoned, left to itself and dependent on its own stamina. And this stamina has diminished to almost nothing.

It is an open secret that the power within the Joint is in the hands of the leftists. Those close to their ideas and their party get a double portion. The allocations are made in a bureaucratic fashion, for there is no executive committee to represent all parties. There is no doubt of the fact that the entire operation is imperfect, but nonetheless, no one leaves them empty-handed. They question only the size of the stipend; they do not dispute the matter of right, the right of everyone to benefit. They may give a little less, but they do give.

March 10, 1940

The gigantic catastrophe which has descended on Polish Jewry has no parallel, even in the darkest periods of Jewish history. First, in the depth of the hatred. This is not just hatred whose source is in a party platform, and which was invented for political purposes. It is a hatred of emotion, whose source is some psychopathic malady. In its outward manifestations it functions as physiological hatred, which imagines the object of hatred to be unclean in body, a leper who has no place within the camp.

The masses have absorbed this sort of qualitative hatred. Their limited understanding cannot grasp ideological hatred; psychology is beyond them and they are incapable of understanding it. They have absorbed their masters' teachings in a concrete, corporeal form. The Jew is filthy; the Jew is a swindler and an evildoer; the Jew is the enemy of Germany, who undermines its existence; the Jew was the prime mover in the Versailles Treaty, which reduced Germany to nothing; the Jew is Satan, who sows dissension between one nation and another, arousing them to bloodshed in order to profit from their destruction. These are easily understood concepts whose effect in day-to-day life can be felt immediately.

But the founders of Nazism, and the party leaders, created a scientific ideology on deeper foundations. They have a complete doctrine which analyzes the Jewish spirit inside and out. Judaism and Nazism are two world outlooks, neither of which is compatible with the other, and for this reason they cannot live together. For two thousand years Judaism has left its imprint, culturally and spiritually, on nations of the world. It stood like a rock, blocking the spread of German paganism whose teaching was different and whose culture was carved out of a different source. Two kings cannot use one crown. Either humanity would be Judaic, or it would be idolatrous-German. Up until now it was Judaic. Even Catholicism is a daughter of Judaism, and the child of its spirit, and is therefore afflicted with the shortcomings it inherited from its mother. The new world which Nazism will fashion is directed toward primitive idolatry with all of its attitudes. It is therefore ready to fight Judaism to the finish.

Here too a political motive is appended, which should be publicized. The British also tend toward Judaism. There is a conjecture that they are the descendants of the ten Israelite tribes. The Jews and the British have made a partnership and have divided the world between them.

It is our good fortune that the conquerors have failed to consider the nature and strength of Polish Jewry, and this has kept us alive. Logically we should be dead. According to the laws of nature, we ought to have been completely annihilated. How can an entire community feed itself when it has no place in life? There is no occupation, no activity which is not limited, circumscribed for us.

But here again we do not conform to the laws of nature. A certain invisible power is embedded in us, and it is this secret which keeps us alive and preserves us in spite of all the laws of nature: if it is impossible to live by what is permitted, we live from what is forbidden. And this is not a disgrace for us. What is permitted and what is forbidden both depend upon common agreement. Whoever fails to ratify an agreement is not bound to it. This is especially true of the permissions and prohibitions of a barbaric conqueror who molds our life in his own image, in conformity to his own murderous and larcenous concepts.

This secret power works wonders in us; as evidence, we don't have cases of suicide. German Jewry collapsed and fell. Its vital strength disappeared immediately. It was gripped by fear. When no way for salvation was found through conversion, it condemned itself to death. Without strength to live, thousands of individuals found sanctuary in the abyss. The same with Austrian Jewry. Each new decree sacrificed thousands of victims on its altar. Entire families voluntarily wiped themselves out when the world became too narrow for them. Proud, filled with self-esteem, thousands of German and Austrian Jews put an end to their lives.

Not so with the beaten-down, shamed, broken Jews of Poland. They love life, and they do not wish to disappear from the earth before their time.

This fact, that we have hardly any suicides, is worthy of special emphasis. Say what you wish, this will of ours to live in the midst of terrible calamity is the outward manifestation of a certain hidden power whose quality has not yet been examined. It is a wondrous, superlative power with which only the most established communities among our people have been blessed.

We are left naked, but as long as this secret power is still within us we do not give up hope. And the strength of this power lies in the indigenous nature of Polish Jewry, which is rooted in our eternal tradition that commands us to live. Polish Jewry says, together with our poet laureate Bialik:

One spark is hidden in the stronghold of my heart,
One little spark, but it is all mine;
I borrowed it from no one, nor did I steal it
For it is of me, and within me.

Even during the bombardments, I did not neglect my diary. I was completely absorbed in my holy task. Isn't it amazing that the most fierce campaign Europe has ever known could not accomplish what a common cold achieved? By great pleading I managed today to get permission from my wife to leave my bed, since the fever has been down for two days. I'm much better, although I am still occasionally bothered by coughing.

Someday the Jewish community of Warsaw will tell all that happened to it during these terrible days. It will know best how to construct its own martyrology of all that has occurred. As long as it is held in the claws of the trampler, it is forbidden to utter even a note of mourning. Sorrowful, silent, in repressed fury, it carries out literally and immediately whatever is ordered. There is no room for bargaining or argument. It is a decree, and must not be questioned.

For several days my divine inspiration has left me. I have neglected my pen, and refrained from any daily entries. The reason is that I have no new impressions. A trouble that lingers loses its original intensity. We are ready—almost willing—to accept any new evil decree with open arms, even before it comes into being. We have been so debased and depressed that we no longer fear what is yet to come. Is it possible that we can still sink lower?

We have become a doormat whose purpose is to be trampled upon. Let the waves rise and swell; let them pass over our heads. If they flood us, we will sink into the deep without crying out against anyone. A society in a psychological state such as this cannot receive impressions. But even so, sometimes the rumbling of a thunder which frightens even us is heard. Then even we, the insensitive, petrified ones, are somewhat impressed, even if it is but for a moment. A tremor passes through our souls and for a short time we are stunned, and then "the silence returns as before."

This year is a Jewish leap year, and so Easter comes about a month before Passover. The end of winter. Sun and ice. And now their holiday of Resurrection has turned into a time of panic for us. The eve of their desire has been made a time of trembling. But this is not the conquerors' doing. Whoever is successful has his work done for him by others, and therefore this is not the conquerors' doing. But it is done with their knowledge and consent, and according to some, under their "lofty" supervision. Never before have there been such days of chaos, upheaval, and confusion in the Polish capital as on the holiday of Easter, which this year fell on March 25. Christian "ethics" became conspicuous in life. And then— woe to us! Someone organized gang after gang of hooligan adolescents, including also little ones who have not yet left their grade-school benches, to attack Jewish passersby and give them murderous beatings. It was simply a hunt, in which Jews were hunted like animals in the forest. And what is there to deny? We are cowards! In cases such as this we have only one choice—to run away. And running away only adds courage to the attacking toughs. There is much ugliness in these attacks in broad daylight, in full view of the authorities, who stand at a distance enjoying the sight of our torments.

March 27, 1940

Here a new chapter of troubles and injuries begins. Operational rules for fighting the epidemics have been set. As is customary in every misfortune, Jewry is beaten doubly. Woe to the tenants of a courtyard where a case of infectious disease has occurred. Even after the sick person is removed, the courtyard is closed for two weeks. At the end of the period of quarantine, they conduct a disinfection of all the apartments. Moreover, they have gotten stricter of late, and decreed that the two courtyards adjoining the infected one must be closed for four days. And at the end of this period, the two "suspected" courts must also undergo disinfection. This is not an ordinary disinfection to eliminate any bacilli that might be present, but rather a disinfection intended to ruin all household goods.

As to animate things, which is to say human beings, they too have not yet been cleansed of their sins. After the disinfection of the apartments, the inhabitants are led to a bathhouse against their will, in order to disinfect their bodies and their clothing. And here the real tortures begin. This is not an ordinary bath, but rather a steam bath. At the time of disinfecting the bodies, they cut off the women's hair and the men's beards, and when the clothing is disinfected, it is returned to their owners so wrinkled and trampled that it is no longer wearable. It simply becomes torn and wrinkled rags, no longer fit for use.

A group of a hundred people goes into the bathhouse and remains there for no more and no less than fifteen to twenty hours. The torture cannot be imagined. Everyone is forced to pass through various stages at each of which he remains for four or five hours. Naked, weak, and hungry, they must wait for the completion of various formalities.

Sometimes you "lovingly" accept all the torments and sufferings and return home "clean." After two or three days, you get a new piece of news; in the courtyard on the right of yours (or on the left, if the most recent incident occurred on the right) there has been another case of an infectious disease, and even if only ten days have elapsed since the last disinfection, your cleanliness is impaired, and you become a candidate for new purification.

March 28, 1940

The conquerors have begun a new political operation. Gangs of young toughs, Polish youth (you won't find one adult among them), armed with clubs, sticks, and all kinds of harmful weapons, make pogroms against the Jews. They break into stores and empty their goods into their own pockets. Wherever there is no loot in evidence, they smash the show windows. The Jews they encounter on the way are beaten and wounded. The Jewish quarter has been abandoned to toughs and killers who were organized for this purpose by some invisible hand. Today, toward evening, I had to arrange an important matter in Nalewki Street and I shall never forget the impression which the whole once bustling area made upon me. In every corner there is the fear of death. Shadows, not living people, pass by. Franciszkanska Street is enclosed by military sentries, and passage through Nalewki Street is permitted only along the sidewalk on the left-hand side (as you come from Gesia Street). The right-hand sidewalk is clear and empty, and military sentries patrol its length. The hooligan youths do not come here, because the stores are closed, having already been emptied and looted, but in the other streets, where a half-open Jewish store may still be found, your ears catch the tinkling sound of windows being smashed by a patriotic Polish youth doing his work under the protection of the conqueror, who stands nearby with his camera, perpetuating all these abominations.

These sons of Ham—just as a year ago they shouted in their patriotic fervor, "Long live Poland! Long live Smigly-Rydz!" they now shout, in their conquered capital, in the presence of the conquerors who destroyed their land, "Long live Hitler! Death to Smigly-Rydz! We want a Poland without Jews!" Is it possible? Yes, I swear that it is so. The accursed youth, walking on the ruins of their homeland, organize demonstrations in honor of the Führer.

March 30, 1940

The mouth which permitted is also the mouth which forbade. Several hundred Poles went mad and perpetrated acts of abomination in sight of the conquerors who boast of their love for social order, and no one blocked their path. For three whole days the streets of Warsaw were turned into fields of chaos and disorder. Robberies and looting in broad daylight, mass attacks on Jewish passersby— with the eyes of the civilized conquerors looking on.

There is great activity in the Zionist circles which aspire to flee from the infernal land. Lack of organization always proves our undoing. Yesterday I visited the office of the HIAS[6] and I came out of there dismayed. Exemplary confusion, chaos, and disorder. In time of trouble everybody becomes an expert at tormenting people. The public servants, so to speak, who have grasped the helm, cloak every activity in the deepest secrecy, and the emigrants who crawl through their doorway are not to be envied. They make up lists of candidates for emigration similar to the list of recommendations submitted to the Jewish Agency for Palestine, and those who make the lists act as if it were entirely their private business. They include whomever they wish, and leave out those who do not please them, and there is no one before whom to cry and complain. But even after you get approval, you do not know that you are saved. For reasons incomprehensible to any intelligent being, it is not the practice of the office to inform you that you have been approved. You must be a constant guest in the office in order to find out by

[6] The Hebrew Immigrant and Sheltering Aid Society of America, organized in 1887, with branches in South America and European countries.

the grapevine that you are one of the lucky ones. Up to now, you have been under the control of the heirs of the "central committee." From here on, you go over to the officials of HIAS, which is to say: out of the frying pan, into the fire.

A big delegation of representatives from the major Polish *Judenrats* was invited to Cracow by Dr. Frank. For what purpose? So far, no one knows. The delegation has already returned, but no one of them wants to say anything. Jaszunski reports that they were treated with respect. What were they told? The delegation refuses to tell until the executive of the *Judenrat* has its meeting. Meanwhile there are various rumors going around the city which contradict one another. Some people saw the members of the delegation and they were happy; some saw them and they were sad. Some say the cruel conquerors have become a little softer toward the despised nation and want to make concessions. Others relate as certain fact that in a few days a ghetto will be established in Warsaw.

CHAPTER FOUR

A WHOLE WEEK without an entry. My ink well has grown tired of lamentations. If I tried to write down everything in order, I couldn't. Nor would I be recording anything new. Robberies, murders, humiliations, deprivations—nothing more.

Our enemy is following a paved road, the one he paved for himself in Germany and Austria. In Austria the Jewish question was solved within two years by "the most successful method." At the time of annexation there were 250,000 Jews there. After two years a sore and oppressed remnant of 60,000 remained. And even this remnant has been stripped of all its possessions and occupations and is awaiting exile. This can serve as an example of what will happen to Polish Jewry.

There is no source of accurate information about the *Judenrat* delegation to Cracow. But from a reliable informant, who works for the *Judenrat* along with members of the delegation, I have learned that for the time being there is no change for better or worse. Six representatives participated in the delegation, four from the *Judenrat* and two from the Joint. In general they were received with due courtesies. However, Dr. Frank himself did not receive them, but rather the director of the Department of National Minorities. He asked them to be seated, and this is a step worthy of special mention, because usually the representatives of the *Judenrat* who come to request a favor are not invited to sit down, and the officer, without really looking at the petitioners, addresses them in the familiar form. All the same the Nazis gave them no promises, merely accepted the memorandum. During the meeting the delegation tried to be frank and not hide anything. Obviously they had to hide a lot. When you stand in fear and trembling before a Nazi administrator, you are not secure in your freedom or your life. There is no form of moral ugliness which a Nazi is incapable of imposing on a Jew.

April 9, 1940

An important change has taken place in the military situation, whose inactivity had become monotonous. The results for the two warring factions cannot be predicted, but it is an occurrence fraught with danger for one side or the other. Germany has violated the "sacred" neutrality of two small countries, Denmark and Norway. With unparalleled cynicism the Nazis justify themselves by saying that it was done to prevent the Western Powers from doing so. Yes, the self-justification of a true robber. All along the German press has accused the Western Powers of not carefully observing the laws of neutrality in regard to the Scandinavian countries and the other little nations near the field of combat. Now, while Chamberlain is still dilly-dallying—conferring with his ambassadors in these countries, preparing himself to issue a written petition to them containing only a request to stop their trade with the Nazis, while it has never entered his mind to force them to do so by military strength—the Nazis have gone and done something. They remain faithful to their program: Grab and take! Grab and take! Possession is nine-tenths of the law.

And the Jewish "politicians" ask in amazement: "Won't America react? Will it remain silent?"

But now I hear the voices of the newsboys peddling an extra. This can only mean that new events have taken place.

April 11, 1940

Every military victory of the Nazis, whether real or imaginary, casts us into melancholy. Every one of us senses that victory for

138

Nazism means total ruin and destruction for world Jewry. True, we have Zionistic complaints against Britain, but that is only a family feud, a private quarrel between us. The mutual friendship—not only historically—between Britain and Jewry cannot be minimized. The British nation is the only friend and the best friend Jewry has among all the nations in the world. I do not refer here to actual favors England does for Jewry, but rather to the friendly position it takes whenever evil is done to us. The downfall of England is first of all the downfall of Jewry, of a despised people whose part no nation takes in its hour of trouble, even to the extent of expressing sympathy in its terrible misfortune. And it must be admitted that the future of imperial Britain, ruler of distant islands and countries, is hanging in the balance. If the Nazis crush its strength to earth, days of shadow and darkness will return to the entire world. And the Jewish people will be the first victims.

For this reason every heart trembles. What if it should come to pass?

When the news came of the conquest of Denmark and Norway by the Nazi army, we were stunned, but less than a day passed before the politicians managed to find various tricks to turn the Nazi victory into defeat, that our souls might be revived.

How? Don't ask! The English radio, which sneaks up on us through the chinks and cracks, consoles both itself and us, and we grasp enthusiastically at every word of consolation and encouragement. Rumors are spreading that twenty-seven Nazi troop ships have been sunk; that thirty thousand soldiers have drowned; that Nazi battleships, whose number is in general very small, were hit and went down in Norwegian waters. In short, an unparalleled defeat! Even if it is imaginary, it comes as a balm for our oppressed souls—particularly since the Nazis themselves admit that two battleships, the *Blücher* and the *Karlsruhe*, were sunk by mines that the Norwegians planted in their waters.

April 12, 1940

Is there any revenge in the world for the spilling of innocent blood? I doubt it. The abominations committed before our eyes cry out from the earth: "Avenge me!" But there is no jealous avenger. Why has a "day of vengeance and retribution" not yet come for the murderers? Do not answer me with idle talk—I won't listen to you. Give me a logical reply!

The end of the first day of Passover,[1] *5700*

"I am black but comely"—even though I am black, it is not a sign of permanent ugliness, which is of natural origin and cannot be changed, for I am "comely." I have had a natural beauty since the day of my creation; but an external reason has made me black.

This phrase in the Song of Songs, which we read for this holiday, is unequaled in emphasizing the individual characteristics of the Jewish community. The synagogues are closed, but in every courtyard there is a holiday service, and cantors sing the prayers and hymns in their sweet voices. As to holiday provisions, without question even the poorest of the Jews does not lack for matzoth. On the eve of the holiday people ran around carrying packages of matzoth as though the sword of sabotage were not hovering over their heads. The whole thing seems somewhat unbelievable. Legally we have nothing to eat but the bread called for on our ration cards, which is such a meager portion that it does not half satisfy hunger. Except for this allotment, one buys or sells bread at the risk of death. In practice, however, there has never been such an abundance of bread for sale as in recent times, and it is not only offered to the buyer secretly, but sold in public as well. In the market on Smocza Street, and the same applies to the rest of the markets, the bread sellers stand in long rows calling their wares. The difference between the days before and after rationing is only that the price of bread has risen fivefold. In short, the conquerors have unintentionally done the black marketeers a favor, and the same applies to all other rationed foodstuffs. The show windows of coffeehouses and even ordinary food stores are filled to capacity with all sorts of baked goods, from ordinary cakes to a variety of the finest pastries.

It is a puzzle, and it remains one. Do the conquerors see this and deliberately close their eyes? Or is it that they have been struck blind, and in the confusion of their minds are not free to direct their attention to breakers of the "law"?

In every Jewish home the signs of the holiday are manifest; perhaps not in dress, but everyone has bought the holiday specialties to the extent he could afford. A sty in the devil's eye!

But the truth must not be concealed. One factor which has not

[1] The celebration of the deliverance from Egyptian bondage.

been mentioned helped greatly in the holiday preparation, and that is the Joint.

But its activities represent a separate chapter in the lives of the Jews of Poland.

The confusion that reigned in the Joint's activities before the holiday was indescribable. Only someone who needed its support in his capacity as a leader of some organization, and who had dealings with its directors—who are like "the servant when he reigneth"—could know the extent of this chaos.

First of all, there is the caliber of the directors in charge of distribution. These are mediocre men who until now were clerks, doing technical office work, and who were suddenly elevated to administrative jobs of broad scope, which are beyond their intellectual and organizational abilities. One of them is a complete villain; the second a good-hearted man; the third—by the way, the most intellectual of all—is neither one nor the other, but rather a man who was a schoolteacher and rose in the world through the force of events, not by his own merits.

The directors don't have regular hours for receiving petitioners. Sometimes you come on foot from some distant part of the city, and the director is busy. He's been called to a meeting. Dozens of people are waiting for his appearance. When will he respond to his petitioners? No one knows. He doesn't choose to say. And everyone leaves, depressed, just as he arrived. Sometimes you are lucky and the director is there, sitting on his throne, receiving. The crowding and congestion at his door are beyond imagination. Suddenly one of the elite goes in out of turn and stays. The people waiting anxiously at the door get angry, count the minutes, curse the day they were born. Then the door opens and the director leaves, wearing his overcoat, with no intention of coming back again that day. The fury of those waiting for him reaches its peak. But in the end—willingly or unwillingly—you leave, embarrassed, full of pent-up wrath, only to return on the morrow, to experience a new trial which saps your blood and substance.

As for the one director who has become known as good-hearted, they don't let anyone near him until credentials are presented through a secretary; and only one person in a thousand manages to get to see him. His practice is to send negative or deferred replies through his secretary, and there the matter ends. You might as well talk to the wall.

Here is something to marvel at: the directors' meetings take place at precisely the times set aside for receiving petitioners. Where did these little men pick up such habits? Even a minister of a great power would not so insult those seeking his favor. The directors of the Joint go into conference at the very time when dozens of upset, stunned people, representatives of the miserable and the oppressed, of refugees and of burned-out, robbed, and beaten people, are gathered on their doorstep. No one is certain that his mission is not in vain; everything depends on chance and on the whim of a director, who is an uneducated person with no learning, no wisdom, no understanding of the realities of public welfare.

None of the directors will take a stand on any Jewish problem, but nevertheless they hold their "conferences." They meet and exchange confidences on how to organize, and the results are always disorganization. Should it enter your mind that after an allotment is approved—one that will be reduced month after month—you can get the money, you are mistaken. Day after day you wear yourself out to get the money which is due you, based on a signed and sealed "order," but it is all in vain. At this stage you suffer new torments. The treasurer, a sadistic little nobody, answers you with special relish: "There's no money." When will there be some? "That is not known." Nevertheless? "Maybe in another three days." When he gives you his dry, terse replies he doesn't look at you as one man to another. Like some misanthrope, he lowers his eyes and averts his head.

Before Passover a holiday project was put into effect. It too should be recorded as a remembrance for future generations. In order to evaluate any project, one should not consider the dry figures which are merely official data, but rather the spirit that colors it. Here I was an eyewitness.

Let one who saw it, then, come forth and testify to what he has seen.

April 28, 1940

I am not responsible for the veracity of this information, but it has come to me by the grapevine that the Joint has set aside a sum of seven and a half million zloty for the support of the Jewish population in the month of Nisan. If it is a little more or less, it makes no difference. In honor of the Passover holiday which occurs in that month, the Joint wanted to demonstrate to the world its organizational powers and its great administrative ability, so it decided to set up a "Passover project" consisting not of financial aid, but of food packages—and here it met its undoing and was unable to create an organized project to achieve its aims. Confusion reigned. The organizers and their supervisors couldn't manage, and the chaos reached such a level that those who were responsible finally gave up, and the project went on under its own power, without supervision by any authority whatsoever. What we saw furnished us an example of exactly how not to run a project of this sort. A negative example, but certainly an example.

The one in charge of the holiday project was a certain Czerski, who had his office in the Tlomackie Judaica Library. In the past all who thirsted for the word of God came to that building; now all who hungered for real bread and real water gathered on its doorstep.

First of all they started the project too late, and they weren't finished by the eve of the holiday, but rather during the Intermediate Days. They finished mostly by chance; the Lord took pity on His poor Jews and the shipments arrived on time, which is to say they came two or three days early and thus, by chance, before the last days of the holiday had passed. Any minor slipup could have detained the shipments for another two or three days, and the packages of matzoth would have reached the recipients after the holiday was all over.

There was a justification for some delay: the conquerors confiscated a large part of the flour and of the baked matzoth. But even this confiscation was the Joint's fault. Instead of giving the baking of the matzoth to the Warsaw bakers, with whom the Joint couldn't come to an agreement on price, they turned part of it over to bakers in the neighboring towns, and part was brought in from Rumania. In the provincial towns the flour was confiscated, and transportation across the border was delayed by the border customs, who demanded that duty be paid on the pauper's lamb.

In crazy times like these, under the rule of a despotic conqueror whose aim is only to injure, it was wrong to scatter their energies and to gather the matzoth from "a hundred and twenty-seven provinces." Anyone with eyes open could have foreseen that this path is full of pitfalls and baited traps.

It is true that the Warsaw bakers want to grow rich from robbing the poor; they are profiteers. But it would have been worthwhile to meet their price, so as to be sure that the matzoth would be ready in time.

May 2, 1940

In a spiritual state like the one in which I find myself at this time, it is difficult to hold a pen, to concentrate one's thoughts. But a strange idea has stuck in my head since the war broke out—that it is a duty I must perform. This idea is like a flame imprisoned in my bones, burning within me, screaming: Record! Perhaps I am the only one engaged in this work, and that strengthens and encourages me.

When the conqueror runs rampant, he makes no distinction between Jews and Poles, even though he knows the Jew has no thoughts of revolt. The Pole is beaten for whatever sin he commits; the Jew is beaten day and night at every opportunity, whether he has sinned or not. When the day of reckoning comes the tyrant lumps them both together, and there is no escaping his wrath.

The prison on Dzielna Street is filled with prisoners, and therefore the entire area around it has become a place ripe for depredations. Gendarmes visit the area frequently, and every one of their visits leaves an impression on the bodies of Jews. The Nazis pass like a storm through the Jewish streets, whose inhabitants know from experience that many of them will come out of it toothless and eyeless. It is an attack of beasts of prey, devoid of any human feeling, upon innocent people walking unaware through the street. And not only upon men—women too are included. Even a mother standing by her baby's cradle is not secure against sudden attack. Sometimes the Germans beat people about the shoulders with long whips while sitting in a car driven along close to the curb; sometimes they pour down their blows while they stand outside the car. Then you see before you animals on two legs: murderous faces; a terrible fury of wild men in destructive rage. Whoever falls into their hands is reduced to a heap of bones. As I say, the Nazis make no distinction between men and women, or, in the case of women, between a young girl and a mother beside a cradle. Today I saw with my own eyes how a Jewish baby's cradle was turned upside down after they had beaten the miserable mother until she fell under the weight of her suffering. Her hysterical screams echoed through the entire street, but the Nazi gendarme carefully finished his "job" before he returned to his car.

Jewish passersby are aware of every appearance of a car whose occupants are the servants of the Führer. When they first notice it from a distance, a flight begins, an escape into the doorways of the houses. In a single instant the street takes on the appearance of a graveyard. In every place they go there is silence, and you won't find a single living soul on the street. Thousands flee, but many are caught. Fear reigns in every corner.

This is the custom every day of the year, so that occurrences of this sort are a fleeting thing, an act of the moment. Whatever happens, happens—and then the danger passes. Everyone returns to his work and his occupation. Life makes its own demands.

May 3, 1940

I stopped my account of the events of the day in the middle in order to gather explicit facts about their causes and results. At the time they took place we were hiding in the innermost rooms, and we didn't dare go near the window for fear of stray bullets. The jokesters among us comment literarily that we didn't look through the windows, but rather we "peered through the lattice."[2] We knew that the sword was doing its work outside, but we could not identify the fallen.

In these mad hours I think to myself: Where are they, where are the representatives of the neutral nations and their emissaries, whom the Nazis invite to their capital to show them their "lofty civilization"? Those nations who become partners of Nazi Germany in spiritual activities, in scientific cooperation, in making exchanges of material and spiritual things—where are they now? Were they to see the depravity of the Nazis and their abominable acts they would surely be ashamed to buy the friendship and amity of psychopathic killers who have no place in human society. Whoever whips a young mother, standing beside her baby's cradle, cannot be considered human.

Sometimes you hear in a whisper: "Stalin has repudiated his treaty with Hitler and has already sent him a declaration of war." A second person adds: "They are already fighting near Ostroleka." The next day they come and give you "an explicit bulletin which cannot be doubted" that "an hour ago Mussolini declared war on

2 Song of Songs 2:9.

145

Hitler and the English radio is playing the Italian national anthem."
And our Jews? They are even competent in matters of military
strategy. The business of Norway is nothing but a trick on England's part; the German army has fallen into the net, and Norway
with its mountains and fjords will be its grave. And so on along the
same line.

May 4, 1940

The Führer's victory in Norway has left me in the deepest depression. Sometimes a terrifying doubt creeps into my heart: What
if their great military might should subjugate all of Europe? Of
course they have now won only a partial victory, and it does not
have the power to turn the final decision in their favor, but this
specific case emphasizes the general situation. It is a sign that the
opposing side is so disintegrated that it cannot stand up against
them. Only a few days ago the Western Powers were shaking the
world with news of their military victories in that same Norway.
What suddenly happened, that one fine day the wheel turned about
on them so that Chamberlain himself admits defeat?

Those who are perpetual believers in the strength of Great Britain console themselves with the slogan: "England may lose a battle,
but she will never lose a war." But this is a vain consolation. In
every isolated battle which has taken place so far, England has been
defeated. And the general concept of a war is nothing more than
the sum total of isolated battles. The whole contains nothing more
than is in the particular.

England has no competent military command. Now the former
military situation has been clarified and it appears that the "Norwegian Action" was an audacious move on the Führer's part; Norway could have been the grave of the German forces, had England
conducted her offensive with ability and intelligence. Churchill
has become an idle talker; his prestige has fallen in the eyes of the
neutral nations.

The German press is jubilant, and it pains me to read all its praise
of the German army, since I realize that reality does not contradict
it.

The destruction of England will mean the ultimate end for the
house of Israel; a "new world" will be created then, in which there
will be no room for the Jews.

146

Sometimes I decide to stop reading the German newspapers, but I confess without shame that it is not because of the insults they direct toward the Jewish people. There is another reason involved: they are full of cheerful items about victories in Norway, and about the great defeat the English suffered which forced them to flee for their lives in their ships, after they had buried a hundred and twenty-seven marine units in the sea within a single month (April), besides the thousands of men who fell in battle. They emphasize every victory *ad nauseam*, whether it is a small or a medium one, and all the more so when it is a great one. I know that all of these news items are tinged with Nazi colors, but nevertheless, to my great sorrow, I realize that there is a kernel of truth to them.

New military tactics have come into being which have totally changed the appearance of warfare, and these changes are to the disadvantage of "mighty" Britain. When I observe the Satanic glee of the murderous Huns when they expound on the details of the battles in Norway, and when I hear their devilish laughter at plutocratic England—which has no sense of reality, and is completely entangled in a network of merchant ships and naval vessels whose time is already past—my heart bleeds. Mockery, flowing from real and actual reality which cannot be denied or contradicted, is as killing as poisoned arrows. It is better for me not to read it.

Whoever recognizes a fact without recognizing its internal causes and stimuli does not understand the situation as it really is. Factual reality creates room for error, and errors of this sort lead to incorrect conclusions. The formal side of any fact is devoid of soul, and it is thus necessary to examine the spiritual side of it in order to appreciate its true nature.

It must be admitted that eight months ago the Soviet government placed an obligation on all the democratic governments by its conduct toward the Jewish fugitives. The democratic countries closed their gates to the most unfortunate of the unfortunate and turned them back into the hands of despotic rulers, while the Soviet government opened its gates wide and gave sanctuary to foreign nationals seeking a place of refuge. Is there any greater humaneness than this? Among the political experts, this fact shook their faith in democracy, which by its nature is obliged to be humane and yet

147

has turned out to be cruel and grudging. It is entirely possible that there were political considerations to Russian "hospitality" as well, but this does not diminish the humanity of it.

From the formal standpoint, this was a good match for both sides—were it not for the fact that both sides were wrong—the Soviets in evaluating the human material. Those who fled to them were armchair communists for whom communism was a sort of exotica at the time when they sat by the fleshpots and enjoyed all pleasures. At the root of their souls they were tradesmen and black marketeers and they persisted in the activities they had carried on in their own country. They did not come to labor but rather to trade; they came to do something that the whole Bolshevik revolution intended to uproot from the world. Thus they caused us embarrassment and heaped disgrace upon us. Many of them made fortunes by smuggling goods from one side to the other, by means of bribes and other ugly acts. The hunger for these goods was especially great among the army men from the interior of Russia who had been brought to the border cities by the conquest. Any badly made, scarce goods found ready customers among them. No price was too much to pay even for a pocket watch made of thin metal that wouldn't last more than a day or two. Ugly speculation reigned without control. Armchair communists reverted to type.

The Bolshevik rulers saw this and were appalled. They trembled at the sight of this ugly speculation which made a mockery of all their teachings, and they ordered that the border be closed.

And now tens of thousands are beginning to come back to us, to those who are "peaceful and contented" in their place. If they are unable to return by permission, they do so without it, but in the past few days it has become known that they are able to return legally, on the basis of a new agreement between the Bolsheviks and the Nazis which permits inhabitants of either country who fled to the other to return to their original domicile. Just as we witnessed the exodus from Poland earlier we are now witnessing the exodus from Russia. They return out of the frying pan into the fire. They exchange garlic for onions. They flee from one prison to another. They do not fear the cruelty, the hatred, and all the various activities in which the Nazis are expert. Moreover, this return flight will furnish the Nazis with a subject for boasting before all nations and peoples.

148

Tens of thousands of Jews who fled to Russia when the Germans came are returning to the conquered territories. This will make a shocking news item. Is it possible?

Nevertheless, it is entirely true.

Up to now people would say mockingly, "In Germany there is order; when they don't give them anything to eat, they don't eat. In conquered Poland, with its inferior civilization, it is different. They are not told to eat—but they eat. Among the new Germans there is nothing more sacred than the Führer, but to us he is a *Verführer*.[3] Who listens to him when he says not to eat?" In Poland there is a great affection for gluttony. A Polish Jew says: "It is enough that I won't eat after I die. Then I'll have no other choice. But as long as I'm alive, let them make any law they like as long as they don't ban eating." When it is impossible to eat legally, they do so illegally.

Our lives, which are so full of sorrow, are not lacking in the exotic. Until now the Jews were being seized to work for nothing; from now on Poles too are to be seized for forced labor—but for wages. The common element in both cases is that both try to avoid it, and whoever is caught bemoans his fate, and woe to him. Be that as it may, the Jews are somewhat pleased: You have been likened unto us. You are equated with us.

In the eyes of the conquerors, the Poles are ingrates and should be treated with the full force of the law. The new proclamation "invites" the Polish population between the ages of fifteen and forty-five, both men and women, to register voluntarily on the list of candidates for transport to Greater Germany to work in the fields. If they don't, they will be forcibly seized and sent involuntarily. And do not think that some sort of injustice is being done to anyone. All in all two hundred thousand farm laborers are now working in Greater Germany, and that is not enough. To satisfy the needs of the populations of the conquered nations, the Germans are forced to bring produce from the Reich, at the very same time when there are men and women roaming around either without work or else engaged in activities of a sort that could be done without. And they will not be forced to work for nothing, heaven forbid. There

[3] A person who leads one astray, a misleader.

149

is a fixed price for work in the fields. In addition to cash, each one receives food and housing. The money he thus saves, he can send to his relatives in Poland. The families of these workers in the fields of Greater Germany will enjoy special privileges. They are under a special administration, and whatever they lack will be supplied them. Thus everything is fine. Yet not a single Pole will register voluntarily. The conquerors are enraged and infuriated. Such an ungrateful lot!

And here the exoticism of our lives grows more striking: in order to avoid forcible capture in broad daylight and transportation to the Reich, many Poles adorn themselves with the "Ribbon of Disgrace" (*Schandeband*) and masquerade as Jews to make sure of not being seized for forced labor.

May 10, 1940

Eight in the evening

The slaughter of nations and the destruction of civilization have begun.

Warsaw is in an uproar. What was spread in whispers throughout the day has become blood-drenched fact. For the second time the Führer has violated the sanctity of neutrality with brazen and unabashed cynicism. The first time it was the neutrality of Norway and Denmark, and now that of the two small states Holland and Belgium, in order to attack France from its unfortified border. More important, together with the order to his armies to invade Holland and Belgium, an order was given by the Führer to begin an offensive along the length of the fortified Maginot Line, which, in the opinion of military experts, cannot be taken.

And so after nine months the "war without war" has ended and the real battles have begun. Tens of thousands of men will fall on both sides. Streams of blood will pour over the European civilization which said, "I am, and there is none else beside me."

If the Führer suffers a defeat there is no doubt that it will be decisive, because the Nazis are being strangled. Their material and financial resources are being depleted, and their first loss will be decisive. But if, heaven forbid, this conflict brings military victory for the Nazis, it will be only a partial victory, because the Western Powers have the capabilities to continue the war for a few more years—until the Nazis' defeat comes from another direction, that of economics

There are many signs that these calculations are correct, that they will lead to the end hoped for by all the nations of the world. The Maginot Line represents a network of trenches and mines that no one can get through alive. It is a labyrinth of forts and fortresses built and supplied with every weapon which modern technology has invented. The Maginot Line is an inferno prepared for the German army, and if in spite of this the Führer has decided to send his army to slaughter and death, it is an indication that he has no time, that he is forced to bring about a quick decision in order not to choke on his Norwegian victories.

This sign is perhaps the only consolation in this world tragedy. My heart foretells that it is not impossible for the Führer to achieve a military victory, and for that very reason the end of the war may be delayed.

May 11, 1940

To our great sorrow, the realization is beginning to penetrate into certain circles that the victory of the Western Powers is not as certain as they once thought.

The debates in the British Parliament last Wednesday after the speeches of Chamberlain and his friends left a depressing impression, and faith in the strength of undefeated England was shaken to its foundations.

The ministers of a mighty power justifying themselves with idle chatter like little children caught in some mischief! The Norwegian defeat of itself diminished England's prestige in the world, but those speeches degraded its honor to the lowest level. In Berlin they rub their hands in glee. One of the British ministers says, "The strength of one division was not enough"; another admits, "The Germans are superior to us in air power"; a third says, "Because of fear of putting the British fleet in danger of being destroyed by air attack, it was impossible to prevent Hitler from bringing new military forces to Norway; thus the Navy did not take the necessary initiative." Finally, Churchill himself beats his breast and confesses: "The air power of Germany, unequaled in might and in scope, has totally changed the situation which was created by the World War. Germany foresaw what was coming, and armed itself completely with the latest weapons, while we were somewhat backward. And you must know that in the future as well we can look forward to bitterness and disappointments."

Ministers of this sort are worthy of praise: they speak frankly without withholding anything. But from that very moment they no longer had the people's confidence as a government.

But the voices of the newsboys are reaching my ears.

Chamberlain has been ousted!

May 13, 1940

In the past few days the conquerors have been making the rounds of the schools for Polish children (Jewish children are still idle and are growing up wild) and taking them out of their classrooms to give blood—since they are elite, red-blooded Aryans born and bred—for use as plasma for the German soldiers. There is great turmoil among Polish parents, and many of them have stopped sending their children to school. The rich were affected first; after a while it became known to the masses, and then the real panic began. The school benches are becoming empty. When the oppressors began invading the children's homes as well, it became customary for the parents to send their Gentile children to spend the night in Jewish homes.

So anyone who says that the Jewish children are not to be envied because they were born in sin and are handicapped by their Semitism, is mistaken. They do envy us; they seek out our friendship—when they need us.

May 15, 1940

The Aryans have been learning much from bitter Jewish experience. They evade and avoid forced labor as much as they are able. They hide in their back rooms and don't go outside except when they must. The Aryan streets, too, are empty, and the silence of a desert is on every hand. The conquerors are not ashamed to make the rounds of their houses; still, as long as one is hidden in his apartment, the danger is not as great.

This week the conquerors did something so humorous that after the war it will furnish material for some theatrical sketch.

In Biala Street, a short, quiet side street, they caught three Jews. They stood them up near one of the buildings and ordered them to dance and sing self-derogatory songs. This mocking scene attracted a great crowd of Gentiles, who enjoyed the moral sufferings of the *Zyds*. While they laughed, they probably thought, Angels of doom don't go on two errands at once; when they are busy with the Jews they haven't time for Aryans. So they thought—but after the entire street had filled up with a crowd enjoying the spectacle of the sadistic game, the street was fenced off at both ends and the festive crowd was surrounded on all sides. They were thrown on trucks and taken away. The Gentiles were taken away as captives, and the three Jews were released and sent home. The entire fantastic business took place only to set a scene whose epilogue was the capture of Gentiles for forced labor.

Sometimes our work is done by schoolchildren. The children of our poor, with whom the streets of Warsaw are filled at all hours of the day, are not afraid even of the despotic conquerors. They remain as always—lively and mischievous. Their poverty and oppression serves to shield them from robberies and confiscations. No one will harm them. Even the conquerors' eye overlooks them: Let the Jewish weeds pine away in their iniquity. But these weeds watch every act of the conquerors and imitate the Nazis' manner of speech and their cruelty most successfully. For them this is nothing but good material for games and amusements. Childhood does much.

Once there came into the ghetto a certain Nazi from a province where the Jews are required to greet every Nazi soldier they encountered, removing their hats as they do. There is no such practice in Warsaw, but the "honored guest" wanted to be strict and force the rules of his place of origin on us. A great uproar arose suddenly in Jewish Karmelicka Street: Some psychopathic Nazi is demanding that every passerby take his hat off in his honor. Many fled, many hid, many were caught for their transgression and beaten, and many were bursting with laughter. The little "wise guys," the true lords of the street, noticed what was going on and found great amusement in actually obeying the Nazi, and showing him great respect in a manner calculated to make a laughingstock out of the "great lord" in the eyes of all the passersby. They ran up to greet him a hundred and one times, taking off their hats in his honor. They gathered in great numbers, with an artificial look of awe on their faces, and wouldn't stop taking off their hats. Some did this with straight faces, while their friends stood behind them and laughed. Then these would leave, and others would approach, bowing before the Nazi with bare heads. There was no end to the laughter. Every one of the mischievous youths so directed his path as to appear before the Nazi several times, bowing before him in deepest respect. That wasn't all. Riffraff gathered for the fun, and they all made a noisy demonstration in honor of the Nazi with a resounding cheer.

This is Jewish revenge!

May 18, 1940

The military victories, which, though they may be exaggerated, nevertheless contain much of the truth, beat upon our heads like hailstones. Today it is Copenhagen, in which there is a Jewish community; the next day it is Amsterdam, The Hague, and Rotterdam, full of Jews who until now dwelt quietly and peacefully in their homeland. Just now the news has reached us that Brussels too has opened its gates to the Nazis. All the military activities of the past nine days prove that the earth trembles under the feet of the Nazis. It seems that these are not chance victories, but rather that the balance of power is such as to make these victories inevitable. Anyone with any perception can clearly see that the Western Powers are incapable of withstanding the military force of the Nazis. This is a gigantic military power in whose path there is no obstacle. And so the day after tomorrow Paris, too, will fall into their hands. And what then? In place of the Versailles Dictate there will be a Paris Dictate, but the dictator will be a different one. Can all this be possible? History is sometimes fond of oddities. It doesn't follow set rules; it moves by strange leaps and sometimes follows serpentine paths.

The conquerors have adopted a new tactic whose purpose is unknown to anyone. Even the mystics freely admit this time that it is an insoluble riddle. At almost every intersection that does not have trolley tracks, the *Judenrat* is putting up—by order of the conquerors, but at its own expense—a thick dividing wall which leaves no room to pass, thus stopping traffic from going from the one street to the other. Warsaw, like Noah's Ark in its day, is full of compartments and partitions that block the roads in the very places where up to now there was the most traffic. Thus for example on the corner of Nalewki and Nowolipki streets, a dividing wall has been made, and a man whose apartment is at Number 2 Nowolipki Street—a distance of only a few steps—is now forced to go around and around, via Nowolipki-Zamenhof-Gesia-Nalewki streets—a half hour's walk. The same is true of the corner of Rymarska-Leszno streets, and so too in all the other fenced-off streets.

It has become known to us that partitions of this sort were also erected in Prague, Czechoslovakia; and this gives support to the hypothesis that this is a military tactic, to diminish freedom of movement in the event of internal revolt. As I said, this is only a hypothesis, but it is a reasonable one.

In any case, beautiful Warsaw has become a jail made up of cell after cell, whose inhabitants are treated like prisoners.

May 19, 1940

Let me not be ungrateful.

I shall try, for once, to speak in praise of the Nazis. The spies in Moses' day started with praise and ended with abuse. Not so with me: here the abuse comes before the praise. The Hitlerian youth were particularly receptive to Nazism's teachings, but many circles among the older generation accepted Nazism because they had no alternative. It is hard to fight against the popular and political current, the creation of a dictatorial government whose rule extends to all spheres of life and which cannot be evaded. Everything is in its hands and it has the power of life and death. All it takes is one slogan like "Whoever does not believe in Nazism is a traitor to his homeland" to make everyone its slaves.

Something of this sort exists in Bolshevik Russia too. You have no right to an individual world outlook. Whatever you need for body and soul is furnished in accordance with a prescribed dose, which cannot be changed. Sometimes you rise up against this in the privacy of your soul, but for fear of danger you don't voice your thoughts.

But in spite of that the spirit cannot be imprisoned.

Sometimes a Jew is seized for forced labor, and the enemy soldier treats him like a human being, even with courtesy. The soldier enters into conversation with him, is friendly to him, like the Germans who were here twenty-five years ago.

A friend of mine who was seized for forced labor testified to me that the supervisor said to him at the outset, "Don't be afraid of me. I am not tainted with hatred for the Jews."

There was another instance. On one of the empty lots in Gesia Street several Jewish boys organized some sort of athletic game; some German soldiers noticed it. When they passed the lot, they addressed the players courteously and asked for permission to join their game. The youths agreed. After the game was over they parted like friends and comrades. It was a miracle. And that is not all.

There was a case in which some Jewish boys were seized for forced labor and transported to their place of work. But instead of work, they were invited to play soccer, and to the Aryans' distress they were beaten by the children of the "inferior race." But they were not humiliated, and for *revenge* they set a time for playing another game.

And the praise of the Nazis is not yet finished.

This week an echelon of twelve hundred Jews who had had their fill of Bolshevism returned from Russia. Full of fear, they awaited their reception by the Nazis. But to their amazement, as well as to their joy and relief, they found they had made a mistake. The Nazis received the Jews returning from exile like human beings who deserve human treatment. The Nazis not only refrained from imposing additional hardships, which is their usual practice; they welcomed the Jews politely and helped them in whatever way they could. They made whatever concessions they could in the matter of disinfection, which everyone crossing the border is obliged to undergo, and they gave them warm blankets. The people who saw this were astounded. "Can the Ethiopian change his skin?"

Not many hours had passed before the secret was revealed. In the course of their friendly conversations the Nazis made inquiries, "by the way," about the condition of the Russian army—its food, clothing, and the places where it is stationed. The questions came out casually, as though they were not premeditated, and the answers too were received in an offhand manner. The naïve among the exiles told what they knew; the more astute understood at once where this was leading and got rid of the Nazis by saying "I don't know." This splendid reception was only for the sake of espionage.

May 21, 1940

The fate of Europe will be decided on the fields of France. Both sides admit to this. This is not a war for a piece of land like the wars that came before it—it is a war over the future of all of Europe. Nazism wants to build a new world in partnership with Fascism. The more outstanding omens of this world which is being created (after the latest military victories in France) are: first, the rule of force; whatever nation has the strength will rule, and in accordance with this there are master nations and slave nations. Second, the rule of race; not all races are equal. There are some among them which are of the loftiest quality, of noble spirit—a superior race; and some among them are of a low degree of civilization, poor in spirit, low and base races since first they were created.

It does not interest me at the moment to prove to what extent this is a doctrine of lies. I wish to show that the Germans received a new doctrine from the Führer. Their old teachings were entirely different. Can a nation reverse its historical doctrines? It is a sign that the doctrines were never mixed into their blood. From this standpoint the Jewish people is truly unique among the nations of earth. Our Torah is an organic part of all our spiritual being. Our Torah permeates our being and we cannot exchange it or replace it with another. The foundations on which our Torah is based are laid out for all eternity; any prophet who comes forth and attempts to give us a new doctrine can be nothing other than a false prophet.

A doctrine which is eternal is the only true one.

I still have a statement made during the German conquest in the First World War. In the days when it was written it, too, gave expression to the German spirit, but it is as far from the spirit of Nazism as East from West. It is almost unbelievable now that this document came from a German's pen.

Its author was "Rittmeister" Stükle, who was the director of the press office in Vilna, and it dates from February 1917. Its contents were made public twice, once in a pamphlet intended only for the attention of the civil servants, and a second time in a public lecture. Here is its content:

One thing which is imperative is a just attitude toward all nationalities. In regard to the future, it is forbidden to make distinctions between one nationality and another, or to discriminate against it to its disadvantage, whether in the administrative field or in the press. We are obligated to rule with strength and fortitude and not to make any distinction between races. All articles must be edited in order to make certain that they do not reflect any national conflicts whatsoever. We must not permit internationally inflammatory remarks in the press. On this principle, it is our duty to be watchful not only in the case of articles dealing with current questions, but in regard to historical articles in our newspapers as well. Here extraordinary supervision must be exercised, so that no national hatred may be emphasized, no undesirable instigation. Only our mighty hand is capable of eliminating harmful attitudes of hatred between various nationalities. It is our duty to see to it that the press arouses no bad feelings between one people and another in any manner, shape or form.

Among the peoples who must not be harmed were the Jewish people. Thus a German wrote in the year 1917.

And in the year 1940?

May 30, 1940

All normal conduct of business has ceased. In place of business, peddling has come, and the place for all such vending is in the street. So the streets are filled with men, women, and little children, as in the good old days, even though all the stores are closed and the houses demolished. Mob upon mob fills the sidewalks until it is as crowded as a market day. And every crowd of vendors is also a crowd of politicians. Every oddity finds listening ears and spreads so fast that within an hour "all of Warsaw" is discussing it. There is no limit to the lies.

Our Jews don't believe in the murderer's victories in France. The newspapers announce victories which cannot be denied, whose truth is apparent—yet the Jews don't admit them. They stick to their conviction: The Germans will end in destruction. They got this far in the years 1914–1919, but nevertheless they were defeated in the end. Knowledgeable people are in mourning, but the masses are happy. They have entered Antwerp? Don't believe them! They conquered Rotterdam? Tell it to grandma. The people's desire doesn't allow them even to consider the possibility that the murderers will win. The entire world will rise up against them. Roosevelt won't sit silently in his homeland; even Stalin will unsheathe his sword. Is it possible that they would extend their hegemony over the entire world? And England? There is no power in the world that could defeat her! She will show her strength yet. Any time England retreats, it is only strategy. Even if the tyrant conquered London, it would no doubt mean that England was luring him into a trap. This is the power of desire. It is the father of all thought.

Thousands of men are dying every day on the fields of death in Flanders. Let us speak the truth: Their deaths have no reason. Just as there was no reason for the deaths of the tens of billions who went before them. Every war is a senseless activity and its participants are, in my eyes, common murderers; when they die it is a pointless sacrifice. Let the slogans about the death of heroes be recited—these have not the power to make the crooked straight. I stick to my convictions: Even a homeland is not reason enough for a man to sacrifice his life, because the whole world is his homeland. For when love and brotherhood reign in the world there is no need for a homeland. Every homeland is a good business for several millions or for several tens of thousands, and the masses are no more than willing slaves for those in power.

It's really amazing. Every death makes an impression, except a death on the battlefield, as though men had made a secret agreement that it is not worthwhile to mourn fools who ruined their lives. It makes no difference whether they did so voluntarily or not.

There is much to be said on these matters. In form they are paradoxical, but there is an inner truth embodied in them. If you say "In such and such a battle, a hundred thousand people were killed," you express your astonishment for a single moment, without sympathy, without the trembling of the soul that stirs you when you see a single individual dying. Everyone knows beforehand that war exists only for the sake of killing or being killed. Its very nature is mutual slaughter. Whichever side kills the most is the one most worthy of praise. The strategy, which is the main thing, beclouds the sacrifice. Who pays any attention to the graves of the fallen, and to the sufferings of the wounded and the dying? They are not important. The important point is whether or not the battle that took place was a successful bit of strategy. Sensation and nothing more!

And I say that this attitude toward the casualties of war is a punishment for the national heroes who call common murder valor. I am the grandson of Isaiah the prophet, and I am at one with my ancestor in that bloodshed is abhorrent to me, in any form whatsoever. You may say that this is cowardice. I am not ashamed of that despicable quality.

German science, it must be admitted, researches deeply into all phenomena both natural and sociological. It is not in the nature of German researchers to set down laws and principles which are not based on detailed and precise studies. All this was before Nazism was born, when there was pure science, without an admixture of politics and partisanship. The scientist was free in his opinions and scientific truth served as a lamp unto his feet. Politics and science cannot live side by side. But in Nazi Germany this is not so. There everything is bound up in the central premise, the principle of race. There is no room for pure science. All the people of Germany are members of one herd, and a herd has no ideas of its own. Only the shepherd standing over them does. Nothing which contradicts the principle of race is to be seen or heard, and scientists have been found who will falsify science and make it subservient to the principle of race. There is no falsification that cannot be proven by means of scientific research. All knowledge is subject to seventy interpretations.

In its disputes with the nations of Europe which it seeks to enslave, Nazism utilizes science as well, which it falsifies and emasculates for its own political ends. In particular it aims its arrows at the Polish nation, whose land it has conquered and whom it has turned into a slave tributary. It is necessary to prove to all the peoples of the world that the Polish nation, besides being of an inferior civilization, is by its origins and ancestry a scion of an inferior race, and as such, its survival as a state is not in the world's best interests.

In May, the annual meeting of the German Society for Legal Medicine and Criminology took place in Innsbrück, under the chairmanship of Professor Buntz, of Breslau, and here the creditor found room to collect his debt. The main item on the agenda was the one dealing with murders by Poles of their fellow citizens of German origin. In German fashion the Nazis brought to the meeting all the copious materials assembled by court physicians, including hospital records, and a complete collection of slides preserved by a Dr. Hallermann.

The various lecturers dove into the mighty waters of pure scientific research and came up, not with a bit of rubble, heaven forbid, but with a complete doctrine on the national characteristics of the Polish people. Opinions were voiced that it is wrong to condemn the entire Polish nation, as a nation, for these murders. Dr. Preisler does not agree with this opinion:

Nations are like personalities, and every personality is responsible for his actions whether before the law or before history. One of the characteristics of the Polish nation is individualism, which reached its peak in the enactments of Radom in 1505, in the phrase *Nie pozwalam!* (I object). Every representative in the Sejm had the right to nullify any decision which did not meet with his approval. Out of forty-eight Sejms, forty-five did not enact a single new law because of this obstacle: there was always someone who did not agree.

And this disagreement did not stem from sound logical reasons which opposed the majority opinion. Rather, the representative was instructed by his constituents in advance not to agree, without anyone's paying the slightest attention to whether the proposed law was in essence good or bad. And this authorization, which is opposed to all political wisdom and all social good, was considered to be a pearl of great price in the constitution of Poland.

Talleyrand once said: All of Poland is not worth a single drop of all the blood we are shedding for her sake. This nation is not competent for anything. With her help only disorganization can be organized. The return of Poland to independent life is nothing but a return to anarchy.

The great slaughter and the terrible murders of German citizens of Poland in the bloody days on the eve of the war, were not the atrocities of isolated murderers who turned into beasts of prey because of the blood-psychosis which reigned in those days, nor even of criminals who were released from jail and committed these acts on their own. All levels of the Polish nation had a hand in these crimes. Out of a group of ten murderers who were caught, two murderers were sixteen-year-old students and four were young apprentices. A second group of thirteen murderers included one forester, one bank clerk, one dentist, and one woman.

More than once the victims were killed by army units who were acting under their superiors' orders; in general, all gunshot wounds seem to have been inflicted by military weapons. There is no doubt that the greatest responsibility for all these events rests upon the former Polish government; on the other hand, it must be stated that since its inception the Polish nation has not been ruled by a government of its own, capable of instituting worthwhile cultural or political activities.

There is much truth in all that was presented and expressed. Witnesses from Przytyk, Brisk, Novo Minsk, and dozens of other cities will attest to this. But the scientific conclusion is dangerous to the Germans themselves; it can thus be concluded that the German nation is responsible for the Führer's actions. And if this is so, there must be death for every German.

Second day of Shavuot,[4] *5700*

The second hooligan has dared, as well! Whether voluntarily or by compulsion it is difficult to say, but the fact remains that Benito Mussolini, the classic traitor, the Führer's minion, the monkey-leader of the Italian nation, has gone to war against England and France.

The French are fighting like lions with the last of their strength. But there is a limit to acts of valor, too. It is dubious that the military strength still remaining to France will suffice to resist the Nazi military might which is superior to theirs in both weapons and numbers. We shudder at the fate of noble and lofty France, the mistress of democracy and freedom. For even though victory will ultimately come, she can look forward to the sufferings of conquest and the destruction of her homeland. And now, suddenly, in so terrible and fateful an hour as this, a knife is stuck in her back!

But perhaps there is some consolation even in this event. From here on the war will spread and will draw new nations and states into its net. And this will speed its end. The eyes of all the world are turned to America and its leader Roosevelt. Will they allow the brown-and-black bloc to win, will they sit quietly at home when they see all of Europe destined to become Nazi-Fascist?! Everyone is almost sure that after Italy will come America. It is not impossible, either, that the small states of southeast Europe will become involved in this conflict. Thus the war is destined to become worldwide.

And in a world war, the defeat of Germany and Italy is certain.

June 14, 1940

The evil tidings have reached us that the enemy has entered the gates of Paris. Everywhere, both among the Poles and among the Jews, there is weeping and wailing. Wherever speech is not silenced, wherever there is political freedom, freedom of expression of both affection and hatred, the masses are demonstrating in the city

4 The Feast of Weeks, commemorating the season when the Torah was given at Mount Sinai.

streets. Pent-up emotions are breaking out and in this they find some moral comfort, since "care in the heart of a man boweth it down." We, however, are forced to be silent and keep our feelings inside us, but our faces show deep sorrow. The thunder of cannons on the fields of France does not reach our ears, but every bomb dropped on France hurts us as well.

Nonetheless, even now a small group of people who see good things in the future remains. They are stubborn: The world will not permit the murderer to triumph. The other side comes and asks: Who is the world? America? Experience has shown that it is air power which is decisive. From here on all Canadian, and for that matter American, production is reserved for England and France. Two hundred and forty planes are being sent from Canada to the battlefield every day, and they will bring defeat to Germany. Thus we argue and debate, wandering aimlessly like shadows.

June 17, 1940

The ways of the wicked prosper. About half an hour before curfew, the capital city was shaken throughout its length and breadth. Since the day I first came to this city, I have never seen such chaos. There is no doubt in my mind that the intelligent ones among the Poles also have this feeling. Their hopes too have been doomed; it is the end for free Poland. People snatched the extras from the newsboys in the street; the headlines were: "France Is Laying Down Her Arms." Even the most extreme pessimists, among whom I include myself, never expected such terrible tidings. Who could have anticipated that the two most stable Western Powers, the wealthiest in gold, in raw material, and in human resources gathered from all corners of the world, with three-quarters of the world (America, Africa, and Australia) available to them, would submit so shamefully and speedily before the murderer?

Will England keep fighting? One can imagine that she too will be forced to sue for peace, and will receive the Hitlerian dictate submissively, which will be even more difficult for England than for France. Because England and France have been pulled apart there will be no peace conference of conquerors and conquered this time; instead of one dictate there will be several separate dictates, each in accordance with the geographic situation of the defeated country—and most important, with the particular benefits that its political and economic submission can bring to Greater Germany, which has now become a reality.

The war is not over yet! England is continuing to fight, and even France will henceforth carry on her battle from the soil of her empire, her colonies in all parts of the world.

And so our hope is not yet lost. The Germans are, of course, the heroes of the war, but they require a short war; as they say in their language, a *Blitzkrieg*. They could not survive a long war. Time is their greatest enemy. Thus the German High Command is restless. For six or seven weeks the battles have been incessant. The enemy is afraid of an additional concentration of forces. In its new form the war will last a long time—and as a result the enemy will be buried. Thus we the foolish experts in war tactics evaluate the world situation.

We sense in all our being that we are drawing near a fateful hour in our history. We might accept any other kind of savagery in the world, but we will not accept Nazi "peace."

Again a disappointment.

We hoped for war, and instead we have peace. Our strange lives sometimes place us in a strange situation, and we begin to hope for things that are against our nature both as a people and as individuals. The Jews are known in the world as lovers of peace— partly because we are sick of murders and bloodshed; partly because our entire survival and our tranquility depend upon peace; and partly because we are the descendants of Isaiah the prophet and are closest to his universal human ideal. But this time peace would be our downfall; we would simply be wiped off the face of Europe.

Will the Bolsheviks come to Warsaw or not? Everyone has a different rumor to relate; everyone furnishes a different proof, in accordance with his taste. People feel that with the entry of the "Reds" there will be another revolution; and as in every revolution, some people are happy and others are in mourning.

The rumors have become so strong that the conqueror's newspaper published a denial in the name of the Bolsheviks, but the time is past for denials to have any effect on the public. There is no doubt of the fact that some negotiations on "border adjustments" are being carried on behind the scenes between the "friend" and the Führer, and it is possible that the capital city, too, will be included in this adjustment.

In theory the war is coming to an end. The signing of a peace treaty between Germany and Italy on the one hand and France on the other, means the end of war in Europe. At all events, it is a step leading us closer to peace. Logic would indicate that civilian life should become more comfortable, more free, but in reality it is becoming stricter, more difficult. Some people attempt to prove on this basis that their victories are not victories. Why isn't joy evident on the faces of the victors? Why isn't there the customary elation that any real victory should cause?

June 27, 1940

We feel in the air that news is coming from the East. Opinion is divided. Some prophesy a war between Stalin and the Führer. Most intelligent people reject this, but the voice is incessant. Others say that the two sides have come to an agreement, and that there will be an adjustment of the borders to the Reds' advantage. As proof: a Russian delegation has gone to Berlin for the purpose of fixing boundaries. The masses even know the time when the Russians will enter—by July 5, 1940.

There is no formal ghetto in Warsaw for the time being, but in practice a ghetto exists. Such conditions of living have arisen that the Jews themselves have unintentionally created a ghetto. In the broad and beautiful Ayran streets not a Jew is to be found—except for assimilated half-, third-, and quarter-Jews whose homes are among the Gentiles. A Jew marked with the "badge of shame" simply restrains himself from appearing in those streets. He is afraid of becoming a subject for disgrace and embarrassment whether caused by Ammon or Moab. The tens of thousands of refugees who fled to Warsaw have likewise settled among their brothers in misfortune in the Jewish quarters. There is no Jewish courtyard whose population has not multiplied. Those burned out of their homes, refugees, fugitives, and exiles have all been added.

And therefore the streets of the Jewish quarters are full of noise, inordinately crowded. The sidewalks are so congested that there is simply no room to pass, and so the human stream is pushed into the middle of the street. A noisy, populous traffic goes on unceasingly from early morning until the hour of curfew. The noise outside deafens your ears, if it is your fortune to live in the midst of this stormy sea.

Moreover, the noisy traffic grows loudest just before evening. At that time, besides the passersby going about their business, there are many strollers among the carefree youths who make no distinction between good times and bad. When parks are closed, theaters are idle, leaving the city dangerous, summer camps are empty, and movies forbidden—everything becomes concentrated in Leszno and Karmelicka streets.

The conquerors are not enthusiastic about that either. They have notified the *Judenrat* that they should try to reduce Jewish traffic in these streets. They are very sensitive, and can't stand the laughter which rings out from the mouths of the Jewish youth—deprived though they are of the right to live, and especially of the right to be happy and carefree—at a time when the German people are in mourning for the loss of the flower of their youth who fell to the enemy's sword.

And while they were about it, they added a warning: If the *Judenrat* is incapable of silencing the busy traffic by its own methods, they will do it by theirs. And we already know the taste of those methods.

June 28, 1940

Some people see mystical proof of the imminent coming of salvation: This year is *Tav-Shin*.[5] It is known that the redemption of Israel will come at the end of the sixth millennium. Thus, according to this calculation, three hundred years are lacking. But that can be explained! Some of those who calculate the date of the Messianic age have already been disappointed; the others too will eventually be disappointed. But this will not prevent people from finding more proofs, nor other people from believing them.

They want the Messiah, and someone will yet come forth who will bring him.

[5] *Tav-Shin*—5700. Hebrew letters have numerical equivalents.

Whatever goes on in the sea goes on on land. Just as there are prophets in Israel who foretell the future, so too are there prophets among the Gentiles who foretell what is to be. The only difference is that Jewish prophecy is religious in essence, divinely inspired, while that of the Gentiles is political, a kind of mental gymnastics.

The destruction of France in so tragic a form has engendered a spirit of mysticism in her oppressed people. Whenever a nation finds itself in darkness, it looks backward to its glorious past and resurrects the words of its seers. Thus one of the French political prophets has now become a subject of widespread interest—the physician Nostradamus, who lived in the sixteenth century. Even in his own day he became famous throughout the world as a political prophet. Charles IX honored him with a visit. Louis XIII and Louis XIV paid their respects to his grave. The prophecies of Nostradamus played an important role in the life of Napoleon III in his war with Germany in 1870–1871. And so in our own day of world crisis, the shadow of the prophetic physician of the Middle Ages spreads its wings over the French nation in its time of misfortune and decline. Here is one of his prophecies:

Seventy years after the establishment of the French Republic [i.e., about the year 1940], Germany will put an end to the great treaty [the Versailles Treaty]. Listen and you will hear, O France! ! You have gone too far and too wide. Why did you not listen to the words of your opponent? The war of France and Germany will shock all the nations of the earth by its stunning swiftness, by its mammoth strength, by its unbounded audacity.

That which we dreaded has happened to us. During the First World War, America showered us with good things, treated us like poor people of noble origins. The distant communities knew of each other only by hearsay, for the descendants of the emigrants of the eighties of the last century were culturally and socially far from the land where their ancestors originated. Only the national-historical consciousness which unites all Jewish communities into one nation remained. Yet our American brothers were asked—and gave. It made no difference to them whether it was for the sanctuary of the Lord or for the Golden Calf. Exaggerated rumors reached them of our poverty, of the economic straits we were in, and they hastened to bring us aid. Everyone stretched out his hand for the American bounty. Everyone wanted to be a philanthropist with someone else's money.

In reality we were not so poor and oppressed. Those were days when democracy reigned and the conquerors did not single us out for evil. A human relationship and a cultural affinity developed between us. All sources of income and livelihood were open to us. Where there was freedom of movement and freedom of commerce the war situation created profits for us. Many became wealthy; the intelligentsia earned large incomes; tradesmen had comfortable livelihoods and as much work as they could handle. Diverse cultural activities developed. We lived and enjoyed life. Yet in addition there came the stream of gold across the sea, and an internal struggle flared up over the money of strangers. Who would be the first to get it? It never entered anyone's mind that it was necessary to organize local relief and make the rich Jews of Poland contribute too.

But in this war everything is turned upside down.

July 3, 1940

The wrath of God has been vented on the Jewish community of Poland. By the force of the terrible edicts raining down upon it, one after the other, it has been reduced to the lowest level. Its human form has been completely erased. Besides expulsions, confiscations, attacks, which have not ceased to this day and which have become a continuing part of our lives, all sources of income have been blocked. We have become the slaves of slaves, and forced labor in one form or another is sucking out the marrow from our bones. We have been eliminated from human society.

This time America's aid is urgently needed to prevent starvation. An entire Jewish community is torn up by the roots and reduced to the last crust of bread. Eighty per cent are in need of charitable support. Yet it is at this very time that the Joint's support has stopped. This time philanthropic America has closed her generous hand and stopped giving us her gold and silver. First of all we look like panhandlers to them. The years 1914–1918 made a bad impression on them, because they couldn't tell whether our appeal came from poverty or was simple panhandling. An entire community that lives on charity no longer arouses sympathy and affection. When begging becomes a business, it ceases to strike a sympathetic chord in the hearts of those who give charity.

Second, the whole business of sending money is not worth their while, or ours. It amounts to nothing more than Jewish support for the conquerors. Every dollar, worth 150 zloty on the world market, is exchanged here in Poland at a rate of four zloty and 80 groszy. For whose benefit is all this activity? Large sums reached the Joint, but they were filtered out into the conquerors' hands.

July 4, 1940

In the past few months the sword of elimination has hovered over the head of the Joint. Rumors have begun circulating that it has no money, that it is in its death throes. The chaos and confusion in its procedure are unendurable. It is true that since its very beginning it has never had an organizer, but as long as the treasury was full the chaos was not so conspicuous. Now that it has become impoverished the Joint is a name devoid of meaning. Only the letters of the English initials, J.D.C., which no one knows how to decipher, remain.

With the disappearance of the rich uncle, we took our fate into our own hands and began to organize courtyard committees. It happens that I am the chairman of ours. The members of the courtyard committees live up to the requirements of their mission. Cultured individuals from all levels of the people have joined this charitable enterprise, and have devoted themselves to their work enthusiastically with no expectation of any reward. But they lack someone to direct and organize them, and this lack is detrimental to the entire project. In the face of rampant disorganization, the committee members are becoming disappointed and, filled with despair, are neglecting their work and going home. Here too the choice of leaders was wrong. They are mostly teachers and journalists, and they are hopeless, totally unable to organize a comprehensive project of this sort.

The project is still in its initial stages. Jews are approached for contributions and give. One gives more, another less, but almost all the inhabitants of the courtyard who have any material means at all, even those who make a meager living, make their contributions. But finally these contributors begin to ask: What is happening to our money? All we see are officials and more officials.

The real needy must wait for an interminable time before they manage to get a meal ticket for the soup kitchen, or a garment to cover their nakedness. It is not worthwhile to cite details, but it pains my heart to see an entire nation degraded, while it is, as it were, held in a prison from which it cannot escape. With all its shortcomings, Polish Jewry never holds back from feeding a starving soul. A tradition of compassion still exists. But the leaders have no experience at all.

July 6, 1940

Again we have the feeling that we are in a period of transition; or perhaps not we alone but the Nazis too. The armistice between the murderers and Pétain's France did not bring about any mitigation, did not engender an atmosphere of peace. On the contrary, the murderer is manifesting signs of inner conflict, of shattered nerves, of privation—and behold, a dream! England has decided to fight for her life. The two sides are fighting with aerial weapons exclusively, and so there is hope that England will not be at a disadvantage as she has been up to now in the battles on land. A rapid victory is no longer certain.

But if the war drags on we are doomed to destruction. As long as the murderer is drunk with his real or imagined victories, Jewry enjoys some respite; when he sobers up, and his soul is empty, the aggression against us, the product of his wrath, multiplies.

A new line of attack has appeared lately; it passes like a crimson thread throughout all sections of the German newspaper *Warschauer Zeitung*. The Jews are combatants and must be dealt with as enemy prisoners. As to the war itself, the Jews caused it, in order to bring destruction upon the Reich. England and the Jews are the two most dangerous enemies of Germany, and there will be no peace on earth until they are subjugated, etc., etc.

And therefore there are more terrible rumors of cruel edicts, which are destined to come to us in order to degrade and debase us still more. The agenda includes a ghetto, degradation to the point of strangulation.

It is difficult to foretell what will happen later on. The important thing is what already exists, or what is in the process of creation—and these prove to us that the pessimists are not mistaken.

July 8, 1940

All contact with the outside world has been stopped, even letters to relatives. An atmosphere of political tension, unrest, of expectancy of great events approaching, has been engendered. Meanwhile the rope around our neck draws tighter and tighter. Obviously, only around the Jews' necks. Apparently things are not going well for the murderers; and every time they are faced by trouble they expend their wrath on us.

The edict about "normal work" in the city, for which the conquerors have made the *Judenrat* responsible and which is known by the technical name of Labor Battalion, has been carried out with full force. As many as ten thousand men a day must be furnished to the conquerors by the *Judenrat*, for various temporary and accidental jobs, besides the hundreds of men seized from among Jewish pedestrians walking innocently in the streets. The *Judenrat* has set up a complete apparatus for this purpose, employing hundreds of clerks and supervisors. Every Jew from sixteen to fifty-five is required to report for work nine days out of each month. In order to increase the *Judenrat*'s income, it is not an absolute requirement; anyone who wants to be exempt from this labor requirement must pay a ransom of 60 zloty a month. It is a good source of guaranteed monthly income for the *Judenrat*. In general the conqueror attempts to increase the *Judenrat*'s income, since "whatever a slave owns his master owns." The murderers have burdened this miserable *Judenrat* with such demands that it is powerless to fulfill them; they have made it into a body of water without fish. Its treasury is empty, but the demands never cease. Unwillingly it supports itself from the misfortunes of the Jews. In the past few weeks fewer people have been coming to work, and so there was a threat. The unfortunate Czerniakow was summoned and warned: Speak to your *Juden* and tell them that if they don't come voluntarily, we will enforce to the letter every one of the stringent provisions of the decree. Czerniakow publicized that warning in every courtyard and the Jews are in turmoil.

One writer in the conquerors' newspaper freely admitted that in every country where Nazi rule is established, the Jews will not be allowed to survive. In such countries they will be completely eliminated. Even though the conqueror is still burdened with the worries of war, he does not forget about the Jews for a single moment; he remembers, always to their detriment.

This week another new edict was put into effect. Again hundreds of Jewish families are barred from the occupations that supported them; they will be impoverished. True to their program, the conquerors closed the printing houses owned by Jews, and as if that were not enough, they removed the presses and scattered the type

171

faces. Thousands more people are reduced to the last crust of bread.

This closure edict will henceforth be applied to the poorest of booksellers, those who peddle books in the street. In place of a store with neat shelves, their goods are on a wagon, out of doors near a street corner. Most of them are Jews. At first the conquerors permitted them to continue in business, ordering them to buy a license for their stand at a price of 150 zloty. So they paid. Now trade in books, even of this sort, is forbidden to Jews.

July 9, 1940

Everyone senses that it is only an accident when a day passes in peace, and therefore no joy is shown publicly about the newspaper item that describes a secret treaty made between Great Britain and the future "Government of Judea" concerning the establishment of a free Jewish state, which will be an English dominion. The oppressors' newspapers publicized it in every detail, and with all the appropriate jibes against England and the Jewish people, as is their evil custom. In normal times we knew how to respond to tidings of redemption, but not in these days. Because of impatience, hard labor, and physical and spiritual sufferings our hearts are consumed by doubt. First of all the news came from a rotten source, because only the Nazi press reaches us. Some say that the government created this rumor for the sole purpose of incitement against the Jews, so that the Arabs will hear about it and revolt against England. This is the opinion of the extreme doubters—no such treaty exists. On the other hand, there are some ardent believers who contend that the Lord's mercies have not ceased, that "out of the strong came forth sweetness," and that the process of the redemption of Israel which was interrupted in the middle has been renewed. The Balfour Declaration was the first stage. Now the second stage will begin. The Eternal will not break His promise.

The cynics question England's good-heartedness in suddenly losing her fear of the Arabs and beginning to show kindness to the Jews. Her strength is broken, her honor defiled. All her lovers, all who esteemed her, have left her. Her allies are fed up with her. Great Britain recognizes that her empire is soon to be dissolved, that a stronger enemy is standing at her gates, and so whatever she is giving away is not hers to give. She has become a philanthropist at the expense of others, and the whole treaty has no practical value.

The entire population senses that it is standing on the eve of some great political event that will totally change its life. There is no end to actual facts, as well as to fabrications.

The hangman's work is incessant.

In the past few days the hand of the cruel conqueror has dealt with us in an unusually cruel manner. The day before yesterday their newspaper announced that the mayor, Leist,[6] who is not cruel or despotic by nature, has issued an order forbidding the Jews to enter the city parks or the municipal promenades. The same applies to sitting on the benches outside them. In addition, certain streets have been set aside where Jews are forbidden to enter; these streets will be marked by signs which will be hung at the beginning of the streets. For the moment, the names of the streets sanctified by this special holiness are not known to us.

Today the frightening news reached us of the expulsion of the entire Jewish community of Cracow, and we are as if turned to stone. The magnitude of the catastrophe has weakened us, deprived us of the moral strength to begin the relief project which is so urgent that it cannot be put off for a moment. But in our great confusion we do not know where to start. We knew that some misfortune was imminent in Cracow, but at first its scope was limited to fifteen thousand refugees who were not natives of the city. Later we learned that its effect was being widened, and the expulsion edict would affect sixty-five thousand Jews. Finally it became known that the edict affects the whole Jewish community without exception.

The "Zyd"[7] newspaper raised the curtain on July 30 with appropriate caution, but every word tore our hearts to shreds:

Our moral duty directs us to clarify the full seriousness of the situation for the benefit of our readers. We must not arouse false hopes, and so we state the bitter truth all at once. It is the wish of the administration, first of all, to require the entire Jewish population to leave the city voluntarily up to the fifteenth day of August. If the Jews do not carry out this de-

[6] The Nazi administrator of the Jewish quarter of Warsaw.

[7] *Zyd* is simply the Polish word for Jew, but it has an abusive connotation.

parture by that date voluntarily, forced expulsion by the police will begin on the next day. The following will be the order of the expulsion: Each day a thousand people will be expelled; first of all, bachelors capable of doing work; next, young unmarried women; and lastly, entire families. Those who leave voluntarily will be able to take all their property with them; those expelled by the police will only be allowed to take 50 kilos of baggage a head.

In order to facilitate voluntary departure, all impeding laws in effect up to now will be suspended. First of all, the demand in effect until now requiring exiles to obtain an advance permit from the *Judenrat* prior to settlement will be eliminated. Based on this, all the territories of the General Government of Poland are open to the exiles. In addition, appropriate orders will be published concerning obtaining exit certificates, and concerning transfer of property by railroad.

Anyone who says that a liberal conqueror of this sort is cruel and barbaric is surely mistaken.

August 1, 1940

The Jewish people have always lived in material and spiritual straits. Our enemies have always engulfed us to destroy us. Yet Jewish creativity never ceased throughout all the days of our exile. Moreover, we created more in the lands of the Diaspora than we did in our homeland. This is the strength of eternal Judaism, that it continues to spin the fiber of our lives even in hiding. Every nation, in its time of misfortune, has conspirators who do their work in secret. In our case an entire nation has been raised on conspiracy. With others the conspiracy is political; with us it is religious and national. We have a special term for this concept: Marranos.

In these days of our misfortune we live the life of Marranos. Everything is forbidden to us, and yet we do everything. Every Jewish occupation is under a ban, yet nevertheless we somehow support ourselves; true, we do it with grief, but we do survive. Public social life has been stopped, but something can still be done in secret. It is impossible to have meetings with the consent of the conquerors, but the Lord of the Nation provided the remedy before the sickness, and the remedy is the soup kitchens, which serve us as meeting halls. After all, the conquerors are in a strange city. If they get no information from Jewish informers, they don't know what is going on.

On the twentieth of Tammuz we organized a memorial meeting

in memory of Herzl[8] and Bialik in the Zionist soup kitchen at 13 Zamenhof Street. We sat in little groups of three or four people at small tables, and various orators spoke, among them some guest speakers from among the exiles of Lodz and Galicia. Everyone sat with bowed heads and eyes filled with sadness, almost as if we were ashamed to look one another in the face. Gatherings of this sort don't enhance knowledge, but the custom persists, and that is the important thing.

August 3, 1940

Anyone who says that there are no exceptions to our general distress is in error.

In every revolution there are opportunities for advancement. Everything depends on luck, and on expert knowledge of the situation. New living conditions create new sources of income for the clever and industrious. The conquerors have sent their own appointees (commissars) into every wealthy and established Jewish business, which means that from the moment the commissar comes in, Jewish proprietorship of the business is ended. The stranger in charge is the only director of the business, and no one can lift a finger without him. The owner of the business is forbidden even to enter the premises. If the net income is sufficient, the owner of the firm, deprived of his business, receives a weekly sum for his own support. But he is always the last to receive, and his salary is by no means guaranteed. In this manner hundreds of Jewish businesses have been taken away from their original owners. It is to them a fulfillment of the curse: "Thine ox shall be slain before thine eyes."

Nonetheless, this is not universally true of all those taken over. There are firms whose Jewish owners have actually grown rich on the basis of arrangements they make with the supervisors. How? A business run by a commissar is entitled to get raw materials for manufacture at low official rates. These businesses buy cheaply and sell at high prices. By law, of course, the sale price is also low, but in practice this is not true. If the supervisor knows what he is about, he makes a secret agreement with the owner of the company, and both of them profit. Most of the supervisors are *Volksgenossen* who know the traditions of the country. A hint to them is sufficient.

[8] Theodor Herzl (1860–1904) was the founder of Political Zionism. The twentieth of the month of Tammuz is the anniversary of his death.

175

August 6, 1940

In times of trouble and hours of evil human beings are not particularly shy, merciful, or charitable. In our irritation, under the hammer blows of our great troubles, we have lost the good qualities for which our people were outstanding throughout history. A man who is embittered tends to become callous to those around him.

We have always paid last respects with particular generosity, and performed the last rites with charity. A public figure was not invariably honored in life, but whether he had worked with sincerity or not, he did receive a splendid funeral. Now, in the difficult days of the conquest, we have even been deprived of this "beautiful death." Every great man or leader of his people who passes on in these evil times is carried to his grave alone, with his death and burial unknown to anyone. Since there are no newspapers there is nowhere to publish death notices. Sometimes a notice is hung on the gate of the house—the wealthy Gentiles in particular have adopted this custom—but only a few individuals among the Jews had taken up this practice, and since the day the Jewish printing houses were closed, even these exceptional cases have stopped. For this reason, in a city as large as Warsaw, no one knows which of his acquaintances are still alive and which are dead. A famous doctor and writer like Gerszon Lewin, of blessed memory, was buried in the presence of only half a dozen friends and relatives. The same happened to Professor Dyksztejn, and to the president of the synagogue in Tlomackie Street, to Szabse Bregman, Dr. Jozue Gottlieb, and other respected and noted people who in normal times would have been accompanied to the cemetery by a great cortège.

August 8, 1940

The community of Cracow is going into exile. This is the wish of the rulers, and nothing happens against their will. There were unfounded rumors that the expulsion was postponed, but the most reliable source—the *Judenrat*—denies this.

The *Zyd* newspaper warns against rumors in its lead article, after which it publishes a notice from the *Judenrat:*

We are standing on the eve of a decisive moment in the history of the Jews of Cracow—of the exodus [they are afraid to say expulsion] of the Jewish community from Cracow. And this is not just a historical event, but a question of life, upon the solution of which the fate of

thousands of families, bone of our bone and flesh of our flesh, depends. So far the percentage of those leaving voluntarily is small. Goods are sent away, while the owners remain in the city. A departure of this sort will not solve the problem. And so we say to all the inhabitants of Cracow, whether natives of Cracow or refugees, natives of other cities, that it is worthwhile to avoid forcible departure, and that they should hasten to leave the city at once, for their own sake, rather than waiting until the last moment.

Those whose livelihood and occupation are not specifically tied to living in Cracow should be the first to leave: people who do not have steady work; the unemployed; those who live on cash; those who have relatives in the provinces, or friends and acquaintances who can support them until the end of the war.

If they do so, they will save their possessions, which they will be entitled to take with them, as well as saving their lives.

Whoever says the conquerors are not entirely humane is mistaken. On the contrary, they will do whatever they can to assist the departures. It is their desire to effect the departure of the Jews from the city without resorting to force, so that the exodus can take place in a humane manner.

For their part they are making many concessions and mitigations for those who leave. Those departing are exempt from paying the head tax. Landlords have been ordered not to withhold the possessions of Jewish tenants who have not paid their rent, so that people can take their goods with them. The savings banks have received an order to pay their depositors a suitable sum for traveling expenses. Lastly, certain sums will be set aside from the closed accounts for a departure fund.

In general, according to the aforementioned newspaper, the conquerors want the departure of the Jews to take place with suitable decorum, and peacefully (!), so as to leave no room for panic or confusion. Obviously, as always, there are exceptions to every rule. For the time being, in addition to the categories already mentioned, the expulsion edict does not apply to those who have jobs based upon contracts, which are registered with the social insurance office, with businesses that bring benefits to the city's treasury. Old people over seventy may remain in the city, as well as the seriously ill for whom the trip would be dangerous; so can orphans and sanitary personnel—doctors, dressers, nursing supervisors, and all other Jews who perform some sanitary-medical service. And so everything is fine.

A short time after the conquest of Warsaw they put the establishment of a ghetto on the agenda. All the preparations were made, and the *Judenrat* was even able to publish a detailed list of the streets where Jews would be forbidden to live. At that time we were not yet accustomed to such edicts. Every decree shook us to our very foundations, and the ghetto decree, which was the most severe of all, did so all the more. Then suddenly the matter was taken off the agenda. We were prepared neither for its appearance nor for its disappearance. The matter was forgotten. This is implicit in the very nature of the thing; whoever is saved from any misfortune tries to make others forget it and to forget it himself. Sufficient unto the day is the trouble thereof.

But the murderers think only of evil every day. They did not forget, it is only that they are putting it into effect a little at a time. The first step has just been taken for the establishment of a ghetto. In connection with this, the matter of the walls dividing the streets, which the *Judenrat* erected at its own expense, is now clarified. A rule has been laid down that, with a few exceptions, all the streets not cut off by a wall are outside the ghetto, and are forbidden to new Jewish residents. As I have said, it is not yet a total ghetto, but rather a half, third, or quarter ghetto.

A new order: the time has come for the closed shops to be reopened. The order says: Every landlord has until a certain date to furnish a list of all the closed stores in his buildings. A store that is open only from time to time is to be considered a closed store. This order caused turmoil among the Jewish merchants. Everyone wants to secure his stand for the days to come, for a merchant who has a store has everything; if he has no store he has nothing. At once they began to check and repair their stores. The sound of hammers never ceases throughout the day in ruined, desolate Nalewki Street. They are returning to rebuild the ruins and to resume business. But they do not make these preparations with complete confidence. The municipality gives a trade certificate to anyone who requests one—it makes no distinctions—but this in itself does not constitute a permit to run a business. Only the conquerors can issue a permit of that sort, and the Jew who invests sizable sums in repairing his store has no assurance at all that he will be granted a permit. So far two hundred and twenty-nine Jews, former merchants, have put in requests for permission to be merchants, while only seven have received permits. At the same time Aryans, without exception, can get one without any difficulty.

It must also be added that Jews may sell only to individuals: wholesale trade is completely forbidden to Jewish merchants.

From now on the newspapers will be able to say that Warsaw is beginning to revive. This will be just one more of the bluffs that the conquerors are so expert in creating.

August 12, 1940

The Eve of the Ninth of Av[9]

Public prayer in these dangerous times is a forbidden act. Anyone caught in this crime is doomed to severe punishment. If you will, it is even sabotage, and anyone engaging in sabotage is subject to execution. But this does not deter us. Jews come to pray in a group in some inside room facing the courtyard, with drawn blinds on the windows.

Today Aryans were seized for work! Their Tishe'ah Be'av came a day early, and they had a day of mourning today. These are the days of the grain harvest in the fields of the Reich, and for this reason innocent passersby are being caught like dogs in the street and sent to the harvest fields. So this has been a day of chaos, especially in the principal streets of Warsaw. When pedestrians disappeared from the streets after the hunt began, they stopped the trolleys and took the male passengers off, whether they were Poles or Jews. After personal interrogation the Jews went home and the Poles were imprisoned.

How good it is to be a Jew!

August 13, 1940

In whispers they are telling one another that the Führer has deigned to say that the Jews will be slaves of the Reich for twenty years. Before the war broke out he prophesied that if war came the Jewish race in Europe would be exterminated. His weakness lies in his prophecies. In his dispute with Churchill, too, he puts on the mantle of a prophet who knows the future, who foresees the end of days (but in his attempt to emulate a true prophet he has not yet deigned to tell what will become of *his* people in the end

[9] Tishe'ah Be'av, a fast day commemorating the destruction of the First and Second Temples.

of days). He foretells that the Jewish race in Europe will be eliminated, that England is nearing defeat, that all his enemies will be thoroughly driven from the earth, that Nazism will reign in the world for a thousand years. And in order for his prophecy to be fulfilled he has already begun to take the first steps in carrying it out: in every part of the conquered territory where Jews live he is forcing them to work at hard labor. In dozens of places in conquered Poland work camps have been created for thousands of Jews who expend their energies and abilities for the benefit of the Reich which spewed them out of it and made them into a thing to be trampled like the dust of the streets.

In Warsaw, the *Judenrat* obligated itself to furnish the conqueror with 8,000 working youths (up to the age of fifty-five) every day. The places of work are usually far outside the city, and the workers must go there and back on foot before and after work. They work eight and a half hours; if you add the two hours' walk it makes ten and a half hours of work for nothing a day. If you multiply this by nine, it comes to ninety-four and a half hours of work a month. And in order to know the over-all sum of hours of work which the Jews perform for their mortal enemies, multiply this by 8,000 for each month, and you will reach the enormous total of 7,260,000 hours of work. All of this is given by Warsaw alone. Using this as a basis, you can estimate what applies to every city and town.

August 14, 1940

Today at my apartment there was a gathering of friends who unexpectedly came to visit me. All were weighted down with worry, their faces lean and pinched, for all have been removed from their jobs. L. has lost 15 kilos. He is bent and crushed, full of despair: How long? When will it end? A whole year without income. He lives by miracles. When will his help come?

P. is an industrious and learned merchant who has read much and studied much and seen much. He was chief clerk of a German firm in Warsaw, his livelihood was assured. He lived in plenty. Right after the conquest of the city he was fired and given three months' pay. He endangered his life by fleeing to Russia. He was a fugitive and a wanderer, and after he had his fill of wandering he again endangered his life by returning. His severance pay is already entirely gone. He too lives by miracles. He waits for the Bolsheviks as for spring rains. His last few cents are disappearing

Next, my good and dear friend K. Formerly—that is to say, last year—he was a rich merchant. A beautiful apartment in Niecla Street. Luxurious furniture in four rooms. He was an official partner in one business and an unofficial partner in another—trips to resorts every year—patron and benefactor of Hebrew writers. And now? His apartment appealed to the conquerors, and they took it from him by main force. He was ordered to vacate within three hours, leaving his furniture. Both businesses disappeared. All income stopped. Fortunately he had some money. He went to live with his sister in a four-by-four room, and lives from his cash savings, which are diminishing. He eats without enjoyment because he is worried about tomorrow. He counts his money every day: how much longer will it suffice? His face is sunken, and his weight is diminishing from day to day. Can this be called life? He has one married daughter, and the couple fled to Russia. He is left alone. His eyes, too, are turned to the East. He is waiting for "them" as for the Messiah. What is your opinion? Will they come?

The fourth of them is my dear friend F., formerly head of an export firm, representing a firm in Danzig which is now defunct because it was owned by Jews. A wealthy merchant—learned, clever, industrious, wise in the ways of the world—he lived in comfort and plenty. Two years ago he set himself up in a beautiful apartment of six rooms in Senatorska Street. Friends and acquaintances greatly respected both in commerce and in public service and Zionism were his regular visitors—a life of ease and comfort. And now? At the time of the bombs and the bombardment his apartment was partially destroyed, struck by a grenade which made a ruin of it. As to the business, what is there to say? Everything is over and done with. He lives from the cash he saved.

And last of all—last of all in life as well—was the Hebrew teacher M., who is one of the best among the Hebrew teachers of Warsaw. Famous, respected, educated, he did not live in wealth in the past, either; his income was meager, but he was a man among men. Free in his actions, secure in his income, he followed his charted course: Hebrew cultural work in the Tarbut school. He never made much, but it was enough for his needs. His environment and his work provided him with material and spiritual fulfillment.

And I bow my head as if to say: I do not know my own fate—how do you expect me to know yours?

This gathering was Warsaw in microcosm. There are thousands, myriads like them. And in truth, what will be our fate? Who is wise enough to tell?

It is not for nothing that our ancestors coined the phrases: "Blessed be the Lord day by day!" "And what one nation in the earth is like thy people Israel?" Who else could bear as we do the burden of terrible sufferings and torments and yet stand upright and tell jokes? Nerves of brass would snap.

Anyone besides the Jews would stumble and fall under the burden of torment. Some of them would lose their minds; some would take to their beds; some would seek alms from door to door. That is natural. But we are fortunate in that we disregard nature. There is no increase in the number of lunatics in Warsaw; if there is it is only because of an influx of them from the provincial cities. In general, laughter is still evident. The youth goes on as always, busy with sports even when they are hungry.

A nation that can live in such terrible circumstances as these without losing its mind, without committing suicide—and which can still laugh—is sure of survival. Which will disappear first, Nazism or Judaism?

I am willing to bet! Nazism will go first!

Concessions have been made to the exiles of Cracow. The rulers want to have their cake and eat it. The *Zyd* newspaper, whose lips are muzzled, which dares not open its mouth, has perforce become their mouthpiece, and so when it expounds on the concessions made to the exiles of Cracow it depicts the ideal of the expulsion in such pleasant and comfortable terms that you forget the tragedy contained in its words.

Nevertheless, the Jews of Cracow are leaving their native city in great numbers. They are afraid to depend on miracles. The tragedy of Lodz has made those who look for miracles wiser. Those who fled in time experienced heaven on earth in comparison to the torments which the residents of the Lodz ghetto suffered: the torments of hell and damnation in the fullest sense of the word.

Having learned from this experience, the Jews of Cracow are hastening to leave the city before the last minute. Everyone wants to save his possessions while there is still time; everyone wants to escape from the eyes of the conquerors so as not to be registered with them.

But where can they go?

In Warsaw we expected a great stream of the exiles. Already the old slogans about "shrouds for the dead and bread for the living" rang in our ears, and those who stand at the helm of charity used the Cracow edict to inspire people to philanthropy. But it is noteworthy that not many of the Cracow exiles have come to Warsaw. They are few for two reasons. First, there is no spiritual affinity between natives of Galicia and natives of Congress Poland. They are of two entirely different types. Neither one is particularly pleasant; neither is outstanding for any particular virtues; but the main difference is one of education, manners, and culture. The Galicians are more cultured, more polite, more European. Civilized Austria educated them and left its European imprint upon them. With the Jews of Congress Poland it was different. All their lives they lived under the oppressive rod of Czarism, which pushed them into a gloomy, dark corner and left them as they were—without bread and without education, and anyone who doesn't have these things cannot be considered a civilized human being. The elimination of the border did not eliminate the spiritual barriers, which still exist even after political union. Two nations of one race in one state. Each has a different mentality; both have a divisive power which keeps them apart.

But this is not the only reason.

Warsaw has gotten a bad reputation in the world, and it must be admitted that it is merited. It makes a business out of anything which turns up. Such an inhuman attitude toward their brothers in misfortune has to a certain extent frightened the Cracow exiles; they refrain from coming to the Polish Sodom.

I must point out that they are doing the right thing: the Warsaw ghetto is full to the brim. The crowding is unbearable. There is no room for the Cracow exiles.

August 19, 1940

The "children's month" project cuts into our world, and the philanthropic noise is deafening. The capital city has been divided

183

into three quarters and my fate decreed that I live in the second, where the Galician Dr. Alter is director.

I am an insider who came from outside. I am not an official with a monthly salary, but I am mixed in with the philanthropic functionaries and, as such, am considered one of those close to the administration. The general impression: a country fair!

The Jews of Warsaw are asked and give. When there are charitable functionaries worthy of the name who know what they are up against, and who know how to lure donations, their work is not in vain. It is true that every cent costs them incessant work, because people give grudgingly; but nonetheless they do give. The public servants have adopted a new technique: Don't ask—demand. This is not charity, it is self-help. Everyone is a separate organ in the collective body known as the Jewish community. When one organ is afflicted, the entire body is afflicted. It is a continuous cycle in life. The enemy doesn't shoot us on the basis of a prior selection. We are all equal in his eyes.

The collectors passed over one resident named Goldman because he was known to be impoverished. They put him on the list of recipients. And this simple Jew was very hurt by this and came to express his protests before the courtyard committee for this slight. "How can it be," he said, "that I have a chance to do a good deed and am not allowed to? It is enough that the Lord has slighted me by keeping wealth from me. You don't have to add to it." And the committee was forced to accept his donation—two days of work a month.

But in contradistinction to Goldman, there are dozens of pigs who live and enjoy every comfort even in these evil times, people with money and large incomes, who have hearts of stone in place of hearts of flesh, and who find it difficult to give the smallest amount from their clenched hands.

Here is a case in point: In the middle of the Jewish restricted area there is one dance hall which is patronized only by Jews. Those people who think only of enjoying life even at a time of trouble go there to spend a pleasant evening. Besides drinks, they can enjoy Jewish music and songs. Yesterday four hundred tickets of admission were sold there at a price of four and a half zloty apiece, while the Self-Aid stamps that were sold among these comfortable people totaled 60 zloty worth. And that only after much pleading, entreaty, and exhortation.

August 21, 1940

Life is becoming too hard to endure. There is a rope around our necks which is being drawn tighter from day to day. We are strangling by degrees.

At the government headquarters in Cracow it was recently clearly stated: The Jews must leave Europe! The Cracow expulsion has come in order to purge the city of the Jewish excrement. What is left for us?

August 22, 1940

"Lowness of race" by itself is not enough for Nazism. It must furnish a pretext for a higher, more sacred aim, the exploitation of Jewish wealth. And so one of the aims of Nazism is to impoverish the Jews, to deprive them of all sources of income, to make them a nation dwelling in solitude. Thus a step is taken toward the establishment of a Jewish economic sector which should properly be impoverished, deprived of all strength.

First of all they instituted a supervisory administration, a veritable government monopoly on the products of the villages. It was the accepted practice for the villagers to bring their produce to the city, to the Jewish merchants, where they would make a double exchange. First they gave produce and got money; that was the first exchange. Afterward they came to the Jewish tradesmen and exchanged their money for city manufactures; that was the second exchange. These exchanges supported the Jews.

What did the Nazis do? They set up a barrier between the villagers and the urban merchants. The economics department of the Cracow administration supervises the various sorts of village products with seven eyes, and the law forbids a Jewish merchant to make contact with the villagers and purchase directly from them. The villager is required to bring his produce to stations set up for this purpose throughout the country. As I say, "the villager is required," but the villagers don't like it, and do it only out of fear. At the official stations prices have been fixed that are not worth their while, so the villagers hide whatever they can from the conqueror, and whatever they can smuggle past his eyes they sell in secret to Jewish merchants at salted prices. Both sides profit by this smuggling.

The Jews have also stopped being productive industrially. Into every Jewish factory worthy of the name the conquerors have

185

introduced supervisors, and so in practice their Jewish ownership is terminated. Every Jewish factory has a closed account. If there is a profit it is deposited into the account, but because it is closed, in the end the funds pass into the conquerors' hands. In this manner two ways in which Jews formerly supported both themselves and other people dependent upon them have been eliminated—salaries to employees and the various services rendered as artisans and tradesmen.

A third group is likewise deprived of their due—the landlords. All of them, without exception, have been deprived of their holdings. Rent is paid to the supervisor, and it is he who is in charge of all income and outgo for the courtyard. From now on rent will be paid on time. Everyone is afraid of eviction!

There is a fourth group which consists of the majority of the Jews of Poland. These are the storekeepers, whose stores were burned in the war or closed down for fear of the looters. Some of them are being reopened because the conquerors are forcing it by threat of confiscation, but not to sell clothing or other manufactured goods, only soda water, ice cream, and candy.

The supply and trade apparatus the Nazis established was set up to take from the Jews, not to give them anything. It was organized with a prior intention of reducing what they had without adding. The money circulating among the Jews in part goes from one Jew to another, but in the main goes from a Jew to an Aryan. Whatever a Jew pays to an Aryan never returns to him either in wages or for services rendered. This is a long, step-by-step process. It made no recognizable impression in its early stages, for sometimes an errant Aryan accidentally brought some profit to a Jew. But in its fundamental outlines, which are still somewhat hazy to us, it is undermining Jewish survival. After the lapse of a certain period of time, the ghetto, the restrictions, the legal disabilities, and all the other edicts will bring about the creation of a Jewish economic sector that will live its own isolated life until it crumbles. If you add robbery, looting, unbearable taxation, and forced labor to all of this, the picture is complete.

August 25, 1940

A Jew can sleep on the bare floor covered with a sheet of paper. The removal of all the furnishings and household goods of the merchant Lehr, who lives at 16 Nowolipki Street, took about three hours, because he was a rich man, with a fine house full of all sorts of nice things.

Before that the robbers had stopped next door and honored Dr. Lajfuner with their pleasant visit. They stole all the furnishings in one room. The robbery at the merchant Lehr's was unique even for these days. They left the man as naked as the day he was born.

Along with the looters came porters from among our Jewish brethren; these are regular porters who serve the Nazis regularly for pay. Not far from the scene of the crime stood street porters, likewise ready to serve their masters upon request, but in the past few weeks the Germans no longer invite Aryan porters from the street in cases of this sort, but rather take regularly hired porters who ride from place to place together with the robbers.

August 26, 1940

The Lodz ghetto, which is a prison for 100,000 miserable Jews who depended on miracles and did not leave the city while its gates were still open, has caused great fear among the unfortunate people of Cracow, and they are therefore not delaying their departure until the last minute.

The information in the hands of the Cracow *Judenrat* shows that in the past few days about 10,000 exiles have left the city. In view of the immense number of exit permits prepared by the government, it is to be hoped that in the time allotted for voluntary departure, all of those affected by the edict will leave. And so the conqueror has attained his shameful goal.

In the main, all Jews must leave the city except those who have a legal haven in one of the mitigating paragraphs of the edict, and who have put in an application based on it which was approved.

From Cracow back to Warsaw. The crown has been removed from Warsaw. It has become only a district city, while Cracow has been built up on its ruins—Cracow, which in the days of the Polish kingdom was only a provincial city. There are many reasons for this. For political reasons the conquerors did not want to maintain the administrative setup which existed before. It has always been the practice of conquerors of foreign lands since ancient times to mix up the internal boundaries. They set up different administrative areas in order to destroy what used to be, and to

187

create different local-geographic concepts. This is a means of establishing and strengthening a new regime.

But that's not all. The conqueror intended thereby to emphasize the fact that the former capital city of Poland is stamped with the imprint of Germanism. Cracow, which was in Austrian Poland before the conquest, fits into this purpose. Its culture is a German one. Ask the German historians, who carry out the wishes of Nazism, and they will prove to you with a hundred different proofs that since ancient times German culture has been the dominant one in Cracow. Its buildings, monuments, and memorials were built by Germans. Whatever was created that was fine and good in all of Poland in general and in Austrian Galicia in particular was fashioned by German hands. If you will, in all of Poland there are only ten million Poles. Nazi science has plunged deeply into the rushing waters and turned up no more than ten million. And it must not be suspected, heaven forbid, of being a false science. It is called "science" for this reason, and there are no proofs beyond those it presents. In view of all this, it is better to establish the government in a city which is half-German than in a city which is foreign in spirit to Germanism. There is a third reason for this choice: communications between the Reich and the conquered areas are easier and quicker between Berlin and Cracow than between Berlin and Warsaw.

The special merit of Cracow led to the destruction of the Jewish community there. A large Jewish population cannot be allowed to remain in the seat of the central government.

But even though Warsaw has been reduced from its political greatness, it does not mean that anything goes in regard to residence there. True, a formal ghetto complete in every detail has not yet been established, but the conquerors have taken the first steps toward fixing the ghetto boundaries. In matters of residence the city is divided into three quarters; a German quarter, an Aryan quarter, and a Jewish quarter. The Jews must leave the German quarter at once. And "justice" demands that they not be allowed to take their furniture with them. The Jews are rejected but their furniture is accepted. In the Aryan quarter, mainly inhabited by Poles, the only Jews permitted are those who already live there. But a Jew from the outside—that is, from another quarter or from another street in the same quarter—is forbidden to set up a new establishment. The status quo may remain, but there is no place for Jews there in the future. In the Jewish quarter, Poles who already live there may remain, but a Pole from the outside is forbidden to settle there.

The boundaries of the Jewish quarter are as follows: From Srebrna Street through Towarowa and Okopowa to Blonska; from Blonska to Stawki; from Stawki and Zoliborska to Bonifraterska and continuing along Bonifraterska-Konwiktorska-Wojtowska-Rybaki-Dekerta-Kollotaja-the Old Market-Swietojanska to the Palace Square. From the Palace Square the boundary leads through Senatorska up to the even side of Miodowa. From there through Krasinski Square to Swietojerska and Nalewki, and from there to Nowolipki-Tlomackie-Leszno-Bielanska-Senatorska-Rymarska-Zabia-Krolewska-Marszalkowska to Chmielna and from there to Srebrna.

August 27, 1940

There is no end to our scroll of agony. I am afraid that the impressions of this terrible era will be lost because they have not been adequately recorded. I risk my life with my writing, but my abilities are limited; I don't know all the facts; those that I do know may not be sufficiently clear; and many of them I write on the basis of rumors whose accuracy I cannot guarantee. But for the sake of truth, I do not require individual facts, but rather the manifestations which are the fruits of a great many facts that leave their impression on the people's opinions, on their mood and morale. And I can guarantee the factualness of these manifestations because I dwell among my people and behold their misery and their souls' torments.

And again I must point out that no day passes whose trials are not greater than those of the last. An entire community of 400,000 people is dying and its psychological state is approaching insanity.

The despots learned that the Jewish teachers are supporting themselves by teaching illegal study groups, and it is their intention to investigate and find out if they are teaching illegally. This causes more panic.

The Jewish carters have now become brothers in misfortune to the scholars. The conquerors became envious of them too, and their horses were taken, their permits voided. It is almost impossible to find a Jewish driver in the streets of Warsaw. They disappeared as though they had never existed.

And if this is not enough, there is the café edict! The best and most successful of the cafés will go to *Volksgenossen* as of the first of September, as happened with the former Jewish pharmacies. Some fine morning one of the *Herrenvolk* walks into your coffee shop and takes over your place. Because you belong to him, and whatever you have is his.

August 29, 1940

It is hard to believe, yet an actual fact cannot be denied. Especially when I myself bear witness to it.

I already knew that Jewish bookstores were forbidden to deal in German books. Their sanctity must not be defiled by the touch of Jewish hands. But that this ban applies to Aryan bookstores as well—that is, that it is forbidden to sell a German book to a Jewish individual who doesn't want it for commercial purposes, but rather for personal use—this no normal person could have imagined. It is the product of warped minds. I find it difficult to figure out the source of this ban: whether it is because of deep, infernal hatred or because of a psychopathic disease that is afflicting the minds of the Nazis. I wanted to order a German book through an Aryan bookstore and they would not accept my order because I am a Jew. The whole thing made me laugh, since I can get the book through other channels. But I was fascinated by the psychopathic side of this strange ban, which is in essence nothing but a stupid protest of hatred, because its practical effect is nil. There is a rumor circulating that this clever ban applies to Polish books as well, but I have not yet had an opportunity to verify it.

The forced-labor edict has finally been put into effect, and our cries reach the very heart of the heavens. This is the forced labor which the conquerors announced last winter, and for which they required all Jews from the ages of twelve to sixty to register, and then, later, to register a second time. This is not just work consisting of performing various services, like carrying loads and moving building materials or loading furniture. This is backbreaking labor draining swamps, building dams, paving roads, and combating floods. Only Jews are required to do this. The Jews will be common laborers without pay, and they will work under paid Aryan supervisors. In camps of this sort military discipline prevails and the workers there are treated like prisoners and criminals, sleeping in field tents and eating 25 decagrams of bread a day. Survival in such circumstances is hard even for strong Aryan workers accustomed to hard physical labor all their lives. All the more so for urban Jews, weak in body, who were never used to physical work in general and to hard labor of this sort in particular. It may be assumed that anyone entering a camp of this sort will never come out again. If he does, he will be completely broken.

September 1, 1940

The first anniversary of the outbreak of the war.

In this year of torments, Polish Jewry has been destroyed. Its property and holdings were confiscated; all sources of income were blocked; its ancient communities were uprooted and exiled; its cemeteries are piles of rubble; its human rights have been erased and annulled; its lives are worthless. Imprisoned, subjugated, and mummified in the narrow confines of ghettos, it is declining to the lowest level of human survival. This is an existence of dogs who lick bones under their masters' feet. Spiritual life is paralyzed. All the libraries, academies, and other buildings which were a haven for the Jewish spirit have been destroyed, and still the enemy is poised to torment us until we disappear from the earth entirely. This is not only in our own conquered country where we have been openly enslaved by the Nazis; the venom of Nazism is poisoning all the communities where the murderers have power. Depraved Rumania, wicked Hungary, audacious and filthy Czechoslovakia— wherever the influence of Nazism reaches, we decline from day to day.

"You Jews wanted a war—well, here is a war; but you will come out of it beaten!"

All of this in a single year. We were mistaken in assessing the murderers' strength, and were again mistaken in assessing our democratic strength. And all the small and great nations who have become working tributaries to Nazism were mistaken along with us. Together with the Jewish people, Poland too is turned into a cemetery.

Today on the first of September, the first anniversary, we were honored with a great holiday. Any time the conquerors celebrate a great victory you can't find a single Jewish soul on the street. This holiday has frightened everyone, especially the Jews. The Poles, too, gathered in their churches and sang the national anthem surreptitiously, with tears in their eyes. The wheel turns. They too are learning what it means to be Marranos.[10]

Theirs was a song of mourning, a sort of Kaddish[11] on the grave of Josef Pilsudski, whose name the conquerors have removed from the most beautiful and representative square in the capital city. Henceforward it will be named after the Nazi leader himself (Adolf Hitler Platz).

September 5, 1940

Watchman, what of the night? Everyone is hungry for news. This is partly because there were never so many Jewish unemployed as in these days. I would not be mistaken if I said that more than a hundred thousand Jewish young people in their very prime, and most anxious for work, are spending their days and nights in total idleness. Small groups of half-starved people, burdened with worries, with pained spirits and dulled eyes, strain their ears for any sound, and the rumors they catch pass in whispers from one to the other, making their way around as open secrets. You will never hear a rumor of good news for the murderers. Always they suffer defeats, always the sword is at their throats. The lying radio that the street corner idlers listen to on the sly builds lies upon lies, which are like a balm to their aching hearts. There are many ready customers for these lies. They want to believe them and so they do believe them.

Any time you meet an acquaintance you hear the stereotyped request: "Open your mouth and tell me what you know. Has anything new happened?" For if there is the slightest hint of any Nazi defeat or political setback it serves as a cure for our bones. A certain stubborn optimism has made its nest among the Jews, and we are all certain that the murderers' days are numbered, that the end of the despot and tyrant will be death. The God of Israel will not betray his people; he will not abandon them.

[10] A term applied in Spain and Portugal to baptized Jews and their descendants who were suspected of secret adherence to Judaism.
[11] The Prayer for the Dead.

CHAPTER
FIVE

September 10, 1940

THE CONQUERORS ARE true to their system. That is the reason they have a reputation in the world as followers of system. This quality of order among thieves has fathered some edicts that a normal man finds it difficult to comprehend.

September 13, 1940

The capital of Poland used to be a beautiful city. Since the Germans conquered it, it has become holy. Jews are forbidden to pass through certain places that are considered especially sacred, and not only on foot—the ban also applies to travel in a car or a trolley.

We have finally gotten an order about schools and vocational training centers for Jewish children. Three days ago Jaszunski came back from Cracow with the news in his pocket.

In the fashion of all the conquerors' orders, it is too ambiguous and too general. Until the regulations for carrying it out appear, we can make nothing of it, because it is totally lacking in programmatic educational information. There is no directive about language of instruction, and nothing about all the other pedagogical problems involved. All that is said is that the *Judenrat* must support schools for academic and trade education for Jewish children at its own expense, and in addition it must furnish teachers for these schools—meaning that it must establish a teachers' institute. Naturally, since these schools are to be supported exclusively by the *Judenrat,* they will be known as private schools. This title makes them ineligible to benefit from the municipal or government treasury. And Jewish children are not accepted in other schools.

Further, all that is spoken of is primary schools, that is, six-year elementary schools. High schools will remain closed in the future as well. Here there is no difference between Jews and Poles. The reason is obvious: a pupil over the age of thirteen is a candidate for forced labor. Besides, the Jews have no need of an intelligentsia to go around complaining and poisoning the Aryan world with their spirit.

For remembrance let me record this too: A rumor is going around that the head of the *Judenrat,* the engineer Czerniakow, received a letter from the conquerors in which there were seventeen paragraphs of new decrees for the Jews. But no one knows what they contain. For embellishment, people add that the engineer grew weak and fainted because of his great sorrow.

Another new catastrophe for the Jews lurks in this cryptic rumor. The details are the products of imagination, but the kernel of truth remains.

September 14, 1940

The conquerors are not always consistent in the matter of labor camps. Frank, in Cracow, once expressed his opinion, which was published in the newspapers, that the entire purpose of the labor camps is to educate—it is necessary to accustom a nation of procurers and middlemen to physical labor. But at the meeting at the *Judenrat* a few days ago we heard its main spokesman, Benjamin Zabludowski, say that in his dealings with the conquerors on the matter of forced labor the rulers promised that the workers would receive food, clothing, living quarters, and medical aid. It is not a punishment, but rather work for hire, because the workers are paid; they receive one zloty and 60 groszy a day. In reality the conquerors treat the workers like prisoners, and there is no food, clothing, living quarters, or medical aid. The camp is entirely dependent on the nearby *Judenraten* who solicit contributions and appeal to the compassion of the Jewish public. The Lublin region was selected for this evil because it has swamps and marshes to drain, forests to clear, and rivers and streams to dam up. The work period will last until November 1, but that is long enough to impoverish both body and soul.

Generally speaking, physical slavery is a new phenomenon for us, one that we never before experienced throughout our long years in the Diaspora. In Czarist Russia in the days of trouble and darkness, when slavery was a legal institution in the life of the state, the Jews were exempted. That was one truth which we attained through fire and water, because we felt ourselves to be free and did not allow ourselves to be chained.

Cursed Nazism now brings us physical slavery as well.

September 15, 1940

The publication of the order about Jewish schools after we had waited expectantly for a whole year has raised a storm among Jewish groups. The troubles that have rained down upon us have not weakened our argumentativeness or our partisan stubbornness. And it must be admitted that the conquerors' policies aid and abet this. They have segregated us as a separate ethnic group, and this separation has made us into a nation living alone with all its cultural, literary, and artistic attributes, which give us all kinds of spiritual satisfactions. Our autonomy has passed into the hands of the *Judenrat*, which has turned into a Jewish government in whose hands everything is concentrated. In normal times we demanded personal autonomy. Nazism has given us autonomy, but not of a personal kind; only a racial one.

The regulations for carrying out the school order have not yet been published, and no one knows its exact meaning because there is only a framework. Since the edict is brief and ambiguous, everyone wants to interpolate his own thoughts into it. Whatever one person postulates in his own mind he transmits to his neighbor as a positive fact. Hypothesis upon hypothesis is being developed, each contradicting the other. Wonder of wonders, even the absence of newspapers is no obstacle, and the ban on assembly doesn't frighten us. We run from meeting to meeting.

The education department of the *Judenrat*, which was closed and is now being reopened, will furnish jobs for hundreds of people. In this area too there is great activity. Big shots, middle-sized ones,

195

and small people race up and down the steps of the *Judenrat*. Who knows—to whom will the Lord show his mercies?

Because it is my duty, I am doing it: I am going to mention in in this entry a thing which does not exist as a fact, but which contains clear indications of a dangerous spiritual state.

Today a rumor is flying that Czerniakow, the head of the *Judenrat*, committed suicide, and that the reason for this desperate act was the seventeen edicts which the conquerors are about to direct at us. By coincidence, another Jew named Czerniakow died the same day, and so it was impossible to stop the rumor.

To the experts, the entire story seemed unlikely. First, who ever heard of a clever public official doing something so stupid? Our public servants may be accused of anything except love for the Jews. It is very doubtful whether Czerniakow's worry and pain over the general misfortune is so great as to be heartbreaking, let alone bring him to a state of spiritual depression so deep that he would commit suicide. As to Czerniakow himself, he is a mediocre man whose education and intelligence combine to make him something of a nincompoop; it is only through the misfortune of his people that he has risen to such eminence. Never before has he been so successful as in these evil hours.

So praise the Lord! "Our" Czerniakow is still alive. As to the seventeen edicts, nothing is clearly known; but if, heaven forbid, they are enacted, Czerniakow will assist in carrying them out, and his heart will not break, nor will he commit suicide.

This is a time of crisis for private schools. Teaching has been my occupation for more than thirty years, and I have stuck with it in good times and bad. But I find that the present moment is the most difficult I have ever experienced.

The conquerors do their work calmly. An inspector for Jewish education has already been appointed, and Czerniakow has appeared before him. Czerniakow wanted to press the administration to spell out its orders, but the entire matter has been put off until the first of October.

Private education is really tottering on the brink. It has no friends or supporters, and no one wants it to survive except the school owners whose income depends on it.

Another psychopathic edict. A ruler with any intelligence could never make laws of this sort. The new order states that a Jewish doctor is not authorized to treat Aryan patients, and an Aryan doctor is not authorized to treat Jewish patients.

A reason is given: It is well known that contagious diseases are prevalent primarily in Jewish areas. If an Aryan doctor serves Jewish patients, there is danger of spreading the disease from one quarter to another. The Jews laugh heartily at this stupidity. It was common for Jewish patients to go in great numbers to Aryan doctors, but this was never so in the case of Jewish doctors and Aryan patients. The latter rarely come to Jewish doctors. So who will lose by this? Obviously the Aryan doctors.

This peculiar order makes no distinction between patients with contagious diseases and those with organic diseases. Jews with heart or lung trouble who were being treated by Aryan doctors must now leave the doctors who devoted themselves to their cure and go to a Jewish doctor. This ban applies to dentists and midwives as well.

This is a preview of the Europe of the future. A partition between one people and the other.

September 20, 1940

Pious Jews who pray in secret will sense tomorrow a new meaning in the portion of the Bible known as the Tokhehah,[1] for all its curses seem to have been fulfilled in us. Sometimes you read a portion of the Bible and understand it; sometimes you read it and feel it. And feeling and comprehension are not the same. Feeling includes comprehension. Sometimes you suspect the Nazis of reading the Tokhehah and using it as a guide.

Up to now there was the furniture trouble. Without notice they came and took the table while you were still eating at it, and the chair while you sat in it. Lately they have gone from the furniture to the apartments themselves. We were sure they would not touch

[1] Literally, warning or admonition. Leviticus 26:3–40 and Deuteronomy 28:14–45.

197

our ghetto apartments. Since no Aryan is allowed to live here, who would need them?

Jews who are eyewitnesses to these incidents begin inquiries— for what purpose was this abomination committed? They learn that in the Aryan quarter a Polish apartment was confiscated by request of a German who wanted it. To provide alternative quarters for the Pole, they confiscated a Jewish apartment. Here too we ask why. Is it not after all forbidden for an Aryan to move into the Jewish quarter? It is hard to find an answer to our question.

September 23, 1940

The *Judenrat* at 26 Grzybowska Street has become the center of life for Polish Jewry. Up to now the Joint occupied first place, and everyone ran to receive at Jasna Street. But when the Joint became poor it lost its importance. No one turns to it and no one waits at the director's door.

The crowding in the halls of the *Judenrat* increases from week to week, even though there they come to give. They give by force, meekly, humbly—but there is no choice because a Jew cannot lift a finger without the *Judenrat*'s approval. Posting of signs requires the permission of the *Judenrat*; railroad travel permits are given by the *Judenrat*; the Labor Battalion is handled by the *Judenrat*—it is the one empowered to send people to labor camps or to liberate them. New taxes have been imposed on the Jewish population and they are collected by the *Judenrat*. The *Judenrat* has turned into a Jewish government, and by order of the conqueror it must now perform governmental functions of a sort that it was never prepared for.

Until recently the *Judenrat* also had a Jewish police force. It wore special badges and was in charge of everything. A few days ago the conquerors stripped it of the insignias of office and its members returned to being ordinary laymen.

September 24, 1940

The president of the *Judenrat* tried again to request a clarification of the school order. This time he made a written application, and an appointment was granted for a somewhat earlier date—the twenty-fourth of September. At the time of this writing, no one knows anything yet. But if there were no hitches, and the appointment took place as planned, we will know the details tomorrow.

We ourselves do not know what is the best course. Will we be better off remaining independent and holding on to our individual proprietorship of private schools, which we will find difficult to run and support—or will we be better off accepting the patronage of the *Judenrat*, which would include our schools in its network and make us into salaried teachers?

In my old age I must change my skin. Instead of being a landlord I shall become a hired hand. But there are two sides to the question.

September 25, 1940

Today private education suffered its first defeat, and the defeat may be charged to my account, because I was the commander and guide of the operation entrusted to me. Some time ago we elected a group of representatives, and five of those chosen became the executive committee. I was its chairman. We went to work—first of all, to inform the *Judenrat* of our existence and organization. I took up the writer's pen and wrote a letter in Polish. Three members were chosen to present the letter, myself among them. Professor Majer Balaban received us and promised us his moral support. He will present the matter to the president in a favorable light. Since my letter lacked a statement about the ideological aspect of the private schools, it was necessary to compose a supplementary letter. This task too was imposed upon me, and Bornsztejn gave it to the *Judenrat* secretary, Hornsztejn, who was formerly the secretary of Ivriah, when I was its vice-president. I used to be his superior—an honorary official—and he, a poor clerk, was servile and always ready to do my bidding. Now the worm has turned. Dozens of people camp on his doorstep, and I among them. When he began talking with me he was neither hot nor cold. Every word was weighed, every statement thought out in advance; he was polite, but without any sign of friendship or amity. It is as I have said—even the best among men become rotten when they get power and become rulers. But that is not important.

Suddenly I found out through L. Bornsztejn of 7 Twarda Street that at 5:30 today a conference would be held at the *Judenrat* in which representatives of the various "trends" in Jewish education would participate. Even before this, Bornsztejn had begun demanding that Hornsztejn permit the representatives of the private schools to take part in this meeting. Hornsztejn suggested that a letter to the president be prepared, and he would give the letter to him before the meeting. That was what we did. I was appointed a representative. I went with Bornsztejn to the meeting, and we were almost certain that our request would be granted and I would be allowed to take part in the meeting. But we were wrong. I had to wait in the corridor in disgrace. We met our big shots there, the representatives of a poor and downtrodden people, who showed us Sphinx-like faces. We tried to talk with those who had been closest to us, and found them distant. Deaf and ineffectual Balaban showed us that he is at a loss, unable to help. A. Wolfowicz replied to my greeting in a low voice, avoiding my eyes. Some advisers went into the president's room and apparently conferred on the matter. After a short time Hornsztejn came out and informed us that we could not participate in the meeting. Insignificant representatives of some party schools were allowed in, but for the representatives of dozens of schools with thousands of pupils there was no room.

The private schools have no friends or supporters. Everyone wants to build himself up on their ruins. We have suffered our first defeat. But it is only the first battle; we must not despair. Things will change to our advantage. Today our president returned from his visit to the *Schulrat* and apparently he has made some progress.

September 26, 1940

Yesterday there was a joint meeting of *Judenrat* advisers and the representatives of the schools sponsored by the various religious and political parties. This is the meeting I mentioned in my last entry, which I was not permitted to attend. The most important thing is that it was decided not to interfere with the private schools. They will be allowed to continue on their own in the future, with no support whatever from anybody, but they will require permits from the *Judenrat*, and must submit to its supervision. The *Judenrat*'s decision makes sense.

The business of the ghetto is cropping up again. When we remember what happened to the Lodz ghetto we are seized by fear. It is a prolonged agony, a lingering death. We have some consolation in the fact that Warsaw, unlike Lodz, has not been made a part of the Reich. But these psychopaths are capable of anything. They punish the Jews for their great crime in fathering Hore-

Belisha in England and Blum in France. The English-Jewish notables sin and the Jews of Niska Street are beaten.

I wanted to sit quietly for one evening without making an entry,
but the wrath of Japan has jumped upon me. Up to now Japan had
never entered into our political calculations. We knew that she
was powerful and had learned from Germany; we knew that she
was somewhat fascistic and somewhat Nazistic, and that she had
recently made changes of personnel in her foreign ministry, changes
in a direction favorable to the aggressors—and that she leaned
toward them. We knew likewise that she is an enemy to her neighbor, North America; and finally we knew that she has been fighting China for two years, and has been making herself at home
there. But these were matters of journalistic politics which had no
connection to real life.

Again it must be admitted that the murderers have scored a great
political victory, for even the politicians in Pawia and Niska streets
could never have imagined this.

Mighty England is left alone and is fighting with what may be
her last strength against a bitter opponent. North America has been
a friend, and has actively shown its affection by supporting her
in a material way. There was basis for the hope that sooner or
later, before the end, when the decisive moment came, America
would stand openly beside England and declare war against the
Führer.

But now, a new diplomatic victory has come like thunder on a
sunny day.

Japan, America's enemy, is threatening her explicitly: If you dare
go to war against my ally Germany, I will stand at her right hand
and my sword will be against you!

Could there be any more depressing and insulting threat?

The Japanese calm the Soviets by telling them that the Tripartite
Agreement was not, heaven forbid, directed against them. The
Tripartite Agreement has a splendid and lofty political objective:
to promote peace in the world. They made secret council between
themselves to make a "new order" in the world—Nazi-Fascism in,
Europe and Oriental Nazism in Asia. Anyone wishing to join forces
with them is welcome. But anyone going to war against one of the

201

three will be attacked by all as one. A clear and explicit allusion to America.

There is no doubt that a decisive moment in the progress of the war is drawing near. Who can foresee its results? I imagine America must be in turmoil. This is an audacious provocation that only an aggressive power would dare to state openly against all nations and peoples.

How will America react? And the Soviets? There is a rumor that neither America nor Russia is sitting idle, and that they are conferring together to rise against the Tripartite Agreement, but we have not yet been informed of this.

If Russia declares war on Germany, we are lost.

September 28, 1940

The prohibition against riding the trolleys with Aryans goes into effect tomorrow. The order has already been published. Jews will be able to ride only in cars marked "For Jews," because two different species must not mingle.

But not every trolley will have a car of this sort. They say that a Jewish car will be added on to every third one, and you will have to wait half an hour until your Jewish car arrives. But the Jews are not upset: "May this be only the last of our worries!" A disgrace? "The disgrace is not yours, but rather your tormentor's."

October 2, 1940

The Eve of the New Year, 5701

We have no public worship, even on the high holy days. There is darkness in our synagogues, for there are no worshipers—silence and desolation within, and sorrow looking on from without. Even for the high holy days, there was no permission for communal worship. I don't know whether the *Judenrat* made any attempt to obtain it, but if it didn't try it was only because everyone knew in advance that the request would be turned down. Even in the darkest days of our exile we were not tested with this trial. Never before was there a government so evil that it would forbid an entire people to pray. But never before in our history, drenched in tears and blood, did we have so cruel and barbaric an enemy.

Everything is forbidden to us. The wonder is that we are still alive, and that we do everything. And this is true of public prayer, too.

Secret *minyanim*[2] by the hundreds throughout Warsaw organize services, and do not skip over even the most difficult hymns in the liturgy. There is not even a shortage of sermons. Everything is in accordance with the ancient customs of Israel. When there is no informer at work, the enemy doesn't know what is going on, and we can assume that no Jewish man, even if he is a Jew born in Poland, would inform on Jews standing before their Maker in prayer.

They pick some inside room whose windows look out onto the courtyard, and pour out their supplications before the God of Israel in whispers. This time there are no cantors and choirs, only whispered prayers. But the prayers are heartfelt; it is possible to weep in secret, too, and the gates of tears are not locked.

And so we give praise to the God of Israel "who kept us alive and supported us and brought us unto this season." During the year many individuals drank the cup of hemlock; many have gone to their graves. The community has been debased and impoverished. But it still exists.

October 3, 1940

The Eve of the second day of the New Year, 5701

The fear of a ghetto has passed. A rumor is widespread that the matter has been postponed—some say for a month, others say for three months. But the very thought of a ghetto has left an impression on our nerves. It is hard to live in a time when you are not sure of tomorrow, and there is no greater torture than waiting. It is the torture of those condemned to die.

And therefore, even now that the matter of the ghetto has been put off, we don't feel ourselves saved. It is not yet complete redemption. I was told that the *Judenrat* had sent a delegation to Cracow about the ghetto, then it was said that the central government knew nothing of a ghetto. It is hard to believe that. But whatever the true situation, for a time we are "saved."

October 4, 1940

Today an order was issued requiring all Aryan maids working for Jews to register. This registration is a prelude to the ban which

[2] Literally, *minyan* means number; the reference is to the number ten, the requisite number of men for congregational worship.

is coming next. It won't be long before Aryan (read Polish) maids will be forbidden to work in Jewish homes. This ban will hurt the Jews less than it will the Aryan women whose livelihood depends on the Jews. Many of them will be left without work, and many of them will go to Polish slavedrivers against their will. At the Aryans' they are handmaidens; at the Jews' they are helpers.

At heart the conqueror hates the Poles more deeply than the Jews. Once the head of the Warsaw district, Dr. Fischer, said, "The Poles we hate instinctively; the Jews we hate in accordance with orders."

The Jews make fun of this decree too: "That's just fine. Now Jewish girls will get their jobs."

October 6, 1940

Within the walls of the *Judenrat*, hidden from prying eyes, Jewish education is being established.

But the matter is not so simple and easy to effect as it might seem to an outside observer. The tired and worried *Judenrat* does not want to undertake a new allotment to support the schools. It was suggested that a special tax be imposed, but no one is sure that the tax would be collected in full and thus be enough to guarantee the education budget. The hospital tax is being collected only with great difficulty, and it is impossible to be too harsh in dealing with people who are totally impoverished. And if they despair of collecting the taxes that already exist, should they now impose new ones in addition?

The president of the *Judenrat* sees himself as a leader, and is not subservient to anyone. He is not sentimental about parties either. You want your own schools? Fine! I approve wholeheartedly. For my part, I will give you all manner of sympathy, except sympathy which involves money.

Even before the schools were set up, a dispute broke out between the teachers and the *Judenrat* about salary scale. The teachers' union had set a minimum wage of 300 zloty a month. This is a semi-starvation salary, and is especially small considering the current inflation; but the president, who is having a lot of trouble meeting the *Judenrat*'s budget, will not agree to such "high" salaries at a time like this. He offers, instead of 300, only 130 a month for the teachers.

Are you any better, he argues with the teachers, than the lawyers and other people with higher education who work in the *Judenrat*'s offices and get only five zloty a day? Their work is temporary; yours is steady.

When they heard this the teachers were furious with the president. No teacher will report for work.

Jewish Joke I:

The Germans are beating the Jews because England doesn't want to make peace; the Poles are beating them because the same England did not prepare herself properly for battle and is being defeated.

Jewish Joke II:

The Führer asks Frank, "What evils and misfortunes have you brought upon the Jews of Poland?"

"I took away their livelihood; I robbed them of their rights; I established labor camps and we are making them work at hard labor there; I have stolen all their wealth and property."

But the Führer is not satisfied with all these acts.

So Frank adds: "Besides that, I have established *Judenraten* and Jewish Self-Aid Societies."

The Führer is satisfied, and smiles at Frank. "You hit the target with the *Judenraten*, and Self-Aid will ruin them. They will disappear from the earth!"

Jewish Joke III:

Frank has ordered that on the Day of Atonement, 5701, the Jews of Cracow must open their stores for business.

One day out of the year he allows the Jews to do business.

Frank came to Warsaw to inaugurate the aid project for next winter. Notices written in German in huge letters joyfully announced his arrival. *Volksgenossen* were ordered to hang out flags in honor of the guest. German Warsaw was jubilant.

And do not be surprised when I say "German Warsaw," even though its German population is only a negligible minority. Here quantity is not important, quality is the determinant. One German outweighs a thousand Poles and tens of thousands of Jews.

The Germans have the power now, and they are the real lords of the city. The war broke out for their benefit, and they were a main political cause of the conquest of Poland and its loss of sovereignty. The whole world was created just for them. Poland is no longer Polish even ethnographically. Don't ask where twenty million Poles disappeared to! German science which serves Nazism has caused them to disappear—and not more than ten million Poles can be found. And those who remain are obviously not worthy to rule. As for the Jews, they don't count at all. They are cattle. When the conquerors' newspapers wrote about Lodz and its industrial development they didn't mention the Jews even obliquely. It was as if they had never existed.

Frank's coming made no special impression on the city. They didn't turn out to see him and his companions; in fact the population pretended not to notice him. Everyone ignored this tyrant whose wickedness and cruelty are even greater than that of the Führer. This is good. It is a sign that the Poles have a political sense. Even though great military and political changes bode ill for their future, they remain stubborn. You will not find one single public-spirited citizen among them who is willing to be the conquerors' representative, to talk to his people and make them realize that they cannot change reality and must accept the yoke of German rule—like Hacha in Czechoslovakia and Quisling in Norway. We could also add Pétain in France, that stupid old man who willingly said Kaddish for his country.

October 10, 1940

Clouds are covering our skies. Racial segregation is becoming more apparent each day.

Yesterday an order was published that the Jews must make way before every German, both soldiers and civil servants in uniform. Making way means that the Jews must step aside until the Germans leave the sidewalk. You must always keep your eyes open and guard yourself against daydreaming and conversation lest you fail to do the proper honor to a Nazi you encounter. Today we have already had our first victims, who were beaten because of the order. You go out trembling, full of panic lest you meet a Nazi.

All people whose ancestors did not stand before Mount Sinai are allowed to walk in the streets until eleven at night. For Jews outside the walls, the curfew is seven; inside the walls, nine. In the morning, no Jew who lives outside the walls can be on the street before eight.

The Jewish trolley is a mockery of the poor. Trolley cars with white trim (for Aryans only) with two cars pass by empty, while dozens of passengers wait at the stop; no one dares to enter the empty cars because it is not a Jewish trolley. In the Jewish tram, the crowding and pushing make it almost impossible to breathe. No one standing can sit down, and no one sitting can get up. The passengers neither sit nor stand, but rather hang—it is like the plague of darkness in the land of Egypt. There is no filthier place, capable of spreading contagious diseases, than a Jewish trolley on a single ride, where everything is infected, when sick people sweat and slobber on you.

Yet with all this the Jews are "content with their lot," and say decisively that the maximal evil has not yet come, that there is some sort of psychological barrier preventing the conquerors from pouring their full wrath upon us. Here the Jews surmise: What will happen to us when a new war breaks out between the conqueror and Russia-America? Then we will simply be eradicated. The Bolshevik land will again be called a Jewish state, and the United States all the more so.

October 12, 1940

End of Yom Kippur, 5701

On the New Year we prayed illegally. The ban on communal worship was still in effect. In secret, in side rooms near the dark, closed synagogues we prayed to the God of Israel like Marranos in the fifteenth century.

But one day before the eve of the Day of Atonement the *Zyd* newspaper reached us from Cracow, bringing us permission for communal worship. This permission was not unconditional, however. It is still forbidden to pray publicly in the synagogues, and they remain locked. The law was relaxed only to permit communal worship in small groups in private homes, on condition that they don't make noise and that there is no crowding.

The Jewish community of Warsaw left nothing out in its prayers, but poured its supplications before its Father in Heaven in accordance with the ancient custom of Israel. To our great sorrow, as the day drew to a close, at a time when the gates of tears were still open, we learned that a new edict had been issued for us, a barbaric edict which by its weight and results is greater than all the other edicts made against us up to now, to which we had become accustomed.

At last the ghetto edict has gone into effect. For the time being it will be an open ghetto, but there is no doubt that in short order it will be closed. In Lodz the ghetto edict was not carried out all at once, but rather step by step, and many signs indicate that it will be the same in Warsaw. After the ghetto plan was postponed two weeks ago, we were almost tranquil. But the enemy of Israel neither sleeps nor slumbers.

This new edict was issued in a somewhat humane form—perhaps for the sake of world opinion—but we know that in its new form it is still the last link of the chain of troubles and misfortunes.

Before the thirty-first of October the Jews who live in the streets outside the walls must move lock, stock, and barrel to the streets within the walls; and all the Aryans (read Poles) living in the streets within the walls must move to the Aryan quarter. To a certain extent the edict has hurt the Poles more than the Jews, for the Poles are ordered to move not only from the ghetto, but from the German quarter as well. Nazism wants to separate everyone—the lords by themselves, the underlings by themselves, the slaves by themselves. The blessed and the accursed must not mingle.

A hundred and twenty thousand people will be driven out of their homes and will have to find sanctuary and shelter within the walls. Where will we put this great mass of people? Most of them are wealthy, accustomed to beautiful apartments and lives of comfort, and they will be totally impoverished from now on. Their businesses and livelihoods were directly connected with the areas where they lived. In leaving their homes they are also leaving their incomes.

The Gentiles too are in mourning. Not one tradesman or storekeeper wants to move to a strange section, even if it be to an Aryan section. It is hard for any man, whether Jewish or Aryan, to start making his life over. And so the panic in captured Warsaw, occupied by harsh masters, is great. As I have said, for the time being we are in an open ghetto; but we will end by being in a real ghetto, within closed walls.

Hundreds of Germans are coming in, refugees from the English bombs, half-mad women with their children. They complain angrily to their fat, comfortable relatives who are enjoying the spoils of a strange land out of all danger. An eyewitness reports that a German soldier dared to write these words on the wall of one of the trolley cars: *"Wir fahren hin un her. Wir haben kein Heimat mehr!"*[3]

Maybe this is the beginning of the removal of the yoke which Churchill is trying so hard to accomplish.

October 14, 1940

There is a rumor that in one of the congregations the prayer leader came and dressed himself in a kittel and prepared to lead his poor and impoverished people in the *Neilah*[4] service, when a boy from his congregation broke in with the news about the ghetto. At once that Jew dispensed with *Neilah*, took off his kittel, and went back to his seat. There was no point in praying when the "Gates of Mercy" were locked.

Has Israel no God? Why has He refrained from giving us aid in our time of trouble?

Even if we use Isaiah's expression, "a day of trouble and of trampling, and of perplexity," we are not fully emphasizing the nature of this "day of atrocities." Nothing like it has ever happened since the day I first settled in Warsaw, forty years ago. The wrath of the conquerors and of our God is poured upon us at once. There were days when I thought that the words of Isaiah were only rhetorical phrases. Today I know that his cruel prophecy is fully realized.

A ghetto has finally been created for the Jewish community in Warsaw, in which there are about half a million Jews. For this ghetto, a place of refuge for tens of thousands of people, a small quarter has been designated which is destined to become a place ripe for all manner of atrocities and evil deeds. This quarter of narrow, crowded streets is full to capacity with refugees from the provincial towns. There is no room in the ghetto—not an empty crack, not an unoccupied hole.

[3] "We ride back and forth. We have no more homeland!"

[4] Literally, closing; the last service of Yom Kippur, the Day of Atonement.

I gazed at the Dantean scenes in the streets of Warsaw, and could not stop thinking: Are we really guiltier than any nation? Have we sinned more than any people? Will we really die? Are we doomed to total destruction? Nobody in the world is concerned for us, nobody shares our plight.

All day long I thought it over. Should I write? Not because of a lack of impressions, but because of too many of them. Only a divinely inspired pen could describe them accurately on paper. A mere writer of impressions could not adequately record all that happened in the boiling chaos of Jewish Warsaw in the first days of the Sukkot holiday, 5701.

Today the official order was published about the ghetto, but the rulers are wary of calling a spade a spade. Instead of a ghetto, which is a medieval concept, they call it a "Jewish quarter." And the fact that the same order refers also to a Polish quarter and a German quarter is supposed to be a sign that the enemy treats them all alike. He even gives a "humane" reason for the creation of the Jewish quarter—because there are so many victims of the epidemics, especially in the Jewish streets, these areas must be quarantined. We know very well that what they are saying is a lie, but we have no way of testifying to the contrary before them. They have doomed us to silence, and we are still.

The publication of the official order has settled all doubts, but to our disadvantage. They took streets away from us that have been Jewish since ancient times, and which no one imagined would be outside the boundaries of the ghetto. Walls had already been erected at the end of them, and this was taken as a clear indication that they would be within the boundaries.

A closed ghetto means death by starvation in a concentration camp with inhuman living conditions. All of the Jewish quarter will be fenced in with walls and barbed wire, and at the gates will be the sword which turns every way, to prevent the prisoners from escaping. In a closed ghetto everything is locked and bolted. No one enters or leaves. Anyone who tries to flee risks his life. The guards of the ghetto do not permit the farmers from the villages to bring any food in through its gates. Babies ask for bread and there is none. In the Lodz ghetto no one had anything hot to drink or any cooked food because there was no wood for fuel. They paid ten zloty for a kilo of onions. The people of Warsaw, who are clever, are laying in provisions to be ready for whatever misfortune may come, and for this reason prices have gone up.

October 18, 1940

When the ghetto was established, we thought we would have things a little easier. After all, this is an infested place in their eyes, and a Nazi would hesitate to risk his life. But here again we were mistaken. There is no more likely place for robberies and murders in broad daylight than the ghetto. Here there is no seeing eye, or listening ear. The Aryans have left, and the Nazis are not ashamed before Jews, who are not considered human.

October 22, 1940

The creation of the ghetto is accompanied by such severe birth pangs that they are beyond description.

When it came time to carry out the ghetto order, everything became chaotic. The Polish side began to haggle—in this suburb they have a church; another is mainly inhabited by Aryans; here is a beautiful school building; there is a factory employing thousands of Aryan workers. How can the rightful owners be driven from all these places? Thus they excised piece after piece, street after street, of the Jewish area, and the boundaries of the ghetto grew more and more constricted.

Even after the official notice was published, and the boundaries of the Jewish area set forth in detail, changes were made the next day. And in this manner thousands of Jewish families lived in panic, imprisoned between hope and fear.

Some unfortunates have been doubly punished. On the strength of the edict they vacated their apartments in the Aryan quarter and took new apartments in the Jewish quarter. The next day they learned that their new apartments too were out of bounds. Thus they must vacate this one as well, and look for new quarters. The inhabitants of the doubtful streets are running in despair to the *Judenrat*. The *Judenrat*'s advisers advise them to wait. But they are afraid to wait. The miserable Jews do not want to postpone the moving of their furniture to the last minute; when it comes to

211

Jews even the time set in the decree is of no importance. The conquerors come and remove them from their apartments before the stated time and do not allow them to take anything at all with them. If we were to observe the conquerors' edicts literally we would die in a day. By law a Jew is not permitted to remove the furniture when he vacates his apartment; in practice, however, the streets of Warsaw are full of carts loaded with furniture.

The *Judenrat* is powerless to grasp the helm in these events. It is true that it has the power to use force, but it is not always desirable or possible to use force. Our troubles are unhinging our minds and weakening our powers of judgment, and in our despair, we do not obey the orders of the *Judenrat*, thus making its work, which is so full of responsibilities, all the harder.

Several days ago the *Judenrat* furnished a questionnaire to all the courtyard committees in which they were asked to give detailed replies to questions about the number of apartments, the number of rooms in each apartment, the number of tenants, and the prices of apartments. On the basis of this information they will confiscate vacant rooms and settle homeless people in them. How many people will be assigned to each room? Some say four, some say six. And so the people are hurriedly renting out rooms to tenants of their own choice. Incidentally, they are raising the rents sky-high. They are afraid that the *Judenrat* will match them up with the wrong people and make them stick to the prescribed rents, so they are hurrying to beat the *Judenrat* to the draw.

Statisticians calculate that a hundred and forty thousand Aryans will vacate their apartments in the Jewish section, and that about a hundred and fifty thousand Jews will have to leave their apartments in the Aryan quarter. They just about cancel each other. But the Aryans who live in the Jewish section are mostly of the poorer classes, and their rents are low. On the other hand, most of the Jews who live in the Aryan quarter have high rents. The Aryans going from one section to the other cannot afford to pay high prices. The Jews driven out of their homes do not wish to live in dark and narrow quarters even though the rent is low. The only thing common to both is that they both are dissatisfied with their lot, and curse the day they were born.

Both sides curse the murderer with the wish that his world darken in his lifetime, just as he darkened their world by ordering them to do something against their will. Never were there such days of sorrow and mourning in Jewish Warsaw as on the days of Sukkot, 5701.

October 24, 1940

The night of Simhat Torah, 5701

The Warsaw ghetto is making its full appearance. Everyone is vacating his forbidden apartment in advance of the deadline, and taking some new apartment in the Jewish area. So long as poverty can be locked in the innermost places, people forget it exists; but when it is brought outside it awakens disgust and loathing. Now we see the used furniture and household utensils of the poor as they search through the streets for a new refuge. There is no sense to this. For what reason are these miserable and oppressed creatures made to roam around like shadows, these who have nothing to keep themselves alive with even under their own roofs?

The naïve among the Jews and Poles ask: Can the world sit silent? Will the evil and the corrupt always have the upper hand? Will the ax fall upon the entire world? O Leader of the city, where are you?

But He Who sits in Heaven laughs.

The torments of the creation of the ghetto are harder, perhaps, than the ghetto itself. At every hour new changes are made regarding one area or another. Thus Zelazna Street, a place of refuge for 60,000 Poles and 26,000 Jews, has been in limbo for several days, and no one knows what its fate will be. Is it ours, or our competitor's? There is a rumor that two delegations, one Jewish (Wielikowski and Sztolcman) and one Polish, went to Cracow, but neither managed to see the ruler, and both returned empty-handed. There are also various rumors about extension of the period of evacuation. Some say it was extended until November 15; others say the original date still stands. Yesterday the radio announced that the time stated before, October 31, remains in effect. Today people in *Judenrat* circles announce that on the twenty-eighth a notice will be published extending the time until November 15.

And an additional doubt is gnawing at us:

Will it be a closed ghetto? There are signs in both directions, and we hope for a miracle—which doesn't always happen in time of need. A closed ghetto means gradual death. An open ghetto is only a halfway catastrophe.

October 25, 1940

End of Sukkot, 5701

In the midst of sorrow, the holiday of joy. This is not a secular joy, but a "rejoicing of the Torah," the same Torah for which we are murdered all day, for which we have become like lambs to be slaughtered, for which we have gone through fire and water. Last year there was darkness in our dwelling places, but a ray of hope still flickered in our souls. We knew the character of the murderers only by rumor, and so we suspected them of having human feelings in spite of all their cruelty and wickedness. Maybe after the first panic of war ended, life would be easier for us, because in their goodness they would grant us an opportunity for primitive human survival. After a year of physical and mental tortures never equaled in history, darkness reigns in our souls as well. The holiday was spent under the impress of the ghetto, with all the sights which accompany its creation and appearance. It is clear to us that the ghetto will be a closed one. They will push us into a Jewish section, fenced in and separated from the world outside, like sinners and criminals.

But we have not shamed our eternal Torah. This was not a raucous celebration, but an inner one, a heartfelt joy, and for that reason it was all the more warm and emotional. Everywhere holiday celebrations were organized, and every prayer group said the wine blessing. The Hasidim were even dancing, as is their pious custom. Someone told me that on the night of the holiday he met a large group of zealous Hasidim on Mila Street, and they sang holiday songs in chorus out in public, followed by a large crowd of curious people and sightseers. Joy and revelry in poverty-stricken Mila Street! When they sang, they reached such a state of ecstasy that they couldn't stop, until some heretic approached them shouting, "Jews! Safeguarding your life is a positive Biblical commandment; it is a time of danger for us. Stop this." Only then did they become quiet. Some of them replied in their ecstasy: "We are not afraid of the murderer! The devil with him!"

The strict ban does not prevent us from calling meetings at which we express our troubles and torments and describe all that has happened to us. Speeches are made whose broad hints enable the audience to understand the situation.

Yesterday, on the night of Simhat Torah, I participated in a Zionist gathering which took place at the Zionist soup kitchen at 13 Zamenhof Street. Established by the Zionists, it serves as a meeting place for refugees from all regions, especially those from Lodz. About fifty people came. It was a warm and pleasant gathering of friends, but by the force of the times through which we are living, there was a change from the normal procedure of proposing festive toasts.

October 27, 1940

As long as the ghetto is open and there is still a gap, no larger than the eye of a needle, through which we may come in contact with the outside world, the *Judenrat* has jurisdiction only over internal affairs; from the time when the ghetto is closed, we will become a foreign national organism, separated from the civil life of the nation. We will stop paying taxes to the government, and be exempt from paying rent. "Sinners and criminals" are not obligated to bear the burden of debts and taxes, because they have been doomed to elimination, and all the arteries of life are stopped up before them. Thus it is that the *Judenrat* will be the representative of the Jewish people both within and without. In a closed ghetto we will not only have cultural autonomy, but administrative autonomy as well.

And in this lies the essence of our tragedy. Out of the frying pan, into the fire. The *Judenrat* is not the same as our traditional Jewish Community Council, which wrote such brilliant chapters in our history. Strangers in our midst, foreign to our spirit, sons of Ham who trample upon our heads, the president of the *Judenrat* and his advisers are musclemen who were put on our backs by strangers. Most of them are nincompoops whom no one knew in normal times. They were never elected, and would not have dared dream of being elected, as Jewish representatives; had they dared, they would have been defeated. All their lives until now they were outside the Jewish fold; they did not rejoice in our happiness nor mourn our misfortunes. Who paid any attention to some unknown engineer, a nincompoop among nincompoops, who was an assimilationist not for ideological reasons but for utilitarian ones. Zionism had already thrown these men over its shoulder, and they moved about among us like shadows. Small minds, artists at poker, schooled in a foreign culture.

How did we come to this state of affairs? Only chance was involved. Even the conqueror didn't choose them, but rather found them already there. After they became his loyal and dedicated minions in heart and soul, he found no flaw in them and left them in their place. The president, moreover, found special favor, and was given an automobile to make his work easier. When the war broke out and the Community Council was orphaned because its advisers and directors fled for their lives, Starczynski thought it over and called the temporary president to rule.

And the president, after being seated on the throne, invited all those he favored to be advisers. Everything was based on the principle of *Führertum*. He didn't consult us, but acted entirely on his own.

To what extent the choice was a good one the citizens of Warsaw will testify when peace comes. During the time when the revival of Jewish education was on the agenda, and veteran social servants came in contact with the *Judenrat*, even my Zionist friends tried to get close to the "Jewish Government" and its leadership. Hundreds of jobs were handed out to all those who appeared before the *Judenrat*. In the Zionist camp there were many out of work, and so our representatives tried to get some of our members into the *Judenrat* too. They were successful to some extent, but generally our members ran from the *Judenrat*. The clean do not mingle with the unclean.

"We won't join with the *Judenrat*," one of the Zionists said, "There is an atmosphere of ungodliness there, of evildoers, of candidates for jail. We have a Zionist tradition to uphold, and will never be a party to this criminal gang called the *Judenrat*. Zionists have nothing to do with these evildoers who belong in the company of criminals who do their work in darkness. The wicked of our people, and the traitors of our nation, are not friends of ours." One thing and another of this sort was said by our representatives— but we didn't dare take a stand.

October 30, 1940

Rents are five times the normal price. Sometimes a man pays eight zloty for two mediocre rooms, and when he comes to rent a single room now, he pays a hundred zloty for it. The exile, whose moments are numbered and who is in fear of remaining without a roof over his head, is forced to pay. Besides that, it has become an unvarying custom to demand three months' rent in advance, and other such requirements. What can the poor do?

The Self-Aid understands what it must do and is marshaling all its forces to bring aid to these needy people in their trouble. But as I have said, its material means are insufficient for even a hundredth of those seeking its help.

Today I was invited to a meeting called by the Self-Aid Center to urge greater activity in the aid project. I didn't hear speeches, I heard eulogies. They didn't speak, but wept. They had no compunctions about openly expressing all the ire pent up in their hearts. The rabbis of Praga wept and groaned aloud, and the audience wept with them. The wrath of the Lord has struck this Jewish suburb of fifty thousand people in particular. Although it has been administratively joined to Warsaw, Praga is actually a city in itself, and they were sure a separate ghetto would be created there. But there is no analyzing the stupidity and evil of the Nazis. By the thirty-first of October, Praga must be empty of its Jewish inhabitants, who were rooted in its soil for hundreds of years. Most of them are poor. They have no money to move their belongings. And where would they move them to? Many Poles drove the Praga Jews from their apartments in advance, before the fixed date.

The scroll of agony which the rabbis of Praga unrolled before us touched our souls. Even the stouthearted ones in the audience could not hold back their tears. One rabbi related, "Today a Jew ran into my home who had been driven almost mad. He was holding a scroll of the Torah: 'My family and I are rolling in the dungheaps; in my home there was this scroll of the Torah. Please, rabbi, take this, my most sacred possession, and guard it as the apple of your eye. Nothing is left to us but this Torah.' "

October 31, 1940

This is the last day for the evacuation of apartments, for both Jews living in the Aryan quarters and Christians living in the Jewish quarter. The conquerors' rag of a newspaper makes everything more difficult of its own accord and on its own responsibility, in order to destroy the nerves of the Jews. Its threats, which had no basis in fact, magnified the weight of the catastrophe. But be that as it may, the open ghetto has already been created. A great herd of half a million people has been compressed and squeezed into a small area where they will live its degrading life in terrible crowding without any income. Rich families who lived in five- and six-room apartments must content themselves with one room. Everyone hurried to insure a place of refuge as well as he could. There was no choice.

Today we learned that the threats were only sadism. The rulers have extended the time for evacuating apartments for another two weeks—that is, until the fifteenth of November. It was officially announced today, clearly and explicitly. All the panic was for naught. Because of this our nerves and emotions relaxed a little. That is always our nature. When we sleep on our troubles for a night we make peace with them. What more could we ask? It is not a ghetto, but a Jewish quarter, not a concentration camp but a quarter of "free men" who are allowed to have dealings with the outside world.

But before we were relieved of the deadline, a new edict was added, again a senseless decree which a normal mind could not conceive. Today there was a new trolley edict. Every Jew who wants to ride on the trolley must pay a monthly tax of five zloty, in addition to the fare. In other words, it is necessary to get a permit to ride the trolley, even in the Jewish car, and you must pay 60 zloty a year for the permit. Anyone without a permit—with a photograph on it—must pay four times over for a ride—instead of 25 groszy, a whole zloty.

The revenues will be reduced to a minimum because no one will pay a whole zloty for a single ride on a trolley—so some people guess. But I say the opposite. They will get used to a zloty, too, and they will ride.

November 2, 1940

The conquerors have no need of a ghetto, in and of itself, from any standpoint. A Jewish ghetto in Warsaw in the traditional sense is impossible; certainly a closed ghetto is inconceivable. Many churches and government buildings are in the heart of the ghetto. They cannot be eliminated, they fulfill necessary functions. Besides that, it is impossible to cut off the trolley routes going from one end of the city to the other through the ghetto. For hundreds of years the great metropolis was built on general civil foundations, and the basis of race was entirely foreign to it. Neighborhoods and backyards of people of different faiths were next to each other, and in spite of all religious and moral differences between them, mutual trade and dealings developed which brought benefits to all. To differentiate citizens of one country according to race, and to erect partitions between them, is a sick pathological idea. From its conception to its execution, it may be considered a symptom of insanity.

Even the fourfold raising of the fare on the Jewish trolley (a zloty instead of 25 groszy) came only in order to "place obstacles in the way of the mercantile 'talent' of the Jews." This was written specifically in the German newspaper. They are not ashamed to state openly, "We want to bring destruction upon the Jews." Not only are they not ashamed; they boast that this is what they have done, are doing, and will do.

November 4, 1940

The face of Warsaw has changed so that no one who knows it would recognize it. People from outside do not enter now, but if a miracle were to take place and one of its inhabitants who fled returned to the city, he would say, "Can this be Warsaw?"

Not even the Poles are in a hurry to rebuild their ruins. The holes and cracks in the burned and destroyed buildings have been patched up with bricks and lime; the rubble of destruction has been cleared; the broken sidewalks shine. The conquerors boast of the order they have instituted. Yes, the order of a graveyard.

But the appearance of Jewish Warsaw is especially changed. There were eras when Jewish Warsaw was problematical, because the Poles, former lords of the land, would not admit it. They objected to any name that tended to forget the Polish ethnography. But since the Jewish quarter was established, Jewish Warsaw has become a city unto itself, with characteristics quite different from those of Aryan Warsaw. Anyone passing from the Jewish district to the Aryan district gets the impression of having entered a new city with a different appearance and a different way of life and having nothing to do with its Jewish neighbor.

Jewish Warsaw has changed for the worse, in the direction of ugliness, tastelessness, and lack of beauty. Here too it is a graveyard, only here the skeletons of the dead walk about in the streets. They have gathered from all parts of the country and come to Warsaw. They came empty-handed, broken and crushed, without

219

a penny, without food for a single meal or clothes to cover their nakedness.

They have begun sending children of various ages to peddle in the streets. I saw a boy of six selling "badges of shame," conducting his business with eagerness and industry. Little vendors like these are hard to catch, because they are fleet-footed and quick to slip away—and when they are caught their liability is not great. So boy vendors fill the Jewish section with their deafening cries. They are either hawking their wares at the top of their lungs or else running for their lives from the pursuing police. Either they laugh raucously or they whine and plead for their lives before the captors who lead them, and their merchandise, to the police station.

The sidewalks are crowded beyond belief. Most of all, mothers take up positions on the sidewalks with their children's cradles, and they lean against the sides of buildings all along the street. The conquerors have closed the city parks to us. Anywhere that a tree has been planted, or a bench has been placed, Jewish children are forbidden to derive enjoyment. It pains the heart to see the sorrow of our little children. Children who have never known what it is to sin are forced by order of the cruel conquerors to stay outside while children their age are romping in a half-empty park. But there is nothing which does not become second nature through use. The Jewish mothers have already gotten used to their bad fortune, and in order not to deprive their babies of the sunlight, they take their stand with their cradles wherever there is a square or a vacant lot, or a sidewalk covered with sunlight.

A second phenomenon—characters out of Mendele.[5] The inescapable beggars and paupers have gathered in Warsaw from all parts of the country. And they are types the like of which you have never seen before. By the thousands they beg for food and sustenance in the streets of the Jewish quarter. They surround you and tug at your sleeve wherever you turn. This is not ordinary panhandling, it is artistry. Every business likes to try new things in order to succeed, and those who work at this one are adept at it, as is proven by their inventiveness and originality in appealing to the hearts of passersby. Thus at one intersection you encounter

[5] Mendele Mocher Seforim, pen name of Sholom Jacob Abramovitsch (1836–1917), a Russian-born Yiddish and Hebrew writer.

a group of children of poverty ranging in age from four to ten, the emissaries of mothers and fathers who supervise them from the sidelines. They sing, and their voices are pleasant and their songs permeated with Jewish sorrow and grief. The music touches your heartstrings. Little groups of idlers and strollers stand near the childish quartet, their eyes filled with tears; they find it hard to leave. At infrequent intervals someone turns up who drops a miserable penny into the hands of the little singers. May the philanthropist be blessed! A short distance away there is a cantor with a complete choir of singers. The synagogues are closed, and they cannot sing before their Creator, so they pour forth their supplications under the open sky. A concert of this sort attracts hundreds of people. They sing prayers and hymns for all the holidays in the year, and since everyone has more than enough free time, the audience grows larger and larger, and the choir does a good business.

Just as there are vocal choirs, so too are there instrumental bands and bands in which vocalists and instrumentalists cooperate. Sometimes a single artist who relies on his own talents goes into business for himself. An excellent basso sings arias of all kinds all day long, and sometimes he is even favored with a penny for his efforts. Aside from artistic panhandling there is physical panhandling everywhere you turn. Lamed, crippled, and blind people; people missing an arm or a leg; all manner of misshapen people who inspire physical repulsion; epileptics and those afflicted with skin diseases; naked people and people dressed in filthy rags; and all of them shouting: "Give! Give!"

This particolored picture represents the Jewish quarter at the present moment. Sometimes you get fed up with yourself and your people. Is all of this symbolic of the "eternity of Israel"? Have we sunk so low? Do these living dead represent national strength? But the bustling, noisy street is not interested in your sad thoughts. Everywhere there is noise, motion; in every corner the pulsebeat of life is unceasing.

November 6, 1940

The day before yesterday the president of the *Judenrat*, the engineer Adam Czerniakow, was arrested!

The bare item, unaccompanied by any details, caused a storm in the city. Those who like to exaggerate embellished the news with the fruits of their imaginations. But even stripped of exaggerations, the fact itself sent shock waves among responsible circles who don't see the shadows of mountains and call them mountains. There is no barbarism of which the conquerors are incapable. To them there is no difference between a Jewish porter and the president of the *Judenrat*. Both are worth no more, in their eyes, than a garlic peel.

We thought that the arrest of the president of the *Judenrat* was an evil harbinger of what is yet to come. This happened close to the time of the creation of the ghetto, at the beginning of an era pregnant with torments, suffering, shame, and disgrace. We waited for new blows, but thank heaven we were wrong. The arrest was not carried out because of orders from high places, it was nothing but an impulsive action by some men of the Gestapo, done without the consent of their superiors. After a few hours the president was freed, and two of his cohorts who had been arrested with him were also released. Again it was a case of "Thy destroyers and they that made thee waste shall go forth from thee." It is the same in every generation. The betrayer was a refugee from Germany, a clerk in the *Judenrat* who had been discharged by the president. Without making any inquiries the Gestapo agents came to the *Judenrat*, arrested the president, and also beat him while they were about it.

This is only a small incident, but it has wide implications. It teaches us that every blackguard among them has the power to desecrate our honor.

An order was issued at one time that "every Jew who meets a German in uniform must make way for him." This makes it clear that we are not required to remove our hats out of respect. But when the Nazi soldiers come to the ghetto, they threateningly demand, "Respect us!" The idiots are not aware that respect through fear is not respect. How can you respect an enemy whose aim is to destroy you and to erase you from under the heavens? But a psychopath has no use for logic, and any Jew who does not bow or remove his hat before the Nazi will come out of it toothless and eyeless.

November 10, 1940

The conquerors' radio emphasized and re-emphasized that this is not a ghetto, but rather a Jewish quarter, like the Polish quarter or the German quarter. In whispers the constant rumor was that

Roosevelt had a hand in these concessions. The oppressed Jewish masses enjoy rumors of this sort. It is good in our terrible troubles to believe that some mighty hand is guiding us, that our sufferings are seen and our sighs are heard.

But we woke up, and our souls were empty.

In our favor there were flourishing, unfounded rumors; against us there were unalterable, hard facts. All the concessions were blown away like smoke. A time extension was given only once, and that was for the benefit of the Poles. We had hopes for Praga, that the edict would be softened in its favor, but it was a dream. By the fifteenth of November not a Jew will be left there. A city of fifty thousand Jews is going into exile.

Most significantly, in all the thoroughfares leading to the Aryan quarters high walls are being erected blocking the paths to the Aryan world before us. At present only the streets united with the Jewish ghetto by car tracks are still open. Wherever you turn the murderers have blocked the way. Moreover, the walls being erected now are higher and sturdier than the ones that were put up earlier. Before our eyes a dungeon is being built in which half a million men, women, and children will be imprisoned, no one knows for how long.

The *Judenrat* is building this great mass grave with its own funds. All of this is a clear proof, because if the conquerors wished to leave the ghetto open they would not need to build high, fortified walls to block the path of life before us.

The *Judenrat* is burdened with much other work in preparing to organize life within a closed ghetto. Under its supervision a Jewish police force is being recruited which will have authority over the buried-alive Jews of the ghetto. Nine thousand young men have already registered as candidates for this force. By the way, each applicant included a five-zloty registration fee, which even the abject poor paid in the hope of being accepted for the ghetto police, although there will be salary for these policemen. Among the other preparations are negotiations with the Aryan owners of pharmacies in the Jewish quarter. In the area set aside for the ghetto there were formerly twenty-one pharmacies, seven of them Jewish, the rest Aryan. As soon as the conquerors came the Jewish druggists were pushed out of their businesses. Now, with the creation of the ghetto, the conquerors intend to leave in the area only eleven pharmacies, which will be under the supervision of the *Judenrat* and will once again have Jewish personnel. The same applies to the management of Jewish-owned apartment houses. From now on there will be no room for Aryan managers. The houses will be turned over to the control of the *Judenrat*, which will employ the agents removed from them by force and deprived of their livelihoods. All of these are bad signs.

The day is not distant when we will be penned in like cattle, forcibly removed from the outside world like a camp of unclean lepers.

November 13, 1940

In their radio programs the conquerors are very careful never to call the Jewish quarter by its right name—ghetto; it is not comfortable for one who wishes to create a "new Europe" to return to the customs of the Middle Ages.

All that is for outside consumption. Here, the walls that will remove us from the world are rising higher and higher. The sight of them brings fear and dread. Your heart says: This is a prison into which I have come before its walls are even finished. Is this not a dream? No, it is bitter, tragic Jewish reality. It is the fate of an entire people.

There is scarcely any doubt that we will have a closed ghetto, although in a form somewhat different from that of Lodz. Four or five through streets will be left, and at these streets military guards will be posted to watch who enters and leaves. Jews may be allowed to leave for several hours each day after they obtain a permit at a certain price. Air will be bought with money.

Just as Nebuchadnezzar came and confounded the world, so the ghetto decree confounded our communal life. The Jewish Self-Aid had, until now, set up six districts for charitable matters. But since the Aryan quarters now have no Jews, the number of charity districts will be reduced. What will the Self-Aid do with their officials who lived off these districts? So as not to deprive them of their incomes, a new territorial division of the charity districts inside the ghetto will be made, and the total number will remain the same. Thus only the total territorial area of all the charity districts and, implicitly, the number of buildings in each, will be reduced. And everything will be as before.

November 17, 1940

What we dreaded most has come to us. We had a premonition that a ghetto life awaited us, a life of sorrow and poverty, of shame and degradation, but no one believed that the fateful hour would come so soon. And suddenly—a frightful surprise! On the eve of the Sabbath of Parashat Vayera,[6] the fourteenth of Marheshvan, 5701, we went to bed in the Jewish quarter, and the next morning we awoke in a closed Jewish ghetto, a ghetto in every detail. In the morning hours of the Sabbath a three-man guard was set up in all the open places where walls were not erected because of the trolley connections. They would not allow Jews wearing the "badge of shame" to cross over into the Aryan quarter. Thus we have been granted "full civil rights" to the extent of having a Jewish police force in the state of Poland, an idea which the Jewish autonomists in every generation hoped for with all their heart and soul. We have entered into a new life, and it is impossible to imagine the panic that has arisen in the Jewish quarter. Suddenly we see ourselves penned in on all sides. We are segregated and separated from the world and the fullness thereof, driven out of the society of the human race.

In reality we have not one ghetto, but two, and there is almost no connection between them. For the sake of accuracy I must point out that actually there is one connection but I consider it nonexistent because it is too difficult to use.[7] This too is part of the conquerors' plan.

November 19, 1940

If it were said that the sun has darkened for us at noon it would not be merely a metaphor. We will molder and rot within the narrow streets and the crooked lanes in which tens of thousands of people wander idle and full of despair.

The matter of food supplies, in particular, has contributed to confusion. Since communications between us and the villages is cut off, our food will be given to us by the conquerors. This will amount to ninety-percent starvation. What good will ten decagrams of coarse bread a week do?

[6] The Biblical portion read in the synagogue on that particular Sabbath (Genesis 18:1–22:24).
[7] The large and small ghettos were connected only by a narrow footbridge above Chlodna Street.

225

Anger at black marketeering has become tremendous. The wealthy, and even the ordinary well-to-do, had hoarded food. Only the poor are left with nothing, because they couldn't afford to stock up. It is they who are the victims of the black marketeers and it is hard to see them in their distress. There is nowhere to earn a penny. Toil and poverty were their lot even in ordinary times, and now a ton of coal costs 800 zloty; a loaf of coarse bread, three zloty; a litre of milk, two zloty; a kilo of butter, 30 zloty. And so on.

November 26, 1940

My pen did not stop flowing even in the most horrible hours of violence. Even the rain of bombs in the siege of Warsaw did not stop me, and more than a few of my diary entries were written in the cellar. Because a daily entry was my obligation, my will conquered my nerves. But in these savage days it is different. I am completely broken. Jewish Warsaw has turned into a madhouse. A community of half a million people is doomed to die, and awaits execution of their sentence.

Six days have passed without an entry. In these days, when the very "stones in the wall cry out," the sheer volume and number of impressions leaves me without the literary power to record and organize them. They have piled up in my brain, but historical moments are being lost. Once again a feeling of responsibility to Jewish historiography begins to make demands upon my conscience.

November 27, 1940

Our constant song—potatoes! This word is repeated a hundred and one times at every moment. It is our whole life. When I am alone in my room for a few moments of quiet, the echo of that word continues in my ears. Even in my dreams it visits me. Once, in the days of peace, potatoes were the food of the poor. The folk song *"Zuntig, Bulbes,"* from the first to the last verse. *"Shabes in a novine a kugele fun bulbes,"*[8] is an elegy mourning the troubles of the pauper who feeds his body all week with this poor fare. And today? Whoever has potatoes stored in his cellar is considered fortunate, and everyone envies him. In the ghetto we have nothing besides this food, which serves the same function as the manna in

[8] Yiddish: "Sunday, potatoes . . . every day potatoes . . . On the Sabbath, for a change, a potato pudding."

the wilderness. It should thus come as no surprise that the price of potatoes has risen from hour to hour, and has reached a hundred zloty for a hundred kilos. But even this fabulous price is no deterrent. A man who could not afford to buy potatoes with ready cash sold some article of clothing to a Gentile (Jews do not buy, out of fear that the conquerors will end up with the item purchased), got the money from him, and at once gave it back to the Gentile for potatoes. All aspirations are gone except for the drive to store up potatoes for the hard and bitter days ahead.

November 28, 1940

The ghetto is empty of all Gentiles and has turned into a Jewish kingdom. The police are leaving and the Jewish police will inherit their place. The same applies to the post office; Jews working for the *Judenrat* will head it and all the jobs there will be filled by Jews. An exceptional concession will apparently be made in the case of the tax bureau, and for the public utility departments—if the cruel conquerors do not forbid us to use gas and electricity. In short, a Jewish state complete in every detail, but a closed, cramped one, imprisoned, mummified within its narrow borders.

November 29, 1940

Polish Jewry has become a self-contained organism. It is forced to rely on its own powers. Despite all its poverty it must support its own destitute. The American "Uncle" of the last war has gone to rest. Willing or not, the misers of Poland are forced to give. The Jewish Self-Aid, which no one believed would succeed at the time of its establishment, has become a far-reaching charitable organization which brings in more than 100,000 zloty a month. Self-Aid is a kingdom in its own right, and from the administrative standpoint it has no connection with its sister, the Joint, which is still alive and functioning in spite of being pauperized, and which is still completely supporting its officials, especially the directors. Its support of the Self-Aid has not yet stopped entirely, but it is stopping discreetly, without publicity. In the eyes of the general public the Joint is bankrupt and no longer has any say. On the other side of the ledger, the Self-Aid has much publicity.

The lowest rung in its broad organization is the courtyard committee. This is a successful organizational invention, of a kind that was never attained in times of peace when a raucous press existed.

At that time no public project percolated down to the masses. This time every Jewish home from great to small has been affected. At the head of the courtyard committees stand men of the people who awaken the drowsy public to give.

Their words, which emanate from simple hearts, penetrate into simple hearts. They find expressions which their listeners can understand, and so are successful. Social action is thus diffused through all levels of the broad public, and there is no boy over ten who does not have some public duty in his courtyard. There is not a tenant who is not among the members of some committee, or in charge of some courtyard duty. Every courtyard committee is divided into reporting subcommittees (financial, sanitary, educational affairs, political affairs, apartments, dress, food supplies, etc.), and each of these is further divided and subdivided, and in this way everyone is kept busy. Self-Aid is a legal organization and it thus gives the legal right to all its branches to call meetings and conferences, and to put their decisions into practice. At every meeting there is a broad field for politics, rumors, and all manner of gossip and slander. Everyone says whatever enters his mind without fear that his words will be carried to those in power. The hatred of the conquerors is so deep that everyone is sure no one will carry anything he says beyond the room.

The Self-Aid is supported by regular monthly payments which the courtyard committees impose upon their "subjects" by the income derived from special projects and drives. Nearly every month it raises a hue and cry about a different rescue project. Once it was a drive to save the children, and the "children's month" became a watchword; then came the "holiday month"; third, there was the "immigration month"; the fourth, which we are presently involved in carrying out, is the "soul ransom" project to raise money for "social improvements." The organization of these projects is not always successful, because it is a time of crisis and everything must be done in haste, without the technical and organizational tools required. But even if they are not a hundred percent successful, the people are satisfied with a sixty percent success. Compulsory giving has served to educate us. The recognition of collective responsibility which was so lacking in our brethren has penetrated to everyone. Everyone has come to realize that he is an organic part of a whole body. Anything good for the whole body is good for him too, and the reverse. This concept was brought to us by the conquerors. That which is good must be accepted from whatever source it may come.

The concept that "all Jews are responsible for one another" has stopped being merely a slogan or a metaphor. It is realized in us.

The courtyard committees operate on the principle that the affairs of their own courtyard come first. And so they impose a double monthly payment upon their "subjects"; one for the benefit of the Self-Aid, which supports the soup kitchens in the ghetto, the other for courtyard needs. This payment need not necessarily be in cash. It may be made in footstuffs, prepared meals, or used clothing.

When the ghetto was about to be set up and people were concerned about the hoarding, the courtyard committees began taking care of all the residents of the courtyard without exception, including even the middle-class and wealthy ones. It was deemed entirely possible that a day would come when all the private hoards would be eaten up and it would be necessary to set up a common soup kitchen for all the residents of the courtyard. So the courtyard committees hastily created a "permanent fund" for the establishment of soup kitchens. At once the necessary (relatively speaking) sums were collected to enable them to buy in advance a certain quantity of foodstuffs, to be stored in a special cellar belonging to the courtyard committee. It will thus remain, ready for whatever trouble may come.

When historians come to write the history of the courtyard committees during the days of the Nazi war against the Jews, let them end their chapter with a blessing of consolation: "May the Lord remember them with favor!"

December 2, 1940

Life in the ghetto is becoming "normal." The chaos lasted no more than a week. When half a million people are locked in a small cage, faced with hunger, privation, epidemics, atrocities, naturally it causes a stir. Even the conquerors were confused. This is a unique political experiment. The intention was to starve and impoverish us in body and in spirit, to segregate us from the outside world; to undermine our very existence. A great project of this sort demands extraordinary exertions and cannot be brought into effect by words alone. But to our sorrow, it must be admitted that the tyrants succeeded.

Entry and exit permits are given only to Aryan officials who

229

hold posts in one of the government institutions within the ghetto. Certain Jews too get permits of this sort, and these include the Jewish Gestapo agents, the destroyers from our midst, as well as an insignificant number of individuals who fill some important position of service for the government in an institution outside the ghetto boundaries. Aside from these, there are also Jewish boys under the age of ten, who, not being marked by the "badge of shame," sometimes manage to sneak across the border, because the border guards do not recognize that they are the children of the inferior race.

These children are clever, and they are sent by their parents to buy food cheaply. Usually they are successful in their mission, and bring home bargains. This week I got a bargain of this sort myself: a quarter-kilo of butter for six zloty, which our relative Emek brought in from the other side of the wall. God bless him!

While the rich were hoarding food the poor were going around mourning and desolate, their eyes expressing anger at those complacent people upon whom the famine had not yet made an impression. This jealousy, which was like a fire contained within their bones, prompted such talk as: "Let them hoard to their hearts' content. When we're starving we will take it by force. Justice does not require allowing the bourgeoisie to enjoy all good things at a time when the people are dying of starvation."

December 3, 1940

The number of street vendors in the ghetto has grown tremendously. There is no avoiding them and their goods. Their cries are deafening, and everywhere you go one follows you like a shadow. What sort of goods are sold thus in the ghetto? Anything from pieces of sugar that have been through the wars to post cards and stamps which are not obtainable either in the stores, because there is no profit in them, or in the post office, because all in all the conquerors have left only two post offices for half a million people, and in order to buy a post card, it is necessary to stand in line for many hours and receive "Jewish blows" from Czerniakow's police who are in charge of maintaining order.

Professional people, deprived of their occupations, are in part sitting idle like penitents, and in part have become attached to some of the posts in the Joint or the Self-Aid office. Artisans are idle because there is no one to give them shoes to mend or clothes to sew. They live on two or three zloty a day. Next come the thousands and tens of thousands who live on charity and eat at the soup kitchens. The latter number a hundred thousand each day.

The ghetto state needs civil servants, and it employs thousands of people. The janitors, the "Lords of the Broom," have left us because they were Aryans born and bred, and Jews have been appointed in their place. Then there are the Jewish policemen with their rubber clubs (they were not given arms). Those who have been beaten say there is no difference between them and the ones carried by their Polish and German colleagues; only they have a special, Jewish flavor. At all events, four thousand Jewish youths who were eliminated from their former jobs were given these new "posts of honor," and thereby an opportunity for living on bribes and food smuggling. Both they and the ghetto dwellers benefit.

The post office employs several hundred people, and the Jewish building agents have returned to their jobs and scared all the tenants. The jokesters have made up a new prayer: "Let us fall into the hands of Gentile agents, only let us not fall into the hands of a Jewish agent!"

The administrative work within the *Judenrat* itself also engages thousands of people. Their salary is small and is never paid on time, but at least they have a foothold.

In short, there is no shortage of jobs, and we will live in spite of the murderers.

December 5, 1940

When Warsaw was conquered, the "Lord of the Broom" was at the height of his power. He literally had power of life and death over his neighbors. At his pleasure he would tell the Nazi robbers, who made the rounds of the gates of the Jewish buildings in search of loot, that rich Jews with a lot of money lived in his courtyard; and at his pleasure he would deceive them by saying that in his yard there are only poor people.

Now that the ghetto has been created, a day of recompense has come for *Pan* Josef as well. He is forced to leave the sinful Jews and move among his pure compatriots, and here his tragedy begins. Where everyone is pure, there is neither honor nor lucre for him, so *Pan* Josef does not want to leave his Jews. Against his will he moves to the Aryan quarter, but every day he risks his life, smuggles himself across the border, and returns to his nest. Here he finds a Jew holding a broom, and tears fill his eyes. I swear that with my own ears I heard a Josef say, "They won't take me away from here alive! If my livelihood is gone, why should I live?"

That is the Aryan side of the coin, but it has a Jewish side that is tragic too. There are thousands of candidates for Josef's glorious job among the unemployed Jews. The courtyard committee, which has the decisive say in the matter, receives dozens of applications from former big shots in which they pour forth their supplications for mercy upon their starving children through their appointment as janitor. Among them are former merchants, jurists, engineers, teachers, and even landlords—and only one in a hundred is awarded the job.

But *Pan* Rubinsztejn is not like *Pan* Josef. The Jews were afraid of *Pan* Josef, and so his income was assured; but *Pan* Rubinsztejn is our own flesh and blood, and so they will support him like a dog.

December 6, 1940

Even within our narrow confines we have no peace. Large signs announce that it is forbidden for German soldiers to loiter in any contaminated place, even outside the ghetto, not to speak of the ghetto itself; and in reality there is no need for any German soldier to come to the ghetto except to loot and plunder. It can be stated as a rule: If you meet a Nazi soldier in the streets of the ghetto, you can be sure he is a thief. Even the black ghetto walls do not protect us. Not only did the robberies not stop when the ghetto was created, they became more frequent. Dozens of families are robbed every day, and there is nowhere the Jews can turn for justice. The thieves among the soldiers make secret agreements with the *Volksgenossen,* and with their racial brethren's guidance they enter any home at will. A Jew does not dare make a sound of protest. There have been cases when courageous Jews were shot in full view of their entire family and the murderers were not held responsible, because their excuse was that the filthy Jew cursed the Führer and it was their duty to avenge his honor.

December 16, 1940

My inkwell lay dormant for a few days because of my mental distress. Every hour there is a new edict, every moment a frightening tiding of Job. Every so often I remember that I am a prisoner in the ghetto; that I am penned within a piece of land four or five kilometers in size, without contact with anyone outside; that by law I am not allowed to buy or even to read a book in a foreign language. When I remember all this I become desperate, ready to break my pen and throw it away.

But this despair does not last forever. The spirit of dedication which had left me in my moments of spiritual agony returns, as though some hidden force were ordering me: Record!

Were it not for my pen, my delight, I would be lost.

We have become accustomed to the miserable life of the ghetto. There are even some few hours when life begins to vibrate again with such strength and vigor that, for a short moment, we forget that we are no longer human beings, that we are members of an inferior race. At first we were afraid—simple, physical fear of the famine knocking at our door. Hoarding of food for evil times to come became a psychosis, and caused terrible turmoil in our minds and emotions. But by now we have come to realize that it was an exaggerated fear. We are not short of any foodstuffs, and if you have the money you can enjoy all good things. In the show windows of the ghetto stores you can find all manner of delicacies, from honey cakes to the choicest wines.

Smuggling across the border increases from day to day. This has become an occupation for thousands of people, both Jews and Aryans, since they have set up partnerships for smuggling food from the Aryan quarter to the Jewish ghetto. Even the Nazis participate in this. Nazi doctrine places no value on money, and the Führer has no need of money, but his soldiers do not listen to him in this instance; instead they agree to feign blindness. Those who dabble in mysteries have even come to the conclusion that the entire motive for the ghetto was to open a source of income for those in the Nazi power circles. But here too there are exceptions. Some of the Nazis are clever in practical matters, but others are fools who know nothing beyond the Führer and his doctrines. Woe to the smugglers who chance to run across a military guard who despises bribes and carries out his orders to the fullest. There was a case of a Jewish policeman who was not careful enough, and attempted to bribe the wrong border guard. First he was beaten with terrible cruelty until he was reduced to a heap of bones; afterwards he was arrested and tried and condemned to die.

Every individual has some field in which he is most proficient, and the same applies to a community or an entire nation. Just as there is such a thing as a monomania, so too there is such a thing as genius in one area. The genius of Nazism is in hatred of the Jews, a hatred as deep as the abyss, in which there is also something of a creative force.

The Nazi genius created not just a ghetto, but rather a Jewish state with all the attributes which pertain to any state. In Lodz, for example, they have put banknotes into circulation bearing a Star of David which are legal tender in the ghetto, but which Aryans are forbidden to accept. The main objective is a complete separation between Jews and Aryans. It must be admitted that in our case their arrow hit the target. The "good days" before the ghetto was completely closed are remembered with nostalgia. Now the only people making a living are the smugglers. They risk their lives, but if they get through unharmed it is worth their while.

The Aryan policemen, big, powerful, with red noses and faces that testified to their drunkenness and coarseness, who would do anything you wanted for a copper penny, have disappeared. In their stead, thousands of Jewish youths have appeared in the streets of the ghetto wearing policemen's caps, their right sleeves wrapped in an amber cloth on which there is an inscription testifying to the fact that the wearer belongs to the public safety service. The residents of the ghetto are beginning to think they are in Tel Aviv. Strong, bonafide policemen from among our brothers, to whom you can speak in Yiddish! First of all, it comes as a godsend to the street vendors. The fear of the Gentile police is gone from their faces. A Jewish policeman, a man of human sensibilities—one of our own brothers would not turn over their baskets or trample their wares. The other citizens of the ghetto are relieved too, because a Jewish shout is not the same as a Gentile one. The latter is coarse, crude, nasty; the former, while it may be threatening, contains a certain gentility, as if to say: "Don't you understand?"

Hanukkah in the ghetto. Never before in Jewish Warsaw were there as many Hanukkah celebrations as in this year of the wall.

234

But because of the sword that hovers over our heads, they are not conducted among festive crowds, publicly displaying their joy. Polish Jews are stubborn: the enemy makes laws but they don't obey them. That is the secret of our survival. We behaved in this manner even in the days when we were not imprisoned within the ghetto walls, when the cursed Nazis filled our streets and watched our every move. Since the ghetto was created we have had some respite from overt and covert spies, and so Hanukkah parties were held in nearly every courtyard, even in rooms which face the street; the blinds were drawn, and that was sufficient.

How much joy, how much of a feeling of national kinship there was in these Hanukkah parties! After sixteen months of Nazi occupation, we came to life again.

This time we even deceived the *Judenrat* itself. It tried to ban the holding of Hanukkah parties without a permit from a special office set up for this purpose. But this too took effect only on paper; the *Judenrat* was fooled. Hundreds of celebrations were arranged and the stupid *Judenrat* did not get a single penny.

Today is the second day of Hanukkah, and I have already taken part in two celebrations. One was a celebration organized by the courtyard committee for both festivity and revenue—more precisely, a celebration arranged by myself and my coworkers, since I am the president of the committee and since I instigated this party, which was completely successful. We enjoyed ourselves and we will give joy to the poor people of the courtyard.

Just now I returned from a celebration at the Zionist soup kitchen. On every holiday the guests here arrange themselves at small tables, sip tea, and nibble on some sort of baked goods. But that is not important. That is only on the outside, for the sake of appearances before strange eyes. The important thing is the presidium, which is headed by Kirszenbaum and Kaminar, to the right and left of whom sit all the leaders of Warsaw's Zionists, who speak and debate with words that go straight to your heart.

This year's Hanukkah celebration was very well attended. We almost forgot that we are only allowed to go as far as the corner of Nalewki and Swietojerska streets. Dr. Lajfuner gave a speech full of jokes and we all laughed heartily. There was one truth in his speech which should be stressed: "In all the countries where they want to bury us alive, we pull the gravediggers in with us."

235

Witness Czarist Russia, Poland, and Rumania. Nazi Germany will have the same fate—and in our own time.

There were also historical and scientific speeches, sermons, and all kinds of talks. Kaminar, Dr. Lajfuner, Kirszenbaum, Dr. Weisman from Suwalki, Bloch, Dr. Schiper, and I all spoke. Everyone used Yiddish except me; I "ruined" the evening by speaking in Hebrew.

January 2, 1941

A new year for savagery. A year ago we expected salvation every day. We did not know our enemy's strength, just as we did not know our friends' weakness. Even those who still hope for ultimate victory see now that salvation will be long in coming. Two giants are contesting, and before one of them overpowers the other, eons my elapse.

January 3, 1941

Informers from among the Jews, or among those of our "good neighbors" who are still allowed to enter the ghetto, brought the matter of Hanukkah to the conquerors, and their faces darkened. Is it possible? We ourselves are drowning in a sea of troubles, yet they are singing? What a rotten nation! The Germans' wrath grew to dangerous proportions. At once they enacted a strict ban on the celebration of the Polish feast of St. Sylvester in the ghetto. The edict was given to the *Judenrat*, which sent special messengers to every courtyard to give warning of the ban against the celebration and to say—apparently this was the *Judenrat*'s own idea—that we must have no lights on that night in rooms facing the street.

For safety's sake, the display of rolls and pastries in shop windows is also banned. This was not an open prohibition, merely a hint. But a hint to the wise is sufficient.

So the rolls have disappeared from view—but that doesn't stop us from eating them in secret.

January 8, 1941

Though we have been deprived of all income, the conquerors do not exempt us from taxes. One thing has nothing to do with the other. Even people without incomes and without human rights must pay their taxes, if they are Jews. Even back taxes that were long forgotten, whose records were long buried in the archives, have been resurrected.

All the churches inside the ghetto were closed and walled up, so that Aryan worshipers would not have to pass through the streets of the ghetto on their way to prayers. There is only one church, in Leszno Street near Solna, which although it is in an "unclean" area remains open, and there the Catholic Godhead continues to dwell. Its doors are wide for all who seek the word of Jesus. It is always full of worshipers who pour forth their prayers before their Father in Heaven, the Son of God.

But do you know who these pious Christians are? They are not Christians by race but Christians by conversion, people born in the Jewish race, whose souls thirsted for the "religion of love" but who remained inferior racially even after baptism. This is a truly unique tragicomedy, that Christians dedicated heart and soul to their faith wear the "badge of shame" on their right hand and the Holy Cross on their left. Even their priest is a Jew, and although he is a priest of a noble deity he must nonetheless wear the "badge of shame." These Christians have no place in the Aryan quarter, since they are considered the same as Jews; so the conquerors assigned a special church for them inside the walls of the ghetto, and said to them: "Your Lord is a Jew also! So both of you go to the ghetto!"

All along the sidewalks, on days of cold so fierce as to be unendurable, entire families bundled up in rags wander about, not begging, but merely moaning with heartrending voices. A father and mother with their sick little children, crying and wailing, fill the street with the sound of their sobs. No one turns to them, no one offers them a penny, because the number of panhandlers has hardened our hearts.

Can we survive? That is the question everyone asks. It is usually asked in a despairing tone, as though in their hearts the questioners already know there is no hope for survival, but they want to confirm it by asking other people's opinions. The stereotyped answer is one you would expect from believers who are the sons of believers: Only God knows!

And at a time like this there is no more efficacious remedy than to be a believer.

237

Logic would indicate that we are going to starve to death. Anyone who spends money without replenishing it ends in ruin, and that is our condition. We need the Gentiles but they do not need us. We buy food from them, and whether it is legal or smuggled we pay for it in full. But the Gentiles are not allowed to set foot in our territory, and for that reason they have no opportunity to buy anything from us. As a result, the money that leaves does not come back. And yet we live.

Just as our ancestors who were imprisoned in the ghetto continued to create cultural values, even though they were hated and despised, so shall we do.

January 26, 1941

Anyone who did not believe in the "eternity of Israel" would be justified in saying that the end has begun for the Jewry of Poland. But even Gentiles are amazed to see our will to live. Let anyone who believes in miracles and individual providence believe; he is fortunate. But even those who deny miracles will admit that there is a certain primal force in us which supports and sustains us.

Today new tidings reached us. Once again hundreds of families have been uprooted from their homes and are coming to Warsaw on foot. Another expulsion in the midst of a bitter winter. There is a rumor circulating that another 72,000 people have gone into exile, and all of them will be coming to the Warsaw ghetto, which is well-schooled in hospitality. Further, there may be a plan behind all this barbarism, for we hear that the murderers have decided to set up three "concentrations" of Jews: the Warsaw, Lublin, and Radom concentrations. Except for these three concentrations, no Jews will remain throughout the area of the General Government. This will make it easier for the murderers to destroy them, not one by one but wholesale. It is not impossible that they will drop bombs on us to finish us off. At all events we will become pariahs, the lowest class in human society, people who resort to crime and felonies for a crust of bread. Disease will destroy us, hunger will breed crime, poverty will raise ignorant boors, and we will end in material and spiritual destruction.

But the guardian of Israel neither sleeps nor slumbers, and good news comes from the dunes of Africa. The Jews continue in their belief that the downfall of the Germans is at hand, that their troubles are greater than ours. Their incompetent partner is already on his knees and will not rise again. It is the beginning of the end. It is obvious to us that we will end in joy and redemption, while they will end in doom and destruction.

January 31, 1941

Today three thousand new exiles from Pruszkow and other Polish cities entered the Warsaw ghetto and it was our obligation to furnish a new shelter for the unfortunates, in addition to the 120 old shelters, which are nothing more than breeding grounds for all sorts of diseases and epidemics.

The exiles were driven out of their beds before dawn, and the Führer's minions did not let them take money, belongings, or food, threatening all the while to shoot them. Before they left on their exile, a search was made of their pockets and of all the hidden places in their clothes and bodies. Without a penny in their pockets or a covering for the women, children, old people, and invalids— sometimes without shoes on their feet or staffs in their hands— they were forced to leave their homes and possessions and the graves of their ancestors, and go—whither? And in terrible, fierce, unbearable cold!

The Warsaw ghetto is surrounded on every side by Aryan districts. When the exiles came to the marked boundary between the ghetto and the Aryan quarters they were searched once more. If anyone had saved anything of value, it was quickly taken away. They even searched the invalids and the sick people in wheelchairs, and if they found a bit of food, it too was stolen.

February 1, 1941

The Jews are deprived of any benefit whatever from any institution for social good, be it governmental, municipal, or public. As a result, even our beautiful hospital in Czysta Street has been confiscated. Up to now it was supported at the municipal expense, and this right was simply a return payment for the taxes which the municipality receives from the Jewish community. And as a community made up mostly of merchants and industrialists, its share in the municipal taxes was greater than that of the others. The Warsaw municipality was anti-Semitic and did not treat its Jewish citizens justly, but even so it was forced to agree to such a social demand.

This hospital was superior in every respect. The Jewish doctors who served it were of the finest and the most renowned. Generations of Jews spent fortunes in setting it up and equipping it with modern apparatus unequaled in any other Warsaw hospitals. The anti-Semites among the Polish doctors (and who among them was not an anti-Semite?) coveted this equipment even in the days of peace. They belittled its internal organization, and they were partly right in this; but in the same breath they could not refrain from praising its equipment and building.

And here the two-act tragedy of the Jewish hospital in Czysta Street begins:

Act I: The hospital is outside the boundaries of the ghetto, because Czysta Street is on the outskirts of the city. Since the building is outside the ghetto, and its budget is no longer the obligation of the municipality, the *Judenrat* was ordered to move the equipment into the ghetto. But no building suitable for a hospital with several services was to be found within the walls, and even if there were, where would the impoverished *Judenrat* find the money to support it? But—seek and ye shall find. In order to supply its budgetary requirements, a special tax was imposed on us, whereby every householder would contribute what he wished and could afford. Every month the courtyard collectors come to receive it, but what with the general poverty they don't collect even half. And so from time to time the *Judenrat* is forced to issue calls for linens, pillows, blankets, spoons and forks. Under these conditions, the sick are not to be envied.

When they began looking for a suitable building, they found themselves in trouble. Although it was hard to find one building, it was easy to find four, so they split the hospital according to its services, and each was moved into a different building. The department for internal disease was moved to the empty school building in Stawki Street; surgery was moved to Number 1 Leszno, to the empty building of the directorate of the whiskey monopoly; contagious diseases, to 78 Leszno, to a building in which there used to be a school, I believe, and later the "quarantine"; gynecological diseases, to Dr. Gurwicz' hospital in Tlomackie Street. Up to this point was the first act.

Act II was also interesting and tragic. When they tried to move the hospital to its various branches, the humane municipality would not let the Jewish doctors remove its expensive equipment which was bought with Jewish funds. You may go wherever you

240

please, but you will go empty-handed; we won't let you touch the apparatus; that is ours. The conquerors did not interfere in this argument between the Jewish doctors and the Polish doctors: they allowed us to move everything. Writers of impressions among the Jewish doctors will no doubt tell future generations all the details of the evolution of the quarrel—I don't know the whole story. But we all understood the tragic element in this. Finally they managed to move all the equipment into the ghetto, but it was done on the sly. The doctors who did it literally risked their lives. Stories are told of the brave and wonderful actions of individual doctors.

The move took about two months, during which the hospital workers knew no rest. It was necessary to plot and deceive in order to save Jewish property from theft and confiscation. To our great joy they have succeeded in moving all the equipment—a Jewish doctor told me—but they did it at great expense, and at the risk of death.

February 14, 1941

Karmelicka Street, which is the only artery of traffic between the Nalewki ghetto and the Grzybowska ghetto, is always ripe for acts of savagery. A few days ago I witnessed a tragic scene of that sort through my window, which faces Karmelicka Street. At first I was startled and frightened by the terrible sound of a mass of people moving, like the roaring of the sea; after two or three minutes I was frightened by the silence that followed. I looked through my window and the street was empty. Not a living soul was there; it was as if all of creation were dead.

In less than a minute a Nazi murderer with a face as red as fire, whose every movement expressed burning wrath, came striding with a singularly heavy step in search of a victim. In his hand was a whip. Behind him, at a distance of a few paces, came his comrade. Both of them glanced in every direction with malicious eyes. The Jews had all disappeared. Near the building at 25 Karmelicka they met a poor ragged peddler, whose every aspect bespoke oppression, standing near his basket of wares. An awful encounter. The unfortunate peddler became a target for the blows of the murdering beasts. He fell to the ground at once, and one of them left him and went away. But not so his companion. The very physical weakness of his victim inflamed the soldier. As soon as the peddler fell, he began stamping on him and beating him mercilessly with his whip. He beat him in various ways, cruelly and sadistically—sometimes on the head, sometimes on the face, sometimes a kick, sometimes a jab. He didn't leave a single part of him unharmed. From a distance it looked as though he was beating a corpse. The beaten man lay flat, without a breath of life. But the tormentor would not let him alone. It would be no exaggeration to say that he beat him without stopping, without pity, for about twenty minutes.

It was hard to comprehend the secret of this sadistic phenomenon. After all, the victim was a stranger, not an old enemy; he did not speak rudely to him, let alone touch him. Then why this cruel wrath! How is it possible to attack a stranger to me, a man of flesh and blood like myself, to wound him and trample upon him, and cover his body with sores, bruises, and welts, without any reason?

How is it possible? Yet I swear that I saw all this with my own eyes.

February 15, 1941

Jewish children learn in secret. In back rooms, on long benches near a table, little schoolchildren sit and learn what it's like to be Marranos. Before the ghetto was created, when the Nazis were common in our streets, we trembled at the sound of every driven leaf; our hearts turned to water at the sound of any knock on the door. But with the creation of the ghetto, the situation improved somewhat. The Jewish teachers engage in their teaching with confidence that they and their pupils are in relatively little danger. The Jewish police are assumed to be reliable; even if they uncover "forbidden learning" they will not betray us to the heathens. In addition, to a certain extent we do have a semblance of permission. The Self-Aid is authorized to open and support "training points" for Jewish children. We are allowed to feed, direct, and train them; but to educate them is forbidden. But since training is permitted, we allow ourselves education as well. In time of danger the children learn to hide their books. Jewish children are clever—when they set off to acquire forbidden learning they hide their books and notebooks between their trousers and their stomachs, then button their jackets and coats. This is a tried-and-true method, a kind of smuggling that is not readily detected.

In the very midst of the infected ghetto stands a varied group of people. It is apparent that no calamity has occurred; on the contrary, their faces reflect surprise and satisfaction at some exotic pleasure. What is the novelty today? The Jews of the ghetto have made a circle around two Nazi officers, and the two faces are friendly. God in Heaven! Have the laws of nature changed?

I guessed that there was no danger, and so I too approached. Nearby I noticed little Jewish children surrounding the Nazis and nearly embracing them. Every so often the Nazis popped candies into their mouths. I was stunned. Was this a dream? Almost against my will I remained in the stream of traffic. I could not understand the explanation of the scene before me and I wanted to linger, although I'm not the kind to hang around street corners. One of the Nazis was lean, the other fat and paunchy. Suddenly I noticed that the fat one was holding a camera. As his companion fed a candy to a Jewish child, he would focus his camera for a picture. The riddle was answered. There is no Nazi without politics. Apparently they need pictures showing friendship to Jewish children for propaganda, to deceive mankind. Anything goes.

February 18, 1941

The Jewish community is on a battlefield, but the battle is not conducted with weapons. It is conducted by means of various schemes, schemes of deception, schemes of smuggling, and so on. We don't want simply to disappear from the earth.

Obviously we are the weaker side. The conquerors have a most powerful machine, and they can direct its force against us at any time. If one method of deprivation is not enough, they immediately resort to another, stronger and more violent.

You have never seen a country fair until you have seen the Jewish post office at work. One post office for half a million people! It is utter confusion. Food packages are always minus some of their contents. Sometimes a quarter, sometimes a third, sometimes half is missing. The cynics claim that the clerks eat their breakfasts from the open parcels of their customers, but it is possible that their Aryan superiors are doing the stealing. Aryanism cannot protect one from the urge to steal. In order not to tempt either the Jewish or the Aryan clerks, the conquerors have banned the sending of food parcels to Jewish recipients.

Parcels from abroad whose value does not exceed 50 zloty may still be received.

It is just before evening in the Warsaw ghetto. Thousands of oppressed and degraded Jews stream like shadows along the sidewalk in Karmelicka Street. At the Dzielna crossing a Nazi murderer appears. He struts around with his head high, his eyes filled with murder and cruelty. In his stupid face you can read the conviction that the whole world was created entirely for his benefit. In an instant the crowded sidewalk is nearly empty; no one wants to encounter this Nazi. But of this vast crowd a few Jews remained, and they took their hats off to the "lord." One of the Jews was beaten on the head while his hat was still in his hands. Taking your hat off is not enough. The Nazi did not feel that his honor was satisfied merely by an ordinary and common mark of respect. Jews are also required to clear the sidewalk before him and to keep a certain distance. Because the Jewish sinner did not do so, he deserved beating.

A crowd of idlers gather around two Jews fighting and wrestling. Each is trying to kill the other. Nobody knows what happened. But if you look closely at the wrestlers, you understand the reason for the battle. One of them was carrying a loaf of bread; the other sneaked up on him, took it away, and started running. The other man ran after him and caught him.

One claims: "I am as hungry as you are, why rob me? Go to the rich people."

The street rabble gets into the quarrel, but the mob is divided into two camps. A student of the Bible decides it: "Men do not despise a thief, if he steals to satisfy his soul when he is hungry."

Everyone agrees that King Solomon was right.

It is forbidden to hold parties with music and dancing. The victims of this order will be the courtyard committees, which live from such spectacles. In its official form the order is not directed against the Jews, but obliquely it contains an anti-Jewish objective.

There is a lot of frivolity in the ghetto, in order to somewhat lessen its sorrow. In the daytime, when the sun is shining, the ghetto groans. But at night everyone is dancing even though his stomach is empty. Quiet, discreet evening music accompanies the dancing.

It is almost a *mitzvah* to dance. The more one dances, the more it is a sign of his belief in the "eternity of Israel." Every dance is a protest against our oppressors.

Will all this end now? I swear that it will not. On the contrary. Stolen water is sweeter.

February 26, 1941

Until now the Warsaw ghetto was not completely blockaded. There was some traffic between the ghetto and the Aryan quarter through the open places left for the trolleys to go through. Jewish smugglers were partners with Aryan smugglers and made a united front to deal with the German guards and the Polish and Jewish police. So the ghetto was filled with good things, and high prices frightened no one. Anyone who had cash left over from the days of peace, or who was making an adequate living (there were some of this sort, although they were few in number), paid whatever was asked at the blackmarket prices.

Smuggling was carried out through all the holes and cracks in the walls, through connecting tunnels in the cellars of buildings on the border, and through all the hidden places unfamiliar to the conquerors' foreign eyes. The conductors on the Aryan trolleys, in particular, made fortunes, earning as much as 200 zloty a day by carrying bags full of smuggled goods hidden in the cars. Aryan trolleys make no stops inside the ghetto, but that's not a handicap. The smuggled sack is thrown out at an appointed spot and caught by trustworthy hands. This is the way they smuggle in pork fat, in particular, which the religious leaders have permitted us to use in this time of destruction. In the Aryan quarter it costs 11 zloty a kilo, and in the ghetto they pay up to 18 for it. Even "pure" Germans, both the natives of the Reich and the *Volksgenossen* born in Poland, are involved in smuggling and grow rich from it. But because of the lawlessness that has developed, the conquerors have grown more strict in separating the ghetto from the Aryan world.

February 27, 1941

Abandoned and alone, Polish Jewry is fighting for survival. There is a paradoxical statement that even if the Jewry of Poland is lost, the Jewish people will survive. This is true. But it is hard to endure the agony of Polish Jewry. If you are told as a piece of sensational news that a thousand men fell on the battlefield, you are not moved. If you hear it while you're drinking your cup of coffee, you quickly turn back to it to make sure it hasn't gotten cold. But anyone who saw the streets of Warsaw when the refugees entered the ghetto would feel his heart burst within him. The process of destruction is worse than destruction itself. The head of the Cracow district, Dr. Wächter, went to Vienna and lectured on the subject of the "benefits and consolations" which the General Government has brought to Poland. Among his other statements he said, "The Jews have been removed from commerce. Judaism is being concentrated."

That is the way of the Nazi murderers. They cloak every cruelty in a beautiful phrase. You are swayed by the prose and pay no attention to the content. Come to us, to the Warsaw ghetto, and you will see how "Judaism is being concentrated." I will lead you to the little square near the Tlomacka Synagogue, and you will see that it is full of trucks just come from the road. They are full of broken belongings, ruined pillows and blankets in which are hidden frozen babies and old men and women without strength enough to stand on their feet, who even after coming to their "rest" are unable to get down. These are the lucky ones since they were able to hire a truck on which to load all their household goods and whatever they possess. They are in the minority among the villagers. Most of them come on foot, and caravan after caravan of them enters the ghetto. Some have knapsacks on their backs, all they have saved of their property. Others carry a little bundle in one hand and a ragged pillow in the other. Their clothes are torn, their feet are wrapped in rags, and there is fear in their faces. What they are looking for I do not know. They are simply coming to their brothers in misfortune. They assume that merciful Jews will not abandon them. But it takes many hours before we manage to gather them all into some refugee point.

February 28, 1941

A Nazi murderer suddenly appears with an iron whip, and in his unholy wrath begins lashing out at the heads of the Jews. In his eyes they are prisoners of war, his mortal enemies, the foes who picked Hore-Belisha to fight against the Führer. The oppressed Jews of the ghetto are responsible for America's aid to Great Britain, and for Mussolini's defeats on the African front.

Today I witnessed a scene of this sort. I too was among the people who ran away and escaped, because I was pushed along with the crowds into one of the courtyards. Terrible fear hovered over us all; everyone ran to hide in a different corner even though the danger was not so great here. The last fugitives who crowded into the courtyard were the injured, their faces covered with welts and scratches. Blood streamed from their wounds, and no spot on their backs was unharmed. But within a few moments the people, even the victims, went on their way. Meanwhile a new stream of crowds passed by knowing nothing of what had happened. Traffic went on as it had before.

My inclination for the exotic drove me to observe the Nazi murderer in secret, so I followed him. Whomever he met he beat with his whip. Anyone who cared about himself hastily fled while the German was still some distance away, thus creating an amazing situation: the part of the street which was in front of him was completely empty, but the area behind him was crowded with people.

Two Jews who were careless and met the murderer were beaten brutally even though they removed their hats and paid homage to him.

March 1, 1941

The exiles of the Warsaw district continue to come to the ghetto. So far the terrible edict affects only the Jewish towns on the left bank of the Vistula; for the present it does not concern the right bank. But no one knows what tomorrow may bring. All of their edicts are published suddenly, and they always come like thunder on a clear day.

The Jews of Cracow are our brothers in misfortune. The expulsion edict for them was published half a year ago, but it was not total at that time. It contained exemptions for certain stated categories, and by means of bribes many people took advantage of them. Thus only those who had no legal reason for remaining, or those who did not have the money to bribe the administration, left the city. Only a few thousand were exiled, and even these would return in secret and live like Marranos. But now it is different. The new edict is being carried out to the fullest extent. The murderers decided to purge the capital city of "Jewish excrement" for three reasons: a) because of "black marketeering"; b) because of their harmful influence on the Christian population; c) because of the filth the Jews bring wherever they go, and with it, epidemic-causing bacilli. So a strict order was issued by Dr. Wächter, dated February 25, 1941, which stated that the residence permits given to the Jews of Cracow would become null and void as of the twenty-seventh of February, and their holders must return them. Henceforward only new residence permits obtained from his office would be valid. To prevent the Jewish swindlers from deceiving members of the administration who are not expert in differentiating between the old, invalid certificates, and the new ones, photographs of both types of certificates were published in the newspapers. They will be very strict about the right of residence in the capital city of Cracow, and will grant it only in an extremely small number of exceptional cases.

But the people of Cracow do not come to Warsaw in any numbers, and that is good. Even in peacetime Warsaw was not outstanding for its hospitality, let alone in these mad times when it is busy with the exiles of the Warsaw district, who have a spiritual and geographic kinship with it. The poor of your own city come first.

March 2, 1941

There are no people as expert in politics as the Jews. Every event, whether political, military, or diplomatic, causes a storm in our world. There is no end to the arguments. One thing is compared to another—one fact to another fact—one statement to another statement—and they build up all sorts of hypotheses from all of them, produce logical proofs, and reach definite conclusions. Our terrible situation has made us sensitive to any sort of change. The fate of the war is our fate here in Central and Western Europe. In this conflict between two worlds, we are in the middle. If democracy falls, we fall forever. If Nazism wins, we are better off committing suicide. And so we weigh in a balance every victory and defeat.

Today we were shocked by the news that Bulgaria has ratified the Tripartite Agreement. We don't know yet, but we have an intuitive feeling that England has suffered a diplomatic defeat, especially since the event was described and explained to us one-sidedly, from the Nazi press' point of view. Undeniably it is full of lies and falsehoods; it is nothing but deceit and deception from A to Z. But the fact alone, which is unquestionably true, speaks for itself, and the entire ghetto is in mourning. Political affinity will lead to ideological affinity. This means a Nazi Bulgaria. Rumania was first, and now progressive, liberal Bulgaria is following. This also means that Greece will fall.

Bulgarian Jewry will be cast into the dust, and its future is tragic. What is more, double and triple evil will come to us as well, for anything that accelerates the victory of Nazism hastens our death. And just when hope was flickering on every face! America . . . fascist defeats in North Africa. Decisive events!

More evil tidings accompanied this bad news. A notice was posted in the Aryan quarter inviting Polish, Ukrainian, and Byelorussian youths to apply for jobs as supervisors of the barracks being erected for the Jews. The questions arise: What barracks do the murderers mean? Are they for the labor camps which will begin working on the regulation of the Vistula when spring comes? Or perhaps we are facing an expulsion from Warsaw? Nothing, no matter how savage, is beyond the murderers. Perhaps it was for just this purpose that they concentrated all the Jews of the Warsaw district in one place?

March 7, 1941

I skipped my entries for a day or two, not because there was a shortage of new events, but because there were too many.

The confusion of life has dulled our human sensibilities, and our hearts are not free for thoughts of revenge. But sometimes a time of calm comes, and anyone who thinks about one aspect or another of our strange lives feels the urge for revenge most adequately.

Since the time of the defeat there have been many apostates among Jews. For people educated in a foreign culture there is no reason for these tortures. Why should they risk their lives for something that is strange to them? Ossified Judaism did not furnish them with the strength necessary to continue their national lives, and even though they knew in advance that race would still be a handicap for them, it did not prevent them from taking the formal step of leaving Judaism. Even if they were not accepted into the foreign milieu at once, they would be after a while, when their entrance was forgotten—especially since priests were found who arranged not only the religious aspects but the racial aspects as well. Just as money purifies bastards, it purified the children of a foreign race. After the priest received a certain sum in cash, he simply wrote out a birth certificate stating that So-and-so is an Aryan from a long line of Aryans. These certificates are assumed to be genuine, and no one disputes their veracity. Those who knew such things say that "proper certificates" of this sort have been given to hundreds and thousands. The priests made fortunes, and these impoverished members of Polish Jewry enjoyed all the rights to which the Aryan race entitles its offspring. They remained outside the ghetto area legally and were treated as genuine Aryans.

Above this group was another category of "Jews," those who were born into Christianity. They were born to apostate parents, and so they don't have the slightest feeling for Judaism, either religiously or racially. But the conquerors checked and rechecked, and the family secrets were discovered. Maybe Jewish informers who were jealous of these Christians' peaceful existence were involved, or perhaps some Pole tipped the Nazis off about irregularities in the family trees of their coreligionists. At all events, the conquerors began a hunt for these *Pans* who originated from the Jewish race and who, in their eyes, are considered Jews in every respect. The Nazis brought a great caravan of them to the ghetto and turned them over to the president, Czerniakow, who was stunned to see them in their ruin. He had known them as the cream of Polish society, people who always showed their hatred for the Jews and who adhered closely to the customs they had adopted. Some of them are the descendants of financial and industrial titans, and some of Polish litterateurs, but neither wealth nor knowledge nor genealogy was of any consequence. Like members of the rabble caught in crime and sentenced to severe punishments, they were led back to the ghetto before the eyes of passersby among the ghetto dwellers. Huge crowds accompanied them to the gates of the *Judenrat*. Like unclean people who have no place in human society, they were removed suddenly from the environment in which they had been born and raised.

Who of them imagined that his origin was in the ghetto? Who of them dreamed that his ancestors stood on Mount Sinai? The good-for-nothing Czerniakow took them into his office with a great show of respect and commiserated with them. I cannot sympathize with their tribulations. One fate for all. I don't doubt that Czerniakow's heart bleeds for them, but fate has made him a leader in Israel, and it doesn't behoove him to spread his wings over apostates and the sons of apostates.

I don't know what their end will be, but one thing I know for a certainty. Their enmity to Israel will never cease.

I have a document before me. It contains no tragic descriptions, only hard facts, but it is a succinct statement of the true situation, without sound and fury, without exaggeration and flights of fancy.

Its simplicity emphasizes our tragic and terrible situation.

It is written by the representatives of the people of Grodzisk to the "Central Committee for Refugee Affairs" in Warsaw, whose address is 58 Dzielna Street. It is numbered 41/43 and is dated March 3, 1941. Here is its text:

The Grodzisk delegation will operate in Warsaw after March 6, 1941. It encompasses the Jews of Grodzisk-Mazowiecki and its environs (Brwinow, Nadarzyn, Podkowa-Lesna, and Milanowek), five thousand people in all.

The neighboring towns were the first to receive the expulsion order, and told to move to Grodzisk. We therefore made the necessary preparations to receive the guests; we were almost certain that we, the householders of Grodzisk, would not be moved from our place. Then a rumor spread that all the Jews of the district would be expelled, and moved to a common ghetto which would be created for them in Zyrardow.

But how great was our sorrow and distress when it was made known to us on the third of February that an expulsion order had been issued for us as well, which required us to evacuate our city by the fourteenth of February. The Jews of the surrounding area, who were expelled earlier and imagined that they would find a place of rest in Grodzisk, had not even had a chance to unpack their baggage before they were suddenly ordered to go to Warsaw. Among the Jews of Grodzisk a great panic arose. By various means they began sending bundles of linens, pillows, and blankets to Warsaw. In the main the parcels were sent either by mail or by the Warsaw-Grodzisk electric tram. Up until then a Jew was permitted to travel on the electric tram only after he obtained a permit from the head of the district. After the expulsion order was enacted, they were not strict in enforcing the requirement for an advance permit; moreover, they helped them load the heavier bundles. Even the Poles did not sit idle; they too helped us in loading our baggage—some out of the goodness of their hearts; others out of happiness, because they were getting rid of the Jews. The conductors respected even those permits granted by the *Judenrat*. Besides the electric railroad, they used carts and freight trucks sending their belongings and household goods; these they loaded to capacity with sacks, both full and empty ones, with furniture, with household utensils, and with provisions. Everyone tried as much as he was able to save many of his belongings and move them to the Warsaw ghetto. Because of the panic there were some who did not bother to procure a permit from the authorities. Illegal wagons of this sort were stopped on the way, in Pruszkow or in Blonie, or else were looted by the street gangs.

Within a few days, whole caravans of wagons loaded down with the belongings of the Grodzisk exiles were wending their way to Warsaw. The city was emptied.

On the fifth of February, the Department of Health of the Warsaw District came to Grodzisk to carry out the "disinfection" of belongings of the remaining Jewish inhabitants, as well as to "steam" them in the bath house. The Jews accepted the edict voluntarily, because they thought that after the "disinfection" in Grodzisk they would come to Warsaw as "citizens purified of their uncleanliness," and would no longer be bothered. Some of us managed to avoid the Warsaw "disinfection"; but the last group (of six hundred people), which remained in Grodzisk until the twelfth of February, was taken to Warsaw like a transport of freight. These were subjected to a second "disinfection" as well as to confinement in Warsaw under unpleasant conditions. At present about sixty Jewish artisans are left in Grodzisk; they are working together at carpentry, completing an order from the military government.

Some of the exiles from Grodzisk have found a temporary haven with relatives and friends in Warsaw; some of them are being housed in the "refugee centers"; and there are some who even now have not yet found a shelter for themselves and a roof for their heads.

As stated above, some segments of the Grodzisk exiles are at various refugee centers (58 Zelazna; 44 Chlodna; 29 Leszno; and 2 Komitetowa), and some are in the prison at 109 Leszno Street. These are mostly old and sick people, who for lack of suitable quarters cannot be moved from there.

Meanwhile many of the exiles from Grodzisk come in masses to their "representatives" with all sorts of requests. They registered at the "soup kitchens"; but because they are unable to pay the 40 groszy price of a "meal," they cannot benefit from them. Our efforts to see that the exiles of Grodzisk received a reduction of the set price were in part successful; but a twenty per cent discount is not sufficient for the needy masses.

Nor is it in their power to pay the other charges placed on the exiles, such as registration with the *Judenrat* and payment for their baggage. These people, the poorest of the poor, were uprooted from their native soil, from the place where their fathers and forefathers are buried. Exiled, oppressed, without a penny in their pockets, or any source of income through either trade or labor, they become attached to the crowds of beggars in the streets of Warsaw. . . .

This is only one short scroll among those which make up our scroll of agony, an official document that for obvious reasons was written to an open organization with the necessary caution, and fulfilled its requirements with a dry recital of facts.

The files of the Central Committee for Refugee Affairs contain tens and hundreds of such tragic letters. Every letter is a sigh; every request is drenched in tears. Under the surface of the cold, official format flutter the living souls of the old and the sick, of babies and women doomed for no crime to undergo the torments of hell in this life.

March 9, 1941

This week a political event took place among the Poles, and even though we are far from the scene, its results are discernible in our lives as well. All the fawning and the compliments that the murderers proclaim in the ears of the Polish public are to no avail, and its hatred of them increases from day to day. This suppressed hatred came to the surface in an attack on the life of a *Volksgenosse,* formerly a citizen of Poland and now a traitor, a spy for the conquerors. For the sake of appearances he held the post of director of the Warsaw theaters, but in reality he informed on the Polish public to the authorities. On the seventh of March he got his just reward as a traitor and a spy, because some anonymous Pole came to his home and killed him like a dog.

It is not known whether the murderer who avenged the Polish public did so on his own or whether he was the emissary of some secret organization, but his death made an impression on the conquerors. In their idiocy they had convinced themselves that they were beloved by the Polish people for their excellent order, and that the Poles were particularly satisfied with the destruction of the Jews, which was done only for the benefit and profit of the Polish public. Suddenly they realized that the earth was shaking under them, and that they had no secure position in this foreign land. At once they decided to requite evil with evil. On the next day large notices were posted, even in the Jewish ghetto, whose inhabitants have no connection with the entire business, stating: (1) In place of the murderer who disappeared, a large number (how many?) of hostages have been taken from among the leaders of the Polish community; if the murderer is not turned in to the authorities within three days, they will be shot. (2) The entire Polish public is responsible for this murder, and as a punishment, the curfew will begin at eight in the evening and continue until five in the morning, instead of from eleven in the evening until dawn. (3) Because there is a suspicion that the murderer came from theater circles, no Polish artists, whether in theaters or in cafés or other places of amusement, will be allowed to work for a month.

This notice caused an uproar in the city. The murderer will not be turned over to the rulers, of that there is no doubt. And so all the notables who were caught will be shot—of that there is no doubt, either. This may be the beginning of more important political events. The people of the ghetto are happy and sad at the same time. They are happy that the Lord created a ghetto for them, for if it weren't for the ghetto, we and the Poles would be in the same trouble, and they are sad that the conquerors lengthened the curfew for the Gentiles, which means a lessening of the chances for smuggling.

In time of disaster a great panic hits the Gentiles and they begin to huddle close to us. This time, too, many Poles escaped secretly and illegally from the Aryan quarter and came to live for a while in the Jewish ghetto. They even wrapped the "badge of shame" on their right arms to disguise their origins. The wise and clever *Judenrat*, for the sake of patriotic prestige, allowed itself to take a dangerous step, and on its own ordered that the curfew begin at eight in the ghetto as well, even though the conquerors stated explicitly in their orders that the extended curfew applies only to the *Polen*.

If the conquerors pay any attention to this restriction we have voluntarily adopted, they may suspect us of being in league with the rebellious Poles, and of being in sympathy with them.

Czerniakow's patriotism will be our undoing.

March 11, 1941

I apologize. The extension of the curfew was not Czerniakow's own idea. We suspected him wrongly. Every time the world is beaten Israel is beaten doubly. This time we are lucky—we are being beaten equally. Although we had no connection with the entire matter and by law the punishment should not apply to us, they cannot show preference for the Jews or grant them special rights. And so this time we have equal rights. Just as the curfew begins at eight in the Aryan quarters, so too in the ghetto. When it comes to punishment, we are equal.

The hostages are said to have been put to death. It can be assumed that most of them, at least, have already found perfect peace in the company of the other Polish martyrs who have been killed in every generation since the day they lost their sovereignty. In spite of their hatred of the Jews, our hearts go out to them. We are all in the same situation: the death of heroes and martyrs.

In reality, we don't have a ghetto, but rather a madhouse. We are imprisoned within the walls and cut off from the entire outside world. Scarcely anyone leaves the ghetto; but it cannot be said that no one enters. On the contrary, they keep on coming. When the exiles from the Warsaw district stopped coming, new exiles arrived: from Norway, from Holland, and from Czechoslovakia. With my own eyes I saw a huge crowd of several hundred of them being led by Nazi gendarmes from the Danzig Station to the prison at 109 Leszno Street.

March 13, 1941

As if to increase fear, the political situation both internally and externally has been complicated. The Poles want to show the world that they are not abandoning their conquered country. This is bravery for the sake of prestige, whose value is nil but whose sacrifices are many. As to the outside, we are afraid of what is coming. Today the radio announced, quoting Tass, that Stalin is mobilizing his forces. In whispers we hear of "the eve of war" between the two comrades who embraced one another up until now. In the event of a war with Russia—which for my own part I do not believe in—we are lost. With plutocracy and communism in a partnership to fight Nazism, the Jews will immediately become the target of revenge.

No one pays any attention to funerals, because for sanitary reasons the hearse is required to go at a fast pace, and the driver urges his horses on until you are no longer able to keep up. Lately the dead have been taken for burial not by horses but by a three-wheeled wagon which the black-clad driver peddles at full strength. The wagon looks like a coffin, but no one turns to watch it or pays any attention to the fact that in the coffin which goes by at such a clip lies one of the victims of starvation. Sometimes several corpses are placed in one coffin, one on top of the other, and all are taken for burial at one time. A wholesale business! And there is one madman in the ghetto who runs after every coffin shouting; "Did the departed leave his bread card?"

Under conditions of this sort we celebrated Purim, 5701. The Book of Esther was not read in the darkened synagogues, because all public worship is prohibited; but we were happy about the defeat of the Persian Haman. We celebrated Purim in the Zionist soup kitchen at 13 Zamenhof Street, which is the center of all Hebrew-Zionist social activity. Here we always find the atmosphere and the warmth of Zionism. Every so often programs are put on with lectures, songs, instrumental music and recitations. When we come here we forget our troubles and all the terrible events taking place outside. Here you can hear debates and sermons, arguments and quarrels as in the good days. And when your throat is dry you can wet it with a glass of black coffee without sugar.

This year we read the Scroll in the Sephardic pronunciation; then we sang the holiday songs accompanied by a piano, and between one number and the other we even had a bite—three pieces of bread spread with butter, a taste of the traditional poppy-seed tarts, and a glass of sweetened coffee.

Credit for this heroic achievement goes to Dr. I. Schiper, M. Kirszenbaum, Bloch, and Kaminar.

We came sad and left sad, but we had some pleasant moments in between—God remember these men with favor!

March 14, 1941

The Jews of Poland are of a low level of culture, but nonetheless they are clever in practical life; in commerce they have unusual talents. By nature they like to see life and enjoy life; they waste money on themselves and are stingy toward others. Whatever they give is given in minute quantities and ungraciously. This is only charity for the sake of reward in the life to come. They lack the sense of brotherhood, of a bond to a community which lives the same life and is akin to them.

But let this be said in their praise: The words of the prophet have been fulfilled by the Jews of Poland: "It is a time of trouble unto Jacob, but out of it shall he be saved." We have been healed by our catastrophe. We have become a social community that realizes its obligations toward its brothers in misfortune. And social servants worthy of the name have been found who fulfill their

256

functions in the highest degree. Out of the little experience with which Starowinski approached his task, the powerful Self-Aid organization which employs hundreds of starving intellectuals has grown and flourished, and its protection now extends to all areas of our social life. Our sufferings have been a balm for our souls—we have thrown away the beggar's pack and become self-reliant.

Half a million zloty to support the needy in a single month! Who would have dared imagine that the Jews of Warsaw were capable of such philanthropy?

No doubt the Self-Aid will find its own historian who will tell future generations of its scope and magnitude, and of the greatness of its influence and its educational value, using facts and figures. I do not intend to compete with him. I wrote this out of my own impressions as someone who is close to it, on the inside, and thus sees only certain aspects of it rather than the entire picture. In January, the Self-Aid stopped collecting contributions and became an institution which imposes taxes that have legal force. Thereby it entered into a new phase. Since then it is developing in a new direction. In my future entries I will touch upon this new incarnation.

March 15, 1941

I wanted to continue what I started: the Jewish Self-Aid in its second incarnation. But meanwhile the wrath of the tyrants has broken in upon us.

This week the Jewish carters were deprived of their livelihood. All horses owned by Jewish drivers—already a remnant of the good horses they once had, but their only source of livelihood—have been taken away—not to work in the camps, heaven forbid, because they were not capable of that, but to make up the losses of the Polish drivers, whose horses were also taken. In this manner the end suddenly came for an occupation that supported hundreds of Jewish families.

Today the Nazi press published the words of the Nazi military governor in Holland, Seyss-Inquart: "The national status of the Dutch has not been touched; but the Jews are not Dutch. They are such enemies that we will never make an armistice or a peace treaty with them. We will strike the Jews wherever we find them, and all who assist them do so at their own risk."

What will be our end if the arm of the tyrant is not broken?

The Labor Battalion was created by the *Judenrat* at the instigation of the conquerors. To our disgrace, the *Judenrat* used it for its own needs and its own budget. The *Judenrat* was ordered to furnish a certain contingent of youths for work, several thousand daily. But a postcript was added to the whole ugly project: If you give a ransom you can go free. Someone who has no money will take your place.

When the ghetto was created the youths of the Labor Battalion were the only ones who left the ghetto boundaries legally and returned legally. Every one of these young laborers brought food from across the border when he returned. The Nazis rarely interfered. So it was that with the conquerors' permission and assistance, the young men brought forbidden food into the ghetto.

With the dissolution of the Labor Battalion, the opportunity for thousands of poor families to bring in inexpensive food was gone.

In the past few days more trouble has developed. That is the matter of the enlargement and condensation of the ghetto at one and the same time. Even in this mass grave called a ghetto they give us no rest. Sienna Street has already been tried by fire. The sword was raised over the heads of its Jews once before, and they ransomed the street with four kilos of gold. But the thieving appetite of the murderers was not satisfied with that. Now they come with a new demand: Divide it! The left side will be for the Gentiles, the right side for the Jews. This time even gold won't help. And so even the mud of the ghetto is raked up from time to time.

In the midst of all this, not only have we maintained our hope for a speedy redemption, but it is growing stronger. Roosevelt is our Messiah. The Nazi press argues with him and contradicts his premises, but in order not to embarrass itself it publishes excerpts from his statements, the excerpts most favorable to it. But we, in spite of their wrath, know of other excerpts which bring balm to our souls. He took words from our own hearts, as though he were in the ghetto and saw how we live, although he didn't mention us by name.

Once, at the office of the Self-Aid, I began a conversation with a clever social servant who had soiled his hands with communal work all his life and knew exactly what was going on. The office was a beehive. New clerks had been added as the clientele grew. When I saw all that was happening, I said, half-joking, "Our business isn't bad!" The social servant answered: "The more clerks there are in the office, the less beans in the pot."

And here lies the source of the trouble. The Self-Aid started on a small scale and set foot on the soil of Warsaw in trepidation, but gradually it grew and developed and achieved greatness. It attained a budget of 150,000 zloty a month. It branched out more and more. It employed hundreds of clerks. And the more the number of refugees and poor people removed from their occupations increased, the greater was its obligation to the unfortunates. It was overwhelmed by the flood. At the same time, when the bureaucratic Joint, the child of American plutocracy, seeing that it did not have the strength to face the waves, passed a sentence of death on itself and almost ceased to exist, the Self-Aid, child of our own community, faced into the cruel waves and its strength for survival increased.

A complex machinery was set up almost overnight. Although it was built on unsteady foundations, it was capable of serving as a permanent basis for the project, and it began doing its work with great success. Hearts were awakened and hands were opened. There was no building in which a courtyard committee was not established to take charge of all the problems. It was able to classify the residents of the courtyard according to their positions and material resources. It also knew which among the residents of the courtyard needed support, and which were obligated to give for the support of others. A sort of *vox populi* came into existence, which judged everyone according to his actions and his philanthropy. If they encountered a "stubborn pig" they softened his heart by various means, some ethical, others coercive. Whoever did not wish to give was considered an outcast in his neighbor's eyes and was publicly shamed. His name was listed on a black-board, which was hung on the gateway so that all who entered the courtyard would know that So-and-so had set himself apart from the community and would not come to the aid of the people. The courtyard committee assessed everyone's material resources and imposed a monthly payment upon each householder. The sums taken in were turned over to the central fund which supported the soup kitchens.

All this was in the early days of its awakening. But it wasn't long before public opinion began to intimate that not everything was right and proper with the Self-Aid, that they were stealing and embezzling, that the soup kitchens were spending a lot but feeding very few, that there was no overall control, that "the whole business is not worthwhile," etc., etc. And the more the backbiting, the less money it took in. It is not my place to judge who is right. As usual, people exaggerate. There is no doubt that the hands of the leaders are clean, but it is possible that some individual official betrayed his trust and stole from the funds. That sort of thing happened even in the days of Joshua.

March 23, 1941

Today I visited the exiles from Danzig, and I came home with my heart torn. There is no shortage of tragedy in the ghetto, for wherever you go there is poverty and oppression, hunger and disease, tears and suffering. We have become insensitive to the troubles of individuals. Yet what I saw at the refugee point for the exiles of Danzig upset me so that even my heart, a heart which has turned to stone, was moved. In the ghetto we are used to vocal tragedy, to loud lamenting, to shouts, groans and sighs, but here, in the giant building of the former business school at 12 Prosta Street, I encountered silent tragedy, victims of a great disaster who sit buried in their own sad thoughts. Their eyes are without a ray of hope or a spark of life.

March 25, 1941

We were all dismayed when Bulgaria entered the Tripartite Agreement, but Bulgaria is nothing. She can do nothing without the approval of Russia. As proof, she has made no move since, because Stalin ordered her to halt. Of Yugoslavia we said, "There is nothing to fear, she will not give aid to the murderers," but to our great sorrow we were disappointed. Today the local radio announced that the Nazis have entered Yugoslavia and that tomorrow her government will announce her adherence to the Tripartite Agreement officially. They expected a military attack in the spring. The diplomatic offensive in southeast Europe began even before spring came. And so again England has suffered a defeat, and England's defeat is ours as well.

Yet in the very midst of this tense situation our will to live grows stronger. May I see them defeated before I die!

The conquerors are famous for their program of *Gleichschaltung:* they are all equal. As opposed to the plutocratic nations, they have no privileged class. Everything is for the sake of the people. Just as everyone's obligations are equal, so too are their rights. Everything depends on local conditions and on the particular despot on whom our fate depends. There are cities and towns in which there is no ghetto, where shrewd authorities are ready to accept bribes. And in places where ghettos have been established, they are not all closed. Tyranny cannot withstand the power of money.

This week the Nazi press published a report on the ghetto in Cracow. It is more than a report. It is an idyll. The conquerors' forte is in cloaking the cruelest barbarism in a mantle of stunning prose. To strengthen the impression, they illustrated the report. Here is a picture of a typical Galician Jew, on whose face contentment is evident. He is no doubt pleased at the thought that he will live alone in the ghetto and have nothing to do with the Gentiles. Here is a second picture: a Jewish youth carrying a suitcase, striding toward the ghetto with great steps that stem from inner happiness. Beside him are two young women carrying a bundle between them. They are smiling happily. The caption under the picture reads:

The transfer of the Jews to the suburbs of Podgorze was done for economic and health reasons. It does no harm to the survival or the habits of the Jews. The faces of the two Jewesses before us, full of joy and contentment, prove that they do not consider the move to Podgorze a means of punishment intended to deprive them of any of their needs.

And so on. Bluff, bluff, and more bluff without end.

Out of the depths, our hope for a speedy redemption flowers. Shadows of victory—in the phrase of the Dutch Queen Wilhelmina —are growing brighter. The past few days have been a time of joy for those Jews who see victory in the shadow of a victory. Good news followed good news. First the revolt in Yugoslavia, then victories in Africa, and finally, a naval battle in which Italian ships were sunk. This had led to all manner of imaginary creations. One refugee from Lodz is already making arrangements for the return trip. And so the terrible oppression which grows stronger from day to day is not making an impression. We have become, in our eyes, redeemed—potentially, at least, if not in actuality. What is an expulsion if it is only temporary? What does hunger mean when satiety is close at hand? But in our practical lives there are only troubles upon troubles.

April 3, 1941

Like the Egyptian Passover, the Passover of Germany will be celebrated for generations. The chaotic oppression of every day throughout this year of suffering will be reflected in the days of the coming holiday. Last year the Joint's project was functioning full force. It was not conducted properly and many people criticized it, but in the last analysis it fed the hungry and brought the holiday into every Jewish home. We lacked for nothing then.

This year everything is changed for the worse, and we are all faced with a Passover of hunger and poverty, without even the bread of poverty. First of all, the Joint has divested itself of all activity in connection with the holiday. In effect it has disappeared from the communal stage, and its voice is no longer heard. Self-Aid support is also a matter of leaning on a shattered reed; and the new taxes did not help to ease its burdens. We thought they would quiet our fears about the support of the soup kitchens, but we were wrong. We Jews are not afraid of a Jewish government. Many evade payment of the tax, and no threat of punishment does any good with the misers. If the Jews of Warsaw who are able to pay had obeyed Czerniakow's decree and turned over the tax of two zloty apiece each month willingly, the problem of feeding the hungry would not be so serious. The courtyard committees who were charged with the assessments had to fight the miserable creatures for every penny. A strong, healthy father of a family of five, who spends 30 zloty a day for the needs of his household and whose home is filled with good things, was ready to put out the eyes of the chairman of the courtyard committee because he would not give him a reduction on his assessment of two zloty per person. "A poor man like me pay ten zloty a month? God in heaven!"

And so there were arguments and quarrels in every courtyard. The members of the courtyard committees are the scapegoats.

The end result is that the collection of the tax goes on with the greatest difficulty. In theory the recalcitrants should be punished, and there is even a special office for this purpose. But this punishment-machine does not function at the necessary tempo. The courtyard committees overlook much, out of their unwillingness to make enemies, and the punishment office overlooks much for personal reasons. The result of all this is that the tax has not improved the situation and the soup kitchens are closed almost every other day.

As the holiday drew near, the Self-Aid made the customary Passover appeal for money for the poor. But this project was born in an unlucky hour and its results will be nil. At present—one week before the holiday—the project's treasury is empty.

What, then, will we eat during the eight days of the coming holiday? I am afraid we will turn our holiday into a weekday. For prayer there are no synagogues or houses of study. Their doors are closed and darkness reigns in the dwelling places of Israel. For eating and drinking there is neither matzoth nor wine.

CHAPTER
SIX

October 8, 1941

End of the first two days of Sukkot

OUR SUFFERING GROWS MORE ACUTE. Even those who anticipate the end and hope for quick redemption are now convinced that we will spend the winter under the Nazis. Last year by a stroke of luck the weather throughout the winter was mild; during the preceding summer we had obtained coal at a reasonable price. Moreover, we were still relatively healthy, and capable of withstanding the inevitable bad times. Not so this year. The enemy became tougher and more effective. Before we have time to utter the *Zidduk ha-Din*[1] over one decree, a more severe edict is hovering over our heads. No relief! No concession! No coal has been stored because of its astronomic cost, 2,000 zloty a ton! But, most important, our physical strength is at a low ebb. Anyone who could still spare a garment has sold it for food. And not only garments but jewels, ornaments, and household goods as well. The Sienna Street expulsion has filled our cup of sorrow to overflowing. The poverty and

---

[1] Prayer recited at a funeral, acknowledging justice of divine judgment.

overcrowding are beyond belief. At first it was rumored that expulsion had been decreed for the whole of the Grzybowska ghetto. For several days thousands of Jewish hearts were trembling in fear. Yesterday the *Zyd* newspaper announced that the edict would not be carried out in full. Our consolation is that only the tenants of the odd-numbered houses of Sienna Street and of the southern parts of Sosnowa and Wielka Streets will be forced to vacate their apartments. Otherwise everything is quiet and calm. Well then, rejoice, children of Israel! Somehow or other, thousands of livelihoods have been wiped out and the soup kitchens founded by the Joint now have a larger clientele.

October 9, 1941

In return for the areas which had been cut off from the ghetto and joined to the Aryan quarter, the boundaries of several streets which had heretofore been outside its limits were attached to the ghetto. Also added were certain streets which stretched to the outermost city limits and until now had been occupied by a very poor Aryan population. To the unenlightened this seemed proper compensation for the areas that had been sheared away. In point of fact, however, the exchange was nothing more than fraud and deceit. The remnants of the streets to be judaized were inhabited by a poverty-stricken group of wagoners, peddlers, and artisans. Their flats are small and very run-down. The houses, too, are old and lacking conveniences. On the Jewish side, however, the dispossessed are well-to-do merchants and the professional intelligentsia. The evicted families are looking for flats on the central streets of the ghetto.

Tens of thousands of people have moved into the area assigned to us. The overcrowding on Karmelicka Street is indescribable. There are always thousands milling about and the uproar deafens the ears and confuses the senses. Staying at home, however, is even worse. Seven families share one flat, every corner occupied by a family, and endless bickering prevails. We must confess that the people lack a sense of unity in times of common catastrophe. When Polish Jews[2] are asked to contribute to charity, they may give, partly for the sake of the *mitzvah*, and partly because they are shamed into it. But if you ask for a contribution to help refugees,

[2] The diarist had a low opinion of Polish Jewry.

the reaction is—here are 5 zloty and let me alone. But should the same refugee come to the contributor to rent a room, then he will deal with the poor unfortunate heartlessly, raising the price and setting difficult conditions. He will demand a whole year's rent in advance and insist on every last penny. Each new decree constitutes a source of income for those not affected by it. Even the tragedy of Sienna Street did not mend the ways of those contemptible creatures who trade on the sorrows of their fellows. First, they raised the rent on the rooms; instead of 60 zloty, they demand 100. Use of the kitchen is strictly limited. Conditions are spelled out regarding the tenants' every move. It is little wonder, then, that people living under one roof hate each other.

There is a Housing Committee functioning in the *Judenrat* for the purpose of fighting the profiteering in apartment rentals. This office threatens and punishes, but its work is ineffectual. Everything is based on bribes, on influence, and on prejudice! Finally, every man does as he sees fit. A Jewish government!

Another curious fact: The Jews, fearful of the tyrant, are very quick to obey all the decrees. In two or three days Sienna Street was vacated. At noon on October 5th not one Jewish soul remained in any of the odd-numbered houses on Sienna Street. Not so the Aryans. They were given until October 10th, and so far not one of them has moved. They are certain they will be granted an extension. For are they not Aryans?

No one enters or leaves the overcrowded ghetto. Leaving it is especially fraught with danger. Only the Jewish dead are the exceptions. True, the road to Praga, which is out-of-bounds, is fenced in; but there is practically no boundary between the cemetery on Gesia Street and the Aryan suburbs. Should some nimble, impudent corpse wish to enter a world in which he does not belong, there is nobody to stop him. Consequently, every corpse being taken for burial in the Gesia Street cemetery is in my eyes a candidate for leaving the ghetto.

Death in the ghetto has become big business which brings great profits. In normal times burial was in the hands of the Jewish community, undertaken by the *Judenrat*, while special cases were handled by the *Hesed shel Emet*,[2] which acted as an auxiliary branch of the *Judenrat*. Not so now. Wherever you turn you see offices for burial arrangements. In front of each stands the black wagon, in sight of all. This is the "quick aid" for human beings who died of starvation and typhus and who now number many tens of thousands.

When death strikes, the mourner turns the "merchandise" over to the burial office, which then attends to everything. So the black wagon proceeds—sometimes drawn by a horse and sometimes pulled ricksha fashion by the employees of the burial office—from corpse to corpse, loading as many bodies as it can hold and transporting them wholesale to the cemetery. Usually the expedition to "the other world" begins at noon. A long line of horse-drawn and ricksha-drawn wagons then stretches along the length of Gesia Street. This death traffic makes no impression on anyone. Death has become a tangible matter, like the Joint's soup kitchen, the bread card, or the raising of one's hat to the Germans. At times it is difficult to distinguish who is pushing whom, the living the dead, or vice versa. The dead have lost their traditional importance and sanctity. The sanctity of the cemetery is also being profaned; it has been turned into a marketplace. It now resembles a "fair" of the dead.

The purification building cannot contain the hundreds of dead. It is filled to capacity and more bodies are brought in constantly. The stables in the cemetery courtyard are also being used as a morgue. There the corpses are laid out with professional skill; a minimum of space for a maximum of "merchandise." They lay the bodies on top of each other, naked, with their emaciated limbs dragging after them. The custom of wrapping the body in a shroud and *talith* has also been discontinued. In place of cloth, which is very costly, paper is used, and that too in insufficient quantity. And the work! In a slaughterhouse the carcasses of the slaughtered calves are handled more carefully than are human beings in the Warsaw cemetery in the year 1941. Even the formalities which always preceded the actual burial have undergone a drastic change. The cemetery department of the *Judenrat* has hundreds of members with vested interests. For some reason which seems incomprehen-

[3] Literally, true loving-kindness for which no recompense is expected.

sible to me, you have to make your payment to the cashier, not of the *Judenrat* but of the cemetery, or, more accurately, to the cemetery attendant, who puts the money into his pocket. This attendant signals an order to bury the body but does not indicate a specific section. The cemetery office does not assign a plot; it only gives permission for burial. Whatever must be done after obtaining permission to bury one's dead must be privately arranged between the mourners and those who do the burying, or the office to which the burial arrangements have been entrusted. Any wagoner can bring a body in his wagon for burial. If you choose, you may even bring your own hired gravedigger from outside the cemetery. And if you are aggressive enough no one will prevent your selecting the best plot available to bury your dead. You won't get an official permit to do so, but if you proceed boldly no one will stop you. Marketplace! Fair! Chaos! I myself witnessed the goings-on; I attended to the burying of one of the dead and, because I was very busy, it was twilight when I brought him to the cemetery. The cemetery office was closed. The attendant wanted to postpone the burial to the following day, but I begged him to let the burial take place immediately and he finally agreed. I paid the required fee but was not given a receipt. He signaled the order for burial but did not indicate where. My dead was lucky for by the merest chance he was given one of the choice plots; I had a feeling, however, that his name was not recorded in the cemetery's books. Several days later, when I came to the cemetery office to inquire, I discovered that I was right: his name had indeed not been recorded and the location of his grave was unknown. I had noted it down for myself so the number and location were now duly recorded beside his name in the cemetery books. Where did the money go?

October 10, 1941

A hint of the "eternity of Israel"—that's how we saw the opening of our synagogues on the holidays. Three synagogues opened their doors for service: the Big Synagogue on Tlomackie Street, the Nozik Synagogue on Twarda Street, and the Lithuanian and Zionist-Mizrachi Synagogue, Moriah, on Dzielna Street. This was done officially, through the *Judenrat*. As for the *Judenrat*, to whom the entire matter was turned over for consideration under certain conditions stipulated by the conqueror, there was nothing to prevent arranging a *minyan* in every house. And many courtyards took advantage of this. Although the endless suffering had produced a great many agnostics among Jews, nevertheless every *minyan* was filled to overflowing. Everyone sought the Hebrew gathering, the companionship, the religious atmosphere that had been missing for the past two years.

I prayed in Moriah, which shone on the holiday with "the light of seven days." The sacred candelabra of the destroyed Danzig Synagogue were now installed in Moriah, where they cast a sea of light. These were giant brass candelabra, marvelous works of art. When the *Judenrat* of Danzig was exiled, its candelabra went into exile with it. Happily they were destined to shed their light once more in the tent of Jacob and not in some Catholic or Protestant church.

In 1939, on the eve of the war, a thorough program of renovation had been started in the Moriah Synagogue. This was no routine job of repairing cracked walls or a leaking roof but a tremendous overhaul which included basic structural and architectural improvements that altered the appearance of the building completely. The work was nearly finished when the war broke out and everything came to a halt; the elders of Moriah forbade the holding of prayer services and the various halls of Moriah were turned into refugee shelters for hundreds of displaced unfortunates. The sanctity of the synagogue vanished; in its place appeared filth and foul odors. Suffering transforms people into barbarians. In their ignorance, they did not spare the building, the furnishings, or the sacred vessels. Everything was either broken or destroyed; nothing was left whole. However, when the time came to "restore our days as of old," all was purified and renewed, and on the eve of the High Holy Days, 1941, the Moriah Synagogue again stood radiant in its purity, its splendor, and its sanctity.

Typhus is destroying us and them. When two friends meet and one tells the other of the illness of a third, he never identifies the disease, for that is understood anyway; it must be *the* sickness that is now prevalent. The same applies when anyone dies; the cause must be typhus. The number of fatalities is enormous. Some families have lost half their number. Everyone knows someone who has succumbed to this horrible disease and there is no end to the toll it is taking.

But God plays no favorites. The poor rally and recover while the rich succumb and die. The poor man's body, toughened by constant struggle, is capable of withstanding even this dreadful disease; but the pampered soul—one touch and he is gone. It is also worthwhile noting another remarkable fact. In their newspaper, *Der Stürmer*, the Nazis state that the Jews are spreading the disease and contaminating the Aryans in their vicinity, adding that the number of fatalities from typhus is greater among the Aryans than among the Jews. We may conclude that German typhus patients are dying as well as Poles. And rich Jews succumb more easily than the Jewish poor. And who is to blame for this situation? The Jews, of course! They are by nature filthy. The overcrowding is nothing. The poverty? The starvation? None of these. What then? The blood of the race—everything stems from the blood. Blood is the man! And *Der Stürmer* continues: The typhus, too, is another Jewish swindler—a form of revenge on the Gentiles!

The sanitary laws that the Nazis have passed serve mainly to provide the sanitation employees with graft, because in return for money anything goes. At the beginning of the epidemic a ten-week quarantine was imposed on any court in which a case of typhus occurred. A policeman was stationed at the gate—sometimes a gentile, sometimes a Jew—to see that nobody entered or left. In practice, however, anyone could come and go freely if he put two or three zloty into the hand of the guardian of the law. Another source of income for the sanitation personnel was the regulation regarding the disinfection of every contaminated flat in the court. Here, too, bribes help. Finally, all the residents of a quarantined court must go as a group, under the surveillance of policemen, to the bathhouse designated for this purpose. A public bathhouse of this type may kill the lice, but it may also infect one with other diseases. Again money talks. The Nazi gendarmes and the police are alike in that both help to conceal, to smuggle, to bribe and commit illegal acts. There was no need to create all these difficulties, especially since nobody could or would observe the regulations. Ultimately, those in supreme authority decided to relax the restrictions. They reduced the quarantine to just one day. But the orders pertaining to the disinfection of apartments and to the purification in the bathhouse remain unchanged.

How fruitless all these sanitary regulations are may be seen from the following incident. I had a tenant in my flat, a refugee from Bialystok. One day he fell ill with typhus and I hastened to inform the Health Department. A week passed and no one came to remove the sick man to the hospital. In the meantime the patient passed away. Again we notified the Health Department so that they might disinfect the court. Some days later, a physician from the Health Department appeared and announced that no disinfection would be carried out in the court but that everyone in my household would have to go to the bathhouse, I at once approached a "fixer," paid him 25 zloty for five people, and so escaped that punishment. I myself disinfected the tenant's room, at my own expense. The world of the ghetto rests on three things: on bribes, on bribes, and on bribes!

October 13, 1941

The Eve of Shemini Atzeret, Tashab (5702)

One year ago on the eve of *Shemini Atzeret* there were already intimations that we were to be enclosed in a ghetto. The Lodz ghetto was a precedent. Our future was unclear and we feared a similar calamity would befall us. A year ago we used many clichés to comfort ourselves. Be strong! We will overcome! No weapon that is formed against thee shall prosper! Previous generations had built homes, planted vineyards, married and had children—all in a ghetto. We wanted to prove to ourselves that we were not inferior to our ancestors. There was, therefore, fear within, but outwardly—a cheerful mien.

Now, on this *Shemini Atzeret*, we have gathered again in a meeting of comrades in suffering to observe the precept: "And you shall have nothing but joy." A year has passed, a year of bitter experiences. We wanted to summarize everything that happened to us and draw relevant conclusions. Again we spoke words of consolation and hope: just as we have withstood everything until now, so shall we continue to withstand all that may yet occur until better days return. But all these comforting declarations lacked conviction. We talked, but doubt was a worm gnawing at our hearts. Of what avail are words of comfort when our strength diminishes from day to day? Wherever we turn we see only poverty, hunger, death. The death rate is now 10,000 per month. To make matters worse, the winter has set in early this year. Snow has already fallen this Sukkot. We have no coal and no winter clothes to ward off the cold. Our bodies have shriveled to half their normal size.

To add to our grief, bad news has reached us from the battle-front. Perhaps it is exaggerated but no doubt it contains a grain of truth. Our enemy is advancing and every victory for him prolongs the war. So we sat at the table like mourners. I attempted to cheer the group by singing "Deliver me, I pray Thee, from the hand of my brother," but there was no response. I changed to "Play Me a Kozachok," but this, too, went unnoticed. Finally, I tried "Lord is Master over all His work," with a Hasidic *bom bom* accompaniment —but this too failed. The gathering broke up with halfhearted expressions of hope. It had been more a wake than a holiday cele-bration.

October 18, 1941

The Nazis continue to advance on the eastern front and have reached the gates of Moscow. The city is still fighting desperately but its fate has been decided—it will surely be captured by the Nazis. What matter whether a Stalin or a Hitler is in power? And when Moscow falls, all the capitals of Europe will be under Nazi rule. The English and Russian broadcasts have misled us and dis-torted the truth. Why, we were almost certain that the murderers' defeat was imminent, that they would disappear into the endless Russian steppes. Now that the Nazi press is again proclaiming cer-tain victory, we wonder what will become of us. A Nazi victory means complete annihilation, morally and materially, for all the Jews of Europe. The latest news has left even the most hopeful among us dejected. It seems this war will go on for years.

The Nazis have calculated that the birth and death rates in the Lodz ghetto show that in six years' time it will be completely wiped out. The Lodz ghetto is situated on the soil of the Reich and enjoys privileges denied to us. The Warsaw ghetto suffers 10,000 deaths per month. At this rate, in fifty months our entire ghetto will die out.

October 21, 1941

Today came another shock. A new break-up of the homes of 20,000 Jewish souls. This time it is the odd-numbered houses on Zelazna and Chlodna streets as well as the alleys branching west from these streets. And no alternative housing is offered. It is impossible to describe the resulting confusion. Twenty thousand people received notice that within five days they must vacate their houses, stores, workshops, and businesses and move—where? Those affected by the order simply went mad.

October 22, 1941

Last year permission was granted to open the schools but this was never put into effect. The reason given then was the typhus epidemic which was still raging through the ghetto. A large concentration of children in one place would be likely to spread the disease. On the face of it, this seemed a justifiable argument. But it was not so much concern for the people's health that motivated the Nazis as their desire to deprive Jewish children of an education. Now, a year later, with the number of typhus victims exceeding that of last year, permission has been granted to the *Judenrat* to open the schools. It is as though last year's considerations had never been. So now we're to have popular education again, the lack of which had so troubled us.

The *Judenrat* has an inflexible rule—to receive but not to spend money. When ordered to bear the expense of popular schooling it simply turned the entire matter over to the political parties. *Tarbut*[4] was given two schools where they can instill their ideology and *Agudat Israel*[5] was given three; CJSO[6] also received a share. There remained, without political patronage, only schools whose language of instruction had always been Polish. This type of school came under the *Judenrat's* own wing and consequently was the last to receive a handout. The party-run schools are not free, however. Tuition is 10 zloty a month, and there is a registration fee of 5 zloty. They expected a large enrollment, but they were disappointed. The poor cannot afford the fees, and the well-to-do are afraid to expose their children to the children of the poor, who might be carriers of disease. Private schooling has not been eliminated, and it continues as before to provide a livelihood for thousands of teachers who conduct classes in their homes.

[4] Literally, culture. An East European Hebrew educational and cultural organization, established in Poland in 1919.
[5] World organization of Orthodox Jews founded in 1912.
[6] The Central Jewish School Organization in Poland.

October 23, 1941

The Berlin and Cracow press occasionally print some item about Palestine, but its contents are invariably distorted and untrue. Whatever the contents they are always full of hate and cutting sarcasm directed at England and "its favorites, the Jews." Nevertheless, we have become experts at sifting the news and separating the wheat from the chaff.

To Zev (Vladimir) Jabotinsky fell a great privilege: the news of his death was reported in all of the Nazi newspapers. Now the sad announcement of the passing of Menachem Mendel Ussishkin has reached us, this time in a private letter from Switzerland. A memorial meeting for Ussishkin was held in the quarters of *Hatechiyah*, 13 Zamenhof Street, the center for Zionist meetings. It has been turned into a soup kitchen and refugee shelter for Zionists who have escaped to Warsaw. M. Kirszenbaum and Dr. Isaac Schiper are the self-appointed patrons of this Zionist soup kitchen, and it is they who see to it that the flame of the Zionist cause is not extinguished.

An excellent appreciation of Ussishkin was delivered by Bloch. He described the deceased as having laid the foundation upon which rested the three principles of our national revival: Hebrew land, Hebrew labor, and the Hebrew language. Bloch was followed by other speakers who represented the Mizrachi, the Zionist rabbis, Zionist women, and Zionist youth. Each of them stressed Ussishkin's characteristic love of the soil and devotion to the Zionist tradition. Yes, Ussishkin's death closed a brilliant era in the rebirth of our people and our country.

November 2, 1941

I have recorded nothing these last few days. They have been days of privation and suffering. The ghetto area is being reduced again, and the frightful crowding increases the spread of typhus. The Nazi overseer, Hans Frank, paid us a visit a few days ago. Every visit of his is followed by "much weeping for generations." His visit in the fall of 1940 brought the decree of the ghetto upon us; his current visit aroused fears we couldn't put into words. Dr. Milejkowski, who represented the ghetto in negotiations with the Nazis, reported to our ghetto physicians the results of his talk with Frank. He had been told: "If typhus doesn't stop among the Jews,

274

they don't belong in Warsaw! Warsaw has no need of the ghetto walls!" Every man among us silently prayed: Any other decree but not expulsion from Warsaw!

As the short autumn day draws to a close, darkness spreads its wings over the whole ghetto, both indoors and outdoors. Outdoors, because of the blackout which has been compulsory since the hostilities with the USSR began; indoors, because the supply of gas and electricity to the ghetto has been cut off. Coal (for cooking—who can even dream of using coal for heating?) is not only terribly costly but is seldom available. Gas has always been cheap and was used in every household. But with the gas shut off how can one prepare a hot meal? Every glass of hot tea will cost a fortune. At eleven o'clock at night, however, long after everyone has fallen into an exhausted, troubled sleep, the electricity is turned on but gas remains unavailable. So our pangs of hunger and thirst sharpen. What sadism!

November 5, 1941

The ghetto which the Nazis have forced us into is far worse than the ghettos of the Middle Ages. In those days, the ghettos were established as a rule in response to the wishes of the Jews themselves, who sought religious isolation. Economic relations with the Gentiles were never interrupted. On the contrary, the ghetto dwellers came and went freely in the courts of kings and princes and amassed great wealth. But the Nazi malevolence has no precedent in history.

This week thousands of people were evicted from Elektoralna Street and crammed into the ever-shrinking ghetto. More than a hundred houses were taken from us, and in return we were given a little over seventy dilapidated ones. It was certainly not a housing shortage that prompted these acts, for the homes they vacated remain empty.

It is rumored that the cemetery of Gesia Street will be declared off ghetto limits and will be joined to the Aryan section. The Nazis do not trust those who accompany the dead. As a matter of fact, their suspicions are well founded. The cemetery fence borders on the Aryan section, thus providing smugglers—both Jews and Aryans —with a broad base in which to operate. Henceforward people accompanying their dead for burial will be denied permission to

275

enter the cemetery grounds. They will be permitted to come only as far as the gate and then strangers will accompany the departed to their graves. Well, I'll bet this won't help either! Were it not for the smugglers, we would certainly have starved to death. Ironically, credit for sustaining lives must also go to the Nazi smugglers who help the Jews. Money is the answer to everything. For a price even a Nazi will bring smuggled merchandise to the Moriah Synagogue and unpack it in one of the storerooms.

November 7, 1941

On Karmelicka Street the congestion grows worse from day to day. Crossing this thoroughfare, which joins two ghettos, you feel that you have been catapulted into a pot that is boiling over. People push and shove and elbow you until you are forced to step down to the cobblestoned gutter. There is a great confusion of pedestrians, street vendors, overloaded porters, carriages and delivery carts, beggars and all sorts of creatures whose proximity you cannot bear for fear of lice. The fear of lice obsesses all of us, for the tiny creatures are the carriers of typhus.

November 9, 1941

Dwellers in the ghetto are like inmates of a roofless prison. Every crevice has been sealed and even an Aryan mouse would find all access blocked. The smuggling center was heretofore Kozla Street because its walls constitute a boundary. As in Rahab's wall in ancient days so here, too, there were apertures in the wall which overlooked the Aryan quarter as well as the apartments of the Jews. When the Nazis became aware of their oversight they ordered iron bars placed in front of the windows. This plan of splitting Okopowa, Zelazna, and Sienna Streets along their full length is a device meant to prevent the smuggling. The side adjacent to the Aryan quarter has been forbidden to Jewish tenants and the opposite side, facing the Jewish quarter, is once again open to them. Well, not only windows but cellars too were used as smuggling points, and the Aryans on the one side and the Jews on the other continue to carry on the smuggling trade. A tremendous building on Leszno Street stands on the borderline of the two adjoining quarters. The entrance is from Aryan Rymarska Street while its cellar windows face Jewish Leszno Street. Here Esau and Jacob make peace be-

276

tween them not only because of their common hatred for the Nazis but also because of their love of money. Partners to this interracial dealing are the Jewish policemen. The Nazis themselves have not hesitated to participate when they could make a tidy sum for themselves. The authorities, finally convinced of their failure to put a stop to the smuggling, have now adopted legal measures. Today large notices were posted on all the ghetto walls, signed by the ghetto commissar, announcing that any Jew caught outside the ghetto without an official permit would be sentenced to death. This applied to giving aid or shelter to such a transgressor. Yet on the very day the death notice went up, I met several Jews who had already visited the Aryan quarter illegally. This is their only means of livelihood, and they will not relinquish it.

November 10, 1941

This is our third winter under the Nazi regime and our second within the ghetto. Contagious diseases and especially typhus continue to take their toll. There is not a family which has not lost one or even several of its members. A strange thing: The weak and the frail rally and recover, while strong, healthy men succumb and die. The women are especially fortunate, and often survive their men. Among the doctors, too, the typhus fatalities are numerous. The notices announcing the death of a doctor refer to his dying "a physician's death," and the public understands what his illness was. Almighty God! Will you destroy the remnant of Israel in this way?

November 11, 1941

The hunger and privation! Even the fortunate ones who have a trade or do clerical work at the *Judenrat* or Joint Distribution Committee or Jewish Self-Aid offices suffer. The price of all foodstuffs is now thirty to forty times higher. Food is available but the only ones who can buy it are the lucky few who earn a good living by today's inflated standards. Because of the exorbitant prices on even essential foods, such as bread and potatoes, most families bring food home from the public soup kitchens. To avail themselves of this privilege, people must show proof of their poverty. Respectable, formerly well-to-do people who never had to worry about matters of food now stand in line next to all sorts of coarse and vulgar characters waiting their turn for a bowl of watery soup. For this one pays eighty pennies.

277

Vanquished and enslaved Poland has accepted its fate, but the conqueror continues to rattle his sword over the heads of the population, both Aryan and Jewish. Occasionally it cuts off an Aryan head, but only when a crime demands the extreme penalty. If the Poles would agree to relinquish their political rights, then no harm would befall the Polish Aryan community. Actually the Nazis are trying to ingratiate themselves with the Poles and pretend an interest in the Poles' welfare. Not so with the Jewish community. The Nazis have condemned the entire Polish Jewish community to death by one means or another. But I am certain that "the eternity of Israel" will not be destroyed.

November 13, 1941

This journal is my life, my friend and ally. I would be lost without it. I pour my innermost thoughts and feelings into it, and this brings relief. When my nerves are taut and my blood is boiling, when I am full of bitterness at my helplessness, I drag myself to my diary and at once I am enveloped by a wave of creative inspiration, although I doubt whether the recording that occupies me deserves to be called "creative." Let it be edited at some future time—as it may be. The important thing is that in keeping this diary I find spiritual rest. That is enough for me.

My wife has been stricken with typhus. I must save her. In order to get doctors and nurses to come to my home it would cost more than 100 zloty a day and my resources are almost gone. The funds of the Joint Distribution Committee and other social welfare agencies are available only to the hangers-on and bootlickers who are always at the directors' beck and call; I must somehow bear the expenses of this illness myself. Besides, I must conceal the presence of typhus in my apartment because it is forbidden to nurse a typhus patient at home. I am alone and must engage a nurse who gets 120 zloty for a 24-hour day. The cost of medicines is exorbitant and the *Judenrat* has put a 25 percent tax on medicines as a source of income for its funds. My wife's moaning tears at my heart. She feels her end is approaching. I soothe and console her as best I can.

My brain is busy with one thing: "Whence cometh my help?" I try to think of the objects of value remaining in my possession that could be sold. During the two years of war almost everything I had was sold in order to escape starvation. Death is lurking at the patient's side, and one suppresses all feelings of sentiment toward even the most cherished thing.

November 14, 1941

Yesterday between ten and eleven in the morning we had a taste of actual war. The Russians came in their planes, dropped several bombs, and disappeared. When hostilities broke out in June 1941 we feared that a front was being created right here in Warsaw and that we would be a direct target for both sides. But we were quite wrong. Day by day the front moved farther and farther away from us until it reached the very gates of Moscow. At the start of the war we experienced a few bad days but they ended quickly. Five months have passed thus. The compulsory nightly blackout seemed superfluous. Then suddenly, one fine day—boom! Bombs were exploding! It was, as we heard later, a direct hit on a house on Sienna Street and it killed eleven people. A second bomb hit the Okenzia Airport. The third one struck a plot of land owned by Narutowicz. The first had been directed at the western railroad crossing, the second at an airplane factory, and the third at a headquarters of the German gendarmerie. None of them hit their targets.

November 19, 1941

All over the ghetto groups of Jews stand in front of wall posters signed by the ghetto commissar, Auerswald, announcing that eight Jews caught leaving the ghetto without permission had been sentenced to death. The sentence was carried out November 17th, 1941. The eight martyrs were six young women and two men. These "criminals" had been caught making quick forays into Aryan territory in an attempt to smuggle food. They were murdered for breaking the law which forbade leaving the ghetto without the required pass. One of the victims, a young girl not quite eighteen, asked the Jewish policeman who was present at the execution to tell her family that she had been sent to a concentration camp and would not be seeing them for some time. Another young girl cried out to God imploring Him to accept her as the expiatory sacrifice for her people and to let her be the final victim.

The representative of the Jewish jail on Zamenhof Street, Mr.

Lejkin, and several representatives of the Jewish police were present at the execution. Their task was to lead the victims to the execution spot and to bind their eyes and their hands. The men refused to have their eyes and hands bound. Their wish was granted. The execution squad was composed of Polish policemen. After carrying out their orders, they wept bitterly. O earth, cover not thou my blood!

December 2–3, 1941

The Kingdom of Israel! That was the magic slogan of the Revisionists. But had they known how this term would be perverted by the assimilationist Jews of Poland they would not have inscribed it on their banners. When the Nazis granted us "political autonomy," they established the *Judenrat* to administer our affairs. When these Jewish representatives were appointed we thought they would be a source of solace and strength for us. In our common tragedy we believed these brothers by race and blood would respond with compassion and love for their needier kin. But these assimilated Jews felt no spiritual ties to the oppressed ghetto Jews. These *"Pans"* (one-quarter, one-third, or one-half Jewish) wanted no part of us. Before the war, they moved in Gentile-Jewish circles, insulting and being insulted. They heaped insults on the Jewish elite, while their Gentile neighbors despised them along with all other Jews. They were strangers to their own people, to its spirit and its culture. It was more than strangeness; in fact, they despised everything Jewish. Their antagonism (to the Jewish masses) was not based on any ideological opposition for they had no ideals except their materialism.

It was these *Pans* who were installed at the head of the *Judenrat*, where they at once began to demonstrate their arrogance. Inasmuch as all aspects of governing the ghetto were involved—the Jewish police, provisioning, housing, the postal service, schools, health, and other matters—these lackeys had a great opportunity to play favorites and amass wealth in the process. The *Judenrat* is responsible to no one except the ghetto commissar, who is himself a partner in all the fraudulent business.

December 9, 1941

War between the United States and Japan! From now on the whole world, except Turkey, is up to its ears in bloodshed. "And

280

every man's sword was upon his fellow!" Ostensibly, three ideologies are clashing in this frightful war, each of which wants to dominate the world. Actually, there is no ideology—only business. Three bellicose worlds are fighting for power: The old democratic, capitalist world, which aims at keeping the markets it already has as well as acquiring new ones. Opposing it is the Fascist-Nazi world, which seeks to annihilate the old and aims at establishing a new world order. The third protagonist in this battle of the giants is the communist world, which would find it most convenient if both the others were destroyed, but at the moment deems it more prudent to join with the capitalist world and benefit from its support. Their hatred for Nazism has led Stalin and the Churchill-Roosevelt team to reach a temporary peace among themselves.

December 10, 1941

From the Germans we learned the value of every scrap, every remnant, every bit of waste material that we used to throw away. Even a torn, ragged sack is a piece of goods which people pounce on eagerly these days. Any worn, patched garment is desirable merchandise that is snatched up instantly. Though it has been turned on all "three" sides, it will be turned again and yet again and put to use. An adult's shabby garment is made over into a smaller garment. This "industry" employs thousands of tailors who were made idle due to the shortage of materials for clothing. These "trivial" things fill your days with annoying worries and irritations until you are quite sick of living. It is a gross, sordid kind of life.

December 12, 1941

What was destined to happen has indeed happened! America's declaration of war on Japan was followed by another war declaration—the USA against Germany. Roosevelt took this step even though the declaration was made by Hitler. Still, let us not be prejudiced: it was Roosevelt who brought it about. The official declaration is merely a formality although a state of war has actually existed between these two powers for some time. Only Roosevelt wanted this situation to continue. Even when he was "neutral," everything he did was to the advantage of England and the detriment of Germany.

Over the radio today came the declaration that "behind Roosevelt stands world Jewry." As always, no matter what the trouble, the Jews are responsible. Henceforth, the stupid Nazis will insist that Germany is at war with world Jewry. They will say that on the one hand is Bolshevist Russia, which was created by Jews, and on the other is plutocratic America, which is controlled by Jews. Herein lies our tragedy. Another reason for revenge on us: ever since the Bolsheviks came to power we have become alienated from Russia. Except for occasional letters to relatives we have had no contact with Russia. Not so with America. Many charitable institutions which are the mainstay of our very existence—especially the Joint Distribution Committee—exist thanks to American funds. And now that America is officially Germany's enemy, the Nazis are sure to vent their fury upon us. The American philanthropic institutions here will be abandoned; the community leaders who had dealings with plutocratic America will be arrested; the soup kitchens will be shut down. Whatever aid we received until now from America will be stopped completely. Furthermore, any American funds now in hand will certainly be confiscated.

But we live with one hope: The Nazis are not strong enough to fight the entire world.

December 14, 1941

The smuggling, which has not ceased—even after the eight Jews were shot to death—is a thorn in the Nazis' flesh. But with the complicated splitting up of the streets weaving through the Jewish-Aryan quarters, smuggling becomes more dangerous. Yet the desperate find a way to evade the police. It seems that every aperture serves as a station for smuggling activities. Most of the windows of the Jewish flats facing the Aryan quarter have become conduits through which smuggled goods are passed. I live on Kozla Street. In years to come you will hear tales about Kozla Street and the smuggling marvels performed there.

A new eviction edict covering the 12th to the 21st of December applied to families living in odd-numbered houses on Elektoralna, Tlomackie, Nowiniarska, Sapierzynska, Mlawska, and certain parts of Franciszkanska and St. Yuska. The houses border on the Aryan quarter and provide good vantage points for smuggling. This eviction has also struck a spiritual blow which affects us most profoundly. The magnificent synagogue on Tlomackie Street is being turned over to strangers. This house of prayer has been our pride and our glory, particularly in recent years when it was a meeting place for all who thirsted for the vision of the redemption. Together with this synagogue, we will also lose the Main Library for the Study of Judaism, whose dismemberment by the Nazis began two years ago when they removed most of the rare volumes. The few that remained, bearing the Nazi stamp, will now be destroyed. Ruin has struck a great national treasure. Since the outbreak of the war the splendid library building had housed the central offices of the Jewish Self-Aid Society, the largest philanthropic institution in the ghetto. Perhaps the building will not be demolished, but its prestige and the dimensions of its work and activities will be vastly reduced.

December 15, 1941

First day of Hanukkah

Our holiday has been turned into a day of mourning. The court-yard of the prison on Dzielna Street was turned into a slaughter-house today. At ten o'clock this morning, within earshot of thousands of people who were jammed around the fence encircling the jail, fifteen people were shot to death. They had been caught outside the ghetto limits. This murder, like the earlier ones, was carried out after a "trial" and "legal sentencing."

Seventeen "criminals" has been brought to trial but one had committed suicide and another was sick in bed. The cries of the victims in the prison courtyard were heard by the throng outside. Rage and frustration turned into mass weeping. Other prisoners locked inside the prison began to shout and beat their heads against the walls. There is nothing more nerve-shattering than the concerted weeping of a great crowd. The wailing at this hour in history was an echo of the weeping and lamentation decreed upon the generations of the people of Israel. It was a protest against the loss of our human rights. The sentence was carried out by Polish policemen in the presence of rabbis and other representatives of the Jews. The Poles fired the shots—and they too wept. They had been given no choice either.

December 17, 1941

This year very few Hanukkah candles were lit. As the day ends, a total blackout settles over the ghetto. There is no illumination on the streets because of the fear of Bolshevik air raids. For the same reason, not a ray of light issues from apartment windows or shops. In many houses the darkness is complete, for most people cannot afford the price of kerosene or even candles. Nevertheless, we've become so accustomed to finding our way in the blackout that the ghetto streets are crowded with people hurrying about their business during the evening hours. Even the street beggars do not pause in their work when evening comes. At times the whole ghetto seems like some eerie underworld inhabited by ghosts intent on strange pursuits.

It is noteworthy that not a scream or a cry is heard on our streets even in the dead of night. There are no acts of robbery or violence. This proves what a highly civilized people we are. Everyone feels his way in the dark, serenely confident that his way is secure and that nothing will happen to him. The sons of Esau would commit robbery when darkness covers the earth, while the sons of Jacob turn away from theft even under cover of darkness when opportunities abound.

December 19, 1941

Friday, eve of sixth day of Hanukkah

A firm conviction burns within us that the beginning of the end has begun for the Nazis. What basis have I for such optimism? A "communiqué" from the battlefield was published yesterday, December 18th, which reads as follows: "Because of the approach of the Russian winter . . . the front line must be shortened. . . ." This is disaster veiled in rhetoric. You don't retreat if you don't have to. After besieging Moscow for three months Hitler finally gives up and turns back his army of fifty-one divisions, wounded and beaten. This is a humiliating defeat for the arrogant German. The broadcasts over the British radio, which we hear secretly at the risk of our lives, add even more fuel to our imagination. They report that the Nazis have suffered a shattering defeat and have been utterly routed; that in their flight they have abandoned enormous amounts of war matériel. To these English exaggerations we add a pinch of Jewish fantasy. Wishful thinking! While one man is saying that the Nazis have already reached Minsk, another announces they're in Baranowicz, and then a wit comes along and reports bona fide information to the effect that Churchill sent a cable to the ghetto, saying, "Let the Jews not run after the Nazis so fast because he has not the strength to follow them. . . ."

These rumors spread like wildfire, wherever people stop to talk, even beside the walls that are being built the length of the streets. That's the way our people are—the bitter reality does not constrain their glowing imaginations: "On the very day the Temple was destroyed, Messiah was born. . . ."

December 21, 1941

Monday, eve of eighth day of Hanukkah

We had a "holiday" today. The *Judenrat* invited us to come to the Femina Theatre to celebrate not the Festival of the Maccabees specifically, Heaven forbid, but the opening of the school year for Jewish children under the aegis of the *Judenrat*. It is ironic that in these terrible times we have at our disposal spacious halls in which hundreds can gather for all kinds of public meetings. The creation of the ghetto unavoidably included many magnificent buildings which in peacetime belonged to the Gentiles and to which no Jews were admitted. These are now put to good use in the ghetto. Originally the Femina was built as a motion-picture theatre but its proximity to a Catholic church prompted the Polish government to forbid its operation. It was a total loss, standing empty and desolate until the ghetto was established and it became quite useful.

Many came to the gathering because they had nothing better to occupy their time and were eager to hear comforting words from their community leaders—all without charge. It was worth braving the crowd just to hear the speech delivered by the chairman. Before he was elevated to his present office he was a *shmendrik* like all the other good-for-nothings of the assimilationist circles. Suddenly he became a lover of the Yiddish tongue, honoring it to the point of recognizing it as our national language. Yet all his words of praise were spoken in Polish. What is more, he criticized the intelligentsia, taking the diploma-holders to task severely and justifiably, forgetting only to mention himself as one of them.

We saw and heard strange things at that assembly. The director of the *Judenrat's* school department at present is A. Alepowicz, who was the director of the *Chinuch Gymnasium* until it was closed down. He is the consultant to the *Judenrat* even though nobody elected him. The *Judenrat* nowadays is composed entirely of appointed officials. Let it be so! He is one of the "Folkists"[7] which no longer exists. His sole virtue is his antagonism to Hebrew; Yiddish is the language of his choice. And yet as chairman of the evening he conducted the assembly entirely in Polish. He even delivered a historical-philosophical talk on Johanan ben Zakkai and Nachman Krochmal[8]—in Polish. Good God, what hypocrites these all-important personages are!

Sitting together at the speakers' table were wolves and sheep, lambs and leopards, and they did not devour one another. Somehow they maintained a truce for the time being. Let us look at the facts: Zysze Frydman spoke of nationalism, confirming its rightful place in Jewish life. A similar theme characterized the remarks made by Szerynski of the Mizrachi, who wove religious and nationalist views together as his party has always done. Both of them spoke Yiddish because they don't know Polish. If they did—who knows?

Menachem Kirszenbaum, the Zionist, read his speech in Hebrew, but what a Hebrew that was! It came out half Sephardic and half Ashkenazic, so twisted and mispronounced that it sounded more like a gypsy dialect. I felt embarrassed before my neighbor but he reassured me with the remark: "In Hebrew, anything goes. No one understands it anyway." I relaxed at once.

All the speakers had one thing in common: Without exception they expressed their pride and satisfaction in securing a Jewish education for our young, overlooking the fact that it is a provisional arrangement adapted to our temporary stay in the ghetto. When the day of our redemption dawns, all this will vanish as though it had never been. With it to its eternal rest will go the chairman and his advisors.

December 22, 1941

New misfortunes are due to befall us at the beginning of the year 1942. The *Judenrat* president knows what they will be but will not release information in advance in order to prevent panic. Some of the guesswork is so funny that one can't help laughing.

[7] A Jewish political party, founded in Poland in 1916, which advocated Jewish cultural and national autonomy in Poland.
[8] A Mishnaic teacher of the 1st Century C. E. and a Galician historian and philosopher, 1785–1840.

Nevertheless, wild stories are circulating and upsetting everyone. Now then, what are the impending disasters? Lend an ear and listen:

1. Jews will be forbidden to marry and bring a new generation into the world.
2. Husbands and fathers will be castrated to prevent procreation.
3. The curfew will be moved back from nine to five P.M.
4. The blue-and-white "badge of shame" with the Star of David as its background will be replaced by the "yellow patch," relic of the Middle Ages. Moreover, instead of one badge we'll be forced to wear two: one in front, the other in back.
5. Jews will be forced to wear shoes with wooden soles.
6. Jews will be required to wear a uniform hat, a *shtreiml* pointed at the top like a pyramid.
7. Jewish currency will be issued. In Lodz it will be called *Chaimkes* and in Warsaw, *Adamkes*, each named for the local *Judenrat* chairman. The purpose of this special Jewish currency is to cut off permanently all contact between Jews and non-Jews.

Woe is me if I laugh, but many of these interdictions are destined to be put into practice with all their tragicomedy. Meanwhile, we cling to the hope that every new decree they inflict on us means they have suffered another debacle. . . .

Today the radio announced that Field Marshal Walther von Brauchitsch has retired. His place will be taken by the Führer himself. This is a sure sign that the Nazi structure is beginning to crumble. Every voluntary resignation is preceded by a defeat. Von Brauchitsch was the central pillar of their high command. His resignation indicates the existence of internal quarrels and differences. Inasmuch as no other general has taken over, all the generals must agree with von Brauchitsch. This news bulletin is the grain of truth on which I base these deductions, but by the time salvation comes, we'll have perished. The giant's last gasp is a long time coming.

December 26, 1941

So far none of the rumored decrees I listed a few days ago has been announced, but the villains struck a totally unexpected blow today. Notices were posted on all ghetto streets ordering the Jews to turn over to the Nazis via the *Judenrat* in the next three days (December 26–28) every scrap of fur they possess. No payment will be made in return. This includes merchandise intended for sale as well as personal apparel. All furs have been declared the property of our enemy. It matters not whether a coat is a luxurious fur or a peddler's old sheepskin—all must be turned over to the Nazis in the next three days. Nor do they stop at fur coats. All fur collars, cuffs, boots, even scraps, must be delivered as tribute. The penalty to any Jew who disobeys is death. There is never a lighter penalty for Jews. For the Aryans, the decree is put in the form of a request: "Won't you please, dear sirs?" "We need the warm garments for our sick who are defending you against the Bolsheviks."

Yet, as in each successive decree, so in this one too we find some solace in the realization that the Nazis are indeed on the run. Their total defeat is imminent and the Russian plains will be their grave. We also have sub rosa information that the German Minister for Military Supplies has committed suicide. All these scraps of news are forerunners of good tidings.

December 27, 1941

The fur decree has raised a great hue and cry in the ghetto. The time limit of three days included our Sabbath. Moreover, the order is deliberately unclear just to confuse and trap us. Nobody knows whether the decree includes the cloth to which the fur is attached. Yesterday, the 26th, their decision was generous: The cloth was detached and only the fur was taken for the Nazis. Today it was mean: Whoever brought the fur only was sent home to bring the cloth as well. For its service and for a receipt the *Judenrat* is collecting two zloty a head.

There are business firms formerly owned by Jews that now function under a Nazi commissar. They employ many Aryan officials who can move freely in and out of the ghetto. This provides them with an opportunity to make profitable deals with the Jewish owners of furs. Every Jew has an Aryan "friend" who is prepared to do him the kindness of holding a fur in trust until the danger is past. The Aryan is not responsible for the coat in case of theft or confiscation. You have to depend on your Aryan friend's honesty and integrity.

December 28, 1941

This is the third and final day of the fur deadline. The whole ghetto looks like a day at the fair. Everyone is hurrying to the

Judenrat, where thousands are standing in line in the bitter cold waiting to turn in their warm winter clothes.

In addition to the "legal" fair an illegal one is in progress. No sooner was the fur decree published than the ghetto was invaded by Aryan speculators who moved in and acquired valuable fur coats for mere pennies. The Jews do the selling without bargaining because time is short and the danger great. The Aryan speculators exploit the situation to the hilt, paying pennies instead of zloty. These sons of Esau have never been seen on the streets of the ghetto before. All of them are elegantly dressed, most of them wrapped in the fur coats they have bought for a song.

But the biggest commotion of all is stirred up by a few Jews who are busy buying up furs at rock-bottom prices, not for themselves but as agents for Aryan customers. The merchandise thus purchased is passed at once from hand to hand, quickly reaching the real buyer who has the cash for payment, and leaving the Jew with his agent's commission. Thus did the Nazis provide certain Jews with a new form of livelihood for a period of three days.

January 4, 1942

The words of the poet have come true in all their dreadful meaning: "'Tis not a nation nor a sect but a herd." Gone is the spirit of Jewish brotherhood. The words "compassionate, modest, charitable" no longer apply to us. The ghetto beggars who stretch out their hands to us with the plea: "Jewish hearts, have pity!" realize that the once tender hearts have become like rocks. Our tragedy is the senselessness of it all. Our suffering is inflicted on us because we are Jews, while the real meaning of Jewishness has disappeared from our lives.

Our oppressors herded us into the ghetto, hoping to subdue us into obedient animals. Instead, however, we are splitting and crumbling into hostile, quarrelsome groups. It is painful to admit that ever since we were driven into the ghetto our collective moral standard has declined sharply. Instead of uniting and bringing us closer, our suffering has led to strife and contention between brothers. The Nazis, possibly with malice aforethought, put us in the hands of the *Judenrat* so that we might be disgraced in the sight of all. It is as if they were saying, "Look at them! Do you call them a people? Is this your social morality? Are these your leaders?"

289

It is not at all uncommon on a cold winter morning to see the bodies of those who have died on the sidewalks of cold and starvation during the night. Many God-fearing, pious souls who, if the day happens to be the Sabbath, are carrying the *tallith* under their arms, walk by the corpses and no one seems to be moved by the sight. Everyone hastens on his way praying silently that his will not be a similar fate. In the gutters,,amidst the refuse, one can see almost naked and barefoot little children wailing pitifully. These are children who were orphaned when both parents died either in their wanderings or in the typhus epidemic. Yet there is no institution that will take them in and care for them and bring them up as human beings. Every morning you will see their little bodies frozen to death in the ghetto streets. It has become a customary sight. Self-preservation has hardened our hearts and made us indifferent to the suffering of others. Our moral standards are thoroughly corrupted. Disgraceful as it may sound, we must admit the bitter truth: Everyone steals! Petty thievery, such as picking pockets or stealing a hat or an umbrella, is common. Because kosher meat is terribly expensive, people have relaxed their observance of the laws regarding the eating of kosher food. Not only atheists and derelicts are guilty of this, but synagogue sextons and pious men as well.

It is Nazism that has forced Polish Jewry to degrade itself thus. Nazism has maimed the soul even more than the body!

January 7, 1942

A certain percentage of the ghetto population has become rich by trading on their brothers' privations. The severe restrictions, which are virtually impossible to observe, give rise to an army of daring smugglers and profiteers. They literally risk their lives but their gains are great. Two kinds of leeches suck our blood: the Nazi leeches who set up the machinery to annihilate us, and their offspring, the Jewish leeches, who thrive on smuggling and black-marketeering. I refer especially to the big-time smugglers who promote schemes in partnership with the Nazis and divide the spoils between them. They can set prices as they choose.

Man's nature is such that in times of crisis the urge to "eat, drink, and be merry" is most powerful. Such people, feeling they "may as well be hanged for a sheep as for a lamb," are in constant pursuit of pleasure. For them an abundance of everything is available. Shop windows display all sorts of delicacies, but who can pay the astronomical prices? Places of entertainment function in the ghetto, and they are full to overflowing every evening. Should anyone venture into the ghetto without knowing his whereabouts and enter one of the luxurious cafés, he would be astounded. Who would believe that the lavishly dressed crowds enjoying the music, pastries, and coffee are the persecuted victims of tyranny? The innocent visitor would never suspect the truth until he looked around outside too. Sometimes at the very entrance of one of these elegant cafés he might stumble on the corpse of a victim of starvation.

Leszno Street has the distinction of being the entertainment center of the ghetto. Operating here are all the pleasure places which welcome the smugglers, the black marketeers, and all those fortunates who live off our troubles. Every child in the ghetto knows who they are and what prices they charge. The well-known Hirshfeld brothers set up a sumptuous café at 64 Leszno Street. One weekday evening I went in there with a friend, seeking to relax for a while and to hear some music. But every table was occupied. There was no room, not even standing room. This was only the front part of the café where they charge popular prices. In the room beyond, where the orchestra plays, the price is double. There is yet a third room—for card players. Here they rent the tables by the hour. People say that the owners' income is 1000 zloty a day.

It is the same with the theaters. There are quite a few in the ghetto. They are filled to capacity every evening. Their repertoire is the vulgar, common variety of *shund* theater on the lowest level imaginable. Heaven forbid that they should touch even lightly on the realities of life. So too the restaurants. Just as people stand in line at the Joint's soup kitchen in order to get a bowl of watery soup for eighty pennies, so do others stand in line at the Hirschfeld brothers' café in order to eat a 20-zloty dinner.

January 15, 1942

The cold is so intense that my fingers are often too numb to hold a pen. There is no coal for heating and electricity is sporadic or nonexistent. In the oppressive dark and unbearable cold your mind stops functioning. Yet even in such a state of despair the human

291

spirit is variable. The call for a free tomorrow rings in your ears and penetrates the bleakness in your heart. At such a moment one's love of life reawakens. Having come this far I must make the effort to go on to the end of the spectacle. It is hard to foretell who will live and who will die, and it is especially hard to depart from this earth without knowing the final outcome. In the face of this battle of the giants one's desire to live becomes overwhelming. In spite of the frightful suffering there are no suicides among the ghetto inhabitants. In these fateful hours, we long for life. "Blessed is he who hopes, he will live to see the restoration of Israel!"

Good news, friends! The ghetto is being honored with a People's University. Sometimes you just want to laugh, a Homeric roar of laughter that will resound throughout the ghetto. But this is not a time for laughter. The tears in your eyes have not yet dried.

The Zionist Menachem-Mendl[9] has never tired in his efforts to convince the entire ghetto that its very survival depends on him. Hence, an organization has been established known as *Tekumah* (Revival), for the purpose of starting a People's University. Actually it is only a ruse to persuade the Joint's directors to allocate a monthly sum for the establishment and maintenance of such an institution. In practice, it will only serve its founders and administrators.

The Zionist Menachem-Mendl does not say "I" but "we" when he refers to the Zionist organization, whose spokesman he has become ever since it ceased to function. Zionism in times such as these is like a disembodied soul, devoid of form but with its good name still intact. It retains sufficient vigor to impress those who scorned it in the good days but turn to it now in hope of salvation. The Zionist Menachem-Mendl is the self-appointed heir to the defunct organization, and this has enabled him to become a close associate of the Joint, coming and going freely in its offices, carrying Zionism as a shield before him. He has a good thing in hand, and being a clever man uses it for the benefit, not, God forbid, of the Zionist cause, but of himself and his entourage. This is a small group of men for whom Zionism in peacetime was an ideal as well as a source of some honors and publicity. Today it provides them

[9] Used by the author in this context as a derogatory term.

with a livelihood. And a livelihood in the ghetto is no small matter. One of the directors of the Joint is Mr. G., who used to be a merchant. He is half assimilated but has no education and can speak only a very bad Polish. He is completely devoid of any knowledge of Judaism. Half non-Jew, half illiterate, this creature has climbed to the post of community leader. This non-Jew held captive among the Jews has been appointed a director of the People's University by Menachem-Mendl, who can manipulate him for his own purposes.

Do you want a Zionist kitchen? Here you are! Menachem-Mendl needs no power of attorney. Nor is it necessary to investigate whether he is persona grata to the majority of his fellow Zionists. Menachem-Mendl has wisely provided himself with devoted companions who accompany him everywhere, two Galician doctors who serve as yea-sayers, their reward being a fine practice in the ghetto.

The Joint requires only a name for an institution in order to put its bookkeeping wizards to work assigning funds in the name of Zionism. So Menachem-Mendl obligingly conceived the *Tekumah* and its offshoot, the People's University. They've drawn up a list of lecturers which, with one or two exceptions, consists of names of people included for publicity purposes. Most of them have never dreamed of delivering a lecture since they are totally unfit to mount even an elementary school platform. The Galician doctors are evidently familiar with all that pertains to a people's university, for are they not Galician? They have also prepared a most impressive list of subjects for the lectures.

When all was ready, they arranged an elaborate opening at which the invited guests were treated to a glass of sweetened tea and a cookie. Menachem-Mendl opened and closed the assembly with his remarks. Sandwiched between, the two Galician doctors delivered speeches in praise of Jewish learning and the newly created institution. The budget will be arranged by Menachem-Mendl. Two of the professors will be Gutgeld for Jewish literature and Nathan Asch for the Scriptures. The Joint director sat with the dignitaries, enjoying the prestige thus added to the Joint's record.

The audience listened in silence to all the gushing nonsense and left the hall pleased with the refreshments, which are very rare indeed in the ghetto today.

Rejoice, ghettoites! You have a People's University!

We have not yet finished with the matter of the furs. The fur and woolen-garments decrees were imposed on the people of Germany too. In the Fatherland too they threatened the violators with the death penalty although they used more civil language. If they had to resort to such dire threats, it is obvious that the people did not want to give voluntarily. In England this was interpreted as a wave of rebellion spreading across Germany. For propaganda purposes, they added that German women stretched themselves across railroad tracks in an effort to stop the trains that were loaded with the winter clothes which had been taken from them.

But, listen and wonder! I do not know what goes on in German cities but I do know what goes on in the Warsaw ghetto. All the furs turned in by the Jews were sent to a disinfection center where, for some unknown reason, a fire broke out and the costly merchandise was consumed by the flames. We learned that the patriotic Germans themselves were the incendiaries who set the conflagration in order to cover up a crime. They had smuggled out the costliest of the furs and sold them. Only the furs of poor quality were delivered to the disinfection center. To conceal the theft and prevent the possibility of investigation and examination, they burned down the whole place. The fire warmed all Jewish hearts, who perceived in it the finger of God.

These are gray days in our ghetto. The new edicts that we expected have not yet materialized, and the previous ones are like old friends by now. Time turns them into normal aspects of our lives. With unrelenting regularity the tyrants shower us with a succession of minor decrees, none of which can kill but each of which spells a deprivation, a sting, an injustice.

According to regulations we are supposed to live on 2½ kilos of black bread per month. Anything more than that is obtained by smuggling and costs ten times as much. Bread obtained legally costs 90 pennies per kilo, while the smuggled bread costs 9 zloty per kilo. These disproportionate prices apply to other foodstuffs as well. Sugar is rarely available and then only at 40 zloty a kilo. Butter is nonexistent, while margarine costs 80 zloty a kilo. Meat is not to be seen. A picture of life in the ghetto today would not be complete without noting the continuing cut in gas and electricity. The bitter cold has also frozen water pipes so that toilets do not function and we are forced to bring in water from the outside.

Yet, in spite of everything, we survive. We live like pariahs but none of us wants to die. It is a fact which puzzles the Nazis not a little—why are there no suicides in the ghetto? Because everyone wants to remain alive under any circumstances just to witness the end of the war and the end of Hitler! That is why this freezing cold which brings us disease and death also brings us a measure of comfort. This same cold is decimating the armies of the Führer on the plains of Russia. It is a hope we cling to.

January 27, 1942

Conquered areas have provided the Nazis with much of the raw material needed for their war machine. Their armies flung across the face of Europe derive their sustenance from the countries they have conquered and subdued. They loot and rob and no one can protest. The taxes and other monetary penalties they inflict on their vassal states are unbearably heavy. What is worse, they commandeer a labor force in each conquered country to produce whatever they require. Here in Warsaw, Aryans have been seized on the streets and sent to forced-labor camps to work without pay and little food.

As the war dragged on, seventeen-year-old boys were called up in Germany. More and more hands were needed in the munitions factories and in the fields. A sharp decline in the number of workers forced the Nazis to abandon their racial principles. If skilled labor was essential for victory, even Jews were acceptable. To this end hundreds of workshops were opened and operated by Jewish contractors who employed thousands of Jewish workers. This brought some economic relief to the ghetto. The Nazis provided the raw materials and the Jewish workers turned out the finished products. As usual, the contractors made money and some even grew rich, while even the most skilled workers remained at the poverty level. Nevertheless, there was no shortage of laborers because free soup kitchens were set up at every workshop by the military authorities. Thus the workshops exist in the hundreds, with Jewish workmen skilled in a variety of trades earning a meager livelihood. A joke is making the rounds that in one of the sewing shops the overseer scolded the men for turning out trousers that were not made in accordance with specifications. The workers answered: "To get killed in, these pants are good enough!"

A strange situation indeed has been created. Instead of labor camps where the work is done for nothing, the Nazis have opened workshops in which Jewish workers earn their crust of bread. Incredibly, the Nazis themselves oversee the shops so that nothing will happen to the Jewish workers. The destroyer of Israel is guarding the remnant of Israel!

January 30, 1942

The wits are saying that England has done irreparable harm by allying herself with Jewry. The news we received from leftist sources about events on the Eastern Front made us think the beginning of the end was already in progress. Everyone was moved by wishful thinking to embroider the reports of Bolshevik victories. There was a rumor that the front had cracked; that all the war matérièl for the spring offensive was captured in Mozawosk; that Riga had been taken; that Lwow was surrounded on three sides; and so on ad infinitum.

Then, like a bolt out of the blue, came the shattering news of the defeat suffered by England on the northern coast of Africa. How can we go on hoping? The defeat of England will be the defeat of Jewry.

February 2, 1942

The latest rumors of new decrees, though they may be exaggerated, must contain some grain of truth.

It is reported that the Führer has decided to rid Europe of our whole people by simply having them shot to death. There is no longer any pretense of legal authorization with all the accompanying byplay. You just take thousands of people to the outskirts of a city and shoot to kill; that is all.

The reports are bloodcurdling:

In Wilno 40,000 Jews were shot to death without a trial or even charges. The survivors number only 10,400.

In Slonim someone killed a Nazi. The Nazi there knew very well that the murderer was not a Jew. But it was a good opportunity for a bloodbath. Eight thousand Jews were shot to death outside the town.

The day before yesterday we read the speech the Führer delivered celebrating January 30, 1933, when he boasted that his prophecy was beginning to come true. Had he not stated that if war erupted in Europe, the Jewish race would be annihilated? This process has begun and will continue until the end is achieved. For us the speech serves as proof that what we thought were rumors are in effect reports of actual occurrences. The *Judenrat* and the Joint have documents which confirm the new direction of Nazi policy toward the Jews in the conquered territories: death by extermination for entire Jewish communities.

Heretofore we were afraid of expulsion. Now we are afraid of death. Moreover, signs of expulsion are becoming evident daily.

The *Judenrat* is arranging for a roll call of ghetto Jews. By January 31, 1942, every ghetto dweller must note on a questionnaire his own and his parents' names; his family status; his address in Warsaw prior to the war and his present address; his occupation before September 1, 1939, and his present occupation. Does not this roll call portend catastrophe?

Exiles from other cities tell us that in their cities, too, the evacuations began with such a roll call. In the meantime, we tremble in fear.

February 22, 1942

Twenty days without recording a word! That is contrary to my habit until now. I must confess it was careless of me to put on paper rumors which were born of certain moods and were not based on solid facts. Our lives have evolved into a set form—needless to say, it is an ugly and tragic one—and for the time being no major changes are occurring within it. The horrors persist and worsen daily. They are accepted as matter-of-fact, everyday occurrences and make very little impression on anybody. In the frightfully cold days during the first half of February, we became inured to the sight of corpses on the ghetto streets every morning. We have long since stopped dreaming of gas and electricity. In place of electricity, we use carbide lamps; in place of gas, wood. These are the conditions that exist and we pray that they do not change for the worse.

Chlodna Street, starting from Elektoralna and proceeding in the direction of Zelazna Street, has undergone many transformations. Each change affects this street one way or another and always to the detriment of the Jews. At the time the ghetto was established, the Jewish section between Elektoralna and Zelazna was declared out of bounds. The area was walled in on two sides, one on the border between Mirowska and Chlodna and the other on the border between Chlodna and Zelazna. That part of Chlodna Street which stretched from Zelazna to Wielka was included in the ghetto. But in the last territorial cut, this segment was transferred from the ghetto to the Aryan section, while that part of Chlodna which stretched from Zelazna to Elektoralna was split into three sections: a Jewish section on the right, about four meters wide; another Jewish section on the left, also about four meters wide; and an Aryan section in the center occupying most of the street. Thus a part of Chlodna Street was divided by two walls. Here, however, a new problem arose from the racial point of view: Such a division would make it inevitable for the two races to meet as they cross Zelazna Street. Consequently, the Nazis ordered the *Judenrat* to construct, at its own expense, a bridge about two stories high with steps leading up from Chlodna and down to the same street. In this way the movement of Jews in the direction of the Grzybowska *Judenrat* is to be channeled over the bridge and thence through Walicow to Grzybowska. Thousands of people now go up and down like the angels on Jacob's ladder. There are fifty steps on each side of the bridge.

The children of future generations will listen to this tale of the Warsaw ghetto and exclaim: "It's only a fairy tale! Could the Nazis really have been such idiots?"

February 23, 1942

We live in fear of the future. The knowledge that we are powerless to combat the decrees which grow more vicious from day to day induces us to magnify the danger beyond the actual facts. Occasionally, terrifying rumors are spread which are simply the products of some inflamed imagination. They are passed along until they reach the ears of the Nazis—who proceed to carry them out. There is a wry joke being circulated that all the decrees were brought about by the Jews themselves. They invent them to incite the Nazis to act on them. "Here is what you've been expecting!"

Under the impact of the bad news from the provinces, we believe the advent of spring will bring some new disaster. I was told by an acquaintance of mine who has seen the official documents that thousands of Jews have been killed by poison gas. It was an experiment to test its effectiveness.

Now that spring is approaching, we fear a new plague because of the frightfully bad sanitary conditions which exist in the ghetto. The negligence of the Health Department, which is under the aegis of the *Judenrat*, has turned the ghetto into a garbage dump and a huge public privy. Frozen water and sewage pipes have forced us to make latrines of stairways and yards. We are surrounded by stinking filth, and when the spring thaws melt the frozen dung heaps who knows what ghastly diseases will be let loose on us then?

February 24, 1942
The *Judenrat* and its shameful deeds are now celebrated in song. Outraged and frustrated, the people are making up songs denouncing Czerniakow and his clique. Even little children sing of "Czerniakow and his ten sons" (an allusion to Haman and his ten sons).

My own experience with this heartless gang dates back to August 23, 1941, when I applied to the Coal Department of the *Judenrat* for a supply of coal and wood for the winter at "normal" prices. I submitted my application early, hoping to set the red tape in motion. Every request must be explained in detail and must prove the applicant's eligibility. I established that I had been the head of a large school and though the school no longer existed legally, I do conduct classes in my own apartment. The fees from these classes provide a living for me and for the private teachers whom I have engaged. In an unheated room it would be impossible to study or to teach. For that reason I submitted my request for my coal and wood ration in good time, long before the cold weather set in.

Knowing how the *Judenrat* operates, I realized that a "recommendation" from someone of importance might expedite matters. I began to make the rounds of leading public figures—what an experience! Every VIP locks himself away in his flat and from behind locked doors the lady of the house will inform you that her husband is not at home and that she does not know when he will return. Finally I met one of the important personages on the street. After much pleading and persuasion, he deigned to write "This request deserves to be approved fully" on my application. Months passed without my hearing a word. Finally, I went to find out what had been the fate of my application. A surly guard informed me that it had not yet come up for consideration.

In the meantime, the weather had turned bitter cold. I decided to turn once again to my influential friend. He assured me he'd speak to the Coal Department about my problem again. Four months and many futile visits later I was informed that I was to receive 125 kilos of "nuggets," 125 kilos of coal dust, and 100 kilos of firewood. This would cost me 170 zloty and I would have to pay within a period of seven days or forfeit my privilege. I was delighted to make the payment.

Let us here note: I submitted my application on August 23rd and received the requisition to the coal warehouse on December 28th. This is being written on February 24, 1942; I have not yet gotten the coal. Teaching and studying in my flat has become an ordeal.

March 6, 1942

A not uncommon tragedy occurred in my family during this past week: My wife's sister and her husband died in the same week four days apart. Death from starvation has become a commonplace in the ghetto. The line of demarcation between life and death has grown very thin. Traditionally the Jew was always bound to life with strong bonds, but not so now! We are on intimate terms with the shades of hell. We keep one hand stretched out to life and with the other try to fend off death. At every turn one sees living skeletons with the skin stretched taut over their bones. The road from life to death is a short one these days.

And the scenes at the cemetery! To witness them is to witness the result of the extermination of a people. Journalists from Switzerland visited the cemetery one day and emerged shaken and horrified, vowing never to forget what they had seen. The Germans "honor" us with visits to the cemetery, cameras in hand. To them it is a pleasantly exotic place where their "Strength Through Joy" (*Kraft durch Freude*) organization brings its sightseers. Representatives of the Warsaw garrison, splendid officers, also pay frequent visits to their victims, now dead of starvation or the epidemic.

March 7, 1942

The size of the ghetto diminishes steadily, and now the Gesia Street Cemetery has been declared off limits for any Jew, dead or alive. For practical reasons, however, it was impossible to forbid the burial of Jews there because sanitation requires that a cemetery be located outside the city boundary. So orders were given to continue to bury the Jewish dead outside the ghetto limits. But free access to the Jewish cemetery is strictly forbidden. No one may enter unless he first buys an admission ticket costing 2½ zloty—a new source of income for the German and Jewish vultures who stand guard at the gate, because they suspect you came not to accompany the departed but to engage in smuggling.

A long line of wagons stretches the length of Gesia Street, each bearing several bodies at a time. In most cases the bodies are naked, without even a paper wrapping to cover them. Where can one find the fabric for two hundred shrouds a day? And who could buy it even if it were available?

The bodies are separated into three categories. In the first are those brought to the cemetery's purification room. Two or three corpses are placed on the same plank. To their credit it must be said that the departed have never been heard to protest, "We're too crowded!"

The second category consists of the bodies that were cleansed and purified in their own homes. Most of these are wrapped in shrouds made of white sheets and the men are wrapped in the *talith*. They are laid at once on the planks which wait row on row in the cemetery yard with the mourners standing beside them weeping and awaiting their turn. The mourners must also keep a strict lookout; otherwise, quick as a wink, the *talith* would be snatched off their dead.

The dead in these two categories are buried in special graves. They are the fortunate ones who receive a halfway decent burial. Nowadays that is a considerable privilege.

The third classification includes all those who died of starvation or the epidemic—and they are the majority! Among them were people picked up on the streets of the ghetto, or who died in the hospital, or starved to death in some attic. These bodies are put into a common grave just as they were when picked up: naked and unwashed. Dozens upon dozens of such corpses are accumulated each day in the cemetery stables to await their burial at sunrise. A thin layer of earth is spread over the burial pit but not in sufficient quantity to cover the limbs, which are left protruding incongruously. In darkness they lived, in darkness they died, and in darkness they were buried. Is this man and this his end?

The day will come when the Jewish people will erect a memorial here, where the common grave holds all these brothers forever. The individual graves of those who were well off in life and in death will be forgotten, but the huge, common "brothers' grave" will remain a national legacy forever. Here lie our "unknown soldiers" whom all of us should honor and remember.

March 8, 1942

Joseph David Bornstejn has passed away, starved to death in his lonely attic. Who was he? The very ones who were responsible for his death eulogized him and did not exaggerate when they said: "Veteran Hebrew writer, brilliant linguist, one of the editors of the *Encyclopedia Judaica* . . . known for research on the Talmud and interpretation of the poetry of Bialik. . . ."

Bornstejn did actually starve to death. Not many people were aware of his genius. He used to visit me occasionally and he would pour out his heart to me. I helped him as much as I could in my limited way with small sums of money for a meal or a few cigarettes. He was by nature humble and modest as befits a true scholar and was not at all impressive in appearance. These "faults" worked to his disadvantage. The dignitaries of the Jewish Self-Aid entertain no special affection for unaggressive paupers. Anyone who can talk big, no matter how ignorant, is welcomed and given assistance. But Joseph David Bornstejn was a simple man, a man of few words, absorbed in his scholarly pursuits like a true *batlan*, impractical creature that he was. For this his reward on earth was death by starvation.

A small circle of his admirers, who valued his profound knowledge of the Hebrew language and his superb researches into the poetry of Bialik, headed by myself and Mr. Fulman (secretary of the Tlomackie Synagogue), undertook to raise some kind of support for him. Even a minimum of economic security would encourage him to continue his creative work in the field in which he was the only (except for Dov Sadan) expert in his generation, Bialik's poetry. Bialik himself had greatly admired Joseph David Bornstejn's linguistic knowledge and had said so publicly. We persisted until we had arranged two meetings to which we invited the lovers of Hebrew literature from the wealthy circles associated with the Tlomackie Synagogue. Many of them volunteered a monthly contribution. There were also some generous one-time donations. We hoped to make this a continuing effort. But the Nazis and their senseless decrees ordained otherwise. The territorial realignments in the ghetto affected the Tlomackie Street Synagogue. Fulman became involved in other problems and also feared that the fundraising for Bornstejn would not be to the liking of the assimilationists upon whom the Synagogue depended. In brief, various problems and apprehensions arose, both ideological and technical, and the matter was dropped. By myself I could do very little. Joseph David Bornstejn returned to his starvation rations again.

Now his only source of support remained the Jewish Self-Aid. Menachem-Mendl the Zionist, who is in charge of the entire assistance program and who has the authority singlehandedly to decide for or against anyone's request, cares not a whit that the destitute man before him is a distinguished scholar. Joseph David Bornstejn is not the type he favors. It required a great deal of pressure on the part of Mr. Franck and myself to extract the promise of a monthly stipend. But Bornstejn never lived to receive it.

Let it be remembered: a remarkably gifted scholar and literary giant was permitted to die of neglect and starvation. In addition to being a brilliant writer he was also a genius in the study of the Talmud. The chapter on the Talmud in the German edition of the *Encyclopedia Judaica* was written by him; it included a list of the Amoraic sages and covered sixty pages. It was our duty to support him and keep him alive. His was a truly creative power, extraordinarily fruitful. Only the *bet midrash* of olden days produced such giants.

But a Menachem-Mendl is incapable of appreciating the stature of a man like Joseph David Bornstejn. He must share the responsibility for this death with the Nazis. Perhaps all of us should, for how can we dare to proclaim: "Our hands have not shed this blood"?

March 22, 1942

Man is a child of nature, raised, instructed and surrounded by it from the moment of his birth until the moment of his death. Nature feeds and nourishes him throughout his life, and when he has

303

breathed his last, then, and then especially, is he united with it in an intimate organic union for all eternity. Mother Nature takes him to her bosom. The deposit is thus returned to the depositor.

Nature's seasonal changes have always been a source of wonder or joy or even sadness, but this year Nature seems to have allied herself with our mortal enemy—the Nazis. Together they are bent on putting an end to us. Spring is on our threshhold—but winter rages at its fiercest. Frost flowers are still being etched on the windowpanes and inside your flat the cold freezes your blood. Today, the 22nd of March, the temperature is 17 degrees, and so it has been throughout the month of *Nissan*. This is not a passing cold wave but a solid winter freeze, settled permanently, with the rights of citizenship. Sometimes an occasional burst of sunshine, radiating light rather than warmth, reminds us that even to this vale of tears called the ghetto, life will some day return. Were it not for that we would be lost. Let the winter be long, let the cold continue—they will bring the Nazis nothing but disaster on the Eastern Front!

Spring finally brightens the world around us but we are "the people who walk in darkness," as the prophet said of us. We do not know in the morning what will happen to us in the evening. We have no definite word as to what is occurring in other Jewish cities occupied by the Nazis. The *Zyd* newspaper is full of stories about soup kitchens and the number of clients who patronize them. Other than that—nothing may be mentioned. It is nothing more than the organ of the charities. That is the only right it has to exist as a newspaper; so the Nazis have ordered.

However, when bad news is in the air the very birds in the sky carry the word. People are whispering horrible rumors which change from day to day according to the moods of the news-bearers. May they be proved false and I a liar, but I am impelled to record them:

First news item: Lublin has been evacuated. About 100,000 Jews were herded into railroad cars and transported—where? Nobody knows. The Lublin community has ceased to exist. One bit of evidence: Someone tried to put a telephone call through to the *Judenrat* of Lublin and the request was turned down with "There is no longer such an institution in Lublin." Then a call was put through to a private home in Lublin and the Jew there answered only, "My wife and I are alive!"

Second news item: In Rowno the entire Jewish community was murdered. Not one soul survived. Why?

Third news item: In Zdunska Wola the Nazis decided to avenge the ten sons of Haman who were hanged. They ordered the *Judenrat* to supply the names of ten Jews who would be hanged to avenge the hanging of Haman's ten sons or—the *Judenrat* members themselves would be hanged. The list was drawn up and the ten Jews were hanged.

To believe or disbelieve? But one thing is certain: The Nazis are capable of the most inhuman acts.

March 23, 1942

Rumors may be flying but we do have some definitely established facts. Litschmanschtadt (formerly Lodz) has been sanctified as part of the soil of the Reich. It is now forbidden to Jews and special laws have been enacted regarding the members of inferior races in that city, namely, Poles and Jews. The Poles in Lodz, too, have been robbed of civil rights but they fared much better than the Jews. The Nazis admit that the Poles are citizens, albeit second-class. Not so the Jews! They were deprived of their citizenship and of all the privileges that it bestows.

The rulers of Lodz decided to eliminate their ghetto with very little notice. That is the method they employ consistently. They surprise the wretched victims of the expulsion so as to create confusion and especially so that they will not manage to get their possessions out in time. In that way the Nazis fall heir to property "legally." In keeping with this method, they called in the president of the *Judenrat*, Chaim Rumkowski, and ordered him to liquidate the ghetto in a period of two to three days. On the heels of this command they immediately proceeded to confiscate all of the *Judenrat's* cash funds (said to be about 2 millions) as well as all the foodstuffs stored for distribution in the ghetto. In effect Lodz is now in another country, and there is no contact between it and the other Jewish communities in the area designated as the "General Government." From now on the post office will no longer transmit letters sent by Jews to the inhabitants of the Lodz ghetto, as though they are no more. Conversely, no letters arrive here from

Lodz any more. It is still possible to request help from relatives in Warsaw by means of a printed form signed by the president of the *Judenrat*. Evidently a meager remnant still exists there and awaits its verdict.

In Lwow the expulsion was conducted slowly but steadily. It had no ghetto, for they did not deem it feasible to create one for just a short period. Before me is a letter which tells that every day 1,100 Jews are evacuated from Lwow. Its famous synagogue has been destroyed by fire. In a matter of weeks that will be the end of Lwow, a city which long had flourished as a great center of learning and education for the Jews of Galicia.

March 31, 1942

Eve of 14th Nissan, Tashab

The author of the Reproof Section of the Bible cursed the disobedient with the classic curse: "In the morning shall you say: would that it were evening!" We, the accursed children of the Warsaw ghetto, say on this eve of Passover in the year *Tashab* (5702): "Would that it were as in previous years!" We have come to see how right our sages were when they taught us "to bless the evil as one blesses the good," because nothing bad occurs that might not have been worse. We are now arrived at our third "German Passover," and we think back longingly to the previous two.

The Nazis continue to chop up and tighten the ghetto into a more and more senseless maze. Their most recent seizure was the square in front of the Tlomackie Street Synagogue and the Main Library for the Study of Judaism. This latest cut was a blow to our Self-Aid, which was left without a roof over its head. The splendid Main Library which had housed it and which was the center of all its charity work is now in unclean Nazi hands.

April 1, 1942

First Seder Night

We have had two historic Pesah festivals: The Egyptian Pesah and the Jerusalem Pesah; now a third has been added, never to be forgotten—the German Pesah.

Hunger rules the ghetto. Anyone who says that living human beings walk the ghetto streets is mistaken; they are all skeletons!

Except for the very few who can afford to enjoy life even in these evil days, most of us have become unrecognizable to our friends. About 60 percent of the ghetto suffers from hunger in the literal sense of the word. About 30 percent are half-starved and what they do eat is harmful to the body. The rest eat and drink and enjoy themselves "for tomorrow we may die." This is true the year round and on Passover all the more so!

This year's German Pesah is only a worsening of the two that preceded it. On Passover pious Jews and even lukewarm observers do not touch *hametz*,[10] obeying the prohibition which demands that "a Jew die rather than commit the sin of eating *hametz*." The *Judenrat*, which holds our fate in its hands, was extremely generous to us this year, giving us a quarter kilo of matzoth per person for the whole week. Last year they gave us nothing. But last year the price of matzoth was 15 zloty a kilo, while this year it is 35 to 40 zloty a kilo, depending on the kind of flour used. The *Judenrat* fulfilled its "sacred duty" and behaved properly. Eating matzoth is compulsory only on the first night of Pesah; on the remaining days it is a privilege. Well, then, here you are, Jews, here is a quarter kilo of matzoth to fulfill your Pesah duty and leave us in peace. And for the remainder of the Passover week? Substitute potatoes! But a kilo of potatoes costs 6½ zloty; who can afford it? But there is another alternative—go hungry!

In normal times Jewish Warsaw on the eve of Passover would be astir with cheerful anticipation. Even the Jewish pauper managed to fulfill not only the precept of drinking four cups of wine but also that of "rejoicing on your festivals" by eating and drinking his fill. This year we can only stare longingly at the shop windows filled with displays of matzoth. Five kilos of matzoth, a two-day supply for a medium-sized family, costs 200 zloty today. Who can pay such prices? No one bought them. On the other hand, large amounts of bread were prepared for the first days of the holiday. Everyone bought it secretly. A grocer would hand a loaf to a customer discreetly, adding in a whisper: "On *hol-hamoed*[11] you'll be able to get more bread if you need it. Don't be shy!" A word to the wise was sufficient. . . .

The war and all its horrible consequences have forced even the

---

[10] Leavened bread.
[11] The intermediate days of the feast of Passover.

most devout Jews to disobey the Torah. The matter of survival alone is what determines their ability to fulfill its injunctions.

I know a certain Zionist, *a talmud haham*[12] to whom the national holidays were always a source of joy. This year he secretly provided himself with three loaves of coarse black bread for the first days of Pesah. His wife is more strictly observant; she is religious rather than nationalist in her views. Eating *hametz* on Pesah was inconceivable to her. All through the Pesach week, therefore, the two never once ate together; the husband ate his bread at one table while at another the wife ate not matzoth, heaven forbid, but ordinary Passover food, prepared in special utensils. This happened in a middle-class home. Poor families remained united—husband and wife sat at one table and hungered together. . . .

And what of the thousands of refugees who had been driven from their homes in other towns on the eve of the holiday—did our Self-Aid fulfill its duty toward them?

That, too, is worthwhile recording for posterity. . . .

April 3, 1942

End of Second Day of Pesah

Our Self-Aid has taken the *Judenrat* into partnership. There is a saying: "When you need a thief, you take him off the scaffold." The role of the Self-Aid differs from that of the *Judenrat*. The function of the former is propaganda, fund-raising, molding of public opinion, thus making its powers limited and frequently ineffectual. The *Judenrat*, on the other hand, is a sort of official body. It is authorized to mete out administrative punishment to those who disobey its orders. It does not request; it commands. Its messengers (the Jewish police) are its law enforcers. One submits to the *Judenrat's* commands out of fear whereas the Self-Aid's appeals can be ignored or answered. Since last year the Self-Aid's funds have reached a critical low. The whole structure began to totter. As the crisis deepened, people began to cut down on their donations and Self-Aid joined forces with the *Judenrat* in order to intimidate the reluctant donors. The *Judenrat* agreed to participate but it seems to have lent the force of its name only.

Be that as it may, the maneuver is succeeding. Dozens of officials

[12] Scholar.

were busy during the winter months with the Winter Campaign and in the end there was not a client of the Self-Aid who did not receive something, nor a reluctant donor who wasn't bullied into a contribution. The trick succeeded and the Winter Campaign brought in about half a million zloty. The offices of the Self-Aid were always full of donors and recipients, givers and takers, collectors and payers, generous and destitute, all hurrying and scurrying on business that never stopped.

April 6, 1942

A sensational development took place this week. Under the supervision of Nazi guards, 2,600 Jewish citizens of Germany were delivered to the outskirts of the ghetto. Their reception as Jewish evacuees from Germany is what made the event so remarkable. People are saying that the Gestapo and the Poles welcomed them at the railroad station with food and flowers. They had been deported in Pullman cars and appeared prosperous and elegantly dressed upon their arrival. In brief, aristocratic exiles. It is also reported that the Nazis had not classified them as members of an inferior race and they were therefore settled in the Aryan quarter. It appears that they will build a ghetto within a ghetto for them.

But who are these people? In racial terminology they are half-Jews. Many of them were born into the Christian faith, their parents or grandparents having converted years ago. Many were children of mixed marriages. Some of the wives are pure German. In other words, in practice they are Christians in every way, full-fledged Germans, who before 1933 occupied important positions in all the professions. What is ironic, is that they despise the Jews as much as the Germans do. If their birth certificates had not betrayed them, they would be more Nazi than the Nazi themselves. Their problem was that anyone tainted with Jewish blood unto the third generation is forbidden to live among the Nazis. Nazi law defines such people as "half-Jewish."

In times of peace they served a useful purpose in anti-Semitic Germany and were left unmolested. Now, with the turmoil inside Germany, it would not do to leave half-Jews in the midst of the war-torn German population. They are still Jews and might even rouse the German public to acts of violence. If they come of Jewish stock they are capable of any act of treason.

But the children of these evacuees, the third Christian-German

309

generation, and perhaps some wives, remained in Germany. The Jewish part is exiled while the Christian part is made to feel at home. Yes, Heine was right when he said: "Judaism is not a religion but a tragedy."

April 7, 1942

Fourth day, hol-hamoed, Pesah

Like the late Joseph David Bornstejn, Ben-Ori too has now gone the way of all flesh and by the same route—he too literally starved to death. Fortunately for him he passed away in a hospital. Ben-Ori was a writer, a man of taste, and a hard worker. When the publishing firms ceased to function, he lost his livelihood.

At the Joint the directors always favored newspapermen over the more literary writers for the simple reason that the influence of newspapermen could be most useful once things returned to normal. Consequently, the Joint and the Jewish Self-Aid distribute their funds where it suits them best. One of the Joint's directors was heard to say: "We are interested only in newspaper people; we need them." He is to be commended for telling the truth. But he forgot that the Joint's funds are only his responsibility and not his personal property. Be that as it may, the funds are in his hands and he administers them as he sees fit. To be sure, the Joint acknowledged that creative writers were worthy of aid, but only on condition that they ranked high in the world of literature. Such writers were sometimes shown particular affection and given a helping hand, whereas ordinary writers were just part of the mass of destitute Jews.

How wrong they are! Literature is not created solely by the famous. Hundreds of educated, diligent men devote their lives to the dissemination of the printed word. They look upon their work as a sacred task and no body of literature could be built without them.

Ben-Ori was such a worker in the field of literature. He was not a specialist in any specific subject, but whatever he undertook he approached with taste and understanding. He was a superb editor. Many so-called "greats" send a publisher their manuscripts sloppily proofread, full of inconsistencies and errors in syntax. Ben-Ori would return such a manuscript corrected, polished, and ready for publication. As a matter of fact, he frequently contributed more by his editing than the authors who had written them.

Ben-Ori was not a professional historian, but his translation into Hebrew of Volumes V and VI of Graetz's *History of the Jews*, published by Central, is excellent. He was no theologian and the philosophy of the Middle Ages was not a specialty of his. Nevertheless, he translated the *Khuzari*[13] and the *Guide to the Perplexed*[14] into Yiddish with a wonderful precision of style and remarkable fluency in language. Ben-Ori's volume of liturgical poetry translated from Hebrew into Yiddish captured the flowery style and reproduced the full beauty of the poems in a simple pleasant Yiddish style. Even those who are fluent in Hebrew enjoy the translation more than the original. His work as a lexicographer was noteworthy. Among his many volumes was a Hebrew grammar, a Hebrew-Yiddish dictionary, a Hebrew-Polish dictionary, a Hebrew-German dictionary, and numerous textbooks and readers.

The directors of the Joint, however, have no use for his kind of literary figure. They prefer the big-name artists whose works they do not read and cannot understand.

April 11, 1942

Until now the borders of the ghetto extended to certain streets and we were not allowed to set foot beyond them. The city had been sectioned off along ethnic lines, but the Jewish quarter retained its winding course as a continuation of the city of Warsaw. Its distinguishing features were the walls erected in open places, at whose gates sentries were posted to guard the passages which connected the Jewish and Aryan quarters.

In the last few days the piecemeal cuts have stopped. A high brick wall now encircles the ghetto, giving Warsaw the appearance of an oriental city. It reminds me of the Arab quarter in Old Jerusalem. Down the center of magnificent Elektoralna Street now runs a hideous dark wall, twisting and turning until it reaches Krasinski Garden. This park, which was in the heart of the Jewish quarter and which for years had served as a place for rest and

[13] By Judah Halevi (c. 1075-1141), Spanish Hebrew poet and religious philosopher.
[14] By Maimonides (Moses ben Maimon, 1135-1204), noted philosopher, Talmudist, and physician.

311

relaxation, has now been severed from the ghetto. Now we can no longer see it. The cage surrounds us completely. A stroll inside the ghetto wall fills one with a sense of helpless fury, a burning rage at the humiliation to which we are subjected.

But the wise men among us say we are lucky to be shut in behind a wall. Perhaps this complete isolation is our one chance of salvation. This is the kind of "evil" on which we must pronounce a blessing as though it were "good." Perhaps it will save us from the kind of disaster that struck Lublin.

April 7, 1942

We tremble at the mention of Lublin. Our blood turns to ice when we listen to the tales told by the refugees from that city. Even before they arrived in the Warsaw ghetto, the rumors reaching us were so frightful that we thought they came from totally unreliable sources. In the absence of newspapers, when all news is relayed by word of mouth, rumor is liable to become a gross exaggeration. Experience has often proved this true. Now eyewitnesses have come who were able to slip away and reach the Lublin community in our ghetto. What they reported was so horrifying that we began to wonder if they too were exaggerating, for surely human beings created in the image of God would be incapable of such evil deeds.

The fact is that reality surpassed imagination by far. Jewish Lublin, the city of scholars and writers, of learning and piety, has been completely devastated. An entire community of 44,000 Jews was plucked out by the roots and slaughtered or dispersed. Its institutions, its synagogues, and its *bet-midrash* (house of study) were wiped off the face of the earth. All their possessions were confiscated or burned. The extermination and evacuation procedures were methodically conducted. First, the murderers raided the Jewish hospitals and killed every one of the patients and staff. Next, they destroyed the Home for the Aged and shot the occupants to death. Finally, children whose parents had died at the hands of the Nazis and who had found shelter in orphanages maintained by the *Judenrat* were slaughtered. With these initial steps executed, the tremendous mass murders and evacuations got under way.

The evacuation order took the Jews of Lublin by surprise, for the Nazis had not dealt too harshly with them until now. As it happened, the officer in charge of Lublin and his advisers were quite decent toward the Jewish population. But Lublin's luck took a sharp turn for the worse when Himmler came to pay a visit. The typhus epidemic had spread to the city, and naturally the murderer Himmler blamed it on the Jews. "Get rid of the Jews!" he ordered. "They are infecting the Aryan population!"

Forty thousand Jews were evacuated; about 10,000 remained. After the first frenzy had subsided, the Jews who stayed behind hoped they would be left alone. But several days later another decree was published declaring that Lublin had to be made *Judenrein*—cleansed of Jews. Today there is not one Jewish footprint in the city of the "Lublin Visionary." The walls of his *betmidrash* were stained with innocent Jewish blood. The *Judenrat* was dispersed but five of its members were detained to serve as eyewitnesses to the liquidation of the *Judenrat*. "They will be shot last!" an officer consoled them.

As Jews tried to escape, the Nazis hunted them down. Heeding the advice of the prophet, "Wait a little until the danger is past," some Jews tried to conceal themselves in obscure holes and corners. Perhaps God would have mercy and spare them? Perhaps the Keeper of Israel would take pity? But the killers discovered the hiding places and swiftly put to death anyone they found. Some of the Jews suffocated in these airless holes even before the Nazis discovered them, for the doors could not be opened from within and there was no one to open them from without because everyone above ground had been arrested.

When the great hunt began, thousands of Jews were rounded up and led—where? Nobody knows. That is the Nazis' way. 40,000 homeless and panic-stricken Jews were taken by the Nazi overlords and led to some unknown place to be massacred. According to one rumor they were taken to Rawa-Russka and were electrocuted there. Immediately after the evacuation all their belongings were removed from the homes and burned—after the valuables had been put aside. The purpose of this was twofold: To eradicate both the plague of the fever and the plague of the Jews.

I do not doubt that there will be survivors who will record for posterity the details of the destruction of Jewish Lublin. Among them there will perhaps be some who carried on negotiations with the murderers, some who even salvaged documents which testify to what transpired. I am far from the scene where the tragedy occurred. The material I have gathered came by word of mouth. I am not familiar with the city, yet I do not feel free of the responsibility of noting down the main points pertaining to the destruction of Lublin, even if only from hearsay. For future generations every word will be valuable. After all, what is important is the seed of history; its buds and blooms will wither anyway.

My notes were made on the basis of what I heard from Lublin refugees, eyewitnesses to that holocaust. Perhaps they are not completely authentic. But the general picture fits the historic truth.

April 18, 1942

The Sabbath eve, the first of the month of Iyyar, Tashab, was a night of terror never to be forgotten in the ghetto. Under cover of darkness the Nazis conducted a massacre, and only when morning came and we found the bodies at the house gates around the ghetto did we discover the extent of the calamity.

For a day or two preceding these killings, the ghetto was haunted by a sense of premonition. Why should Warsaw fare better than Lublin? Lending credence to our fears was the rumor that the battalion responsible for the killing in Lublin had arrived to conduct a similar massacre in Warsaw.

The immediate cause for concern, however, was that a certain Aryan named Yonak had been killed on the Aryan-Jewish boundary of the ghetto. He was a tough outlaw type who lived by robbery and smuggling. Some of these thugs are Ukrainian and German. The one who was killed was a German whom another thieving villain had murdered at the height of a violent quarrel over a matter of smuggling. The killer was known to the authorities, but that did not prevent them from inventing the pretext that a Jew was involved. When word of this episode seeped through to us, we knew that disaster threatened. On the Sabbath eve, eighteen Jewish policemen who could speak German were invited to accompany the murderers on their rounds. A wave of unrest swept the ghetto but the Jewish policemen quieted the aroused crowds. "Not one hair of your heads will be harmed!" they assured us. At midnight the massacre began. Carrying a list of names, four killers to a group, with a Jewish policeman showing them the way, set out for the homes of those who had been condemned to die. In their hands they carried pistols while machine guns were slung on their hips. They rang the bell at a gate. Wherever the killers did not have to cool their heels waiting, the life of the concierge was safe. But a concierge who delayed opening on the instant became the first victim of the bullets. Six gatekeepers lost their lives in this manner although their names were not on the list. Strangely enough, the Nazis were very courteous on this deadly mission. They began with a polite "Good evening," then asked the condemned man to step into the courtyard. With a powerful flashlight lighting the scene they stood the victim against a wall and with a shot or two put an end to his life. They left the body at the gate and hurried on to the next place.

How many murder gangs fanned out across the ghetto we do not know, but we do know that more than 50 people were killed. The morning light revealed the inert bodies beside the gates. Officially they were not charged with any crime. In darkness the list was drawn up and in darkness the sentence was carried out. No one knows the reason for these murders. It was a night I shall never forget.

At 36 Nowolipki Street a man by the name of Goldberg was killed. He was a barber in peacetime, and when the war broke out he went to work in the quarantine house. His wife worked there too. When he was killed his wife set up a terrible wailing and would not leave his side. To silence her, they killed her too. Both were left lying by the gate. In death as in life they remained inseparable. The baker, David Blajman, on Gesia Street, was murdered in the same way. They came to take the husband but the frantic wife ran after him. To rid themselves of this hindrance, the murderers killed her along with her husband. The morning light revealed both bodies at the gate. At 52 Leszno Street, Linder was killed. At Number 27 on the same street a father and son were killed. So it went down to the last victim.

The news has spread through the ghetto and the president of the *Judenrat*, Czerniakow, has come before his flock with words of consolation: "Calm yourselves! Don't be distressed! Those who were punished were involved in some illegal activity. Let everyone return to his work!"

The ghetto Commissar, Auerswald, sent word: "Tell the Jewish population to calm down! No one threatens their lives! Let them remember just one thing: Do not get involved in affairs that do not concern them. . . ."

What affairs? He did not say.

On the morning after the massacre the Jewish police gathered up the bodies scattered throughout the ghetto. The whole city was stunned by the deliberate manner of the massacre. Even the Aryans who have entrée to the ghetto were uneasy, for in times of crisis the Germans do not distinguish between Aryans and Jews.

When the initial shock began to wear off and the panic had subsided a bit, we began to wonder about the episode. Why that particular kind of selectivity? What was the key to the list they had drawn up? The victims came from every level of our ghetto society: Well-to-do merchants like Blajman, the baker, former officials, small shopkeepers, even some from the very poor. Why was one baker selected and not another? We concluded that Jews were somehow involved, that the names and addresses of the victims had been supplied by the Jewish Gestapo. But again, why the selectivity?

It became quite clear after some careful digging into the matter. It seems that the people marked for death were guilty of putting out an illegal political bulletin called *Das Blettl*. All that the deceitful Nazi press wanted to conceal this bulletin revealed. The idea had come from the *Bund*[15] and a group of men from every walk of life had helped them to carry it out by providing money, paper, typesetting, printing, and distribution. These courageous men got their reward on the eve of the Sabbath, First of Iyyar, Tashab.

The political terror does not let up. After the night of the massacre the Nazis attempted to reassure the ghetto through the president of the *Judenrat*. He ordered telegrams to be sent to all branches of the Jewish police in the ghetto advising them to announce that such things would not happen again. But the ghetto public did not believe them. The collective heart felt that this would not be a unique punishment meted out just once for a specific crime.

Our fears proved to be right. The Nazis have begun to look for past "political crimes" committed by Jews. Only two days later seven more men were shot down like dogs in broad daylight. The Gestapo killers made no charge against the condemned. They

[15] An abbreviated name for the Jewish Socialist Party.

simply put a bullet through their hearts on the spot. At 41 Leszno Street a mother and son were killed.

Today a German automobile traveled up Okopowa Street and stopped beside a ditch. A Nazi officer jumped out followed by a Jewish youth. The German pointed to the spot where the Jew was to stand. The youth obeyed. The officer then drew his pistol and put a bullet into the Jew's heart. The German got back into the car and drove off as if nothing had happened.

The sound of shots continues through the day and into the night. Early this morning people saw about 50 black coffins brought out of the Pawia yard and taken for burial in a common grave. Rumor has it that the wave of political terrorism has swept over the Aryan quarter too. Today something happened in Zoliwosz that will certainly affect the Aryans. A man shot and killed a German gendarme. He then attempted to escape by jumping on a tram. Someone noticed that he was confused and nervous and, suspecting nothing, asked him what was wrong. The killer, in panic, thought the stranger was a police agent and shot him to death. Now, the killer, in a real frenzy of fear, jumped off the tram, ran to a nearby rooftop, and jumped to his death. His suicide, however, did not serve as atonement for his fellow-Aryans. Hundreds were immediately arrested on Kerczelli Square and its vicinity.

April 25, 1942

The preceding report should be corrected. The reason the German gendarme was killed was not politics but robbery. The killer was a robber who tried to rob the Spolem Bank on Zoliwosz and the gendarme interfered. The rest is as stated above.

The odor of political revolt is in the air. The members of the former Polish Socialist Party are spouting high and mighty words. So we are told. There is reason to believe they received a hint from the enemy to incite the public to rebellion. What a rebellion that would be! Hundreds of victims would be sacrificed on its altar—in vain. It would be a repetition of last year's events in the conquered countries, which brought nothing but bloodshed. The result of the Czech uprising was that the Jews became the target of the Nazi revenge even though they played no part in it. The Nazis, of course, will put down any sign of a civilian rebellion and inevitably there will be innocents who, eager for the prestige attached to such a nationalist action, will be caught in the net of revolutionary propaganda. The instigators know full well that this is only playing at rebellion. Nevertheless, they will not cease their provocations because they want to attain a strategic aim: to keep military forces in the rear, engaged in putting down the "rebellions" and thus weakening the forces at the front. It is only the old Jesuit strategem that "the end justifies the means."

In the meantime, in order to prepare for the coming events, the Pawia is being filled with hundreds of prisoners, all Aryans. During the curfew hours the ghetto is like a cemetery. Black darkness pervades everything. Not a living soul is about. Everything is locked up; no one enters or leaves his home. The latest acts of terror, which have continued since the night of the massacre, have cast fear into the hearts of all the ghetto inhabitants. During the curfew and the darkness all is plunged into an awful stillness. Every knock at the door portends danger. Even in the innermost rooms we speak only in whispers. In this threatening silence one can hear clearly the rumble of the military vehicles as they make their way from Leszno Street across Karmelicka toward the prison on Dzielna Street. They are bringing the political suspects like sheep to the slaughter. After a day or two they will be executed. Most of the prisoners are Aryans who refuse to accept the "benefits" the Führer has brought his new Europe.

But that is not the Nazis' way with the Jews. The Aryans are put to death after a short period of arrest; the Jews are killed without even a pretense of arrest. Why go to the extra trouble? No preliminaries exist for the Jews. The murderers burst into a home in the middle of the night and put an end to a life. Sometimes they take a man out into the courtyard and shoot him at the gate. At other times they put a bullet into his temple on the spot, in front of his wife and children. If the woman begins to wail, she shares her husband's fate. Even babies are killed if there is any chance that they may cause a disturbance. Gorka, the chairman of the Invalids (41 Leszno Street), was shot in his home in his mother's presence. As soon as the killers left, she started down the stairs to fetch the physician who lived in the same house. As she ran, she cried, "Doctor, he's still alive! He's still alive! Hurry! Help him!" Her cries reached the ears of the murderers. They immediately sent a Jewish policeman to find out whether the victim still lived. He returned saying the man was still alive. Whereupon they went up and finished the job.

Yesterday they shot the wealthy tanner, Rosen, who did business outside the ghetto limits. He who lusts for money never has enough. Even though he was very rich he risked his life repeatedly and he was finally caught. They transferred him from the Aryan area, where he was arrested, to the Pawia, but he did not reach the inside. As soon as they reached a gate on Dzielna Street they killed him with a single shot. They were legally correct. That's the way to deal with a Jewish criminal.

Another vignette: Starting at Chlodna Street, along the length of Zelazna toward Sienna, there is a mass of pointed, jumbled barbed wire serving as a fence in place of the usual brick wall. A Jewish boy, about fourteen years old, dared to cross this barbed-wire border and became entangled in the wires. A Nazi gendarme noticed him and before the boy could extricate himself the Nazi took out his pistol and killed him.

Terror and murder fill the ghetto air. Nobody knows when he lies down at night if he will be alive when morning comes.

April 26, 1942

My friend F., who is a sensitive man with no illusions about what the future holds for us, has nearly lost his mind with fear. "All this is not accidental," he insists. "There is method here. I remember that before the Danzig expulsion there were similar episodes." And this clever man, who is a successful merchant, has given up everything and resigned himself to a hopeless slothfulness. "I have no need of business," he declares, "because in any case I am condemned to death. One day I will be seized and my fortune will be confiscated. Am I better than the Jews of Lublin? Why should Warsaw fare any better than Lublin? Standing on the brink of an abyss a man need not concern himself with business affairs. . . ."

Luckily this sort of pessimism affects only a small segment of the ghetto population. The majority still make every effort to survive, to continue their business affairs, even to seek pleasure.

The Nazis employ three kinds of terror. The first is the terror of shooting. Any Jew who commits the slightest misdemeanor is punished on the spot—without warning, without inquiry, without trial. The second type of terror is beatings. They will suddenly pounce on

319

a Jew who is walking along minding his own business and, in view of stunned passersby, beat him up brutally. If a Nazi crooks his finger at a Jew, that gesture is a command to approach immediately so that he can receive a merciless beating. The third form of terror is humiliation, which, as a matter of course, is accompanied by physical violence. I met a Jew on Dzielna Street whose face was bleeding and the right half of his beard had been cut off. He and three other Jews had been seized on Smocza Street and dragged to a gate where the Nazis began to abuse them. They devised all kinds of "sport" to insult and humiliate the Jews, culminating in the sacrifice of the beards.

The shoemaker Zilb and his family are neighbors of mine. He is a wealthy man, a pious *hasid* and the father of several sons. One of them, a lad of about twenty, left the house yesterday and did not return. The family searched for him all over the ghetto and finally notified the police, with no result. Today a policeman informed the family that a corpse had been found whose appearance fit the description of the missing son. He was right. The Zilb lad had been seized in the street and taken to the Pawia, where he was shot to death. Today he was buried, taking the secret of his death with him to the grave.

The *Bund* violated the law but the whole community will have to bear the guilt. As far as we know, *Bundism* and Zionism have nothing in common, but the Nazi "sandwiches" them together and "eats" them as one.

Because of the terror, the Zionist *Oneg Shabbat*[16] no longer takes place at the Tarbut School at 22 Nowolipki Street. "Satan denounces men in times of danger." The weekly *jour-fixe*, the Sabbath, which the Zionist Menachem-Mendl always observed, has now ceased. He and his sycophants now have to seek a night's lodging at the homes of friends. They fear the night visits of the Nazi murderers.

April 30, 1942

Not only are the sword, the plague, and starvation our lot under the Nazis but mass wanderings and exile as well. Entire communities have been uprooted and transferred to places unknown. Where

---

[16] Literally, Sabbath celebrants. The secret name of the "Society of Brothers," organized to preserve the records of the time and the people for posterity.

did the 40,000 Lublin Jews disappear to? Of course many were put to death and many died en route to wherever they were banished, but even the survivors have disappeared and no one knows their whereabouts. Aryan emissaries have been unable to trace them. During the past two weeks we were witness to a procession of German and Czech Jews coming into exile in our ghetto. One morning I heard the voices of Jewish policemen ordering the closing of all entrances from the adjacent streets to Karmelicka Street and the clearing of Karmelicka of all passersby. A large transport of German and Czech exiles was to pass through Karmelicka to Leszno. Standing at a distance were local Jews in little groups, looking at their brothers and sisters in race, blood, and religion, shaking their heads and weeping over their fate. Over whose fate? That of the exiles as well as their own. Each one is thinking: Who knows? Is Warsaw next?

Terrible rumors about Warsaw are flying thick and fast among the ghetto dwellers. A non-Jew from outside the ghetto has brought news that a quarter of a million Germans living in Lübeck, Rostock, Köln, and Kiel, whose homes were destroyed by the English bombardments, were marching toward Warsaw in order to take over the Jews' homes.

The half-Jews and converts who came in the first transport from Germany were given shelter in the spacious buildings which the local Jews were forced to vacate. These were the buildings in the court of the Tlomackie Synagogue and the building of the Library for Jewish Studies. Everything was arranged for these German exiles with remarkable speed. They are served coffee several times a day. At noon a hot meal is brought to them from the kitchen of the Jewish Hospital which is now located at 1 Leszno Street. More than 160 of their men have already found employment, and with Jews at that. There are many professional, highly qualified men among them who will have no difficulty finding jobs. These "fortunates" live in a ghetto within a ghetto and have nothing to do with us. They probably consider us lepers.

The fate of the Czech exiles is not known. For the time being they are going through the first stages experienced by all exiles: disinfection, the bathhouse, and then—the struggle to survive.

The process of discrimination between the Jews and other peoples intensifies daily. It is now forbidden to a Jew to drink at the fountains of Aryan wisdom and culture. In order to implement this prohibition fully, the Commissar of the ghetto, Auerswald, published an order which, on pain of all kinds of harsh penalties, strictly forbids the ghetto cafés and theaters to use any literary, art, or musical work produced or composed by an Aryan. As a matter of fact, this prohibition has been in existence for a while, but it was honored in the breach more than in practice. Now the Nazis have begun to enforce it rigorously. To this end a special bureau was opened at the *Judenrat* with Czerobinski in charge. Every review and every piece of musical and artistic work must first be examined by the bureau. Nothing can be brought before the public until a permit is granted.

Curiously enough, even the works of Mendelssohn and Rubinstein, who were of Jewish descent, are proscribed. Czerobinski had better pray that no mishap occur because of him. Who knows, he may err sometimes in determining the racial origins of some grandmother or in calculating the number of Christian generations in an artist's family.

The Jews are hilarious over this prohibition which only a stupid *Yekke* could conceive. The main thing, they say, is that there should not be an evacuation of Warsaw. As for musical productions—let him kiss, if you'll pardon me....

May 2, 1942

With the coming of spring, a wave of exorbitantly high prices engulfed the ghetto. Even the rich now have to give up certain foods which they had been able to afford until now. The cost of bread has climbed from 8 to 14 zloty for a loaf weighing one kilo. Butter, if it can be found, costs 160 zloty a kilo. Lard, which had been used a good deal in the ghetto homes, is not available even among the Christians. The Nazis have commandeered lard and sugar for themselves and removed them from the private market. As usual, the penalty for disobeying this regulation is death. Whatever is left in the ghetto shops from earlier smugglings is dearer than the gems of Ophir.

Until now the penalty of death applied only to a Jew who was caught outside the ghetto limits; from now on it will also apply to the Aryan who ventures over the border without permission. When it comes to the death penalty the Nazis grant the two races equality.

In general, the hearty friendship which seemed to exist between the Nazis and the Polish population has declined considerably. Even the distinction they conferred on themselves as the saviors of Poland from its Jewish foe did not help. Moreoever, there were political reasons for the antagonism. As a matter of fact, it had never ceased but in certain periods it was concealed while at others it came to the fore for all to see. What especially irked the Nazis was the fact that the Polish populace did not behave like Quisling of Norway or Mussert of Holland—two traitors who put their local governments at the disposal of the Nazis. The terror began with the Jews and ended with the Poles.

CHAPTER
SEVEN

May 3, 1942

Gajewski the Pole has been put to death. His crime was that as
the owner of a luxurious coffee house he fed rolls to the public
illegally. Fifty-nine Polish stores that were selling food on the sly
at high prices were closed down and their stocks confiscated. There
is some element of consolation for us in this, but it increases the
starvation within the ghetto. As long as the attitude of the government toward the Gentiles was lax, the Jews also benefited; but
since their wrath has been directed against the Gentiles too, the
condition of the Jews has worsened sevenfold.

As always, every sorrow has sorrowful offspring. The mother
sorrow gives birth to sons and daughters. Since the dreadful night
of mass slaughter,[1] the terror has not ceased. The caretaker of the
Jewish cemetery is the most reliable witness in such matters, and
he testifies that there is no day when tens of people killed by
shooting are not brought to burial. And here is one basic principle:
When someone dies by shooting, it is the handiwork of the Nazis,

[1] The night of Friday, April 18, 1942, when fifty-two people were shot down in
the streets of the ghetto. This began a wave of killings in Warsaw and other
Polish towns.

324

because no one else has any firearms. The walls of the Pawiak[2] know all the secrets, but we have not yet seen the fulfillment of the words of the prophet: "The stone shall cry out of the wall." No one brought into its gates comes out alive. This is the operational center of the Nazi slaughterers. The vicinity of the Pawiak strikes terror into the hearts of passersby, and the inhabitants of the neighboring houses are in constant danger. The windows that look out on the Pawiak are shaded even in the daytime.

I have mentioned all this for the sole purpose of showing the extent to which the terror is upon us. And the real terror has given rise to a fabricated terror for the purpose of extorting money from the frightened Jews, who will give all they possess in exchange for their lives. Sometimes a group of armed Nazis comes to take someone in the middle of the night. This is an invitation to death, and the fear of death begins to hover over the house. A wail breaks forth. It is followed by pleading. All of this is in vain. After the pleas, an offer of substance; a ransom of life. Here the hangmen become more amenable, and in the end there is a compromise. Such a case occurred two days ago at 27 Leszno Street, and a second one at 18 Nowolipki Street. The head of the courtyard committee was nearly taken and paid a ransom to save his life. Another interesting detail: When he was invited to go he began getting dressed. As he started to put on his shoes the killers said, "There's no need for that. You can go barefoot!" Instead of putting on shoes, he was asked to empty his moneybag—that was needed.

May 4, 1942

The hour of twilight is harder to bear than the hour of total darkness. We are on the eve of great events—perhaps decisive ones. The Nazi press admitted this after the Salzburg meeting of the two leaders, but we, dwellers in darkness and gloom, have no need for that sign. We sense a movement of unrest among the conquerors.

In the stillness of the night the echoes of shots in the house of slaughter (here read the Pawia) reach our ears. Creeping and crawling things may be shot without law or sentencing.

All our troubles have intensified; there are more and more de-

[2] The Pawia prison on Pawia and Dzielna streets, in the middle of the ghetto.

crees, and this time the Aryans are also affected. Now the Poles as well have begun to suffer confiscations and sudden evictions from apartments. Yesterday they confiscated the goods at the Pakulski Brothers' store. Sometimes they order the evacuation of an entire building, and hundreds of families are left without a roof over their heads. We have mixed feelings about this. On the one hand our enemies, those who segregate us, will taste of our sufferings. On the other hand, to the extent they are flogged we are flogged doubly. A rumor is circulating—and it has some basis in fact—that German refugees from the British bombs will be brought to the evacuated Aryan houses, and the Poles who are left without a roof over their heads will be brought to the houses of the ghetto, after the Jews are expelled from them. Behold—the Warsaw exodus!

This flourishing rumor, which may be nothing but the product of a frightened imagination, makes our lives more bitter. After Prague, Berlin, and Lublin, is it not possible that Warsaw will come too? Even if it is only a partial expulsion—we are lost, lost, destined to die.

After the massacre the *Bundist Bulletin* stopped. Nevertheless the birds of heaven brought us the word that the Allies have begun an offensive on the Eastern front and have succeeded in chasing the Nazis out of Kharkov and Smolensk. The truth will out. Even the radio, which hides twice as much as it reveals, has admitted that "heavy fighting has broken out in the East." This is a good sign. The whole world was sure that with the coming of spring the Nazis would begin an offensive war, and they were all atremble and agitated at the thought of its results, but in the end the hunter became the hunted. Is this not a sign of weakness?

But all of these are hypotheses and assumptions, a bit of comfort in our grief. We do not know the situation as it really is. What is clearly known to us is the inflation which grows from hour to hour and eats up half our substance.

And behold this wonder: In spite of the inflation which causes a diminution in food, the typhus epidemic has abated with the coming of spring. For that matter, the death rate in general has declined. Instead of two hundred graves a day, as there were three months ago, now only about a hundred are buried each day, and they are mostly the poor and the aged. At the time the plague was rampant the wealthy and the young died too. But complete exemption is impossible. Diseases, too, shed one form and assume another. Tuberculosis has inherited the place of typhus. It is that which multiplies the fallen among the ghetto dwellers. This is the chronicle of famine.

Out of the depths of our current troubles our longing for our old troubles has increased. How good things were a year ago, and all the more so two years ago! It would be as Rashi[3] commented on the verse: "At even thou shalt say: would it were morning!" By morning is meant yesterday morning.

May 7, 1942

The inflation sucks out our blood and the marrow of our bones. From day to day it grows in intensity. The price of bread has doubled. Unrefined bread costs up to 15 zloty a kilo, and your teeth are ground down trying to chew it. If it is white, the price goes as high as 30. Before the war, the price of onions was ten groszy; now it is 12 zloty. When the housewife goes to market with 20 zloty in her pocket she brings home a kilo of bread and a kilo of potatoes. The reason for the high costs? The ghetto which is fenced in on all sides. Everything comes to us by means of smuggling, and smuggling endangers the life of the smuggler. Whoever is caught outside the ghetto boundary is doomed to die.

Today I was a witness to an ugly scene which taught me why the price of onions has gone up to 12 zloty a kilo. I made a visit to the cemetery in Gesia Street. The dead are privileged in that they go outside the boundary without the Nazis' killing them anew, but the living must buy a pass for two zloty and 50 groszy. This is a new revenue for the beloved *Judenrat*, which takes in tens of of thousands a month. To get into the cemetery you have to pass through two gates, and under the staff of Nazi policemen, armed and clad like brave men of war, and of the Jewish policemen who assist them. Besides the Nazi guards fulfilling their obligation to the Fatherland and the Führer, their friends also come there for a stroll and for a little worldly pleasure.

The cemetery is a place which allows for small, petty smuggling. The poor come here to smuggle—the impoverished and pauper-

---

[3] Rabbi Solomon Yitzhaki (1040–1105), French rabbinical scholar and Biblical commentator.

ized youth whose occupation is to bring in a few kilos of potatoes or onions. A whole family sustains itself from this. In order not to endanger the lives of the grownups, young children are sent in their place, even children of six or seven. Whoever sees them recognizes them immediately. Their bodies are clothed in rags and tatters—even their feet are wrapped in torn rags—and their faces attest to abysmal poverty. Besides their poverty they have another distinctive characteristic. All of them bear humps on their backs after the custom of camels. Anyone who didn't know their occupation would think them deformed. But the connoisseurs of smuggling know their secret. This in an artificial, manufactured hump whose inside is filled with potatoes and onions. The hands of a smuggler must have freedom of movement, for when his hands are burdened, his feet cannot run quickly. In time of danger he is forced first of all to throw away the smuggled merchandise.

The time of my visit to the cemetery today was an unlucky one for the smugglers. They were all caught near the gate of the cemetery, and here the Nazis found a broad area to demonstrate their devotion to the Führer. The Nazis made a present of a brutal beating to the smugglers (and the Jewish policemen helped them), and the youths who were smuggling made the Nazis a present of their smuggled onions. Almost all of them had filled their humps with onions, and when they were caught they were forced to empty them out. There were no sacks, and therefore the onions were dumped on the ground, near the gate. Bit by bit the treasury filled up. This fund of onions was stolen from poor people, who this time will lose not only the profit but the principal as well. They earned only the sturdy blows given them by the angry Nazis, and in particular by the Jewish policemen, for whom the entire matter is good business.

The end of this whole affair will be that the confiscated onions will be turned over to the Jewish policemen for resale. They will take the place of the young smugglers and will sell them at the price of 11 zloty a kilo, and the money realized will be divided, according to an established rate, between the two races.

I now understand why onions are so very expensive, and also the correct meaning of the words, "The oppression of the poor and the sighing of the needy."

The Jewish imagination is inventing "news" which never was and never existed. In the end the news is proven false, but meanwhile it is enjoyed. Today a rumor spread that Mussolini has been killed. The details are unknown. It is safe to assume that this is a complete falsehood, but it is my duty to record it.

A second piece of news belongs in my diary, but without quotation marks, because this one is real. The ghetto dwellers are sure that the end of the war is drawing near, and that its end will be the overthrow of the Nazis. But the Nazis apparently think otherwise. Frank once said that no power on earth can drive them from this land, that it is part of Germany from days of yore. Faithful to this tradition, the Nazis are settling in for millennia to come. Their rule is being established on permanent and stable foundations, as though this were not an occupied territory but rather a land annexed after the signing of the peace treaty. All areas of life are being established not in a temporary fashion, but for eternity. After the Jewish ghetto a Polish ghetto is now being established, though not a closed one for the time being. This week boundaries were published for the German quarter, which is set aside for the elite, those who are not only Aryans born and bred, but German Aryans, whose blood is purer.

Thus the Polish Aryans, who are second in the loftiness of their ancestry, are obliged to uproot themselves from the German quarter and find a resting place outside its boundaries. Inferiors must not mingle with their betters. A special housing office was established to organize the exchange of apartments. We have already tasted of this more than once. Now the Poles too will taste of it. One more minor detail: In the Nazi decree the Poles were barred from Saski Park, even though they don't wear kaftans. A believer would see the hand of Providence in this; the unbeliever will see in it the rule of the strong.

In the past few days the apartment situation has changed for the worse. The changes are very new, and we have not yet seen their practical results, but our minds and hearts tell us that they will bring evil upon us.

Up to now a German overcommissar was in charge of all the confiscated Jewish apartment houses; below him were Jewish commissars for every twenty or twenty-five houses; and below them were local administrators for every house or every two houses. The administrators collected the rents from the tenants and turned the money in to the commissars, who sent it in to the central fund. Relations between the tenants and the administrators were on a personal basis. Sometimes the collectors made concessions on deadlines for payments; sometimes they made reductions for one person or another when it was merited—all according to their whims and according to the size of the bribe which they received. Every request to the commissar about repairs or reductions in rent required the endorsement of the administrator, and he would always support such requests when it was worth his while.

Then Jews who were looking out for the Nazis' interests and their own came and demonstrated with figures that it is possible to manage the houses in more rational ways and thereby reduce costs. The administrators are to be replaced by collection agents and the ghetto will be divided into sections with a hundred houses in each. In each section a central office will appoint agents to collect rents and do nothing more. This will be a bureaucratic apparatus for collections—and for evictions if the collection doesn't go well. The collector comes once a month and brings you a reminder and a warning at the same time. If you pay, well and good; if not, he reports to the central office of the section that So-and-so isn't paying.

And afterward? Afterward the main evil comes—a report to the overcommissar who will authorize the eviction of the tenant. Bypassing the law courts and the entire judicial process, they can come and remove you from the apartment with the authority of an administrative order which has the force of a court order. The root of the evil is that the new arrangement will increase income and lower costs by twenty-five per cent. Whatever is good for them and bad for others the Nazis will accept from anyone, even a Jew, and the new arrangement was approved.

So far, central offices for three sections have been set up. At their heads are Jews: Abraham Gancwajch, a man from Lodz who is now the Gestapo's right-hand man; a certain Lüdtke; and the third is Tauber. Each one is in charge of a hundred houses. The number of administrators has been reduced by half. The personal bargaining has ended.

The Nazis and their three Jewish advisers benefit; and for the Jews—darkness and gloom.

Cruelty is a disease. Man's natural inclinations are good from childhood, and the feeling of compassion is embedded in him from the day he leaves his mother's womb. But I speak of a normal man. When a man is lacking in humane sensibilities, it is a blatant sign of a sick mind. A man who takes pleasure in tormenting one who is weaker than he stands accused of having a diseased psyche. The victim of cruelty deserves pity; the object of torment merits sympathy. The sadist too is a miserable man, but he does not deserve of pity. From this standpoint the Nazi is a sick and miserable person. Before this we had seen cruel individuals, but from the time that Nazism came into being, cruelty became the disease of an entire party, and perhaps of an entire nation. Even the sadists used to be tempered with a sense of shame; their cruelty was perpetrated in secret places, not in public. But since the coming of Nazism public shame has ceased, and the more one practices cruelty in public, the better.

In the last few days the terror, cruelty, and savagery toward the Jews have reached a climax. There is simply no air to breathe. The only consolation is that Nazism is insanity—but this is no consolation to a Jew who is bruised and bleeding.

In Dzielna Street they expect special punishment, because the jail for political prisoners is located there. The traffic of the Nazi hangmen in that street never stops, and every time a Nazi car goes by, its passengers beat the Jews they encounter with the whips they carry in their hands. And while they do so, they laugh heartily.

Sometimes they order several Jews to get into the car. If you don't get in, you are shot at once. Inside the car they make fun of the captives and torment them. Bearded Jews emerge with half of their beards shaved off and the other half smeared with tar. The Nazis prepare the necessary tools and materials in advance.

This week they have invented a new torture. Whoever hears of it doubts its veracity, yet this has happened—

First they captured a few dozen young and beautiful women and transported them to a certain Jewish ritual bathhouse; afterward they captured some strong, powerful, virile men and brought them to the same bathhouse. Both sexes were forced by means of intimidation and whiplashes to remove their clothes and remain naked; afterward they were made to get into one bath together and were forced into lewd and obscene acts imitating the sexual behavior of animals. The captives who underwent this ordeal are ashamed to relate the details of the abominable acts. Any sensitive person would be nauseated not only at seeing them, but even at hearing of them. And all this was done for a purpose.

While one Nazi cracked his whip over the heads of the captives, his partner set himself up in a corner with a camera. Henceforward all the world will know how low the Jews have fallen in their morals, that modesty between the sexes has ceased among them and that they practice sexual immorality in public. Such acts, which offend the moral sensibilities of man and which are intolerable to the pure soul, are the customs of a lewd and degenerate people that is not worthy of being let alone. There is no place for them in civilized Europe, and by implication their property must be confiscated and taken possession of. And don't think this is a libel: "Here you have a living photograph!"

There is no limit to the diseased imagination, and the storehouse of disgraces and depredations has not yet been emptied. Gas is a necessity in every house. Without it neither the poor man nor the middle-class householder has a hot meal. Therefore the magistrate has been ordered to exercise hairsplitting fussiness toward the Jews in the matter of gas. If one of the neighbors doesn't pay his bill on time, the flow of gas is cut off from all the other tenants' apartments too. All Jews are responsible for one another. Moreover, besides the amount of the unpaid bill, the other tenants of the house are required to pay a penalty. The amount is not the same all over. The house at 30 Elektoralna Street had to pay a penalty of 1,500 zloty. A different appraisal is set for each building. The officials justify themselves before the Jews, and repeat again and again: "Don't blame us for your troubles. They force us to behave like this toward the Jews."

Another detail: Even after you've paid the bill and the penalty they still withhold the gas from you, sometimes for a month, sometimes for two. Sometimes they shut it off for good. And all this because some stranger didn't pay his bill of three zloty and 30 groszy.

May 16, 1942

Life in the ghetto is stagnant and frozen. There are walls around us; we have no space, no freedom of action. Whatever we do we do illegally; legally we don't even have permission to exist. Our sources of livelihood are all tenuous and temporary, based on chance. As many as sixty per cent are starving in the full sense of the word. Up to thirty per cent are in a state of terrible deprivation and hunger, even though it is not apparent from without; only ten per cent are exceptions, making their living from the misfortunes of Israel. These are the smugglers, the bakers, the traders in produce, and the functionaries of the *Judenrat* and those who revolve around it. Our lives—if this can be called living—have taken on their inert, monotonous forms and no changes occur in them. The only ones who bring some activity into the sordid life of the ghetto are the killer and his friend death—the killer with his decrees which are renewed from time to time, and death with his scythe. Today one person died; tomorrow another. When their names are mentioned people wake up for a moment and sigh out of fear for what may befall them tomorrow, then life returns to its usual course. The same is true with a new decree. When a new decree is made it stuns the soul for a moment. Thousands of families fall victim to its cruelty and barbarism, but in the end we "make friends" with it too.

This week there were a few days of shock in the ghetto. The stinking mud stirred from its place. First of all Menachem Kipnis died—an author, singer, and poet who acquired great fame in his lifetime. Even the uncultured knew his name and enjoyed his folksy songs and satire. After Sholem Aleichem, whose fame has reached across the seas—in fact to every place where a Jewish foot had trod—Kipnis is second in Poland. What was unusual about his death was that he did not die like everyone else here, of hunger and privation. On the contrary, he was considered a wealthy man as writers and journalists go, and he died of a stroke. This is a good death because it is a quick one. In the ghetto everyone wishes a quick death for himself because a death from hunger is a slow one; its final agony is long and its sufferings great. Even though Kipnis was a journalist, he was true to his word this time. A day or two ago he was the subject of complaints from his friends the writers who are rotting in their poverty, and who were hoping for their stipend which came from him. Out of bitterness of soul he lashed back at them: "If you leave me alone, well and good; otherwise you will see 'speedily and in our own days' that you will accompany me to Gesia. I have no more strength! I'll be rid of you beggars!"[4]

What do they argue about in the ghetto? About whether the downfall will come quickly, during this summer, or next summer. As usual, there are those who rush the end and those who put it off. But this is not the main point. What concerns us is whether we will live to see that debacle. Alfred Rosenberg has stated explicitly: "The Jews are awaiting the end of the war; but the Jews will not live to see it. They will pass from the earth before it comes!" Vilna, Kovno, Lublin, Slonim, and Novogrudok have proved that the Nazi may be relied upon to keep his word.

In short, these are historic days. We are within their orbit and revolve with them; therefore we haven't the perspective to see what's coming.

May 19, 1942

In Thy book all is inscribed!

When an individual is afflicted with a psychological illness it is a private matter for the doctor who is treating him. But when an entire community has been afflicted with a psychological illness it is a sign of the times, and is of interest to historians of the future as well. This I swear to: The Nazi is not a normal human being, and it is open to question whether he is human at all. Perhaps he is nothing but the missing link between man and the animals. Let me relate a psychopathic manifestation to which we were eyewitnesses today in the ghetto.

The goring of the Nazis is worse than that of a killer bull. People fear them as they would a lion. When a German appears in the streets of the ghetto, everyone crosses over to the opposite sidewalk, just as one keeps his distance from a beast of prey. And this, as a matter of fact, is not cowardice. When a Nazi meets a Jew, the outcome is harm, and if you escape your Jewish obligation of death by accepting a blow from a stick or a whiplash you are among the fortunate. Sometimes the Nazis invite you to follow them—and then your life is in danger. We know a basic rule: All those who are led to the Pawia are being led to slaughter. Just yesterday an event of this sort occurred. Several killers went out

---

[4] "Speedily and in our own days" is a phrase from the Kaddish, the Prayer for the Dead.

hunting in the streets of the ghetto; a Jew was caught; and this morning he was taken out free—but dead. This is a basic rule: Every Nazi is a killer by nature, and when he is in Jewish surroundings he spreads death and destruction.

But today—wonder of wonders—at ten in the morning three trucks full of Nazis, laughing, friendly, with complete photographic equipment, stopped near Schultz's famous restaurant on the corner of Karmelicka-Nowolipki. It was evident that they hadn't come for murder and larceny this time. They behaved in a friendly manner toward whomever they met, and entered into personal conversations with the ghetto dwellers.

Why the difference today? Today they came to take photographs of the ghetto and its inhabitants, and the pictures must mirror the abundance and good fortune in the ghetto. And since in the ghetto there is poverty and famine, there is nothing to stop them from creating a temporary, artificial abundance and good fortune, made by the Nazis themselves. First they detained every beautiful virgin and every well-dressed woman, and even some who were not beautiful or well dressed, but who were made up and somewhat elegant. The women were ordered to move around gaily and to look and sound animated. This was recorded on the film, so that the mouths of the liars and propagandists against Nazi cruelty will be stopped up. Behold life in the ghetto! How lighthearted and joyous it is!

Starving people are incapable of showing the laughter and lightheartedness that come from the zest of life and great good fortune. The Nazis detained every fat Jew and everyone with a potbelly which had not yet had a chance to cave in. Jews overloaded with flesh are almost nonexistent in the ghetto, but among tens of thousands of passersby even this kind may be found. Even plutocrats, those serious men so hated by the Führer, were good material for the film. On order, they crowd up and push their way into Schultz's while at the same time a waiter shoves them back because of lack of room. All the tables are taken, and other plutocrats sit around them eating rich meals and enjoying sweets and dainties. The Nazis are footing the bill because it is worth their while.

Thus nothing is lacking in the ghetto. On the contrary, every delight is enjoyed, for the Jews of the ghetto have attained paradise in this life.

Why did the Nazis do this? No one knows, but one can guess

that it is for propaganda abroad. Before the Cracow ghetto was created, they showed us how the happy Jews were running to the ghetto with gladness. Whoever saw them in the newspaper picture would say: These are people who are contented with their lot. And the same will be true this time. This is the way of the deceit, lies, and falsehoods of Nazism. Nazis distort the truths of life, and the unfortunate Jews are forced to help them.

A few days ago the Nazis came to the cemetery and ordered the Jews to make a circle and do a Hasidic dance around a basket full of naked corpses. This too they recorded on film. All of these are segments of some anti-Semitic movie, which upon being spliced together will emerge as a gross falsification of the life of the Jews in the Warsaw ghetto.

Just as Nazism itself is a lie and a distortion, so everything it produces is a lie and a distortion. All of Europe is fighting against England! Hasidic Jews dance around their dead!

May 20, 1942

A case of martyrdom.

Melech Czerniakower is a young man of thirty-eight, in his very prime. He dresses in Hasidic garb because of his family origins, because of habit, and because of his trade, for he is a slaughterer. But this is done illegally and discreetly, because immediately upon their entry the Nazis banned Jewish ritual slaughtering. And for the very reason that it is a forbidden occupation, it brings in a handsome profit.

But under the Nazi regime no one's life is secure, least of all that of the "cursed Jew." Yesterday Czerniakower's luck brought him face to face with a Nazi whose blood boiled at the sight of his Hasidic garb, and for no other reason he was arrested and brought to the Jewish prison in Gesia Street. There they searched him and found a ritual slaughter knife on his person—he had been on his way to slaughter an animal—and here the Nazis found a "legal" ground to accuse him of sabotage. Czerniakower was thus punished for the crime he hadn't committed; he was shot to death immediately, and today he was brought to burial. When a Jew transgresses, everything is done summarily on the basis of appearances with no judicial proceedings. The executed man left a wife and three children.

People say that Czerniakower was slaughtered with the knife they found on him. I do not vouch for this rumor.

"Were the skies parchment, were all the reeds quills," we would be unable to count the deeds of the beloved *Judenrat*. All its ramifications and all that accompanies it (and its branches are many and its entourage vast, because its functions in the ghetto are those of a government) are ugliness and destructiveness. After the Nazi leech comes the *Judenrat* leech. There is no difference between the one and the other but that of race.

Do you wish to consider its ethical quality? Read it from the book of Isaiah: "Thy princes are rebellious, and companions of thieves; everyone loveth bribes, and followeth after rewards; they judge not the fatherless, neither doth the cause of the widow come unto them." The *Judenrat* has conducted a program of taxation which has no parallel anywhere in the world. Out of every zloty you spend on household expenses, you "contribute" about forty per cent, through fraud, for the benefit of the *Judenrat*. A tax of forty per cent has been placed on medicines, and for every zloty of the basic price, you pay one zloty and 40 groszy. Even postage stamps are not free of a high tax for the benefit of the *Judenrat*, besides an additional charge for every official manipulation. All this is by law. But illegally, when you need any service from the minions of the *Judenrat*, you can never arrange your affair without behaving in accordance with the principle that one hand washes the other.

There is no end to the tales of its mischief and abominations. All along I have been careful not to write them down for fear of exaggeration and overstatement, until I saw for myself. On my honor, I do not exaggerate in the slightest.

Once an entire delegation from the *Judenrat* entered my apartment (of three rooms and a kitchen) to requisition one of the rooms for a family of refugees. The reason? I am charged with occupying an apartment in an illegal way. Instead of twelve tenants, only seven tenants are registered in my apartment. The delegation was armed with every possible kind of formality. The secretary, who had a whole portfolio of documents under his arm, presented a letter to me—a requisition signed by the august president himself. Beside him was a Jewish policeman. The third was also a representative of the *Judenrat*, but I don't know what his function was.

And behind them was a fourth, the roofless refugee whom I was required by law to take into my home.

This visit occurred at a time when my wife was sick with typhus. I opposed the demand of the delegation on the ground that the room was occupied by a woman with a contagious disease who was sick to the point of death. But the delegation stuck to its demand. The sick person will be transferred to the hospital. The room will be disinfected and the requisition will take effect in accordance with law. This audacious demand infuriated me and we began a bitter, angry argument. I told them decisively that I would not allow anyone else to come into my home; that blood would be spilled; that you can't move a deathly ill patient who would die on her way to the hospital. But the quarrel didn't last long: while we were still arguing, the refugee signaled that he wanted a word with me, and in private he bared his soul. There is no one more miserable than he, for his whole family is embracing the dungheaps, but I have awakened his pity, and he agrees that a healthy family shouldn't be brought into an unclean place. But what? This whole matter cost him money. If I will reimburse him for his expenses, he will backtrack and inform the delegation that he will forgo this apartment.

When I heard his proposal my eyes lit up. But I bargained with him. The refugee demanded 100 zloty; I offered 20. In the end he agreed to accept 20. Right away the delegation found an excuse to make light of the whole affair. They drafted a protocol that the apartment was full and their requisition nullified. Later on I found out that I need not have been so afraid. This is the way the delegation acts with all of its creatures. They hadn't come to confiscate, but rather to receive 20 zloty. The "refugee" was hired for the occasion.

Last night was a night of watching. The Jewish police made the rounds of Jewish homes and awakened about eight hundred young men from their sleep to take them to the labor camp. Again turmoil and confusion. The police justify themselves: We are compelled by the conquerors' order to supply so many young men for labor, and we must obey orders.

The captured youths were led to the place designated for them, but half of them returned—specifically, the wealthy among them. This was a mystery. Later on, the secret was revealed; they were ordered to supply not eight hundred but four hundred. For greater security and for greater income, eight hundred were arrested, among them four hundred wealthy ones. The wealthy ones ransomed themselves and returned home; the poor ones were taken and are destined for hard labor and lingering death.

This is only an indication of what the *Judenrat* does. The rest will emerge in due time.

May 26, 1942

To go from one matter to another on the same subject—from the *Judenrat* to the Nazis; that is, from the actions of one degenerate to those of another degenerate; they are both on the same ethical plane. The nightly terror never ceases. There are lists of "suspects," and for everyone on the list the sentence is death. The condemned is not arrested beforehand, nor interrogated and examined, nor brought to judgment. Following their list, the killers enter his home and order him to go—they don't say where or why. When they get outside, the one marked for death is ordered to walk ahead, and the executioners remain behind him. Not many moments pass before a shot is heard. The sentence has been carried out wordlessly. The killers disappear. The corpse of the victim lies in the dust of the streets until the morning light. When day breaks the Jewish police comes to clear it away from the public place and take it for burial.

Thus the members of the ghetto are punished and die.

Sometimes the greedy Nazis conspire with some worthless Jew. They share one pocket; both lie in wait for the loot of innocents and for their blood; both fill their houses with the wealth they have stolen and robbed. But robbing doesn't last forever, and when the partnership breaks up it is not convenient for the thieving Nazi to have a Jew know his secrets. The remedy for this is to get rid of him. Let him not remain among the living, an eyewitness to his larcenies.

Thus Perlmutter, the president of the *Judenrat* of Mlawa, was killed by his German overseer, whose hand had never left his while both of them looted and robbed and grew rich. And so it was with the "Thirteen."[5] In their time they were the slaves of the

---

[5] A group of Gestapo informers headed by Abraham Gancwajch, so called because of the building at 13 Leszno Street. Among their activities was the management of a great number of ghetto apartment houses.

Gestapo, partners to all kinds of abominations and monstrosities. Now the partnership has been dissolved, and no memory of what existed must remain. If there is no partnership, what need is there of partners? Thus it is that they are caught at night, and their former partners send the bullets into their hearts.

The heads of the "Thirteen" made an error in their calculations. They thought that they could live in the shadow of the Gestapo, that it was a special privilege to be close to an iniquitous, wicked regime. And behold—they have gotten their just deserts. Thus may they be destroyed!

The best-known automobile in the ghetto, the one the school kids talk about, is that of a Nazi named Schultz. He passes by several times a day, driving through the streets of the ghetto in the direction of the prison on Dzielna Street. Besides Schultz, the chief killer, there are three or four comrades with him in the car, and they all have clubs. As they go by they club every Jew they encounter. Every time tens of people are struck and injured.

At first we thought it was only an isolated occurrence. This is the way the Nazis torment the Jews, and who pays attention to such incidents as these? But the killer Schultz runs the business of beating Jews according to a system. Not once does he enter the ghetto idly. He and his friends stand holding their clubs, their hair wild, their teeth protruding, the look on their faces one of murder and pillage. The echo of their laughter is heard throughout the ghetto. People are struck and injured without distinction for sex or age. This is a punishment for the Jews of Karmelicka Street because England is unwilling to give up her empire for the benefit of the Nazis. This is the revenge on the Jews because they are calling on all nations of the world to war against Germany.

But in our war the victory is that when Schultz and his cohorts appear in Karmelicka Street, the street becomes deserted. Passersby hide in the courtyards and there is not a living soul to be seen. Schultz becomes very angry; the Jews are sabotaging him.

May 27, 1942

Today the whole ghetto seethed with excitement. Of course we have become accustomed to the abominations and monstrosities of the Nazis, but the abomination committed today surpasses them

340

all. In its nature it is larceny; in its form—no adjective can describe it, because you couldn't find ugliness of this sort even in a robbers' den.

The only place where Jews and Aryans can meet one another without breaking any laws is in the courthouse in Leszno Street, which has two entrances: one on Ogrodowa Street for the Aryans, and one on Leszno Street for the Jews. Thousands of people come and go, and not all are on legal or tax business. A great part of them are there for the business of smuggling. At the entrance, to be sure, there is some inspection, but it is not especially strict because of the great number of people who come in. One just has to show a summons to court or some such paper. As I said, many come on such legal matters and many to pay taxes. The members of the ghetto are deprived of their income but not of their obligations.

Today Nazi justice reached its climax. All who came to pay their taxes were robbed in public by the Nazis in full view of thousands of passersby, and no one dared interfere. People who happened to be there today were surrounded by guardians of the law who searched their belongings and stole whatever was in them, whether cash or valuables. And a Jew in the Nazis' talons is like a lamb going to slaughter—he doesn't open his mouth or show any signs of protest. He is saying: My property is yours; just give me my life.

In the first year after the entry of the Nazis, and to some extent even in the second, acts of robbery such as these were perpetrated discreetly, in the dark of night or in the shelter of some gateway. Today the restrictions have been removed and the robbers rob, not just in a public place but in a government building, in broad daylight before the eyes of thousands of people, and in the place of "justice and righteousness." And more: the robbed man receives change in return; beatings, blows, and kicks. The affair is carried out with German strictness.

It is impossible to imagine the chaos that broke loose among those standing in the lines waiting their turn. Whoever was fortunate enough to manage it fled and disappeared. Whoever sensed what was happening around him, and had not yet been surrounded and seized by the robbers, hurried to the window and paid whatever money he had with him as an advance against future taxes. And whoever didn't manage to do one or the other was robbed and looted, and also beaten.

341

The entire ghetto is a huge dunghill. The Jewish janitors do as they please, and there is no one to reprimand them. There is no limit to their impudence. The local wits say that the Führer knew their character and nature in advance and for that reason he appointed such rulers over us.

The residents of the courtyard stifle their bitterness because almost all of them make their living illegally, and nothing is hidden from the janitor. They give in to every impudent demand —anything not to irritate him, heaven forbid—and for this reason neglect of the courtyards is classic. The steps are littered and full of filth and grime, and when an order comes from high places to clean and wash them the janitor makes the rounds of the tenants and takes up a collection "for the benefit of cleanliness." The time of curfew begins at nine. The janitors in the ghetto close the gates at seven. The day is far from over; the traffic in the streets reaches its peak at precisely those hours, and everyone is obliged to pay for the opening of the gate. The *Judenrat* has ordered that the gates remain open until nine, but no one pays any attention to the decision, and the same thing applies to sanitation.

However, if anyone thinks that only the janitors are corrupt, he is greatly mistaken. Not for naught did Solomon say, "When the king accepts a lie, all his servants are corrupt." Everyone who holds a responsible position in the *Judenrat* is openly or secretly prepared to do your bidding—for a price. A perfect example of this is the health department established under the auspices of the *Judenrat* to maintain standards of sanitation, cleanliness, and health. In this instance you are not dealing with vulgar, dull-witted janitors, but with apparently highly intelligent, cultured doctors. Yet even here money purifies all filth and covers all iniquities.

Outwardly no one is more zealous than the officials of the health department in enforcing sanitation. Periodically the "visiting committee" comes to your apartment and thoroughly examines every piece of dandruff and every single louse in the hair of your head. During the examination no one is favored, and nothing overlooked. At times you are even told to unbutton your shirt and show your undershirt. Is it clean or not? You have to answer for every tear and tatter—and should a grease spot be found, then death is too lenient a punishment for you! Everything the committee finds in your apartment, to your favor or to your disadvantage, is written down.

However, nothing is revealed to you. The procedure is as follows: After a few days the courtyard committee receives notification from the health department that due to below-standard conditions of sanitation in the following apartments, disinfection is necessary. What does disinfection entail? Only the initiated can possibly know. It entails the complete ruin of all your possessions with the sharp disinfectant they use. After disinfection you are clean all right—clean out of clothes, bedding, and woolens.

In my courtyard the following incident once took place: A disinfection was announced and the disinfectors came with their paraphernalia, not to disinfect but to haggle over the size of the bribe. For a full hour they stood on their price. During that time the bargaining would stop and start periodically, not secretly but publicly. In the presence of all the residents of the courtyard, the disinfectors negotiated their deal. Finally they agreed on 400 zloty. Every apartment that was supposed to have been disinfected paid its share. Once the money was handed over the courtyard was out of danger, as far as sanitation was concerned, since the health department would receive a duly signed report that everything had been carried out according to plan.

May 30, 1942
Outside—annihilation; inside—terror. Woe unto us for we are lost.

Another night of slaughter. This time the victims numbered only eleven. Once more pain and worry on every face; once more the quaking of the heart with the arrival of the evening shadows. Will you live to see the light of dawn? Every echoing footstep, every rustle in the immediate surroundings casts the terror of death over you. You are certain that the death sentences have already been drawn up; it is merely a matter of awaiting your turn—your turn to die. Perhaps it will come tonight, perhaps in a few more nights, but you will not escape your fate.

The Führer is a man who speaks with assurance; he is not one to engage in trivia or make meaningless pronouncements to the whole world. And he has explicitly stated: Whether the war ends in victory or defeat, the Jews of Europe will be wiped off the face of the earth. Now, apparently, the order has been given to all the occupying forces to carry out his pronouncement.

The eleven people who were killed walked in our midst only

yesterday and never thought it was their last day. They were shot like dogs, in the darkness of the night next to some gate, with their corpses left in the dust until daybreak. The worst part of this ugly kind of death is that you don't know the reason for it. They come and greet you with a "good evening" and invite you to follow them. Which means: You are going to the slaughter.

As an example, take the Wilner family from 11 Mylna Street. Before the war they owned a brick factory in Grodzisk, near Warsaw, and were quite comfortable. When their livelihood was destroyed they migrated to Warsaw and made a living by privately administering the provisions department of the *Judenrat*. Yesterday at midnight, all the males of the family—father, son, and son-in-law —were taken to be killed, and no one knows why. That there is no rationale to the murders is proven by the following incidental fact: Together with the three members of the family, a fourth male found in the house was also murdered. He was a stranger who had sublet a room and had no intimate dealings with the Wilners at all. His residence with them was only temporary; nevertheless, he too was killed. One of them—I don't know which one—was thrown to the ground from the fourth story while still alive, because he was paralyzed and unable to get out of his bed.

And then there was the student, the Jewish policeman Rabino-wicz. The murderers came to his parents' home and couldn't find him. When they asked where he was, the family at first answered, "In the police station." But the policeman's sister quickly corrected the error and said that her brother was on duty at the hospital on Leszno Street. They then commanded her to go with them to point him out, which she did. When they arrived, the victim was told to remove his hat and badge and follow them. After they had gone some distance they ordered him to walk in front of them. As they approached Number 3 Leszno Street, they shot him in the back and he fell dead.

Among the murdered men there were also a dentist from 32 Pawia Street, a barber, and a baker and his son, none of whom knew each other or had anything in common socially or economically.

The lack of reason for these murders especially troubles the inhabitants of the ghetto. In order to comfort ourselves we feel compelled to find some sort of system to explain these nighttime murders. Everyone, afraid for his own skin, thinks to himself: If there is a system, every murder must have a cause; if there is a cause, nothing will happen to me since I am absolutely guiltless.

But my friend Hirsch,[6] who is a very clever Jew, thinks differently. The system is a lack of system. The guiding principle is the annihilation of a specific number of Jews every night. They go to the files, indiscriminately draw out a card, and whoever is picked, is picked: he is destined to die.

Hirsch's opinion has earned him many enemies. People do not want to die without cause.

May 31, 1942

We have pondered the destruction of Lublin. Why did the Nazi hand fall so much more cruelly and arrogantly on her than on the other cities of the General Government? And now the curtain is raised a bit. The newspaper *Warschauer Zeitung* printed a letter from Lublin today, written by some sort of literary hooligan. Everything is to be found in his report, including lies, perversions, and simulated science. Every sentence is a sword pointed at the heart of Polish Jewry; every word, poison. It is nothing more than the loathsome babbling of some scribbler who knows nothing of what he is judging. The whole thing is based on zoological hatred that perverts truth and subverts historical facts. But the article does have one good point—in a roundabout way its reveals something of the reason for the deportation from Lublin.

The stupid Nazis consider Lublin the spiritual center of Polish Jewry, whence ideological, intellectual, and legal ties to world Jewry are maintained. It was therefore necessary to snap these ties, which are a danger to all Aryan peoples. From the historical point of view, there is some justification for the Nazis' thesis. Yeshivat Hahmei Lublin is a Talmudic academy whose thousands of graduates are dispersed throughout the entire world, and thus play a prominent role in the spiritual life of Diaspora Jewry. According to the Nazis, this great Yeshivah is the foul Talmudic fountain from which its students, the ideological agents of world Jewry, drink. In this style the writer goes on and on.

And therefore an end to this stinking Yeshivah. This muddy source that floods the whole world with its evil waters must be

---

[6] It would seem that Hirsch is an imaginary personage, invented by Kaplan to present the dark, hopeless, but realistic aspect of the situation.

stopped up. And the Nazis deserve credit for carrying out this work that benefits all mankind.

The Nazis recognize only the Jewish community and its representative, the *Judenrat*—not the individual. When several hundred Jewish youths are needed for slave labor, ultimately to be released broken and crushed, the Nazis turn to the Commissar for Ghetto Affairs and he to the *Judenrat*. The *Judenrat* makes a nice business out of this. There have been instances when someone was released for ten zloty, for a sum that is not enough for a whole loaf of bread. Any way you look at it, both sides are benefited. Long live the war!

June 3, 1942

As much as the first expulsion excelled in the cruelty, horror, and tragedy that accompany such total terror as this, the conquerors at least allowed the deportees to remain alive.

Now it is different. The deportees are transported as prisoners in tightly sealed freight cars under the supervision of Nazi oppressors. They are in the care of these angels of destruction until they come to the place of execution, where they are killed. Many of the deportees, among them mothers and their infants, are put to death along the way; the remainder are brought to some secret place, unknown even to the hawk, and there killed in satanic fashion, by the thousands and tens of thousands. The community of Lublin has lost all its sons. About 40,000 Jews of Lublin have disappeared, and no one knows their burial place. Aryan messengers were commissioned to search for them through the entire General Government, but they found not a trace. It is as though the 40,000 had been swallowed up by stormy waters. But there is no doubt that they are no longer alive.

Lublin was the first to drink the cup of sorrow to the dregs, but not the last. Since then not a day passes without some Jewish settlement being completely wiped off the face of the earth. Take Wlodawa! Take Tluszcz! Both of them were emptied of Jews. The Hasidic rabbi of Radzyn was killed. The deportees were put into the hands of Nazi S.S. men who murdered them along the way. The beautiful girls and women were herded together and then shot down. "The Jews do not need beautiful women!" S.S. men on horseback led the deportees along the road. Maliciously they prodded their horses on and then commanded (actually forced) the hundreds of deportees not to lag behind. In the lead, galloping horses swallowing up the distance. Behind them storekeepers, mothers with their babes, old people on crutches—everyone comprising a provincial household—compelled to keep up on foot. Their *Judenraten* too have disappeared and no one knows if the deportees are still alive.

A joke is making the rounds: Rabbi Stephen S. Wise is helping. He has ordered the American Jews to say the memorial prayer for the departed souls of Polish Jewry. His foresight is accurate.

June 7, 1942

Never were we so hopeful of the final Nazi downfall as during these days, days in which our tribulations grow worse from hour to hour. The transports do not cease, and the Nazi sword rests against our throats, wreaking havoc amongst us. But we were always a nation bound by hope—and so we shall remain. Jewish faith is marvelous; it can create states of mind that have nothing to do with reality. Like the believing Jewish grandfather who in anticipation of the Messiah always wore his Sabbath clothes, so we too await him, "and, though he tarry, I will wait daily for his coming." The English radio, whose listeners endanger their lives, strengthens our hope. We listen to Reuters with great respect. Every word gives us courage; every small detail that points to any military weakness is carried through the length and breadth of the ghetto as though on eagles' wings, with even children talking about it. When the news doesn't tell us what we want to hear, we twist and turn it until it seems full of hints, clues, and secrets that support our views. We no longer count weeks, only days; and some have even started to count hours. Everyone asks everyone else about the news, certain that this time the report will be favorable. And the news from Reuters always contains a certain intonation or expression to satisfy and comfort a spirit thirsting for a speedy and quick redemption. A stubborn people!

Hirsch, my wise friend, is an exception. He is the only one who sits like a mourner among bridegrooms. "Idiots!" he shouts, and his face becomes red with anger. "Your hope is vain; your trust a broken reed. All of you are already condemned to die, only the date of execution has yet to be set. We are doomed to pass from the world without seeing the Nazi downfall because the physical annihilation of European Jewry is one of Nazism's cardinal princi-

347

ples. You have eyes and yet you do not see that the fulfillment of this horrible goal has already been started. What hope do we have that it will not be carried out? Over half a million Jews who used to live in Poland have already been murdered; some by hunger, some by disease, some by the Nazi sword. Jews have been deported from hundreds of small communities, and no one knows their whereabouts, simply because they were killed along the way and never reached a new destination. Optimistic fools! Where is the great community of Lublin, and the hundreds of other smaller communities? Where did their deportees settle? The Nazis created ghettos in order to annihilate us but their plan did not succeed. Now they have decided upon the "final solution," annihilation through murder. Those of you who are worried about money— it's a futile concern; you trouble yourselves for naught since Warsaw will not escape the sword of the Nazis. As for the intellectuals who are busy acquiring rare books because they are inexpensive— it is truly amazing! Can you really prevent your eyes from seeing? What do you need books for if you will never live to read them?"

And thus he goes on and on. Would that Hirsch's predictions prove to be untrue.

June 9, 1942

The Jewish section of Warsaw has become a city of slaughter.

We have endured three more nights of butchery, and we have almost become accustomed even to this. It is impossible to determine the exact number of victims; the opinions range from 21 up to 115. No matter. The executioner was kept busy enough. Some tens of Jews died a dog's death, in the German manner, and the murderers continue to come with lists in their hands. Moreover, as a byproduct of their job, they also kill others who are not even on the list. A Jewish porter was killed because he answered no when the murderers asked him if he had seen anyone escape. He was immediately shot down on suspicion of sympathizing with the escapee. It is standard procedure with the murderers to take relatives and neighbors in place of an absent victim.

Habit becomes second nature, even in matters of life and death. We are so used to the idea of being shot to death that this entire horrible matter no longer frightens us. Because no one knows what will happen to him at night, there are those who set their households in order before they lie down "to sleep"; they caution their wives in a quiet and practical way that should it happen—and of course it will not—but should the Nazis come, they must not make an outcry because it would frighten the sleeping children. Devout Jews utter their last prayer and whisper, "In thy hands I entrust my spirit."

Tremendous intellectual effort is expended to find some motive behind all the slaughter. If there is a motive, there is a possibility of estimating the proximity of individual danger. But none of the theories have a leg to stand on; there are always incidents that do not fit the alleged motive, that are beyond calculation and unbounded by logic.

Now there is an effort to substantiate the theory that the Nazi murder-machine strikes only at fugitives; but this theory is contradicted by the fact that an artist who voluntarily came from Vilna was put to death. Among the victims there are those who illegally fled from the ghetto of Lodz, but as far as a motive is concerned, it is the motive of Haman: to destroy, to murder, to annihilate. These are the only reasons.

It is now three years that the Nazis have held power over us, and their arrogance and cruelty toward the Jews grow from month to month. In their awful anger they follow no standards of government; never before in history has any tyranny ever allowed itself to proclaim publicly that it is preparing to annihilate an entire people. In their bitterness they wreak all their anger upon us, and as their defeats increase so will their persecutions.

Today the news was received that a deportation decree was issued to Biala Podlaska. Of a Jewish population of 8,000 people, 6,000 must leave within three days. The rest work for the German army, and will therefore remain until they complete their work. After that they too will be deported. Where will the deportees go? No one knows. However, perhaps my "no one knows" is no more than self-deception. Where to? To a place from which they will not return. The deportees are not free, they are the prisoners of the Nazi S.S. men who lead them, and their path can only be the path of death. The difficulties of the road, the weariness and afflictions of the deportation do their job; the murder-machine does the rest. Here it is quite possible to find a motive: the deportees are forced out with premeditation, in order to annihilate them. No pity is shown to infants or the deformed, invalids, old people, or the infirm. On the contrary, they are killed first in order to facilitate travel. The Nazis steal babies from their mothers' breasts and kill them before their mothers' eyes.

During the deportation from Pabianice there was one mother who fought like a lioness and refused to turn her baby over to the murderers. They immediately grabbed the baby and hurled it out the window.

June 15, 1942

When the shadows of evening begin to cover the skies of the ghetto, fear begins to penetrate into all its empty places. From curfew on, the killers prowl over its length and breadth in search of prey.

There is no system to the Nazi killing, but nevertheless the most obvious objective of this carnage is to purge the ghetto of smuggling. In the main, the victims of the shootings are smugglers. The smallest shadow of suspicion that So-and-so is engaged in smuggling is enough to make him a candidate for murder. Jews are not judged, they are merely punished, and there is no lighter punishment for them than death by shooting.

There is continuous war between the cruel, dim-witted Nazis who have condemned us to subsist for a whole month on two kilos of bread apiece and the members of the ghetto who want to live. Even the death penalty has not reduced smuggling. If you can afford to pay 25 zloty for a loaf of white bread, someone will throw it into your mouth any time, at any hour you wish. And the same is true of any other delicacies you may crave. The victims among the smugglers fall like barley behind the reapers, but the quantity of smuggled produce in the ghetto does not decline. Every crack is being sealed up; every hole filled in—and the miserable Nazis are dissipating their energies on chaos and vanity. The smuggling doesn't stop. There are even instances of Aryans sneaking into the ghetto to buy produce that is lacking in the Aryan quarter.

And now for the clincher! The Nazis themselves are engaging in smuggling, because it is worth their while. The mice of smuggling, the miserable creatures who smuggle small quantities of produce through the wall, are put to death by the tens, and their death is their penance. This is not the kind of smuggling the Nazis abet. The real smugglers sit at home and no danger awaits them. The Nazi gendarmes receive vast sums of money from them when no one is looking, and the smuggled goods are brought in on loaded trucks through the four entrances that these selfsame gendarmes are guarding. Both sides benefit, and the third side, the ghetto, pays. But it too benefits.

June 16, 1942

My Hirsch cannot be budged from his opinion: A catastrophe will befall us at the hands of the Nazis and they will wreak their vengeance on us for their final downfall. The process of physical destruction of Polish Jewry has already begun, but it is possible that Warsaw will be the last. When the Führer announced to all the world that the Jewish race would be eliminated from Europe, we said, "He is only tormenting us. It could never happen." After him, his servant Goebbels came and repeated his words. Who is more important, the master or the servant? I'd say the master. But even so, the words of the servant shook us to a greater degree than those of his master, because by the time they were said they had already been fulfilled.

Now this is no longer a prophecy for the future, but a terrifying, horrible reality. Not a day goes by that the Nazis do not conduct a slaughter. It is simply murder and destruction in their elemental sense. The rumors that reach us from the provincial towns are worse than the tidings of Job. Every day entire communities are uprooted from their native soil and their members are slaughtered in the hiding places of the forests or in desolate deserts, and no man knows their resting place.

These are disjointed rumors that reach us in fragmentary form, and their details have not been properly investigated; but in each one of them there is a grain of truth and that is sufficient. Seventeen thousand Jews are missing in Cracow. They are lost, and are no more. Here read: They were killed upon their departure into exile. Their trail has disappeared because they are no longer among the living.

About 40,000 people are missing from among the Jews of Lublin, almost all of those who were exiled. Our Aryan messengers could not find their trail, but their relatives would not rest until something of the fate of the exiles became known to them. Thus we learned that they were taken to some forest and killed to the last man. They dug their graves with their own hands while they were still alive—a great, giant mass grave. They were made to stand at its rim to be shot. Was anyone saved? And if one was saved, would he risk becoming a chronicler of impressions?

The remnant of the community of Lublin was divided among four concentration camps. This is only a waiting room for death, for in a concentration camp no one lasts longer than eight weeks. The strength of mere flesh and blood is insufficient to sustain him longer.

The Jews of Hrubieszow were killed to the last man. The fact is genuine, its details unknown to me. The last two thousand people were exiled from Biala Podlaska. Where were they taken? We can rightly assume that they were taken to their death, for no remnant of them is left.

In Mlawa, twenty-two smugglers were hanged before the eyes of the entire Mlawa congregation; and among them were four women. When the Nazis had tortured the captives to their hearts' content, they ordered the Jews of the city to build a stage in the market place. The stage was a scaffold. In front of thousands of people ordered to be present, the Nazis hanged the builder's relatives and the members of their congregation. Here too details are lacking, but as to the fact itself there can be no dispute. And so it is in other towns and villages: expulsion, destruction, and the sword.

My Hirsch is screaming: "Cowards! A whole community of millions of people stands on the brink of destruction, and you keep silent! You delude yourselves out of hope that the evil will not reach you; you have eyes and see not. Are you any better than the people of Lublin? The people of Cracow? The people of Lodz? If not today, then tomorrow or the next day you will be taken out like lambs to slaughter. Protest! Alarm the world! Don't be afraid! In any case you will end by falling before the sword of the Nazis. Chicken-hearted ones! Is there any meaning to your deaths?"

June 17, 1942

The members of the ghetto, condemned to die, want to enjoy life as long as breath remains within them. But herein lies the trouble, for the people of the ghetto are limited in their ability to find the enjoyment they long for. Like the Nazis we utilize substitutes. You cannot imprison human desires.

The ghetto is girded on all sides with a medieval wall. Of all the beauties of nature only one remnant is to be found in its

352

possession—the blue of the sky over our heads. Even our pleasure in this is somewhat limited, for the horizon we see reminds us that in the open spaces of the burgeoning world of nature outside the wall there are trees and beautiful plowed fields, forests and streams, hills and valleys, "full of splendor, they radiate brightness." But we have made peace with the idea that they are forbidden for our enjoyment.

It is now three years since we have seen grass growing and flowers in blossom. Even before we were shoved into the ghetto we were forbidden to enter the city parks. Inside the parks there was space and breadth. Outside, the Jewish children—beautiful little ones, the children of the masses—would find a place for their games and toys on the stone sidewalks outside the fence, in the traffic of the street and in the dust heaps of the noisy, stinking ghetto. Then we were taken away even from outside the fence. Within the limits of the ghetto there is not a single garden. Moreover, Krasinski Park, which was originally in the ghetto, was declared outside the boundary and a stone wall now hides even a treetop from our eyes. We have been robbed of every tree and every flower.

When we saw that was the way it was going to be, we invented substitutes—first of all, the Aryan gardens within the ghetto that were abandoned by their original owners when they were forced to move to the Aryan quarter. There aren't many, but there are enough. Among them are some that formerly belonged to the municipality and some that were connected to Aryan coffee houses. Now the coffee houses have all passed into the hands of Jewish tenants, and become our country places and our summer resorts. Is there a tree in them? Not necessarily. Have they wide-open spaces and freedom? Nothing of the sort. Desolate, lonely lots, surrounded by high walls at the backs of courtyards or planted in the space between the houses of the wall, have been turned into "gardens." Mothers and children fill them. For space for a baby's cradle they pay 50 zloty a month, and if any member of the family besides the mother accompanies or comes to visit the child, he must pay an additional admission charge. Old people and invalids who want to relax and enjoy the "beauties of nature" pay two zloty a day. The unemployed young people play games there, and fill the garden with gaiety and lightheartedness.

I have forgotten the main point.

Nursery schools bring their infant charges to the gardens, and older children have their lessons there. In short: an arrow in the Nazis' eyes! The arteries of life do not stop pulsing. We are schooled in life, skilled in the art of living; it is like the words of the prophet: "When thou walkest through the fire thou shalt not be burned; neither shall the flame kindle upon thee!"

June 18, 1942

Squeezed and locked within the ghetto, we have no dealings with other human beings. Gentiles are scarcer than hen's teeth. Our souls yearn for the sight of a Gentile face, but you could look for one with candles and not find it. We have dealings with only five Gentiles; besides these, we haven't even a memory of one. These five are a Gentile who collects the monthly payments for the electric lighting, a Gentile who collects the monthly gas bills, two Gentiles on the Jewish trolley, and a Gentile tax collector. And whoever is privileged to be haled into court has the joy of seeing the face of a sixth Gentile, the judge. Assimilation—who mentions it? And if it exists, it does so only among the "*Pans* of the faith of Moses" who are assimilated into Judaism against their will.

The ghetto is exotic, very much worth seeing. In normal times it provided material for newspapermen and other writers looking for sensational material, but now is a time of destruction, and tourism has naturally declined. No one comes to visit us. Once some Swiss journalists came into the ghetto to visit the cemetery; what they saw they couldn't put down on paper because a Nazi honor guard wouldn't leave them alone for a moment. And therefore the sensation in the ghetto was all the greater when all at once there suddenly appeared among us a few Gypsies for whom the Nazis had made room in the Jewish ghetto. One must admit that this is an excellent match. Just as the Jew is a wanderer, so is the Gypsy, and the main thing is that the Nuremberg Laws fall on both of them, and marriage between them and "Aryans" is forbidden. For all these reasons the two can dwell together. The impure can't defile the impure.

The local comedians say that the faces of the "*Pans* of the faith of Moses" lit up especially at the sight of the Gypsies. From here on the *Pans* will stop assimilating with the Jews whom they despise, and will return to assimilating with the Gentiles they adore. In the last analysis, even the Gypsies are, in the main, Gentiles.

And how will the Gypsies make their living? The men will trade horses; the women will tell fortunes; in short, their old-time occupations. And most important, they will help the Jews in the business of smuggling.

Until they get established, they occupy themselves by stealing from the Jews, their brothers in the ghetto. Today a Gypsy stole a coat from a Jew before the eyes of thousands of passersby, and Karmelicka Street was in an uproar.

June 19, 1942

Our "blessings" have always come in pairs: two rabbis, two languages, and two kinds of study (Hebrew and secular). In the ghetto we are blessed with a new pair, two kinds of police. One is the unarmed Jewish police who are merely a force to keep order, and the other is the Polish police who fulfill all the functions of a normal police force: catching lawbreakers, executing sentences, making investigations in criminal affairs. They are the middlemen between the conquerors and the ghetto in all civil, criminal, and administrative matters.

Above both of these is the Gestapo, whose very name inspires fear and horror. When it comes to a Jewish house it brings with it destruction and ruin. Its emissaries are angels of death.

And now come and hear what befell me today:

At five o'clock in the morning, when we were still sunk in the slumber of dawn, there came a knock at the door. Every knock makes the heart tremble. This time it was the police; and to be exact, the Polish police. My wife, who had opened the door for them, slumped and nearly fainted. "Is Ch. A. K. here?" "He is here." "Where is he?" "He is sleeping in there." Immediately they shut the front door and came into my room.

"Are you Ch. K.?"

"I am."

"Get dressed and come with us." Trembling seized me. I struggled to understand why, wherefore. I asked the policeman and he answered, "You'll find out at the Commissariat."

May you never know such an experience! I suspected myself of every kind of crime in the world. I called to mind the prayer, "For the sin . . ."[7] and contrary to the custom of the world, I found

---

[7] The penitential prayer of the High Holidays, in which all one's sins are itemized.

355

myself guilty. I got ready to go at once, and the policeman led me to the Commissariat. I was entered on the list of captives and was locked in a cell with several other prisoners. From half past five until nine-thirty I sat and waited, paced and waited, thought my mournful thoughts and waited.

When the hour of redemption came I was informed that I was called only as a witness in a judicial inquiry and would be cross-examined in the matter of the death of an acquaintance of mine. My eyes lit up with relief, but I was almost uncontrollably angry. For what purpose had they frightened me? Was it necessary to wake me up for this? For this I was seized and locked up? For this purpose did I lose five hours?

Afterward the secret was revealed to me. The judicial interrogator to whom I was to give testimony lives outside the Jewish section, and for this reason I was turned over to a policeman who would be the one to take me out of the ghetto and deliver me to the Aryan quarter, and then take me back. I was a part of the policeman's body. Without him they wouldn't have let me enter the Aryan quarter and without him they wouldn't have let me leave it, lest I might have entered it illegally. I spent almost an entire day in idleness and in an overwrought state of mind, and all this in order to answer: Was the late G. a quarrelsome man? Did he have disputes with people during his lifetime?

But in the wake of my misfortune I came into my reward. I was privileged to be in the Aryan quarter after being separated from it for nearly two years. I saw it and was again convinced that the world would not exist but for the merit of the Jews. The Aryan quarter is like a cemetery. There is no life and no traffic in it. In the stores there is not a living soul. Everywhere there is cleanliness, but it is the cleanliness of a ghost town. "Is this Warsaw?" its people ask. There is no income, no traffic and no life. The policeman who accompanied me sighed and said as we parted, "If God does not have mercy on us we'll all die like flies." I thanked him but deep in my heart I took revenge for my sufferings.

June 20, 1942

These are days of great activity in the ghetto. Those condemned to ruin and destruction have found an opening as small as the eye of a needle through which to escape with their lives, and they have all awakened at this news.

There is an instinctive feeling that some terrible catastrophe is drawing near for the Warsaw ghetto, though no one can determine its time or details. This time the masses are relying on the authority of the great hooligan: that in forty days ultimate destruction will befall the Jews of Warsaw, because in this week's *Völkischer Beobachter* it is expressly written that if battles begin on a second front, the end will come for Polish Jewry within forty days. And since Churchill has flown to Roosevelt to discuss the matter of creating a second front, and since both of them take their orders from the Jews, it is obvious that our days are numbered.

But now, suddenly, a ray of light has appeared, the drowning man grasps at a straw. There is a chance that we can escape with our lives. Therefore make haste! Hurry! Hurry to the *Judenrat* to sign up among those who hope to emigrate to North America, South America (except Argentina and Chile, which are at peace with Germany), and Palestine!

Before, when such rumors got started no one knew their source or how to act on them. Now the whole thing is clearly stated in a circular the *Judenrat* put out for the courtyard committees. Palestine has made a particular impression, as though everyone is certain that it is the most secure place for an impoverished people. The categories of those who will be permitted to travel are quite numerous: a woman to her husband; children to their parents; parents to their children—and, the Gestapo added orally on the telephone, brothers to brothers!

The circular was received and the ghetto became filled with movement and activity. Out of their great despair the masses don't ask for details, or how anybody expects to implement the thing. They rush about, and rush first of all to the *Judenrat* to sign up. Long queues of thousands of people beleaguer the rescue office that the *Judenrat* opened for this purpose. They have no hesitation about the expenses which might be implicit in this *Judenrat* monopoly as long as they are saved. Who hasn't a son or a daughter or a brother or a father overseas? The Jewish family is scattered over the four corners of the earth. And if there were no external deterrent, we would all leave this land of Tophet, young and old alike.

But every rose has a thorn. This time too, we do not lack people who see the black side and set the whole business at naught. And their rationale? The whole thing has come about only for the

357

purpose of making exchanges between the warring factions: you give me my *Deutschen* and I'll give you the Jews in their place. Some people say it will be one Jew for three *Deutschen*. In Palestine, according to them, there are altogether nine hundred and eighty *Deutschen*, none of whom have the slightest desire to go to their Führer. The result is that the number of people who will be privileged to go to Palestine will be small.

That's one problem. Second, as is the custom of Poland, nothing will be run properly. In the end, only those who can spread a lot of money around will be privileged to make this journey. Everyone will exploit you to the last cent and the last crumb. First of all there is the Jewish policeman who takes a service charge for letting you stand in line and giving you a chance to submit the questionnaire. Next comes the *Judenrat* itself, which is beginning with a five-zloty registration fee and will probably end up charging several thousand. Afterward, the Gestapo and everyone connected with it.

Some people add that the whole business is nothing but blackmail and that some misfortune is afoot here for those who sign up. As an example they cite what happened in Mlawa; all those registered were arrested, and their end was an evil and bitter one. I don't believe this rumor, but I do believe that only money will open the way to Palestine. And I further believe that first of all the *Judenrat* and the Jewish police will profit from the whole affair. The community will get registration fees from thousands of people. The police will get service charges from thousands of people. And the registered people? They too will gain—disappointment.

May they be sustained in their illusions.

June 22, 1942

The latest fragment of the tragedy of the ghetto:

The wall of the ghetto surrounds the Jewish quarter almost from end to end. It is of unlimed brick and at the top of the wall its length is sown with pieces of broken glass. Thus it continues onward beginning from the Jewish cemetery in the direction of Leszno and Zelazna streets to the corner of Chlodna. From there it branches off across Sienna and across Elektoralna-Rymarska-Przejazd-Nowolipki-Nalewki-Swietojerska-Bonifraterska streets. At the corner of Bonifraterska-Muranowska it was cut off and awaited continuation. Now a third segment is to be built, cutting out the little area from Bonifraterska, corner of Muranowski, to Muranowska, corner of Pokorna, which encompasses eighteen buildings with six hundred families. The wall is now being extended until it meets the Pokorna wall. Then the work of the wall will be completed. Whoever has not seen the sorrow and anguish which are poured over the faces of the new exiles, for whom finding a new apartment will be harder than the parting of the Red Sea, has never in his life seen a mass misfortune. In front of the houses which are being emptied of their Jewish inhabitants, the entire Muranowska Square is full to capacity with the furniture they have moved out of their old apartments and have not yet taken to new ones because they can't find any. Stacks upon stacks of used furniture await an apartment or a buyer, for almost all of those affected by the decree are forced to sell the greater part of their belongings. Either they must move from a large apartment to a small one, or they have to sell their furniture to put down six months' rent in advance on a new place, which is the Polish custom. Those who are not affected by the relocation decree want to re-establish themselves via their brothers' misfortune, so they treat them harshly. They raise the rents, demand the six months' payment all at once, plus cash security at the rate of two months' more, forbid the use of portable stoves, and make other prohibitions at which the gracious daughters of Warsaw are experts.

And so Muranowski Square has turned into a furniture market. There are no private buyers in evidence, but those who traffic in this hastened to come. By the tens they walk leisurely around eying everything, and everyone recognizes them by the slates on their chests with the Polish inscription, "I buy used furniture." Opposite the square so full of trading are the bare windows of the empty houses.

I remember the office of the Lovers of the Hebrew Language, which used to be at Number 14, on the third floor. In those days we were still naïve enough to dare to think of the Jewish role in the Diaspora, of reviving a language, and of rebuilding a land and a nation. And now behold, O God, and see our disgrace!

June 25, 1942
Every day Polish Jewry is being brought to slaughter. It is estimated, and there is some basis for the figures, that three-quarters of a million Polish Jews have already passed from this earth. We

are imprisoned within double walls: a wall of brick for our bodies, and a wall of silence for our spirits. Whatever happens or is done is cloaked in total silence. The *Zyd* newspaper will tell you all about soup kitchens; it refrains from mentioning expulsions and destructions. On paper everything is going on as usual. But the rumors are awesome.

The Nazis kill Jews by various means. Some of them are sent to a labor camp where they survive for a month at the outside. More than that would be beyond human strength. Some are shot; some are burned; some are poisoned with lethal gas; some are electrocuted. Before the Lublin expulsion the critically sick people were put to death first; after them, the old men and women from the home for the aged; and lastly the children from the boarding schools. The patients in the mental hospital at Otwock were killed to the last man. The Nazi world has no use for them and these unfortunates haven't the right to exist in it. As for healthy people, if they are over sixty years old and not working for the benefit of the Nazi camp, the rule is death by shooting; their portion of bread is needed for the productive workers from whom the Nazi regime derives benefit. The Jews among these are the last Jews to be shot. The Führer is putting into practice the principles that Friedrich Nietzsche and Houston Chamberlain preached about the Jews.

In the past few days death has begun to stroll about in the streets of the ghetto even during the daytime. A military car drives into Orla Street in a great hurry. An officer and a very splendid lady get out of it. When they alight, the officer stretches out his hand to the lady and takes leave of her. The lady walks on ahead; the officer lingers behind her. Not many moments pass when a shot is heard. The officer has murdered the lady, and she falls to the ground and dies. A woman is killed in broad daylight in the sight of hundreds of passersby and the thing makes no impression. There are various rumors about the reason for this incident, but they are beside the point at the moment.

A car stops near Number 4 Nowolipki Street. A young man gets out; in fact he is a non-Jew. The Nazi who accompanies him takes him into the gateway and ends his life with a shot. This too is in broad daylight, while hundreds of ghetto dwellers are witnesses to the drama.

Of what value is a human being—especially if he is a Jew. The fear of death looks out from every corner. Everyone tries to make himself inconspicuous, so that no one will notice him and he will not be included in some nightly list. People fear strangers and they fear the Jewish police, their "brothers in misfortune."

Like stranger, like brother! Both of them are plotting evil for you.

June 26, 1942

Death paces the streets of the ghetto. Everyone wants to escape; everyone is jealous of his relatives and friends who have succeeded in saving their lives.

And suddenly came the news of registration for travel to North America, South America, and Palestine. Could there be any greater good fortune than this? One who escapes from the hands of the Nazis is as one who has escaped from the hands of a thief and a murderer, and here a door is opened for salvation. When the *Judenrat* circular (June 21–23) stated that three days would be allowed for the registration, the despairing masses hurried to the registration office by the thousands and tens of thousands, and long queues of people who got up early to get a place in line formed even before the sun rose.

Never before have we had such days of activity and alertness as on the days of the announcement of registration. I myself was sought out by people I hadn't seen in a long time. They turned up for the sake of friendship and also to ask advice. As usual, some people approve and some are against the emigration. Some believe the Nazis will take them to Palestine, and there are instances of parents refusing to register their children because of suspicion. They believe that only evil can come from evil people, that the Nazis cannot be trusted to behave humanely toward the Jews, and that therefore whoever registers is walking into a trap.

The Jews' nerves are ragged. They have no patience or ability to think rationally. After the enthusiasm had somewhat subsided, an opposing movement arose. Just as they rushed to register before, they rushed later to have their names erased. I met a Jew who is close to the kingdom, an adviser of the *Judenrat*. According to him, he signed up his son for emigration to Palestine, but after a few hours he regretted the whole affair. Why? He doesn't want his son's name to be found on a list that will pass into the hands of the

Nazis. It is better to remain hidden, in the shadow. As soon as he realized this he hurriedly took his son's name off the list.

Thus we are shunted from hope to fear, from despair to consolation and back again.

June 27, 1942

It is now almost three years since the outbreak of the war. The days of combat between the sides were few, for within a week the enemy had reached the gates of the capital city. In the days of the air raid which preceded the conquest, we saw death face to face, and when the city was taken, the Nazis spread their rule over us. Since then there has been no day whose trouble was not greater than that of the previous one. Our ancestors, who knew trials of this sort, gave a true expression of this: "Our lives are diminished by sword and captivity and plague and epidemic and by every trouble and sorrow." And there is no exaggeration in this, for the conquerors have set us aside for evil, and sent all their plagues to our hearts.

But with it all, we have lived. It has been a hard life of hunger and austerity, a life of poverty and sorrow, of suffering and sighs, a life of degradation and shame—and even so we were able to survive. Day followed day and they became weeks and months and years, but with all our trouble and sorrow, we did not feel the burden of life so much. On the contrary, we felt a little easier, because as the days went by redemption came nearer. But now it is not like that. I do not exaggerate when I say that we have reached a state of lack of breath. There is simply no air. Every minute is like a thousand years. Every day is a never-ending eternity.

Up to now we were supported by the material and spiritual forces which were stored up, products of days gone by. Today we are poor and empty. Our supporting forces have already been dissipated and no new ones have been granted to help us continue our existence. The candle of our souls is still flickering but we sense that in a moment it will be extinguished. Is our strength the strength of stones? Is it in the power of a human being to endure hardship in this degree? We had one consolation in our lives: our faith in the victory of democracy; our belief that its powers were greater than those of the other side, the enemy of the Jews and the enemy of humanity.

We consoled ourselves that the Nazis' downfall was drawing near, that their military victories were only of the moment, that their strength was imaginary. The evidence? The Russian front. The Nazis remained as though bound in their winter positions, and did not attempt an offensive against Leningrad or Moscow because they were convinced that it would not succeed. When we saw all this we began to become impatient. We even set dates and hours for the end of the war. It was clear to us that the war was approaching its end this very summer, that we would not spend another winter with the murderers; that the redemption was near at hand.

And now, another disappointment. Rommel arose in Africa and confused our calculations. England has suffered a defeat and is fleeing to Egypt. And once the war is in Egypt, who will wager that it will not spread from there to Palestine as well? There are plenty of signs that Rommel's offensive is a powerful one. The Führer wants to mend the error he committed last year when he attacked Russia instead of falling upon the Suez Canal. This year his goal is Suez. England has been dealt a blow from which she will not be able to recover soon.

Perhaps here too Israel is at the heart of it. Our luck has caused it. You don't go into partnership with *idiots* and *failures*. The sum total is, then, that the war will drag on. We will winter behind our walls. And who can survive one more winter with Hitler?

The terror is increasing. Since that first night of slaughter it has not stopped. Around midnight, night after night, the Nazis come out to stalk their prey. Sleeping people are brought to death like sheep to the kill. Last night fourteen people were shot to death in the streets of the ghetto. In the morning their naked corpses were found near the gates of the houses. Yes, naked; for the Nazis strip their victims. All the possessions of those killed by the regime are forfeit. Two of those killed fell victim right before the window of my house, near the gate of 25 Karmelicka Street.

These lines are being written after midnight, and out of the silence of the night, the rumble of the wheels of the cars hurrying on their way to Pawiak, the house of slaughter, reaches my ears. A ray of light showing through the window would endanger my life.

The victims are bound inside the cars. This very night they will ascend the scaffold. God of Gods! Shall the sword devour thy sons forever?

Tonight (dawn 7/1) was also a night of slaughter for us. At first such nights were something out of the ordinary; but when they went on and on, we stopped counting them. But there was something new in tonight's tragedy. Among the corpses there were only ten Jews; four of them were Aryans, Poles born and bred, who were in partnership with Jews in matters of smuggling. In their lifetime the Nazis allowed them to dwell among their people and take pride in their Aryan ancestry. But when they were caught in the crime of smuggling, they were equated with their lower-race partners and were buried with the rest of the dead of Israel in the Jewish cemetery.

The war against smuggling is at its peak. The size of the ghetto was reduced only to reduce smuggling! The wall was built only to strengthen the watch and eliminate the smuggling! A special brigade has been created to guard the wall from within, and these watches are stationed inside the ghetto. Every watch is responsible for an area of fifty meters. Although most of the victims of the nights are smugglers, the smuggling never ceases. Number 30 Nowilipki Street was turned into a slaughter house last night, when five or six people were killed, among them the wife of the janitor. The whole courtyard is tracked with blood. All this took place in the middle of the night. Twelve hours later, a car brought smuggled goods into that same courtyard, a load worth tens of thousands of zloty. The roof is in flames and the clock strikes on!

And this is the rule. The Nazi dole to the Jews is only two kilos of black bread a month per head. What then should the ghetto dwellers do if they don't smuggle? In any case they die, but they prefer death by the sword to death from hunger.

The importance that the Nazis attach to the war against smuggling can be proved by the fact that for capital punishment they have made the races equal. An Aryan who is caught smuggling is not killed at the scene of the crime; they bring him into the ghetto and kill him there.

The management of the Jewish cemetery in Gesia Street received an order to dig a mass grave for two hundred people as quickly as possible. While the work was going on, the Nazis came and found an Aryan policeman looking around. One Nazi became angry at this and asked wrathfully, "What is this lump doing here?"

At once the Nazi collected the fifteen Jewish gravediggers and took them outside the ghetto. For what purpose did the Nazis do what they did? Nobody knows for certain, but common sense would indicate that they didn't take the gravediggers to raise the dead, but rather to bury the dead. Thus it appears that Aryans too are being slaughtered, only the Nazis prefer to bring them to a Jewish grave, so that they may find perfect peace under the shadow of the divine presence of Israel. Digging a mass grave in the Catholic cemetery would be too conspicuous an activity; it would stir up the people and cause bitter demonstrations. Better for the Aryans to disappear among the dead of Israel, so no one will know of their death and burial. Since the conquest of Poland, we have attained equal rights. After death!

July 2, 1942

From birth a feeling of esteem toward the wealthy man is implanted in us. Even scholars honor the wealthy. And therefore Roosevelt and Churchill, who are wealthy, know what they're about. Would Roosevelt lie? Would Churchill make promises and not keep them? All the treasures of the world are in their hands; they rule immense realms; and at their hands will come the complete overthrow of the killers. Churchill spoke, and Roosevelt orated, and we forgot that a beautiful oration cannot keep Rommel out of the desert.

Suddenly we have awakened. It was but a dream. The news of the past two days has depressed our spirits to a degree unequaled since the day the war broke out. Our prophecies have not been fulfilled. Realities contradict them, and our hopes are shattered like a reed. The murderer has grown stronger. Instead of weakness, he shows incredible strength on every front. Rommel is before Alexandria; the British are fleeing weakly before their pursuers; Sevastopol has been captured; and along almost the entire length of the Russian front (except for the Leningrad sector) an offensive has begun of a sort that we may assume will end in victory. For were it not so, they would not be announcing it so loudly to the whole world.

Where is the mighty British army after three years of preparations? Where is the power of mighty America? Where is the second front? The Suez Canal is in danger, and isn't it the lifeline of the whole British Empire? If England's strength is insufficient to protect Suez, the most treasured possession of the Empire, what hope have we in our aspirations for its ultimate victory?

Besides all this, we fear for Palestine. The one spot in the world in whose shadow we believed we could seek protection is close to being destroyed by the same killer who destroyed the lives of all the Jewish communities in Europe. Two bombs have the power to demolish Tel Aviv as Sodom and Gomorrah were demolished. And if she is conquered, her sons and builders will be exiled and the Arabs will have dominion over her. It will be total destruction for the hope of a people.

Wherever the Nazi plants the soles of his feet becomes his eternal domain. In every place he has created a culture; everywhere he has built. His works are recognized in every field of human endeavor. Only one small step further is necessary: Jesus who lived in the "land of the Gentiles" was racially an Aryan, and Christianity was the vision of his spirit. They will pay a professor, and he will prove this with scientific signs and portents.

As we sat together like mourners, discussing our worries, Hirsch suddenly appeared, and his voice was like thunder: "Worthless ones! Do you know what has happened tonight? A hundred Jews have been killed; and ten Jewish policemen have been added to their number. You're worried about Palestine? Worry about your ghetto! The days of your life are numbered and counted. The sword bereaves from without, and there is fear within." There were those among us who refused to believe the entire story. Such a thing is impossible. But not many moments passed before large announcements were posted declaring publicly that in fact 100 *Juden* were put to death by shooting for some unspecified crime. But the sin is not essential here. The sin will be found, if not before the shooting then after it.

July 3, 1942

The announcement of our hundred and ten dead was written and signed by Auerswald, the ghetto commissar, who has power over life and death. The ruling power of the government was not ashamed to call this killing by its right name—revenge. Which means that the dead were not cut off from among their people for a crime they had committed, but were brought as a sacrifice to prove to the inhabitants of the ghetto that the hand of the government is all powerful, "and if acts such as these are repeated in the future, the sword of vengeance will devour you right and left."

The hundred were killed for quite insignificant crimes. They had been caught and taken to the Jewish prison in Zamenhof Street, where they were awaiting trial. Then it was decided to kill a hundred Jews as an act of revenge. Why should the Nazis put themselves out to make the rounds of the houses to find people when they have a ready supply? The prison administration was ordered to select a hundred from among the prisoners. A special room was allocated in which to choose those who would live and those who would die. At first the prisoners didn't know why one man was being separated from another, but a man's heart tells him. They didn't know, but they sensed it; and once they sensed it their terrible tragedy began.

The fate of the ten policemen was the same as the fate of the civilians. Their names were entered on the revenge list even before they were arrested, while they were still fulfilling their functions as free men. As they did every day, they had scattered to all the corners of the ghetto to stand watch, and they were taken from their places of vigil to their death. Four of the men set aside for death could not be found at their posts, and at once others were brought to take their place, men who were neither suspects nor originally intended for the revenge-sacrifice. One of them had been married just a month ago, and 4,000 zloty from the dowry money had paved his way into the police force. Five minutes earlier he had gone to stand his watch, and his fate was sealed. At dawn on Thursday, the seventeenth of Tammuz, 5702, at an hour when all was dim, before man could distinguish between white and blue, they were all led out like invisible wraiths to the old cemetery in Praga. They dug a grave for themselves, and the Nazis sent bullets into their hearts.

What event brought about this revenge?

The Nazis themselves tell it in their announcement: Recently there have been many times when the Jews have shown opposition to orders from the police, and sometimes they have opposed the police with force. As for the Jewish police, they have failed to uphold the loftiness of their mission. Some offer bribes; some help the smugglers; some are guilty of insubordination.

And thus the sin is expiated with a hundred civilians and ten policemen.

July 6, 1942

We have had a bit of relief. We learned that Rommel has been somewhat delayed on his way to Alexandria, that the British have amassed a large force and blocked his path. Perhaps this coup will benefit England. It will teach her the basic fact that you can't conduct a war in little bits, that war is not a dance of forward and back, a game of cat and mouse. In every case the British came with small forces against a mighty enemy, and in every place they met defeat. Because of this the front is growing longer, but the result is a strengthening, not a weakening, of the enemy. Through the conquest of new territories the Nazis' power is increasing. The African front offered England many opportunities for a decisive victory, but her ineptitude caused her to lose the advantage. The English have a tradition that the final victory will be theirs, a sort of "eternity of Israel"—English version. But just as the eternity of Israel did not deter the Führer from bringing physical destruction to a million Polish Jews, so the British tradition, which is a historical optical illusion, will not deter him from chasing Great Britain out of Europe and off the coast of North Africa.

Historical events do not repeat themselves in their original form. One can no longer rely on the customary saying that England loses battles but wins the war. The foul-souled Goebbels correctly asked: "Is it possible that a whole string of defeats can lead to a final victory? Why should the last battle be set apart from its predecessors?"

The indications are that this time England will concentrate forces on the African front which will beat Rommel bloody, and make his victories as meaningless as bubbles on the face of the waters.

There are echoes of the incident of the "revenge of the hundred," and they are frightening, sorrowful echoes. The Valley of the Vision was 36 Nowolipki Street. From this courtyard two porters suspected of smuggling were taken out to be killed, and with them was a friend named Izraelit, a tailor, who had come by chance to spend the night. There were two killers.

The three candidates for death, however, defended themselves. They were virile men with strength in their loins, and they did not want to die in spite of the Nazis. Thus in the dark of the night a terrible wrestling match began between those who were defending their lives and the killers. The porters fought with the strength of their bodies, without weapons; the killers were armed and confident of their superiority. At such times there is no rational thought. Instinct comes in its stead. In time of danger the latent, hidden powers of a man burst out and are exposed; and in particular when one finds oneself in a condition of "in any case we will die." And therefore, before the killers had time to act, the condemned men pounced on them and tried to seize the pistols. One of the pistols went off and wounded the tailor in the leg. Then the porters grabbed the Nazis by the throat and tried to strangle them. The two sides wrestled until their strength waned, and in the end the killers, who still had their weapons, were victorious. Izraelit the tailor cleared himself before the killers with a document showing that he was working in a factory for the German army. With the dawn, he was taken to the hospital.

On the morrow, the Nazis avenged the mutiny of the two porters with a hundred and ten Jews. They were put to death for the sins of men who had never laid eyes on them.

July 10, 1942

The prison on Dzielna Street is fenced in and blocked off from every side and direction. No one comes in or goes out except the corpses of the "criminals" taken out for burial, and the living skeletons brought in for slaughter. The gates of the houses along the length of the entire prison are closed off even to their tenants, whose entry and exit is through Nowilipki Street. Their windows are darkened even when the sun is shining, and whoever peeps through them forfeits his life. And in spite of it all, the abominations of the Nazis rise up to the sun. The hidden things are revealed.

My friend Hirsch worried constantly about the disappearance of the 40,000 Lublin exiles whom our Aryan messengers never found. Finally one refugee managed to escape alive and reach a human habitation. We learned certain dreadful details from his lips.

It has been decreed and decided in Nazi ruling circles to bring systematic physical destruction upon the Jews of the General Government. There is even a special military unit for this purpose, which makes the rounds of all the Polish cities according to the needs and the requirements of the moment. But a total slaughter such as this can't be put into practice in one day; one can't kill tens of thousands of laborers and artisans who are adept in various trades needed by the German army. Besides that, it is necessary to give the whole matter an organized and semi-human appearance. Therefore the Nazis have established a gigantic exile center for three hundred thousand people, a concentration camp located between Chelm and Wlodawa, near the village of Sobowa.

Jewish exiles from all the conquered countries are brought to this exile camp. All the exiled Jews of Czechoslovakia were brought there, and all the German Jews affected by the expulsion decree; and they continue to bring in whole camps—now the Jews of one village, now those of another. An Ingathering of the Exiles on foreign soil! The lost and oppressed Jews of Lublin also found a resting place there—and their grave.

The exiles at Sobibor are fortunate in that they have no shortage of food. Whoever has the money can buy produce from the farmers nearby, as the exiles in the camp are their only customers. This concession is made for the sake of the farmers—not, heaven forbid, for the sake of the exiles.

The great camp, which stands amid dense forests and swamps, is completely surrounded by barbed wire and is heavily guarded. After the exiles are taken there, the real tragedy begins. The young and healthy ones, those who are strong and under sixty, are taken for work. Throughout the region there are labor camps for various crafts. There the prisoners work at hard labor, and for all their toil they receive only a crust of black bread and the water of oppression. In the end they go to their death, for it is not in their power to survive and endure for longer than six months under such living conditions. This is the segment which is condemned to die, but slowly, after they have given their strength to their mortal enemy and aided his victory.

The fate of the other segment is even more tragic—they are condemned to die at once. Those who are over sixty or are incapable of physical labor because of some bodily weakness, as well as young children and their mothers who "eat and do not produce"—they go to death wholesale, in a "civilized" way, by poisoning with lethal gas or by electrocution. There is no pity, no measure of mercy. They are superfluous people who are not to be kept alive and fed. Their portion of bread, even though they buy it with their own money, is needed for the workers, from whose labor the Nazi regime benefits.

In general the Jew has no right to live, but it is possible for him to postpone his death for a while as long as there is need for his work. Upon the conclusion of the work, he too goes to death.

The killing of thousands of people has turned into a business that employs many hands. After the souls expire, they strip the corpses. Their clothing, shirts, and shoes are not wasted, but are collected in piles upon piles and turned over for disinfection, mending, and repairs. Hundreds of Jews are employed in these tasks. The Nazis, who are lovers of truth, admit it, and say that the work of the Jews is quite satisfactory. They are efficient, intelligent, and quick to catch on. This merit has stood the Jewish workers in good stead, for their death has been deferred to an unspecified time, and they will be the last to be shot.

All that has been said refers to the Jews of Poland. And the Jews of the Ukraine? And the Jews of Russia? And the Jews of Lithuania? If they are still whole, they are on the brink of destruction.

July 11, 1942

The stories of the refugee shed light upon the matter of the physical destruction decreed for us in conquered Poland. We knew that the process of destruction had begun, that tens of thousands of Jews had already been brought as sacrifices upon its altar; but the manner of its realization was clouded in mist. The lost exiles sank like lead in mighty waters, so that their voices were not heard again among the living, and other sources of information were sealed off from us. As long as there is no knowledge, hope still flows in the heart, but from now on everything is clear, and all doubt of our future is removed.

And this is a terrible, awesome future. Death is hard; harder still are the moments before death; and even hardest of all is being condemned to a death which is inevitable, but whose time has not been set.

Everyone must wait until his turn comes. That is when life becomes too hard to bear. The desire to live grows stronger at just that point. On the very eve of their death, the masses in the ghetto worry about their routine affairs as though they still had a long life ahead of them. But the intelligent and perceptive walk around like mourners.

Indeed, this is not the first experience of physical destruction in Jewish history. In every generation they have risen up against us to destroy us. The experiences known to us from our history are not, however, like the current experience. There is no similarity between physical destruction which comes about as a result of a momentary outburst of fanatical mobs incited to murder and this calculated

371

governmental program for the realization of which an organized murder apparatus has been set up.

Day after day new Jewish exiles are brought to the camps, and day after day new victims are taken out from among them, either for hard labor or to face the sword of the angel of death. The murder *machinery* does not stop for a single day. And this is not, heaven forbid, illegal murderous work. On the contrary, the program has been proclaimed throughout the world; it has in effect received formal sanction.

The Lublin fugitive escaped, but he put himself in mortal danger, for if he failed his life would be forfeit. But out of despair, and feeling that he had very little choice, he decided to make the attempt. If he succeeded, so much the better, and if not, what was the difference between an early death and a later death? He is a native of Germany who was exiled with the rest of the German exiles. In his wanderings he had lost his wife and child. Chance brought him near a large truck on which they were loading the clothes of the murdered ones to transport them to the shops for disinfection or repairs. Out of his earlier fortune he had managed to hide a few jewels, so he approached the driver and offered him a jewel to save him. "How?" the driver asked. "I'll stretch out on the loaded clothing, and you load more clothes on top of me and cover me. If I suffocate, fine, I'll suffocate; may my death atone for my sins." The driver agreed. The refugee didn't suffocate on the way, and he wasn't caught.

July 13, 1942

The Nazi press is gloating over great victories on the Eastern front, against General Timoshenko, who, having been struck a decisive blow, will not rise again; about the sinking of the Anglo-Saxon ships carrying war matériel and armaments to the Soviet "comrades" across the seven seas; and about Rommel, who is working wonders along the coast of North Africa.

The noise of victory is necessary for the Nazis. They need to strengthen their national spirit, which began to wane as the winter and spring passed by uselessly. But we have an intuitive feeling that these are victories made in Berlin by Goebbels, that they are ministerial victories in the offices of the Ministry of Propaganda, rather than military ones on the field of battle.

The Jews of the ghetto, for their part, say that the Nazis' downfall must and will come. Their victories on paper make no impression. A weakening is apparent in comparison with their power and might of last year. Here is proof: During the entire two weeks since the day the new offensive was launched, the Nazis have hardly moved. The conquest of Voronezh was only a foot in the door; following it up is fraught with danger. Not only is the Russian front not tottering, but the "beaten" Timoshenko is mounting a new offensive with great force in another place. Rommel's hand, too, has withered. He remains standing on the border between Egypt and the desert. The members of the ghetto have already encircled him, attacked him, and left him as an eternal ruin.

There are additional details to the "revenge of the hundred." First, there were ten women among those killed. When it comes to taking lives, the Nazis put women on an equal footing with men. More so— in their eyes it is preferable to sacrifice a woman. She will stop giving birth to children who would bring destruction upon the enemies of Israel.

Second, in this killing too the Nazis tempered judgment with mercy. As atonement for the sins of the ghetto, the Nazis demanded that the *Judenrat* compile a list of a hundred well-known people, the élite of the Warsaw block, to stretch out their necks for slaughter for the transgression of the entire Jewish community. The *Judenrat*, stunned, schemed to turn up substitutes: let those be taken who have already been caught in their sins. In a list prepared by the *Judenrat* according to the Nazis' original order, the President's name would have been found at the top. To make a long story short, the substitution was successful. Thanks to this "success," one hundred innocent people were killed.

Third, the murdered ones were not buried in Praga, but rather in Babycz. They dug a grave for themselves, and Jewish gravediggers, who were brought to the place of slaughter in advance, buried them.

Daughter of Germany! Blessed is he who will seize your babes and smash them against the Rock!

The past ten days have been days of tumult and confusion in the ghetto.

The decree concerning "labor camps," which are merely a prepa-

373

ration for death, has been renewed. Since the day when war with Russia broke out, the camps had been idle and the ghetto had quieted down. Now the edict has been renewed. There is weeping and wailing in every house. The *Judenrat* was ordered to supply 1,500 youths, and the Jewish police began to make the rounds of the candidates' doors during the night. Their coming was accompanied by cries and wails, but the police, in spite of their being Jewish, harden their hearts and do their duty. Since every edict is in essence nothing but a business to its executors, so here too there is a business. Instead of 1,500, 2,000 are taken out of their home; 1,500 are turned over to the Nazis, 500 set free after paying a ransom to the Jewish police. This time the edict is more severe; even the crippled and deformed are taken. The healthy and the strong go to work; the crippled and the weak go to destruction. Before this, the Nazis used to make a distinction between the healthy and the sick; now no one is exempt. I have an acquaintance in my courtyard whose son is a hunchback. It would have been possible to ransom him off, but my acquaintance didn't want to pay for the very reason that since his son was deformed, he was sure that they would release him in accordance with the law. He was wrong. The boy was taken and did not return.

July 15, 1942

There is a well-known folk saying: "A worm that lives in a horseradish thinks that it is sweet." We have been like prisoners since the time we were pushed into the ghetto. The life of captivity, the yoke of edicts which never cease and are daily renewed, the degradation which has been our daily fare, the poverty and depression which grow as the sources of sustenance are cut off—the whole martyrology which is devouring us on every hand, and which has reduced us to objects of contempt unworthy of being thought of as men even in our own eyes—these things have made us into possessors of noble virtues; into people who are hurt but do not strike back, who hear themselves disgraced but do not react; and most of all, into people who are content with little.

Every ray of light which is reflected to us from afar unsettles our souls. Every ember of hope which begins to sparkle on the horizon of our life encourages us to believe that we will surely survive and return once more to our past glory. We have already been rescued from real freedom. A crumb of freedom is sufficient to make us happy. We acquiesce to the harshest living conditions, if only to be privileged to reach the end.

Today the Nazis granted us a concession. They reduced the cur-few by one hour. "What is this that God has done to us?" Would a tyrannical and barbaric regime, which is forever planning to destroy and demolish us, whose sword cuts among us right and left—allow us even a minute to relax? Don't let this surprise you. Whenever you see a Nazi doing good for the Jews, know that he is doing good for himself. This time too the Nazis' intentions were not for the good of the ghetto dwellers, but to lengthen the workday in the factories. When the curfew begins at nine, the workers stop at eight, and when the curfew begins at ten, they stop at nine. Hence an extra hour of work a day.

The Nazis' preparations for the winter season are going on full force. It will be necessary for them to spend another winter on the steppes of Russia, and for that reason they all have their hands full with work. Every day more and more factories for various trades are being opened, and it is the intelligent and knowledgeable Jewish worker who is preferred by the Nazis. The starved and oppressed Jewish worker accepts seven zloty and a sip of soup for twelve hours' work a day, as long as he has some assurance of not being exiled.

The registered worker benefits from special "privileges." The Nazis care for him in a manner reminiscent of the relationship be-tween a carter and his horse: he feeds and waters the horse to enable him to bear his yoke; without his horse the carter is as good as dead.

A decree has been prepared to expel seventy thousand Jews from the ghetto, but the German firms who had a vested interest in the ghetto dwellers, and who couldn't get along without them, opposed the expulsion. They served as our advocates and protected us with all their might. This is a tragedy as deep as the abyss—to help your enemy with your own hands, to save him from his misfortune so that he may turn around and kill you.

July 16, 1942

A decree has struck at the thousands of Jews who are foreign citizens, who had preferential treatment and availed themselves of special privileges before the outbreak of war with Russia and the United States. First, they were exempt from wearing the "badge of shame"; second, no one interfered with their crossing borders and the like. They were given special treatment so that the governments protecting them would not take retaliatory action.

Now the wheel has turned upon them. They have become the prisoners of the Nazis, and whoever falls into those hands does not rise again. When registration for Palestine was opened, the foreign citizens—excluding only exiled and deported German Jews, Czech Jews, and former Polish Jews—were not forgotten. In their case registration was mandatory. They had already been required to register once, but that was not enough for the Nazis. This time a special amnesty was offered to those who had failed to register earlier. If they met their obligations now, their crime would be forgiven.

The second registration omitted no one, and we learned its outcome yesterday. All foreign citizens were required, on a few hours' notice, to take with them a hand valise weighing no more than ten kilos, as well as 20 zloty in cash, and go over to the Pawia. What their fate will be no one knows. Will they be exchanged and transported by the Nazis to Switzerland, as it is said, through the International Red Cross, or will they be imprisoned as enemies of the Reich and transported to some concentration camp?

If I were a student in a Yeshivah today I would ask my Talmud teacher: What is the law concerning a Gentile who is buried among the dead of Israel? When the resurrection of the dead comes, will he too rise to his feet and live? Or when it is written, "Your dead shall live," does "your dead" mean only the dead of Israel? There are daily instances of Polish youths being taken into the ghetto in broad daylight in a military car, and shot to death in a public place before the eyes of thousands of passersby. One of these cases occurred in Orla Street the day before yesterday. Who was the victim? He was an Aryan, of that there is no doubt. The reason for his death cannot be ascertained, but we can be sure that he was one of the smugglers. The business of smuggling brings the Aryans and the Jews together. It unites them in joy and in sorrow. Why was this man brought to the ghetto to be killed? In order not to irritate the Aryans. An ugly killing such as this would have incited them. His relatives know only that he has been arrested, not that he has been killed, and his body is taken to the Jewish cemetery as soon as he has breathed his last.

As to the question of the "resurrection of the dead," it bears study.

July 19, 1942

Once you let fly a rumor, it makes wings for itself and soars from one end of the ghetto to the other like an arrow from a bow. A few moments pass and it comes back to you so distorted, its form so changed, that you cannot recognize it.

Everyone is panic-stricken. Will he too be deported? Will he die a cruel, ugly death at the hands of a foul-souled Nazi gendarme? The emotional climate is feverish. In the morning hours the decree is final, and not to be rescinded. In the afternoon, the *Judenrat* negotiates. At this very moment a conference is going on in which Auserwald, Czerniakow, Heller, and the Gestapo representatives participate. The terrible decree is left in suspense—things can go either way. They argue back and forth, and are constantly in touch with Berlin. While one person is still telling you this another comes and relates that Czerniakow is offering 10,000,000 zloty to nullify the decree. You are transfixed between fear and hope. It is hard to believe that all this is merely blackmail for the sake of spoils. The Nazis don't have to resort to blackmail to extort money from Jews. If the edict is, according to Nazi opinion, for the good of the state or the good of the race, money will be of no avail on the day of wrath. Considerations of profit and pleasures don't enter the picture.

But it cannot be denied that if you manage to spend the night in peace and live to see the light of morning, you will find a large announcement posted at the street corners stating that the categories itemized below will be forcibly uprooted from the ghetto within twenty-four hours.

The ghetto is suspended over nothingness.

July 20, 1942

The ghetto is quiet. All the terrible rumors are false. *Judenrat* circles deny them, saying that no proposal for expulsion has been made. All the canards about meetings and bribery are invented. The masses are in a panic for their very lives, and in their eyes potential danger turns into active danger. When the rumors reached the ears of the Nazis, they were angry. One Gestapo man deigned to say: "The sin of anyone who spreads rumors like this is too great to be borne. We will initiate an inquiry, and whoever is caught in this

377

transgression will be shot." This time the lie was started by some *Judenrat* group which had a particular interest in broadcasting it. For what end? This is difficult to determine with certainty. There are no grounds whatsoever to suspect one circle or another. When we are privileged to reach better days then these many secrets will be revealed to us, and among them even the secret of the panic which arose in the Warsaw ghetto on Sunday, the fifth of Tammuz, 5702. Who fathered it? From what source did it emanate?

July 21, 1942

The destruction of the sword is rampant in the streets of the ghetto. We shall perish. The day before yesterday there was the panic of deportation. Yesterday the furies abated for a while. Today, again the panic of the sword.

This time we are not dealing with written laws, with a legal code like the Nuremberg Laws, but with German custom—mob rule— where every gendarme and every Gestapo officer acts on his own, but in perfect harmony with the spirit of hatred which permeates the laws themselves. Here is an actual example that occurred right in front of my window. Like an earthquake, it breaks the body and the spirit in one blow.

At 17 Nowolipki Street lives Dr. Sztejnkolk. He is a popular doctor and an important personage, without vices or flaws—tall and personable, one of the shining lights of the ghetto. To our sorrow and to his misfortune he left his house at an inauspicious time. Near 26 Karmelicka Street, he was accosted from behind by four killers. Two of them were *Volksgenossen* and two were gendarmes. One of the policemen kicked Dr. Sztejnkolk, a thing he was used to doing to Jews, and the good doctor, bitterness apparent in his face, turned and asked: "Why do you strike me? Am I guilty of some sin?"

At once one of the killers ordered him to go into the gateway. He went through and never returned. The Nazis immediately took a rifle and shot him in the temple. The honored and righteous doctor died instantly. A quick death and a mass funeral: Karmelicka Street is a center of traffic and the shootings in broad daylight attracted a huge crowd. The killer went on his way wiping his mouth. He had done no crime; he had only killed a Jew.

The same day a Jewish policeman was put to death. A gendarme found some fault with him and punishment immediately followed crime, with no trial intervening. When he neared the place of execution he was ordered to walk with his hands clasped behind his neck. This is neither the law nor the custom, but the killer wanted it that way. He's sure to get a medal.

And at 13 Nalewki Street, the janitor was killed. A Nazi gendarme was chasing a youth. The fugitive eluded his pursuer and disappeared, presumably into the courtyard of Number 13. The janitor was killed for not revealing the supposed hiding place of the hunted man. A life for a life.

And on the same day, at 20 Chlodna Street, an entire family was put to death in their home. I have no precise details of this family tragedy, but there is no doubt of the fact itself.

Near the bridge at the intersection of Zelazna and Chlodna streets everyone who passed by, coming or going, was searched. Traffic stopped in an instant, everyone fled for his life, and the street was emptied at once. The Nazi officers were left without work. But in the interim they had managed to detain and search tens of people and carry them away. It was as if these people just disappeared from the earth.

But the biggest sensation is that the great dragons were arrested, that is, the elite among the heads of the communal department of welfare. They include A. Gepner, Wielikowski, Sztolcman and some others. This is unquestionably a bad omen for us.

All this happened to us on the eve of the Ninth of Av, 5702. "On this night my sons will weep."[8]

July 22, 1942
I haven't the strength to hold a pen in my hand. I'm broken, shattered. My thoughts are jumbled. I don't know where to start or stop. I have seen Jewish Warsaw through forty years of events, but never before has she worn such a face. A whole community of 400,000 people condemned to exile.

What we dreaded most has come. The people had an instinctive feeling that some terrible misfortune was impending, but our official circles denied it completely and presented happy, smiling faces to the populace. "Expulsion from Warsaw? Nonsense! The Jews are sentencing themselves without reason. The Nazis will hear what they say and do just that." They persisted in this deception in order to avoid a panic. But it was useless. The news was carried by the birds of the heavens and the people felt that

[8] From a dirge recited on the eve of Tishe'ah be'Av.

expulsion was imminent. Even before the notices were posted in the streets of the ghetto, we knew we were being tried in absentia. The *Judenrat* building on Grzybowska Street was surrounded by police and closed to visitors. The *Judenrat* leaders met with the Gestapo for a final session about the expulsion. We were even able to determine the exact moment when the order was signed. From dawn to late afternoon we spent the most tense hours of our lives. The spark of hope flared up and then died. And at four o'clock the notice was posted. Our fate was sealed! They say that Himmler is visiting in Warsaw and that this is the gift he is leaving for the Jews. His visit also preceded the decree in Lublin, and for that reason they see a precedent. They also say it was his idea to promulgate the decree on the eve of the Ninth of Av, a day of retribution, a day fated for mourning through all generations. But all that is irrelevant. In the last analysis these are accidental, momentary manifestations. They did not cause the decree. The real purpose is deeper and more fundamental—the total destruction of the Jewish nation.

The order merely verified what we knew without it; the evidences of expulsion were visible earlier. The Jewish police execute the orders, and they live among their people. The first sign was the abolition of the refugee centers. Like passing shadows, their inhabitants were taken away to an unknown place. In the transports were not men but shades. These are the remnants who survived typhus and famine, but now there is no refuge for them. No one doubts that they are going to their death.

The second sign—the removal of the prisoners from the Jewish prison in Gesia Street. They too are going to their death.

The third sign—the moving of all the divisions of the Jewish hospital, which were scattered in various places, to a central location, the hospital in Leszno Street. The patients too are going to their death.

And a fourth category was also among the first to be deported: the street beggars. They were captured by the hundreds and taken away on transports. Where to? No one knows, but everyone understands: to the kingdom of death. Their cries and wails ascended to the heart of the heavens. But who hears cries in a time of such destruction?

These blatant signs boded evil. The notice only added the details to what was known without it. There is one interesting item in the announcement. It was not composed by Auerswald, the Nazi commissar of the ghetto, but by the *Judenrat*. Later we learned that the commissar had already been fired. The reason for his removal is not known. The *Judenrat* issued the order and will execute it. The Jews console themselves with this, but only by means of tortuous reasoning. They grasp at straws.

It is not a total expulsion. There are certain categories for whom concessions were made, and the expulsion decree does not affect them. In the next entry I shall itemize these. I will stop now, and go to my night's repose, but it will be a sleepless night, for I am one of those affected by the decree. I have no special status. Is it possible that I shall not be privileged to end this chronicle on a note of consolation?

July 23, 1942

Today's impressions require an artist's pen. They are so great that they are not subject to forgetfulness, for what is carved deep, deep within the soul is not easily forgot. Their vividness will not be lessened if I write them down tomorrow. Today let us hear what the Nazis have to say:

In comparison with the Lublin expulsion we have before us a liberal document, even though its essence is a savagery and barbarism such as never before existed.

The categories not affected are set forth: Jews who work in the German shop-factories, and the officers of the *Judenrat* and all its agencies. This paragraph exempts hundreds of officials from expulsion, and with their families, thousands of people. It encompasses the Jewish police, the hospitals, the welfare department, the cemetery administration, the post office, and the House Committees. This is in effect a small state and its various divisions carry on state functions. One paragraph is ambiguous: "All Jews qualified for labor are exempt from deportation and may remain in the ghetto; those Jews who were not heretofore included in the labor force may henceforth be included. They will be taken to barracks where they will work."

Finally a very important note: At a meeting which took place in the *Judenrat* building on the twenty-second, the official in charge of the deportation granted the leaders of the Jewish Self-Aid Society the right to be considered on a par with *Judenrat* officers. This means that they too are exempt from deportation.

The deportees are forbidden to take bundles weighing more than ten kilos. Silver, gold, and jewels may be taken without restriction. This is understood: All of that will be stolen from them, not on paper, but on the road. This tactic is already known to us. The time of deportation will begin at twelve noon on the twenty-second day of July in the year 1942. Exemptions apply only to immediate family—wife and children. No more. An aged mother will be exiled, a senile crippled father will be deported.

Now could anything be more humane? The ghetto residents found some consolation in the paragraph which speaks of "all Jews qualified for labor." Labor—that can mean both physical and mental; no age limit is specified. That means even men who are over sixty. Everyone suddenly became eager for work. Everyone is prepared to give up hot meals and a comfortable bed at home to go live in barracks, if only to stay put. To be deported means to prepare for death, and it is a lingering death which is the hardest kind of all. The deportees are, to begin with, taken for killing. They are not qualified for work. And as to food, even if a crust of bread were available, would the Nazis give it to them? It has become known that the Nazis flay their corpses, remove the fat, and incinerate the bodies. This accords with a prestated plan: The strength of the healthy and productive are to be exploited for the needs of the German army; the weak, the crippled, and the aged are to go to eternal rest.

Such a plan could have been invented only by Satan.

This is no more than a curiosity of history. The Jews aid the Nazi victory so that the Nazis can expel them from Europe and destroy them. Their cynicism is such that the Nazis say this bluntly. Sometimes a laborer's work pleases them; then they praise him and say, "May you be recompensed by being the last one to be shot."

The industriousness of the ghetto is a credit to everyone. It produces three times what was demanded. This is skillful and industrious work which produces goods for the use and enjoyment of the Nazis. The Jewish worker is compensated by having his relatives deported to a valley of death and destruction, while he is left locked within the walls of the ghetto.

The expulsion has already begun. It is being carried out by the

Jewish people under German supervision. On the first day the Jewish police furnished the requisite number of 6,000 people; the second day of the expulsion, the police could round up only 4,700 men, women, and children. The Nazis filled in the deficit. We remember the words of the elegist: "On this night my sons will weep." In these two days the emptiness of the ghetto has been filled with cries and wails. If they found no way to the God of Israel it is a sign He doesn't exist.

July 26, 1942

The terrible events have engulfed me; the horrible deeds committed in the ghetto have so frightened and stunned me that I have not the power, either physical or spiritual, to review these events and perpetuate them with the pen of a scribe. I have no words to express what has happened to us since the day the expulsion was ordered. Those people who have gotten some notion of historical expulsions from books know nothing. We, the inhabitants of the Warsaw ghetto, are now experiencing the reality. Our only good fortune is that our days are numbered—that we shall not have long to live under conditions like these, and that after our terrible sufferings and wanderings we shall come to eternal rest, which was denied us in life. Among ourselves we fully admit that this death which lurks behind our walls will be our salvation; but there is one thorn. We shall not be privileged to witness the downfall of the Nazis, which in the end will surely come to pass.

Some of my friends and acquaintances who know the secret of my diary urge me, in their despair, to stop writing. "Why? For what purpose? Will you live to see it published? Will these words of yours reach the ears of future generations? How? If you are deported you won't be able to take it with you because the Nazis will watch your every move, and even if you succeed in hiding it when you leave Warsaw, you will undoubtedly die on the way, for your strength is ebbing. And if you don't die from lack of strength, you will die by the Nazi sword. For not a single deportee will be able to hold out to the end of the war."

And yet in spite of it all I refuse to listen to them. I feel that continuing this diary to the very end of my physical and spiritual strength is a historical mission which must not be abandoned. My mind is still clear, my need to record unstilled, though it is now five days since any real food has passed my lips. Therefore I will not silence my diary!

We have a Jewish tradition that an evil law is foredoomed to defeat. This historical experience has caused us much trouble since the day we fell into the mouth of the Nazi whose dearest wish is to swallow us. It came to us from habit, this minimizing of all edicts with the common maxim, "It won't succeed." In this lay our undoing, and we made a bitter mistake. An evil decree made by the Nazis does not weaken in effect, it grows stronger. The mitigating paragraphs are increasingly overlooked and the more severe paragraphs intensified. At the beginning, the time of the "negotiations," a directive was issued to the *Judenrat* to deport 6,000 a day; in point of fact they are now deporting close to 10,000. The Jewish police, whose cruelty is no less than that of the Nazis, deliver to the "transfer point" on Stawki Street more than the quota to which the *Judenrat* obligated itself. Sometimes there are several thousand people waiting a day or two to be transported because of a shortage of railroad cars. Word has gotten around that the Nazis are satisfied that the extermination of the Jews is being carried out with all requisite efficiency. This deed is being done by the Jewish slaughterers.

The first victim of the deportation decree was the President, Adam Czerniakow, who committed suicide by poison in the *Judenrat* building. He perpetuated his name by his death more than by his life. His end proves conclusively that he worked and strove for the good of his people; that he wanted its welfare and continuity even though not everything done in his name was praiseworthy. The expulsion proclamation posted in the city streets on the afternoon of July 22 was not signed in the usual manner of *Judenrat* notices, "Head of the *Judenrat*, Certified Engineer Adam Czerniakow," but merely "*Judenrat*." This innovation astonished those circles who examine bureaucratic changes in notices. After the president's death, the reason became clear. Czerniakow had refused to sign the expulsion order. He followed the Talmudic law: If someone comes to kill me, using might and power, and turns a deaf ear to all my pleas, he can do to me whatever his heart desires, since he has the power, and strength always prevails. But to give my consent, to sign my own death warrant—this no power on earth can force me to do, not even the brutal force of the foul-souled Nazi.

A whole community with an ancient tradition, one that with all its faults was the very backbone of world Jewry, is going to destruction. First they took away its means of livelihood, then they stole its wares, then its houses and factories, and, above all, its human rights. It was left fair prey to every evildoer and sinner. It was locked into a ghetto. Food and drink was withheld from it; its fallen multiplied on every hand; and even after all this they were not content to let it dwell forever within its narrow, rotten ghetto, surrounded with its wall through which even bread could be brought in only by dangerous smuggling. Nor was this a ghetto of people who consume without producing, of speculators and profiteers. Most of its members were devoted to labor, so that it became a productive legion. All that it produced, it produced for the benefit of those same soldiers who multiplied its fallen.

Yet all this was to no avail. There was only one decree—death. They came and divided the Warsaw ghetto into two halves; one half was for sword, pestilence, and destruction; the other half for famine and slavery. The vigorous youth, the healthy and productive ones, were taken to work in the factories. The old people, the women, the children all were sent into exile.

The president, who had a spark of purity in his heart, found the only way out worthy of himself. Suicide! In the end the Nazis would have killed him anyhow, as is their custom in the areas from which they expel the Jewish population; nor would the president have been the last to be shot. From the moment of his refusal to sign the expulsion order he was a saboteur in the eyes of the Nazis and thus doomed to death. With a president one must be very exacting. In any event, he did well to anticipate the Nazis.

He did not have a good life, but he had a beautiful death. May his death atone for his wrongs against his people before becoming president. There are those who earn immortality in a single hour. The President, Adam Czerniakow, earned his immortality in a single instant.

July 27, 1942
Anyone who could see the expulsion from Warsaw with his own eyes would have his heart broken. The ghetto has turned

385

into an inferno. Men have become beasts. Everyone is but a step away from deportation; people are being hunted down in the streets like animals in the forest. It is the Jewish police who are cruelest toward the condemned. Sometimes a blockade is made of a particular house, sometimes of a whole block of houses. In every building earmarked for destruction they begin to make the rounds of the apartments and to demand documents. Whoever has neither documents that entitle him to remain in the ghetto nor money for bribes is told to make a bundle weighing 15 kilos—and on to the transport which stands near the gate. Whenever a house is blockaded a panic arises that is beyond the imagination. Residents who have neither documents nor money hide in nooks and crannies, in the cellars and in the attics. When there is a means of passage between one courtyard and another the fugitives begin jumping over the roofs and fences at the risk of their lives; in time of panic, when the danger is imminent, people are not fussy about methods. But all these methods only delay the inevitable, and in the end the police take men, women, and children. The destitute and impoverished are the first to be deported. In an instant the truck becomes crowded. They are all alike: poverty makes them equal. Their cries and wails tear the heart out.

The children, in particular, rend the heavens with their cries. The old people and the middle-aged deportees accept the judgment in silent submission and stand with their small parcels under their arms. But there is no limit to the sorrow and tears of the young women; sometimes one of them makes an attempt to slip out of the grasp of her captors, and then a terrible battle begins. At such times the horrible scene reaches its peak. The two sides fight, wrestle. On one side a woman with wild hair and a torn blouse rages with the last of her strength at the Jewish thieves, trying to escape from their hands. Anger flows from her mouth and she is like a lioness ready for the kill. And on the other side are the two policemen, her "brothers in misfortune," who pull her back to her death. It is obvious that the police win. But during the fight the wailing of the captives increases sevenfold, and the whole street cries with them.

But isolated incidents don't hold up the operation. The police do what is incumbent upon them. After the completion of the arrests in one house, they move on to another. The *Judenrat* prepares a daily list of houses in which blockades will be made that day. And here a new source of income is opened up for the graft-chasing police. The wealthy and the middle class have yet to be brought to the transports. For those who have no documents, banknotes turn into documents. There is almost a fixed price for ransom, but for some it is cheaper, all according to the class of the ransomed one and the number of people in his household.

Two actual cases are known to me. One of the members of our family ransomed himself off with a substitute for money. In place of the ready cash which he didn't have at the time of the hunt, he gave a silk umbrella as a "gift" not to be returned. An acquaintance of mine, a Hebrew teacher, a downtrodden pauper with a crippled son, was forced to give 300 zloty—his last nest egg, since he has no expectation of new earnings from teaching Hebrew. In this instance the price was high, for expulsion of a cripple means expulsion to the gates of death. Sick people and cripples are killed by the Nazis while still en route.

But from the time they began to hunt down passersby on the street, the sorrow of the expulsion became even greater. For this barbarism the beloved *Judenrat* will find no atonement. One who is seized in his apartment supplies himself with some clothing and food for the journey. His loved ones take their leave of him, fall on his neck. Not so one who is seized on the street. He is taken to the transport as he is, without extra clothing, without food and sustenance, and usually without a penny. No entreaties avail him. He is led out to the transfer point like a lamb to the slaughter.

Life in the ghetto has been turned upside down. Panic is in its streets, fear on every face, wails and cries everywhere you turn. Trade has ceased; bargaining has been silenced; and most important, smuggling has stopped. When there is no smuggling, costs go up, so that the price of bread has reached 60 zloty. Prices have increased tenfold, all businesses have ceased to exist. Everyone's staff of bread has been broken. From whence cometh our help? We are lost! We are lost!

July 28, 1942

The situation grows graver by the hour. Through the window of my apartment near the scene of the "hunting," I beheld those trapped by the hunt, and was so stricken that I was close to mad-

387

ness. For the detainee, the thread of his life is cut in an instant, and the work of an entire lifetime in which his best efforts were invested becomes abandoned property.

Before my very eyes they capture an old woman who walks with a cane. Her steps are measured, and she makes her way with great exertions. She is unable to straighten up. On her face there are marks of nobility and signs of a family status now past. She too was arrested by a lawless Jewish scoundrel. He needs clients, and even this old lady counts, "as is," without clothes or linens, without even food. She will be sent "to the East." She will be fortunate if she doesn't live long.

A young mother of two little children from 19 Nowolipki Street was caught and sent off. The dear children were left orphans. There is no comfort for her husband and their father. And there are similar victims by the hundreds. Today about 10,000 people were taken. They are shoved into freight cars which have no places to sit and no sanitary facilities. If anyone survives that journey, it is nothing less than a miracle.

In truth we have reached extremity. Death is precious when it is quick and swift, when it takes your soul and you pass on into your eternity. But a death which comes by the agonies of starvation and the tortures of the oppressor, who prolongs the death agony and turns his victims into living skeletons—this is the cruelest of punishments. Have we truly sinned more than any nation; have we transgressed more than any generation?

Never in my life had I known the pangs of hunger. Even after I was pushed into the ghetto I ate. But now I too know hunger. I sustain myself for a whole day on a quarter-kilo of bread and unsweetened tea. My strength is diminishing from such meager fare. At times I can't even stand up. I fall on my bed, but rest eludes me. I am in a state of sleep and am not asleep, of wakefulness and yet am not awake. I am plagued by nightmares. Fear and worry preoccupy me—fear lest I be seized and deported; worry about where to find my bread. My income has stopped. The sums owed to me by others are lost. Besides what he needs for food, no one has a penny to his name, and payment of debts isn't taken into consideration at all.

But the main thing is fear of expulsion. The only ones partially insured against expulsion are workers in the factories that German firms have taken under their protection. Many factories accept workers skilled in their trades, and even those who are unskilled but have money. Thus a new economy has begun in the lives of the ghetto Jews who have not yet been expelled.

I am tired. The sequel will come tomorrow, if I'm not caught.

July 29, 1942

The expulsion is reaching its peak. It increases from day to day. The Nazis are satisfied with the work of the Jewish police, the plague of the Jewish organism, and the police too are satisfied: the Nazis, because through industry and cruelty the police have succeeded in supplying exiles above and beyond the daily quota originally specified, and close to 70,000 people have already gone into exile; the police, because they are lining their pockets. This income is fortuitous and apparently not dangerous. The Nazis don't bother about details. Give who you will, as long as there is no shortage of human material for expulsion. In any event, the respite that the bribe creates is only temporary. A house which is blockaded today can be blockaded tomorrow too, and the next day, and so on ad infinitum. A man who was released once can be caught again—even by the same policeman who let him go the first time—especially since the police have nearly 2,400 dogs. The wiles of the policemen know no bounds. Besides taking bribes, they also steal and rob. How? They order the inhabitants of the house to go down, while they themselves remain in the unguarded apartment. Thus they profit from all that is abandoned.

This criminal police force is the child of the criminal *Judenrat*. Like mother, like daughter. With their misdeeds they besmirch the name of Polish Jewry which was stained even without this. At the transfer point where the exiles are collected, the policemen traffic in bread. These loaves of bread, which the police force gets in abundance free of charge, are sold to the hungry and oppressed captives at 80 zloty a loaf. For delivering a letter, ten zloty. They are growing rich on these profits, and for the time being they are experiencing the eternal reward in this life—until the Nazis take pity on them as well. Their day will come, and they too will be destroyed, but they will be the last.

Nazism is not original. They took everything from Bolshevism, only that they expanded its rottenness. This is the same Bolshevism in black paint. There is no difference but that of color. Bolshevism came and said: "Everyone must work!" Nazism came after it and said likewise: "You are idle! Go ye unto your burdens!" But Bolshevism spoke out of its desire to improve the world; Nazism spoke out of hatred for the Jewish people.

With one stroke of the pen the face of Warsaw was changed. They made an end of its peddlers; its beggars and paupers and down-and-outers were collected; its stores were closed; its streets were emptied. Everywhere there is the silence of the graveyard. Everything has passed away—disappeared in one day. It is as if the earth had opened and swallowed up all its crowds and noises, its secrets and vices, and the entire tribe of ants that scurried through its streets from dawn until curfew.

When the Nazis decreed expulsion for the "unproductive population," people went into hiding as though they had been erased from the face of the earth. Now there is hunting for the sake of expulsion, where once they traded and bartered.

The unproductive population included most of the ghetto dwellers. In the eyes of the Nazis, anyone who doesn't take a needle or a shovel in hand is in no way productive. Based on this, the entire population of the ghetto was scheduled for expulsion. They therefore tried to save themselves by a change in approach: You want us to work? By all means—only allow us to live. One is not overscrupulous about the means in time of danger. Immediately a great movement arose to set up factories to work for the good of the German army, and the German commandant invited German firms to establish branches in the General Government. The Jewish shop-factories received raw materials from these firms and began to manufacture for each one what was required to meet their obligations to the commandant. In this way factories for various trades were opened which employed tens of thousands of people. Thus the expulsion decree caused people who had been storekeepers, tradesmen, peddlers, servants, teachers, lawyers, engineers, and all kinds of other middle-class people to stream toward the factories. Henceforward, only one who is enrolled as a worker in one of the factories under the protection of some German firm has the right to remain in the ghetto. A certificate (*Ausweis*) granted by a firm of the Reich has the power to save its bearer from expulsion and from all the other troubles that have attached themselves to us. Within a week, tens of thousands of tradesmen, peddlers, unemployed men, idlers, spreaders of false rumors, and bums have been turned into creative workers, into a productive element; they sit hunched over a needle, sewing buttons on a pair of army pants.

The entire ghetto is a mammoth factory producing for the good of the German army. We have become a laughingstock!

July 30, 1942

The seventh day of the expulsion. Living funerals pass before the windows of my apartment—cattle trucks or coal wagons full of candidates for expulsion and exile, carrying small bundles under their arms. Their cries and shrieks and wails, which rent the very heavens and filled the whole area with noise, have already stopped. Most of the deportees seem to be resigned to their fate. Only an occasional sound, the tear-drenched echo of a protest, is heard from some unfortunate seized while she was engaged in the activities of everyday life. Misfortune descended upon her unforeseen. She knew that there was an expulsion, but she was almost positive that it would never come to her. And behold, it is come! Woe to her! Alas for her soul! But her shrieks and plaints are sown upon the wind. It is finished, decided. She is going toward a new "life."

Amid all the tragedy of sudden expulsion, one minor detail is perhaps the most tragic of all: People come to the transfer point voluntarily, saying: "Take me! Save me from the quagmire of the ghetto! I will die anyhow; there is famine in the ghetto. Comfort the dying!" But these are the words of a small minority of people with no roots in the soil of the ghetto.

Besides the blockading of houses and hunting in the street, there is still a third method of expulsion—premiums. Large posters have been put up in many courtyards to say that all those who voluntarily come to the transfer point for expulsion will receive three kilos of bread and a kilo of marmalade to take with them in their wanderings. They are given until the thirty-first of July.

Today I haven't gone outside the house, because the sword of expulsion strikes in all the streets of the ghetto. They take everyone who comes to hand, those dressed in finery and those dressed in cast-offs—all of them, all of them swallowed up by the wagon. They are not even paying attention to the certificates of those who work for the German factories, which should be a protection for them.

The soothing rumors that the expulsion will cease, that only a certain percentage will be exiled, that the many factories abetting the victory of the German army will enable the rest of the Jews to remain in the ghetto, have not materialized. Nothing of the sort. The tempo of the expulsion increases from hour to hour. On every hand there are catchers. Besides the uniformed Jewish police and the nonuniformed auxiliary police, pure Germans have also come to this task. They dress in civilian clothes so that people won't spot them.

All day long the ghetto has been deathly silent. During the working hours in the factories the number of passersby decreased to a minimum. Those who have not yet managed to be accepted in some factory are afraid to stick their noses out for fear of being caught. They hide until the wrath shall pass. Perhaps salvation will come! Perhaps there will be a change for the better! But for the time being, the oppressor does not stay his hand.

There is one category among those "insured" against expulsion whose eyes reflect fear, who despite the documents in their pockets never go out of the doors of their houses and, within their houses, hide in inner rooms. These are the "officials" of the Jewish Self-Aid Society, who numbered over two thousand at the outbreak of the catastrophe. It is the strength of the Jewish people that in time of disaster they invent something out of nothing, build bridges out of paper. If it works, it will work; and if not, what have you lost? Before the expulsion, the Self-Aid employed about four hundred people who were registered with the labor office, and there were also full-time officers who held work cards in accordance with the laws of officialdom. Suddenly, the calamity! Thousands of people were left without legal protection and doomed to exile. Accordingly the directors of the society, with the consent of the *Judenrat*, decided to provide their friends with a legal haven in the form of "legitimizations," documents stating that So-and-so was an official of the society. They based their plan on the fact that the expulsion decree had a paragraph which stated specifically that officials of the Jewish Self-Aid Society would have privileges comparable to those of officials of the *Judenrat*. A veritable factory for legitimizations was set up. Anyone who had had any connection whatever with the activities of the society from the time of its establishment to the present day, whether as a salaried employee or a volunteer, received certification as one of its officials.

Within three days, over two thousand certificates were prepared and distributed— a tremendous job, even for a well-equipped and refined technical apparatus, let alone an organization as inefficient as the Self-Aid. Here no one stood in long queues, but rather on top of one another. The pushing and crowding of hundreds of people with the fear of death in their eyes reached horrible proportions. Mobs pushed their way into the officials' offices and urged them to speed up their work. The result was exactly the opposite. Order was disrupted, work was interrupted and delayed: anger and hysterics from both sides. No one had any assurance that such a certificate would be legally accepted, but it is good to have something in writing to lean on. People seek comfort in the fact that for the time being the Jewish police are handling everything, and the police are under the orders of the *Judenrat*, which considers these certificates legal. Everyone said, "It carries no real guarantee. In the end it will come under censure and be nullified. But for the time it has validity in the eyes of the Jewish police, and that's enough for me. I'll at least be able to go and look for a more secure hiding place." In point of fact it did save many people. They were seized and later released. I too find refuge in the shadow of a certificate. Blessings upon the Self-Aid!

I have just been informed that 57,000 people have already been deported. The teacher and writer Aron Luboszycki, a refugee from Lodz, was among them.

July 31, 1942
The hunting goes on full force. The living funerals never cease. The Jewish police are fulfilling their humane duty in the best possible manner, and the Nazis are so pleased with their work that some of them are being sent to Radom and Kielce, where expulsions have now been ordered as well. These cities are both smaller than Warsaw, and local elements are not particularly desirable for this sort of operation, so the strangers from Warsaw come where no one knows them to carry out the Nazis' wishes.

Yesterday and today were "days of awe"; no *Ausweis* was honored. Workers were taken out of factories protected by the German firms of Többens, Schultz, Mangesten, and the like. Thousands of people were seized whose documents were questionable,

393

having been given only as protection from the destroyers, and whose bearers were not expert in the trades ascribed to them in their certificates. These are documents given out of kindness, like those of the Self-Aid Society, and are of no value. Sometimes they help if by a miracle you chance to meet a policeman who shares the distress of his people—but the Nazis are insatiable.

The sum total is that there is no Jew who has not insured himself with some piece of paper, and there is no Jew who doesn't hide in the inner recesses of his house, certificate and all. It's just that with a certificate in your pocket, hiding is more comfortable.

More factories are established every day. This is the only source of salvation now, even though every one of them is built on sand. Many people scurry to register for the factories. Merchants and tradesmen, intellectuals and Menachem-Mendels,[9] are turning to handicraft in order to be saved from deportation. Everyone is pushing his way into a "shop" and is prepared to sell all his possessions and give away his last cent, if only to be considered productive.

How great the panic of the factories has become! Everyone fights to be enrolled in them, and everyone gives thousands of zloty for this privilege. For a genuine laborer it is enough if he brings a sewing machine with him, but a business or professional man contributes ready cash in place of a machine. None of the newly erected factories has any validity or future unless they are incorporated into the network of factories of some German firm; and this privilege too must be bought with cash from the Germans, who demand immense sums in return for the right to work for the German army. But no one has scruples about the size of the sum. A man will give everything he has in exchange for his life. The whole matter is clouded in doubt and no one knows what the day will bring; but the people of the ghetto, who see death face to face, are seeking security not for a day, but for an hour.

Be that as it may, we are like rams and sheep bound for sacrifice, except that it is hard to determine the exact instant at which one will be put upon the altar. The sword has already been removed from its sheath, but we haven't yet stretched out our necks for the slaughter.

My powers are insufficient to record all that is worthy of being written. Most of all, I am worried that I may be consuming my

[9] From a character created by Sholem Aleichem—an impractical dreamer.

strength for naught. Should I too be taken all my efforts will be wasted. My utmost concern is for hiding my diary so that it will be preserved for future generations. As long as my pulse beats I shall continue my sacred task.

August 1, 1942

The enormity of the danger increases our strength and our will to save our lives, like a fever which gives strength and power to one who is dangerously ill. But all this is merely a momentary relief; afterward the weakness returns sevenfold.

Yesterday the murderers from the S.S. came to assist the Jewish police, and within two hours, i.e., from seven to nine in the evening, the entire Jewish population of Nowolipie Street—from the corner of Karmelicka to Smocza—was forced to leave its homes and go into exile.

Blessed is the eye which has not beheld all of this!

The expulsion decree is a twofold one: expulsion for the nonproductive, and after this the terrible edict of evictions. A command is suddenly given to evacuate an entire block of apartment houses within a single hour. This starts an uproar, a turmoil that Dante could not have envisioned. It is the Nazis' intention that every decree come as a complete surprise. Hundreds of families hurt by this decree become frantic from the enormity of the misfortune. Where will you go? What can you save? What first? What last? They begin to pack bundles in haste and fear, with trembling hands and feet which refuse to do their bidding, and to take their belongings outside, for they no longer have a home. Hundreds of women and swollen infants rend the heavens with their cries. The sick are taken outside in their beds, babies in their cradles, old men and women half-naked and barefoot.

At seven in the evening the S.S. arrived and ordered the Jewish police to blockade an entire block. They made an announcement in each courtyard: "Prepare bundles weighing 15 kilos and go down into the courtyard. No one is exempt!" Terrible fear gripped the whole area. Everyone sensed that his fate had been given over into the hands of insatiable murderers. With the Jewish police the inhabitants could come to a compromise in one way or another, but this time the decree was inexorable. Submit yourselves to your bitter fate!

About 10,000 people were deported and disappeared.

Jewish Warsaw is in its death throes. A whole community is going to its death! The appalling events follow one another so abundantly that it is beyond the power of a writer of impressions to collect, arrange, and classify them; particularly when he himself is caught in their vise—fearful of his own fate for the next hour, scheduled for deportation, tormented by hunger, his whole being filled with the fear and dread which accompanies the expulsion. And let this be known: From the beginning of the world, since the time when man first had dominion over another man to do him harm, there has never been so cruel and barbaric an expulsion as this one. From hour to hour, even from minute to minute, Jewish Warsaw is being demolished and destroyed, reduced and decreased. Since the day the exile was decreed, ruin and destruction, exile and wandering, bereavement and widowhood have befallen us in all their fury.

For five days now the Nazis have been "helping" the Jewish police. Since then the expulsion has begun to leave a trail of innocent blood behind it. A man who is ordered to leave his apartment must go as he is, for if he tarries a single moment he is put to death at once.

After Nowolipie, henceforward to be known as Schultz Street, came the turn of Leszno Street from the corner of Zelazna to Solna. The population of Leszno was not struck by the evacuation order, but rather by the decree of expulsion. A blockade was made on Leszno Street, and within two hours about 2,000 people were brought to the transfer point. All of them went forth empty-handed, naked and half-dressed. Woe to that family which must be routed out by the Nazis or their minions, the "alert" Ukrainians and Lithuanians. The victims emerge beaten and sore, naked as the day they were born.

Today the population of the "little ghetto" drank the cup of hemlock. At four the murderers set upon their task, and at seven a crowd of 5,000 people was led out through Smocza to the transfer point. All their possessions were left in the hands of the enemy.

Jewish Warsaw is turning into a city of slave laborers who have nothing of their own. The German companies that own the factories concentrate their employees in one section. To achieve this, they confiscate all the houses near a factory and settle the workers and their families in them. Without them there would be no Jewish community. Every activity in the ghetto, and all its establishments, are being brought to an end. Jews who are not employed in one of the factories will be expelled from Warsaw. For the time being they are busy with schemes and plans for hiding until the wrath passes, but the wrath of the Nazis never passes. On the contrary, it increases. Concessions granted on paper never materialize in practice. All of the various *Ausweisen* are voided and nullified. In the end, everyone will be expelled.

Today I heard from Dr. Lajfuner, who in turn heard it from rumor, that the houses from 12 to 21 Nowolipki Street will be confiscated and turned over to the workers of a brush factory. This news will affect us both, for he is a resident at Number 14 and I at Number 20. If the rumor proves true I shall have no place to lay my head. And his fate is like mine. We shall both sleep out of doors —until we are caught and deported. Meanwhile we are without food—not even enough for a single meal.

We have no information about the fate of those who have been expelled. When one falls into the hands of the Nazis he falls into the abyss. The very fact that the deportees make no contact with their families by letters bodes evil. Nothing that is related—and many things are related—is based on exact information. One person says that a certain family has received news of one of its members who was deported, that he arrived in the place intended for him alive and well—but he doesn't name the place nor give his address, and he doesn't ask them to write to him. Certain other unconfirmed reports are widespread, but no one knows their source nor lends much credence to them. Nevertheless, there is some local information about one segment of the deportees—the sick, the aged, the crippled and the other invalids, the weak ones who need the care and help of other people. They have returned to the city, not to the living but rather to the dead—to the cemetery. There they have found rest for their oppressed souls, and there they attain eternal peace. I have not yet verified this information myself. I record it as I heard it from the rumor.

August 4, 1942

During the morning hours

I spent yesterday in hard and tiring work, packing boxes and making bundles of pillows and blankets, and particularly in hiding my library, the joy of my life and the delight of my soul. My block is insecure. We are on the verge of expulsion and the confiscation of our houses. It is a time of danger. Our living in Warsaw has become illegal; we await calamity at any moment. The houses are being confiscated for the factory workers, to whom the idlers must give up their apartments. And I, and all those like me, are idlers, for we haven't a place in a factory. Therefore it behooves one to be ready for the coming catastrophe.

I packed my possessions to send them to a relative of mine who has succeeded in getting a "worker-status" (*Placowka*) outside the ghetto for 2,000 zloty. He is more secure in life and property than I. An apartment was even set aside for him at 15 Leszno Street, a building whose inhabitants had already been expelled. He thus becomes my savior and refuge in my time of need. The furniture, glassware, and other household goods will remain where they are and strangers will inherit them for themselves. It is obvious that my privileged relative can protect only part of my property; there is no one to protect my life and my liberty. My life is forfeit and suspended over nothingness.

Yesterday, the third of August, they slaughtered Zamenhof and Pawia streets. They did not confiscate houses, but blockaded the entire block for expulsion. The S.S. killers stood guard while the Jewish police worked inside the courtyards. This was a slaughter in proper style—they had no pity even on infants and nurslings. All of them, all, without exception, were taken to the gates of death. The fabricated papers of the Self-Aid Society were as useless as though they did not exist.

In the Zamenhof-Pawia blockade, unlike the Nowolipki disaster where hundreds perished, innocent blood was not spilled on the spot, because the S.S. did not go through the apartments.

The rabbi of Radomsko and his entire family—six people in all —who lived in Nowolipki Street were murdered.

In the evening hours

I have not yet been caught; I have not yet been evicted from my apartment; my building has not yet been confiscated. But only a step separates me from all these misfortunes. All day my wife and I take turns standing watch, looking through the kitchen window which overlooks the courtyard, to see if the blockade has begun. People run from place to place like madmen.

On the very day that I packed my possessions to turn them over to the relative who is my protector, my friend M. from Nowolipki Street brought me some of his belongings because he had heard that his block was in danger of blockade. My friend M. is "kosher" by virtue of the fact that he has an administrative position at the *Judenrat*. His documents are valid and carry full privileges. But the size of the ghetto is being steadily decreased, and there is therefore a danger that the function of an administrator will cease to exist. What did he do? He looked for some kind of factory, and found one, but only upon payment of ransom. Because he had no cash, he gave its equivalent, a precious stone worth several thousand zloty. This was the last of his savings for the bad times to come. When he handed over the stone he was destitute.

My lot is even worse because I have neither money nor a factory job, and therefore am a candidate for expulsion if I am caught. My only salvation is in hiding. This is an outlaw's life, and a man cannot last very long living illegally. My heart trembles at every isolated word. I am unable to leave my house, for at every step the devil lies in wait for me.

There is the silence of death in the streets of the ghetto all through the day. The fear of death is in the eyes of the few people who pass by on the sidewalk opposite our window. Everyone presses himself against the wall and draws into himself so that they will not detect his existence or his presence.

Today my block was scheduled for a blockade with Nazi participation. Seventy Jewish policemen had already entered the courtyard. I thought, "The end has come." But a miracle happened, and the blockade was postponed. The destroyers passed on to the Nalewki-Zamenhof block.

When the danger was already past I hurried to escape. Panic can drive a man out of his mind and magnify the danger even when it no longer exists. But already there is a fear that my block will be blockaded tomorrow. I am therefore trying to lay plans to escape with the dawn. But where will I flee? No block is secure.

Thousands of people in the Nalewki-Zamenhof block were driven from their homes and taken to the transfer point. More than thirty people were slaughtered. In the afternoon, the furies subsided a bit. The number of passersby increased, for the danger of blockade was over. By four in the afternoon, the quota was filled: 13,000 people had been seized and sent off, among them 5,000 who came to the transfer of their own free will. They had had their fill of the ghetto life, which is a life of hunger and fear of death. They escaped from the trap. Would that I could allow myself to do as they did! If my life ends—what will become of my diary?